Toward a New World: Articles and Essays 1901–1906

Historical Materialism Book Series

The Historical Materialism Book Series is a major publishing initiative of the radical left. The capitalist crisis of the twenty-first century has been met by a resurgence of interest in critical Marxist theory. At the same time, the publishing institutions committed to Marxism have contracted markedly since the high point of the 1970s. The Historical Materialism Book Series is dedicated to addressing this situation by making available important works of Marxist theory. The aim of the series is to publish important theoretical contributions as the basis for vigorous intellectual debate and exchange on the left.

The peer-reviewed series publishes original monographs, translated texts, and reprints of classics across the bounds of academic disciplinary agendas and across the divisions of the left. The series is particularly concerned to encourage the internationalization of Marxist debate and aims to translate significant studies from beyond the English-speaking world.

For a full list of titles in the Historical Materialism Book Series available in paperback from Haymarket Books, visit: www.haymarketbooks.org/series_collections/1-historical-materialism

Toward a New World: Articles and Essays, 1901–1906

On the Psychology of Society, New World, and Contributions to *Studies in the Realist Worldview*

Alexander Bogdanov

Translated, edited and introduced by
David G. Rowley

Haymarket Books
Chicago, IL

First published in 2021 by Brill Academic Publishers, The Netherlands
© 2021 Koninklijke Brill NV, Leiden, The Netherlands

Published in paperback in 2022 by
Haymarket Books
P.O. Box 180165
Chicago, IL 60618
773-583-7884
www.haymarketbooks.org

ISBN: 978-1-64259-788-2

Distributed to the trade in the US through Consortium Book Sales and
Distribution (www.cbsd.com) and internationally through Ingram
Publisher Services International (www.ingramcontent.com).

This book was published with the generous support of Lannan
Foundation and Wallace Action Fund.

Special discounts are available for bulk purchases by organizations and
institutions. Please call 773-583-7884 or email info@haymarketbooks.org
for more information.

Cover art and design by David Mabb. Cover art is a detail of *Variant
5, Morris, Vine / Popova, Untitled textile design*, paint and wallpaper on
canvas (2006).

Printed in the United States.

10 9 8 7 6 5 4 3 2 1

Library of Congress Cataloging-in-Publication data is available.

Contents

PART 3

Contributions to *Studies in the Realist Worldview*

Translator's Introduction

From 1901 to 1906, the period in which he wrote the articles contained in the present work, Alexander Bogdanov (1873–1928) was a leading participant in the revolutionary Social-Democratic movement in Russia.

Bogdanov had declared himself to be a Marxist in 1896, but he was unable to participate in the formation of the Russian Social-Democratic Labour Party due to his arrest in November 1898 for 'social propaganda among workers' and subsequent five years of provincial exile. Even in exile, however, Bogdanov kept abreast of party matters. He was in communication with *Iskra*, the official journal of the Russian Social-Democratic Labour Party (RSDLP), beginning in 1901, and when the Bolshevik-Menshevik split occurred in 1903, Bogdanov sympathised with the Bolshevik position. In the autumn of 1904, as soon as his exile was over, Bogdanov went to Geneva, Switzerland where Lenin, Krupskaya, and other Russian Social-Democratic leaders were living. In August 1904, he participated in the 'Conference of the 22', the founding conference of the Bolshevik fraction, and he was elected to the Bureau of Committees of the Majority, the leading organ of the Bolsheviks.

Bogdanov returned to Russia during the 1905 Revolution where he wrote tactical leaflets about armed uprising, edited the Bolsheviks' two periodicals, served on the Bolshevik bureau in St. Petersburg, and was in fact the most senior Bolshevik in Russia at the time.[1] He was also a delegate to the Third Congress of the RSDLP in 1905, at which he was elected to the new Central Committee of the RSDLP. In the autumn, when the Revolution reached its height, Bogdanov was in St. Petersburg, deeply involved in party work and serving on the Executive Committee of the St. Petersburg Soviet of Workers' Deputies. In December he was arrested, along with the entire Executive Committee, when the Soviet was suppressed. He remained in prison until May 1906, and, after his release, Bogdanov went abroad. It was in the years that followed that his famous split with Lenin occurred.[2]

Meanwhile, during this same period of political exile and revolutionary activity, Bogdanov pursued an ambitious intellectual agenda: to develop a comprehensive worldview that would explain all of nature – including human life – according to the principles of historical materialism. The many books

---

1   White 2019a, p. 113.
2   For thorough coverage of Bogdanov's life and thought, see James White's superb biography, White 2019b.

and articles he wrote in this pursuit fall into two main groups: a positive, non-polemical exposition of his scientific philosophy and worldview; and a polemical struggle with Russia's Marxist revisionists in which he both dismantled their arguments against the principles of historical materialism and explained how his philosophy answered the objections that the revisionists raised, thus further developing his own worldview.

Bogdanov's pursuit of a systematic, scientific philosophy began with *Basic Elements of the Historical View of Nature* (1899),[3] in which he presented a picture of reality as a single, dynamic, interconnected flow of processes based on the monism of motion (or 'energy') as 'one and eternal'. He explained how nature, life, the individual human psyche, and human society are all parts of the same interconnected reality and are subject to the same laws of nature. He particularly emphasised the concept that all processes of the individual psyche, as well as those of whole societies, are determined by external influences of the natural world – i.e. that existence determines consciousness. Another notable feature of *Basic Elements* was Bogdanov's replacement of the concept of dialectical change – development through contradiction or of the transformation of quantity to quality – with the concept of a dynamic equilibrium of forces and the notion that quantity and quality are entirely commensurable.

In his next book, *Cognition from the Historical Point of View*,[4] Bogdanov focused specifically on the question of how the human psyche is conditioned by its environment. He explained how cognition 'arises from non-cognitive processes' and how phenomena both inside and outside the processes of cognition are part of a determinist system. In the course of doing so, Bogdanov denied Kant's notion that the categories of cognition are inherent in the human mind and argued that such categories of thought as space, time, and causality are psychical forms – abstractions – that have been produced by humanity over its long history of cognitive activity and that are imparted to individuals by society. Thus, cognition is not an individual but a social process, and 'cognition plays the same role in the life of the social whole as consciousness does in the life of the individual'.[5] Moreover, consistent with his Marxist outlook, Bogdanov asserted that 'the social labour struggle for existence, or the process of production, is the basis on which cognition arises and develops'.[6]

---

3 Bogdanov 1899a. It is Volume 1 of the Bogdanov Library.
4 Bogdanov 1902a.
5 Bogdanov 1902a, p. 135.
6 Bogdanov 1902a, p. 115.

It must have become clear to Bogdanov that 'motion' or 'energy' was as inadequate a basis for a monist outlook as metaphysical materialism, since the notion that some 'thing' is the cause of sensations (and so, ultimately, of cognition) leads inevitably to a dualism of exterior and interior, physical and psychical. Bogdanov found a solution to this problem in the neutral monism of being and cognition advanced by Ernst Mach and Richard Avenarius – the idea that the 'physical' and the 'psychical' are two sides of a single reality. As Mach put it, sense elements (of colour, sound, pressures, space, time, etc.) are the only reality. They are called 'psychical' when taken in relation to the physiology of a person's sensory apparatus and 'physical' when they are taken in relation to complexes in the physical world.[7]

In a series of articles that became the first two volumes of *Empiriomonism*,[8] Bogdanov applied this neutral monism to the worldview he had developed in *Basic Elements of the Historical View of Nature*. His continuing task was to explain how the operations of the human psyche are interconnected with the rest of nature and are ultimately caused by external stimuli, and he sought to 'systematically reduce all the gaps in our experience to the principle of continuity'. These gaps included the gap between 'spirit' and 'matter', the gap between 'consciousness' and 'physiology', and the gaps in the field of experiences that separate the individual from the universe and individuals from one another.

In the third volume of *Empiriomonism*, Bogdanov dealt with the question of how his scientific philosophy related to Marxism. He began by explaining the superiority of his empiriomonism to the outdated theory of knowledge of G.V. Plekhanov, the self-styled defender of 'orthodox' 'dialectical materialism'.[9] He went on to show how empiriomonism substantiates the basic principle of historical materialism, that a society's economic base determines its ideological superstructure. What Marx referred to as 'the material forces of production' Bogdanov called 'the technology of productive labour' and what Marx referred to as 'the production of material life' Bogdanov called 'the assimilation of energy from the environment'. For both Marx and Bogdanov, the process is the same: the mode of production determines social, political, and intellectual life. As Bogdanov put it, the technological process 'is the genetically primary realm of social life and all social development can issue only from it'.[10]

---

7   Mach 1897, p. 15.
8   Bogdanov 2019.
9   The term 'dialectical materialism' was never used by Marx or Engels to designate their outlook. It was coined by Joseph Dietzgen and popularised by G.V. Plekhanov.
10   Bogdanov 2019, p. 328.

Bogdanov concluded by insisting that empiriomonism is a Marxist philosophy developed in a Marxian way. It is 'the ideology', he said, 'of the "productive forces" of the technological process',[11] and it was arrived at by abstracting the worldview of workers in machine production. In short, empiriomonism is the ideology of the industrial working class. Bogdanov further insisted that his 'point of view, while not being "materialist" in the narrow sense of this word, belongs to the same order as "materialist" systems'.[12]

In the second group of works in this period (all of which are contained in this volume), Bogdanov used polemics with Russian Marxist revisionists as an opportunity to further elaborate his own philosophy.

Ironically, the starting point of the Russian revisionists – most notably Peter Struve, Nikolai Berdiaev, and Sergei Bulgakov – was the same as Bogdanov's: the search for a scientific philosophy that would support the principles of historical materialism. However, whereas Bogdanov had begun with the neo-positivist, empiricist trend in contemporary scientific philosophy, the Russian revisionists adopted neo-Kantianism.[13] And whereas the logic of Bogdanov's radical empiricism led him to a rigorous and consistent monism, the logic of the Kantian outlook led the revisionists to dualism, idealism, and religion.[14]

This latter possibility was not in the least foreseen by Peter Struve, one of the intellectual leaders in Russian Marxism in the 1890s and a collaborator with G.V. Plekhanov and V.I. Lenin until the turn of the century. Struve became famous with his first book, *Critical Remarks on Russia's Economic Development* (1894), which was devoted to proving that Russia was on the path toward capitalism on the European model. In this work, Struve took what he thought was a thoroughly Marxian position, with one exception. 'We cannot but recognise', he wrote, 'that a purely philosophical foundation of this doctrine [historical materialism] has not yet been given'.[15] He then proposed to build that foundation with the help of the German neo-Kantian philosopher, Alois Riehl.

At the time, this did not seem unreasonable. As a scientific philosophy, Riehl's variety of neo-Kantianism had a great deal in its favour. Riehl claimed to be a 'critical monist',[16] and he was one of the few neo-Kantians to take the

11   Ibid., p. 407.
12   Ibid.
13   For discussions of the quest for a scientific philosophy at the turn of the twentieth century, see Richardson 1997, 2008, and Howard 2004.
14   The most complete discussion of Struve's intellectual development is in Pipes 1970. Struve, Bulgakov, and Berdiaev are discussed in Kindersley 1962 and Mendel 1961.
15   Struve 1894, p. 46.
16   Heidelberger 2006.

standpoint of materialism, in the sense of treating matter as the cause of sensations.[17] Riehl's philosophy must also have been attractive since it appeared to have much in common with radical empiricism; in Russia Riehl was often studied in connection with Richard Avenarius.[18]

Nikolai Berdiaev and Sergei Bulgakov, two rising stars in Russian Marxist circles, followed in Struve's footsteps, and, from the mid-1890s to the end of the century, Struve, Berdiaev, and Bulgakov used arguments taken from Riehl and other neo-Kantian philosophers to develop their Marxist outlooks. What they did not realise, however, was that they were stepping onto a logical slippery slope toward idealism. They failed to appreciate that the metaphysical materialism of Kant's *Critique of Pure Reason* inevitably brought with it the dualist idealism of his *Critique of Practical Reason*. If a 'thing-in-itself' is the source of human perception, then it must be different from and independent of perception, and two realms of being must therefore exist: experience and transcendent being.

This, indeed, *was* Riehl's position. Following Kant, he distinguished between the world of experience, in which science sought objective truths, and a transcendent world of free will and ethical reasoning. Riehl believed that epistemology could clarify how scientific truth is arrived at, but he did not think it could provide a philosophical outlook or a picture of the world. The realm of philosophy, he said, 'is not the real but the possible, that which may be created by the will and the power of man'.[19] '[Philosophy] refutes the fatalistic meaning that is generally given to the conception of the universal reign of law in nature, and shows men how to assert and to extend their rule over nature'.[20] Thus, the same work – *The Philosophy of Criticism* – that the Russian neo-Kantian Marxists used to justify historical materialism could equally well have been quoted in order to refute it.

The slippery slope toward dualism (then idealism and ultimately religion) began with the question of morality and free will. Even as they continued to claim commitment to the Social-Democratic movement, the neo-Kantian Marxists began to adopt principles alien to historical materialism. By 1897, Struve defended Kant's separation of the realm of experience, in which causality prevails, and the realm of subjective ideals, in which freedom rules. Ideals come from outside science, he said, and people have free will to pursue their

---

17   Heidelberger 2007, p. 29.
18   Vucinich 1970, p. 251.
19   Riehl 1894, p. 22.
20   Riehl 1894, p. 23.

ideals.[21] In 1901, Berdiaev, even while asserting that the social ideal of Marxism was objectively necessary, insisted that it must also be subjectively desirable and objectively ethical, and ethics, Berdiaev said, 'must take Kant's critique as its starting point'.[22]

Russia's neo-Kantian Marxists were soon swept up in the rising tide of idealism in Russian culture. The process began with their association with the Moscow Psychological Society, which had been taken over by neo-Kantian philosophers seeking a metaphysical alternative to the traditional positivist, materialistic, and scientistic outlook of the Russian intelligentsia.[23] Its journal, *Voprosy filosofii i psikhologii* [*Problems of Philosophy and Psychology*] became a venue for articles by Struve, Berdiaev, and Bulgakov at the same time it was publishing articles by Christian philosopher Vladimir Solovev.

Solovev had sprung to fame in the 1870s as a bitter critic of European positivism,[24] and by the late 1890s he had developed a religious philosophy that could hardly have been more hostile to the principles of historical materialism. He countered empiricism with intuition, materialism with idealism, determinism with freedom, and atheism with Christianity. Solovev celebrated the absolute value of the individual and combined idealism and liberalism in the notion of *lichnost* or personhood. 'Human personhood', he said, 'possesses in principle *unconditional dignity*, on which is based its *inalienable rights* ...'.[25]

Solovev inspired the 'new religious consciousness' in Russian culture at the turn of the century, which was manifested in the work of the symbolist poets of the 'silver age of Russian poetry', religious-philosophical societies that formed in Moscow and St. Petersburg, and various groups of self-styled 'god-seekers', mystical anarchists, etc.[26] He exercised a profound influence, as well, over the Russian neo-Kantian Marxists, who enthusiastically adopted his notions of absolute values and the sanctity of individual personhood.

The watershed event in the rise of idealism in Russian culture was the publication in 1902 of the symposium, *Problems of Idealism*, which was organised and edited by Peter Struve but was sponsored and published by the Moscow Psychological Society. It was also a watershed moment for the Russian revisionists, since the contributions by Struve, Berdiaev, and Bulgakov to the symposium signified their final abandonment of historical materialism. Struve announced

---

21   Struve 1897.
22   Berdiaev 1901, p. 71.
23   Poole 1999.
24   Solovyov [Solovev] 1996.
25   Solovev 1896, p. 868.
26   See, for example, Rosenthal 1975 and Read 1979.

that he had 'openly passed to metaphysics, that is, having broken with positivism, in the *philosophical* sense, [he] ceased to be a Marxist'.[27] Berdiaev, too,
stood 'on the ground of philosophic idealism'[28] and argued that the struggle
for human liberation was essentially an ethical task and not a natural necessity.[29] Bulgakov declared that participation 'in the current social struggle' 'will
be motivated not by egoistic class interest, but by religious duty, by an absolute
order of the moral law, by a dictate of God'.[30]

Even though they had abandoned – and even argued against – the principles of historical materialism, however, the Russian revisionists continued to
present themselves as Social Democrats, in the same way that the Bernsteinian
revisionists remained within the German Social-Democratic Party. Although
they argued that the contradictions of capitalism were being 'blunted' and
although they gave up *Zusammenbruchstheorie* – the idea that capitalism must
inevitably collapse in socialist revolution, they claimed to still believe in the
principles of socialism. Their difference from revolutionary Marxists was that
they conceived of socialism as an ethical ideal and the path toward it as a
moral endeavour. The difference between the Russian and German revisionists was that the Bernsteinians remained in the Social-Democratic movement,
while Struve and his colleagues did not. After the 1905 Revolution, the Russian revisionists abandoned Social Democracy entirely. Until that time, Russia's
revolutionary Marxists – Bogdanov included – bitterly condemned them as
renegades. After 1905, when they no longer pretended to be Social Democrats,
they were simply ignored.

Bogdanov makes rather contradictory claims in his introduction to *On the
Psychology of Society*. He says that the 'struggle with theoretical "idealism" ...
provided the immediate occasion for the appearance of the articles that comprise this work' but then asserts that 'the principal content of this work is not
a critique of or a polemic with "idealism"'.

That these articles are polemical is unquestionable. In them Bogdanov subjects articles by Berdiaev and Bulgakov to withering critiques. He ridicules
the notion of absolute truth and absolute values and criticises the idealism of
Immanuel Kant and Vladimir Solovev. On the other hand, the most important
aspect of this polemic is that it provided Bogdanov the opportunity to elaborate and develop his own scientific philosophy. For example, one of the ways

---

27   Poole 2003, p. 156.
28   Poole 2003, p. 162.
29   Poole 2003, p. 189.
30   Poole 2003, p. 118.

in which he discredits the idealists is through the application of his concept of sociomorphism[31] – the idea that methods of thinking of a given era reflect its methods of social production. Thus, Bogdanov debunks the notion that the idealists are pursuing eternal, absolute ideals by demonstrating that their way of thinking is not timeless and absolute but is the specific manifestation of their social and economic status. Idealism, he argues, is the ideology of an intelligentsia that hopes to serve as the spiritual leader of a society that is based on the exchange relationships of modern capitalism

Furthermore, Bogdanov not only criticises the ideology of the idealists, but responds to *their* critique of Marxism, and in the course of doing so he provides a more thorough explanation of how his historical view of nature and empiriomonist philosophy substantiate the principles of historical materialism. He pays particular attention to the relation of economic base and ideological superstructure and to the precise causal process through which changes in the relations of production produce changes in ideology.

The same considerations apply to the articles in *New World*. Bogdanov's polemic against the idealists continued, but he now turns his attention to the future and a discussion of how his philosophy envisions future socialist society. Bogdanov first deals with extreme individualism, arguing that it is caused by the specialisation and social antagonisms of exchange society, and he explains, in empiriomonistic terms, how socialism will bring social fragmentation to an end – how the 'narrowness and incompleteness of human beings that has created inequality, heterogeneity, and the psychical disconnection of people' will be overcome. Bogdanov then takes up the problem of moral norms. After explaining that compulsory norms of the present originated in the process of production and serve as conservative supports for the status quo, he argues that in the future norms will take on a scientific form. They will be goal-oriented or *expedient*: 'if you want such and such, then you must do such and such'. Thus, since members of the working class will all share the same goals, they will voluntarily pursue them without compulsion. Finally, Bogdanov explains that questions regarding 'the meaning of life' will become irrelevant to people who have taken charge of their destiny and who are using their knowledge to master the forces of nature. They will become 'harmonious and whole people who have been freed from contradictions and compulsion in their practice and from fetishism in their knowledge'.

---

31   Bogdanov developed the concept in this time period, but he did not use the term 'sociomorphism' to refer to it. I am not aware that he used it before he wrote *The Philosophy of Living Experience*. See Bogdanov 2016, pp. 219–21.

Bogdanov also attacked idealism in 'Legal Society and Labour Society' (in *Studies in the Realist Worldview*), a review of *Economy and Law* by the neo-Kantian philosopher of law, Rudolf Stammler.[32] In that work, Stammler had argued that society is created by laws and norms and is fundamentally moral. Law regulates the economy, he said; the economy does not determine the law. In his review, Bogdanov continues both to criticise the neo-Kantian outlook and to develop his own scientific philosophy. The essence of social life, he says, is the process of collective labour in people's struggle for life and progress. Legal norms are only organising adaptations that are worked out in the labour process, and they have only conditional and temporary meaning.

The turn toward philosophical idealism was not the only deviation from historical materialism on the part of Russia's Marxist revisionists. Like the Bernsteinian revisionists in Germany at the same time, some Russian revisionists abandoned the labour theory of value and adopted the theory of marginal utility.
     The theory of marginal utility, which takes the value of commodities to be a function not of the cost of production but of the effect of consumer demand on production, first appeared among neo-classical economists in the middle of the nineteenth century as an alternative to Adam Smith's and David Ricardo's labour theory of value. It did not become a problem for Marxists, however, until 1894 when volume 3 of *Capital* was published. Two years later, Eugen Böhm-Bawerk, an Austrian economist, published *Karl Marx and the Close of his System*[33] in which he pointed out what he thought was a contradiction between Marx's treatment of value in volumes 1 and 3 of *Capital*. He took Marx's assertion in volume 1 that 'all value is based on labour and labour alone, and that values of commodities [are] in proportion to the working time necessary for their production' and contrasted it with the statement in volume 3 that value is relative to the costs of production, that 'individual commodities do and must exchange with each other in a proportion different from that of the labour incorporated in them, and this not accidentally and temporarily, but of necessity and permanently'.[34]
     Struve and Bulgakov were the first Russian Marxists to address this issue. First, they defended the labour theory of value, then they accepted Böhm-Bawerk's analysis but argued that marginalism is actually compatible with the labour theory of value, but they ultimately abandoned the labour theory of

32   Stammler 1896.
33   Böhm-Bawerk 1949.
34   Böhm-Bawerk 1949, pp. 29, 30.

value completely and adopted marginalism. Marginalism was also adopted by two important Russian (former) Marxist economists, Semen Frank and Mikhail Tugan-Baranovsky.[35]

Bogdanov made specific rebuttals to Frank's and Tugan-Baranovsky's critiques of the labour theory of value,[36] but he also defended the labour theory of value in general terms in 'Technology and Exchange' in *Studies in the Realist Worldview*. Bogdanov first explains how his own historical view of nature substantiates the labour theory of value and then dismantles Böhm-Bawerk's arguments against it. Of particular note is Bogdanov's expression of Marx's conception of the labour theory of value in terms of the universal system he had established in *Basic Elements of the Historical View of Nature*, i.e. that production and distribution are social adaptations in the struggle of society to survive and that social labour should be considered as a specific aspect of the general expenditure of human energy. Moreover, Bogdanov introduces a new understanding of the 'material' basis of society and social development. Whereas Marx treated the changing means of production and ownership of the means of production as the key to economic and social change, Bogdanov treats the changing technology of production and mastery of the technology of production as the basis of change.[37]

The Text and Translation

The first two sections of this volume consist of the contents of two books of collected articles, *On the Psychology of Society*[38] and *New World*.[39] *New World* appeared in three editions – 1905, 1918, and 1920 – and was published for a

---

35   Kindersley 1962, pp. 154–72.
36   Bogdanov 1899b, 1900, 1901a.
37   Bogdanov would expound this concept in greater detail in Chapter 9, 'Historical Materialism', in the third volume of *Empiriomonism* (Bogdanov 2019). What Marx refers to as 'the material forces of production', Bogdanov calls 'the technology of productive labour' and what Marx refers to as 'the production of material life', Bogdanov calls 'assimilation of energy from the environment'. But for both Marx and Bogdanov, the process is the same: the mode of production conditions social, political, and intellectual life. As Bogdanov puts it, the technological process 'is the *genetically* primary realm of social life and all social development can issue only from it' (p. 328), and the purpose of the technological process is to produce an energetical balance – the preponderance of assimilation over expenditure of energy. The ideological process is genetically secondary or derivative, since its function is to remove contradictions from the technological process.
38   Bogdanov 1906a.
39   Bogdanov 1905e.

fourth time in the collection, *On Proletarian Culture: Articles 1904–1924* (1925).[40] I used the 1905 edition to be consistent with the time period in which all the other articles in this volume were written. However, I have compared the 1905 edition with the 1925 edition, and I make note of all revisions in footnotes.

The last section consists of two articles Bogdanov wrote for a collective work, intended as a response to *Problems of Idealism, Studies in the Realist World-view*,[41] which he edited. *Studies in the Realist Worldview* was published in 1904 and reissued in 1905. I have translated the 1905 edition, although I have not found any difference between them except for the foreword to the 1905 edition.

The order in which Bogdanov published these articles is as follows:
    'What is Idealism' (Bogdanov 1901b)
    'The Development of Life in Nature and in Society' (Bogdanov 1902c)
    'A New Middle Ages: On *Problems of Idealism*' (Bogdanov 1903a)
    'Authoritarian Thinking' (Bogdanov 1903b)
    'In the Field of View' (Bogdanov 1903c)
    'A New Middle Ages: On the Benefits of Knowledge' (Bogdanov 1904a)
    'A New Middle Ages: Echoes of the Past' (Bogdanov 1904b)
    'The Integration of Humankind' (Bogdanov 1904c)
    'A New Middle Ages: A Philosophical Nightmare' (Bogdanov 1904d)
    'The Accursed Questions of Philosophy' (Bogdnaov 1904e)
    'Exchange and Technology' (Bogdanov 1904a)
    'Legal Society and Labour Society' (Bogdanov 1904b)
    'Norms and Goals of Life' (Bogdanov 1905a)
    'Revolution and Philosophy' (Bogdanov 1906b)

In the introductions to my translations of *Empiriomonism*[42] and *The Philosophy of Living Experience*,[43] I have discussed in some detail my approach to translating Bogdanov and how I translate his key philosophical terms and concepts.

As far as the articles in this volume are concerned, there are several terms that I feel require a comment.

One is *zakonomernost*, which in ordinary usage means regularity, conformity to a pattern, obeying rules, etc. As a philosophical term, however, *zakonomernost* means 'conformity to the laws of nature' consistent with the idea that physical reality is governed by cause and effect. This, indeed, is what Bogdanov

---

40   Bogdanov 1925.
41   Bogdanov 1905a.
42   Bogdanov 2019.
43   Bogdanov 2016.

had in mind, except that, whereas he conceived of the processes of the universe as invariably subject to cause and effect, he understood 'laws of nature' to be human formulations, the truth of which are relative to their time. Consequently, although I translate *zakonomernost* as 'regularity', the reader should keep in mind that Bogdanov uses the term to mean that nothing occurs without a cause and every occurrence has a necessary consequence.

Moreover, *zakonomernost* was a particularly sharp point of contention between 'materialist' and 'idealist' Marxists because of its implication for the question of determinism versus free will. Bogdanov's frequent use of the term would have been an obvious affront to the idealists, who specifically and emphatically denied that human beings were subject to *zakonomernost*. In his excellent translation of *Problems of Idealism*, Randall A. Poole has translated *zakonomernost* as 'determinism', which is exactly what it meant both to the idealists and to Bogdanov.

Another term is *lichnost*, which in ordinary usage can mean person, personality, individual, individuality, etc. However, as noted above, Vladimir Solovev employed *lichnost* as a key concept of his philosophy, using it to refer to the sanctity of individual personhood, and it was adopted and celebrated by Nikolai Berdiaev, Sergei Bulgakov, and other Russian idealists. I have chosen not to translate Bogdanov's usage of *lichnost* as 'individual personhood', which would be quite awkward and not always relevant, but either as 'human individuality' or 'the human individual', and I leave it to readers to decide if in any given instance Bogdanov intends to contrast his usage of the term with that of the idealists.

The term *sobiranie*, which is of crucial importance in Chapter 10 – 'Sobiranie cheloveka', in Russian – does not have an agreed-upon translation. Robert C. Williams has translated it as 'collectivising'.[44] In Biggart, Gloveli, and Yassour's bibliography of Bogdanov's works, it appears as 'gathering'.[45] And in his biography of Bogdanov,[46] James D. White has translated it as 'integration'. Before I read White's book, I was leaning toward 'coming together', but White has convinced me that 'integration' is even better. The 'coming together' of humankind that Bogdanov had in mind was the 'gathering' of humanity into an integral whole, and the notion of integration – whether of an integral worldview or an integral personality – was an important one in Russian culture of the nineteenth and early twentieth centuries. Translating *sobiranie* as 'integration' thus indicates Bogdanov's connection with the culture of his time.

---

44   Williams 1986, p. 39.
45   Biggart et al. 1998, p. 107.
46   White 2019b, p. 90.

Finally, Bogdanov conceives of a society based on an exchange economy as one in which labour is divided between *organizatory* (singular: *organizator*) who organise production and *ispolniteli* (singular: *isponitel*) who carry out an *organizator*'s directives, and he uses this concept to explain the dualistic thinking that is typical of exchange society. (It is this dualism, by the way, that will be overcome in the 'integration of humankind' that socialism will accomplish.) Translating *organizator* as 'organiser' makes obvious sense, and that is what I do. However, I feel it would be confusing to translate *ispolniteli* as 'executors' or 'executives', which is the dictionary definition of the term. The notion of a society divided into 'organisers' (who are very knowledgeable and have great responsibilities) and 'executors' or 'executives' (whose training is only sufficient for carrying out directives) would be at great variance with how these words are used today. I therefore translate *ispolniteli* as 'implementers' not 'executors' and *ispolnitelskii* as 'implementational' not 'executive'.

I am once again indebted to Evgeni V. Pavlov, the real *organizator* of the Bogdanov Library, for his invaluable advice and encouragement.

PART 1

On the Psychology of Society

∵

From the Author

The storms and tempests of the Great Russian Revolution[1] temporarily moved questions of theory to the side lines, even within Social Democracy. Meanwhile, right now, the democratisation of knowledge in general and the spread of Marxist ideas among the masses in particular are proceeding with unprecedented speed and are creating a real and robust basis for the theoretical development of Social Democracy in our country, and this development is becoming more necessary than ever before. The novelty and complexity of the political positions and social groupings that have sprung up in the course of this, the greatest and most distinctive of the revolutions that we know of, are such that only the greatest specificity and precision of our basic points of view can safeguard our young party from programmatic and tactical errors – errors that are infinitely more harmful and dangerous in an era of revolution than in peaceful times. The broader and more complex that practical work is, the more important is the role of the theory that illuminates and oversees it.

A few years ago, when the whole Great Revolution was still in the future, the strikingly rapid growth of the proletarian movement had already made it obvious – and not only to Marxists – that this revolution would soon arrive and that it was precisely the working class that would be the force that would lead and organise it. At that time, progressive bourgeois groups began systematic attempts to assert their practical and ideological leadership over the proletariat. If they had been successful, the Great Russian Revolution would have repeated in full measure that same picture of blatant political exploitation of the proletariat by the liberal bourgeoisie that was so characteristic of the of the nineteenth-century revolutions in Western Europe. But our young Social Democracy succeeded in smashing these attempts one after another. It was able to do away with both 'economism',[2] which disparaged the political and class consciousness of the proletariat and handed hegemony over the political struggle to the bourgeois parties, and 'idealism',[3] which undermined prolet-

---

1 The Russian Revolution of 1905 [trans.].
2 'Economism' refers to the first open schism in Russian Social Democracy, which had to do with the relationship of the Social Democrats to the working class. In 1899, E.D. Kuskova wrote an article arguing that workers should fight only for economic demands and should leave the political struggle against the autocracy to the middle classes. G.V. Plekhanov and V.I. Lenin called this 'economism' and used the label to denigrate Social Democrats who emphasised economic over political appeals in mobilising the working class [trans.].
3 'Idealism' is how Bogdanov refers to Marxist revisionism of the day – the idea that socialism could be achieved through democratic methods rather than revolution. By using the term

arian class theory and substituted pathetic bourgeois ethical idols for the great class ideal of Social Democracy. All this has so far allowed the revolutionary proletariat to preserve its leading position in the people's common struggle.

Both 'economism' and 'idealism' were not smashed immediately, however. They enjoyed a period of relative influence on broad layers not only of the 'intelligentsia' that gravitated toward Social Democracy but even of the advanced elements of the proletariat, and, from the perspective of the logic of class development in social struggle, this is not surprising. Moreover, due to the unequal level of development of different layers of the militant proletariat and due to the dual nature of the specifically 'intelligentsia' part of its ideologists, the tendency to opportunism and eclecticism that are fully and clearly expressed in these past attempts will survive for a long time in Social Democracy, albeit in a weakened and moderated form. New moments of temporary triumph of these tendencies are possible, and our struggle with them must continue for a long time.

I personally did not have to participate directly in the struggle against 'economism'. Prison and exile placed me too far from practical work during its heyday. But neither prison nor exile posed a huge obstacle for the struggle with theoretical 'idealism', and this struggle provided the immediate occasion for the appearance of the articles that comprise this work.

The principal content of this work, however, is not a critique of or a polemic with 'idealism'.

The success of 'idealism' was especially remarkable since the ideologists of this trend were notable for being of a far from high calibre. In part, they were representatives of the philistine type of scientific specialisation (such as Messrs Struve, Bulgakov, and Tugan-Baranovsky)[4] that under normal conditions is organically opposed to the ideologists of the proletariat and, in part, they were people who simply had ignorant and frivolous attitudes toward ideological work (such as Mr Berdiaev),[5] and I could not but arrive at the conclusion that no small part of their success must be directly ascribed to the 'theoretical unconcern' of the majority of politically active Social Democrats against whom Comrade Plekhanov has always justly been up in arms. People who have committed themselves to practical work have for the most part devoted so little time and attention to questions of general theory that they have not been able to

---

'Idealism', Bogdanov emphasises the neo-Kantian philosophical and ethical concerns of the revisionists [trans.].

4   Petr Berngardovich Struve (1870–1944), Sergei Nikolaevich Bulgakov (1871–1944), Mikhail Ivanovich Tugan-Baranovskii (1865–1919) [trans.].

5   Nikolai Alexandrovich Berdiaev (1874–1948) [trans.].

quickly understand the scholastical twaddle and epistemological references of Messrs 'Idealists', who have emphatically sworn that they are 'also Social Democrats' and are only 'underpinning' Marxism with a 'philosophical foundation'. In addition, some of these gentlemen do deserve credit for their struggle with the reactionary side of Narodism in the past. Others deserve no such credit, it is true, but they have displayed all the greater aplomb. All this has made an impression on the inexperienced and has increased their confusion. It is a graphic illustration of the old saying, 'whoever has a club in his hands is a corporal'.

In the given circumstances, it was obvious that first-hand polemics with the 'Idealists' was the least important aspect of the task facing a theorist. The main task consisted in explaining and popularising basic principles that would provide a point of view from which it would be easy to judge the vital meaning of any ideology, even the most abstract. This was the only possible way to avert any future 'abstract-theoretical' deviations toward ideologies that are alien to the proletariat – deviations that pave the way to confusion in practice and opportunism in tactics.

What was required was, on the one hand, to clearly formulate the real meaning of ideology in general, and, on the other hand, to present the meaning of different *basic ideological types*. And it was necessary to state these ideological types specifically enough so that it would be possible to easily match to them one or another concrete ideological manifestation – to one or another doctrine, theory, religion, etc. This was the principal and *positive* task of my work, and the larger share of the articles of this collection are devoted to it.

In explaining the role of ideological forms as organising adaptations of social life, I tried to show how necessary it is to correlate these forms to social practice. In establishing historical types of ideology and of the authoritarian, social-fetishistic, and synthetic[6] forms of ideology, I pointed out their connection with specific social formations and classes and with the development and degradation of those formations and classes. This automatically produced firm criteria for evaluating progressiveness or reaction in life – for evaluating the 'truth' or 'falsity' of different ideological forms, right down to the most abstract forms such as philosophical or religious theories.

The remaining, smaller number of articles in this book are of a predominantly critical and polemical nature. They are directed against 'idealism' and 'critical' scholasticism. At the present time, as everyone knows, Messrs 'Ideal-

---

6   To avoid the tsarist censorship of this time, Bogdanov used 'synthetic' to mean what he later called 'socialist' [trans.].

ists' no longer bother Social Democracy with their sympathy. They are unmasked and have already found their place – for the most part taking shelter
under the right wing of the liberal 'Kadet' party.[7] But, all the same, I think that
my critical analysis of their ideas will still prove useful from time to time in
the future. Bourgeois tendencies strive to permeate into proletarian ideology
by various paths and from various sides, but they themselves are not particularly varied in their forms, and the same basic motifs constantly appear with
very little variation. At present, theoretical motifs of this kind have retreated
for a while in the face of practical ones. One does not hear about 'idealism', but
instead the 'blunting of contradictions' and the 'uniting of all classes against
the common enemy' make their appearance in countless nuances and aspects.
The course of events is slowing down, life is becoming less stormy and troubled,
and, along with this, interest in theory is growing in wide circles of Social Democracy. 'Absolutist' attitudes and 'idealist' and 'critical' theories will appear on
the scene once again. They will probably take on some new outward forms but
will have the same essential content as ideologically organising forms for the
practice of compromise and the 'blunting of contradictions'. And then it will
be useful to recall that all this has happened before and to use an old, proven
tool along with new techniques that issue from new conditions ...

Pursuant to these considerations, I added to this second edition of this work
not only the article 'Revolution and Philosophy', which concisely summarises
the relationship of the most 'abstract' ideology to the most 'concrete' practice,
but also two small critical articles ('On the Usefulness of Knowledge' and 'A
Philosophical Nightmare') that depict two distinctive aspects of ideological
degeneration.

Let the calm voice of theory not be lost amidst the awesome roar of the great
storm of life.

20 June 1906

---

7   The 'Constitutional Democratic Party' (abbreviated as the KD or Kadet Party by combining
    the initial letters of its name, *Konstitutsionno-Demokraticheskaia Partiia*) was created during
    the Revolution of 1905 by a coalition of liberal groups. It was a party of middle-class intel-
    lectuals and professionals, and its philosophical basis was indeed supplied by neo-Kantian
    idealists (see Poole 2003) [trans.].

CHAPTER 1

In the Field of View

... Es ändert sich die Zeit ...[1]

∶∶

In olden times, people lived better ... That is, not actually better – of course not better – but ... easier. And not easier in the sense that there was less toil and suffering – no, there was plenty of that – but people did not have to *think*. Other people thought for them. But these other people also actually did not think because a third set of people thought for them, and, similarly, a fourth set thought for the third set, and so on. It would seem that at the very beginning of this chain of 'not thinking' there must have been some kind of 'thinkers', but that was not the case. The fact of the matter was that there was no end to the chain. The whole chain of living people was connected with the chain of the dead, the dead did the thinking for the living under the guise of 'precepts of the ancestors'. In exactly the same way, still more dead people did the thinking for these dead people, and the chain continued back until it was finally lost in the depths of time. Undoubtedly, the creative thought of humankind did indeed exist in this chain of chains – otherwise life would long ago have come to an end. But this creative thought was spread along the entire chain in such infinitely small doses that they were imperceptible and therefore did not tire people out. If creative thought manifested itself in a great amount at any point on the chain – becoming noticeable and therefore tiring – the chain convulsively curled and shattered the manifestation into dust. The chain then untwisted itself, and everything went on as before. This is how it was, and it seemed to work well.

Everything was simple and clear and so well defined that it was easy for it to be kept within the confines of one or two formulas. One can find these formulas in their purest and most regular from in philosophy: they were *absolute*

---

1 This phrase is taken from a line from Friedrich Schiller's *William Tell*, 'Das Alte stürzt, es ändert sich die Zeit, und neues Leben blüht aus den Ruinen'. 'The old collapses, times change, and new life blossoms in the ruins' [trans.]

and categorical imperatives. Thinking was determined by the absolute; actions were determined by the categorical imperative. Both of them applied not only to important things but also to trifles. Every link that was higher on the chain was absolute for every link that was lower on the chain because it was the representative of all the rest of the chain that was unwinding endlessly upwards and into the past. It was known as authority, and each of its manifestations was considered to be an expression of the eternal will that lay at the beginning of the chain. It was appropriate for absolutely everyone to be commanded and to be commanded categorically, i.e. without giving reasons and without any conditions. This makes sense: if a command were not a self-sufficient category, if it were subject to explanations or limiting conditions, then it would be necessary to think about it, and it was precisely this that was forbidden.

This is how it went. Humankind was given a specific directive from the nearest absolute – how to live, what to believe, what to do. These directives had no explanation. They were therefore incontestable, and there was therefore no thought of criticising them. In much later times, when there were several absolutes side by side, the categorical nature of their commands was still not prevented. Because their roles had been assigned to them, they did not come into conflict with one another. One indicated what to think, what to believe, and how to feel for one realm of life, another absolute did the same for another realm of life, a third for a third realm of life, etc. They mutually acknowledged one another because they had a common starting point in the absolutes that stood higher, just as those higher absolutes had a common starting point in the ones that stood even higher than them. All the links in the chain did not think, but each of them had available completely sufficient information in order to manage without thinking. Each link was given, first, a certain sum of categorical commands from higher links and, needless to say, the lack of any doubt that these commands were obligatory, second, a profound feeling of the infallibility of *its own* absolute and categorical commands to lower links that corresponded to its faith in the infallibility of the higher links, and, third, a certain spontaneous will that caused an immediate and decisive reflex when the necessity arose to give a categorical command when the circumstances were not foreseen and specified in advance. All this was sufficient for all the needs of life – for the kind of life, of course, that did not think. 'Imperatives' did not always turn out to be wise – sometimes they resulted in starvation and devastation and annihilation. But this did not shake the infallibility of the various links because infallibility was supplemented with inscrutability. The possibility of doubt was replaced with a formula; this meant that it had to be. There could be no breaks in the chain since the human power of reproduction is limitless, and the people who were destroyed were replaced by exact copies.

It is clear that there was really no need to think, and thinking was for people who were not in their right mind. This was so clear to everyone that the phrase 'to be lost in thought' served to designate a mental disorder.

But life grew and the chain stretched out, and there finally came a time when it had to burst. Something new arose, and this new thing was called human individuality.

In the depths of social life, where its roots branch out into boundless nature, an invisible work was going on. Living cells of a powerful plant were building up their strength. They grew and became constrained, since both trunk and branches were entangled with countless loops of a chain, each link of which was – absolute. The living cells crowded together and pressed on the chain, now and then encountering pressure in return. Human individuality, harshly colliding with other people, began to contrast itself to them as a single entity with its own, special interests. Thus, human individuality was born. The pain of constrained life and the hostility of the spontaneous struggle for elbowroom were its midwife. The baby was healthy and energetic; the future belonged to it.

When the human individual tried to stand up to their full height, the links of the chain cut viciously into their body, and one of two things happened: either the chain stifled them or it burst. The former happened more often; the latter had more important results. Stifled individuals either died – as they would have died a little later on, anyway – or turned into an exact copy of the species of 'human' as it had always been before. The broken chain had to be reconnected, which made it shorter and its pressure even greater. It had to be stretched out even more tightly than before, and it now burst not one connection but several new ones. And this continued.

There was no possibility of holding on to the past. The same thing happened at each step: one or another of the countless representatives of the absolute, fulfilling their natural purpose, announced the categorical imperative to life. And what resulted? Something unheard of and unbelievable: the question 'why?' – the demand for a justification. The representative of the absolute could not even understand this. Bewilderment turned into animosity, and struggle began. Once doubt was raised, what had been indubitable ceased being so. Once it was possible to ask a question about the absolute, the absolute was no longer absolute. Once the realisation of the categorical imperative became dependent on specific conditions – whether or not there was the power to impose it – it lost its categorical nature. *This* was now irreparable.

Thus, the principle of human individuality had to be victorious because the spontaneity of social development was behind it, because the principle of individuality was an organic expression of the growing material forces of society.

But to be victorious – to destroy the obstacles in its path – still did not mean that everything was done. The principle of human individuality was born from the struggle of the individual against others, from the contradictions of the life of society; it embodied the creative power of that struggle and of those contradictions. But this creative power was limited. Opposing other people in this struggle, human individuality first stood up against the impersonal, stereotypical human being; here the individual did not contradict itself. But as soon as it won, what was the result? Now, instead of stereotypical impersonality, it faced another human individual; it was opposed by *it* and struggled *with it*. This was now a real contradiction, and in it the principle of human individuality found a boundary to its creative work. Each individual represented an element of the growing life of society, of its power in overcoming nature, and now all the elements of society struggled amongst themselves. Life that was growing turned against itself, and life, in its progressive movement, brought itself to a halt.

A new principle, a new form was needed in which this radical contradiction would disappear and the forces that were engendered in its depths would not waste themselves in fruitless and superficial struggle. This new form is the merging of individual lives into one grandiose whole that is harmonious in relation to its parts and that harmoniously arranges all its elements for one common struggle – struggle with the endless spontaneity of nature. Such a form is immeasurably more complex than either a chain of identically repeating links or an anarchical flood of harshly colliding atoms. It will take a huge amount of creative activity – both spontaneous and conscious – to accomplish this task. Only humanity – and not just one human – is capable of the task, and it was only while working on that task that it became humanity for the first time. This chapter of history began long ago, but no one knows exactly how far away or how near its conclusion will be.

The social life of people is not as even, consistent, and uniform as the abstract depiction of its changing types. The field of social life, on which so many seedlings of the future appear, is, at the same time, littered with debris from the past. *Human individuality* has still not completed its creatively destructive work and is still is tangled up everywhere in fragments of the old chain. And the individual is now incapable of completing its task *itself*; it is incapable of cutting through and throwing off the last of these fragments *itself*.

Those classes whose entire strength comes from the spontaneous-atomistic struggle of one human against another, cannot abandon the principle of this struggle – the principle of human individuality with its private interests and egotistical desires – for the sake of a superior ideal. This would mean to abandon *themselves*, to cease to be themselves. New classes now step forward demanding a higher ideal, and they declare it with increasing energy. They want to destroy the spontaneous collision of social atoms; they want to make it so that all atoms move harmoniously toward a common goal, so that they become elements of an orderly whole. The old atoms do not like this; they are afraid of losing elbowroom for their accustomed movement. It is not in their nature to understand what they might gain from full participation in the limitless and powerful movement of the whole, since they do not have and have never had this, and they naturally think that they will lose everything that they now have. It seems to them that the new relationships of life are worse than the old chains.

The atomistic classes – the middle, intermediate classes of our society – then change their battlefront. In order to find a support against the flow of time, they have no objection to grasping other surviving fragments of the old chain. They are, of course, as hostile to those immediate links that cut into their body as they were before, and, as before, they are prepared to protest against them. But now they ponder how to create a new chain that is more suitable for sufficiently restraining the new life that is being born. Recalling the strength of the previous chain, they now find it useful to attach their new chain to the remnants of the old one – not to those that still constrict themselves but to those that lie a little further away, preferably to those that have retreated fully into infinity so that they do not pose new dangers. Thus, the return to idols is accomplished.

This picture is unfolding before our eyes. The new idol worshippers begin by placing a series of huge, misty absolutes under life, and they explain that they are the goals of life and that the meaning of every movement of every atom is contained in them. They attach the end of their new chain to these absolutes, which are made, by the way, from very old material that they call 'duty'. They then unwind this chain and point out to all observers that it is completely safe to travel forward on it, since it is endless. They then begin to coil this chain around human nature while allowing the absolutes to pull on the other end. But since they themselves create both the chain and the absolutes, it is clear that this is what happens: the absolutes pull in a direction so that human individuality is torn from the old cruel and uncomfortable chains, but the coil is arranged in such a way as to more firmly distinguish each person from all other people in all their highest feelings, so that the very idea of merging with other people in life is eliminated as completely as possible. Thus, the struggle for individualism proceeds on two fronts – against the enemy on the right and against the enemy on the left.

All this stands for a little while, and it has a fleeting significance in the great struggle of social forces. Playing with absolutes is really advantageous for the atomistic classes only where society is filled with remnants and memories of the era of the absolute and where society, according to habit, thinks about new content in old forms. It is there that it ameliorates the transition from old forms of life to new ones and slows the development of the newest ones. At further stages, the social struggle is stripped of its misty shell and the atomistic classes, having attained real domination and having cut themselves off from the enemy on the right, cease trying to lull their enemies on the left with beautiful phrases. They then say to this enemy – with noble openness, not lacking in cynicism and arrogance – we are *beati possidentes*,[2] and we oppress you because it is profitable for us and power is in our hands.

For us, this time has not yet arrived, and, in the meantime, a whole saturnalia is unfolding before our eyes, in which yesterday's slaves, having become conscious of themselves as autonomous atoms, are enthralled with whirling in metaphysical-mystical dances with phantoms of the past, not noticing in the festive thrill the more than considerable growth of their dancing partner. Whoever does not want to participate in the saturnalia is reproached for being cold and arid, for being prosaic and coarse, and whoever tries to point out the artificial colour on the cheeks of the dancing partners is accused of hating the bright colours of life and of wanting to paint the whole world one drab colour. All this is done without any dissimulation; the ardent knights of the archaic ladies are sincerely convinced that they are infinitely above prosaic interests and class cravings. They have heard, of course, that there were people who taught everyone to treat the ideas and phrases of themselves and others objectively, who taught everyone to search for the practical, vital strivings that were hidden behind those ideas and phrases, and who taught everyone to uncover the unconscious basis of the work of consciousness by asking the question 'to whom is it useful?' But the knights of the painted phantoms have nothing to do with this coarse teaching; they do not ask the question 'to whom is it useful?', since even the interests of humanity are too narrow and petty for them. For them, only absolute ideals have value, and if the corollaries of these ideals were profitable for their own classes above all, then this was not a concern of theirs – it is the will of the absolute that was chosen by their prophets. And they continue to prophesy.

But there is no prophet in our fatherland, and the knights of the shadows find many opponents even from among people of *their own* classes and tendencies. Some are people who are by nature more rigorous and logical, and who hate the past too much to feel sympathy even toward its innocent phantom reflections. Some are people who fully feel the growing force of real life, pin their hopes on it, and do not want to seek a support anywhere else. Finally, some are

---

2   Latin, 'blessed are the possessors'. It means that the law favours the possessor, and it is also
    expressed by the phrase, 'possession is nine points of the law' [trans.].

more concerned with a conclusive victory over the past than with preventing an unattractive future. But people such as this are becoming ever fewer, and they are not the ones who will supersede the current 'heroes' of the day.

New voices are resounding, calm and self-assured, filled with self-satisfaction and the spirit of the golden mean. They say that clarifying ideas is not important and struggling against the mists of the absolute is superfluous. They advise dealing only with the practical conclusions of the priests of the absolute, and they find these conclusions useful in practice. That people's heads are clogged with the debris of the past seems really trivial to them, and from their point of view they are correct, since faith in the ghosts of the absolute does not decrease the rate of surplus value by even one per cent, and it often even makes the maintenance and growth of surplus value easier. These worthy people jeer more maliciously than anyone at those whom they take under their protection. In sympathetically deliberating the practical price of 'absolute' values and in seriously pointing out the real benefits of the 'ideal', they disclose more mercilessly than anyone the true meaning of their actions. A business-like mood appears on the scene that has nothing against the increasing mists but nevertheless does away with them all the more certainly by making them hopelessly laughable. People of such a frame of mind are tomorrow's 'heroes'.

Fortunately, the matter will not end with them. Suppressed voices are ringing out ever louder ...

Postscript of 1906. The 'tomorrow' that was spoken of has arrived ... People of the 'golden mean' form the real nucleus of Russia's liberal party – made up for the most part of the 'business-like' Kadet elements who come from the landed gentry. The time of conversations about 'idealism' has even passed, although later on, as circumstances change, these conversations will undoubtedly be renewed. The 'suppressed voices' of the struggling people cannot be suppressed any longer. Twice already they have drowned out all the old authorities with their roar, and the third time ...

CHAPTER 2

What is Idealism?

> ... Dogmatism necessarily has a *ready-made absolute* that does not move forward and is gripped in the one-sidedness of some logical definition; it is satisfied with what it has, and it does not progress on the basis of its principles, but, just the opposite, its principles are an immovable centre, around which dogmatism walks in a circle.
>
> A. ISKANDER[1] (From a letter about the study of nature)

∴

I

It has long been said that the only truths that are accepted without debate are those that do not affect anyone's interests. If the proposition 'two times two is four' had led to practical inconvenience for a certain part of humankind, then it still might not be universally accepted. And it has often happened that a truth, having succeeded in occupying an apparently lasting position in the system of scientific knowledge, has been subjected to new assaults and has been forced to carry on a new struggle for existence when practical conclusions were drawn from it and applied in life that were not desirable from the point of view of the interests and wishes of some social group. Attacks of the vulgar economists against the science of the classical economists can serve as a typical example of such 'relapses of ignorance' – attacks that continue to our day.[2]

This dependence of knowledge on the practical interests and desires of one or another social group need not boil down to the simple baseness of human nature, to the conscious predilection for a profitable lie over an unprofitable truth. No. Although it sometimes happens that people consciously betray truth for the sake of petty considerations, this is unquestionably not a general rule but only an exception. Usually, people's interests govern their thinking in a way that is utterly unnoticeable to themselves. People are not themselves conscious

---

1   The pseudonym of Alexander Herzen (1812–1870) [trans.].
2   For Marx's distinction between 'vulgar' and 'classical' economists, see the 'Afterword' to the second German edition of *Capital* [trans.].

of how the 'selection' of conceptions and ideas in their psyche is continually accomplished in a specific direction – to be precise, toward the greatest harmony with practical desires. The work of thought travels the 'line of least resistance'.

In addition, one must keep in mind that it is not only people's interests that are different but their entire experience of life. The division of society into countless groups that are differentiated according to their social role in the process of labour and distribution leads not only to a conflict of interest of the different groups, to a contradiction of their desires, it also leads to a dissimilarity of the material upon which the thinking of the group operates. Situated in different conditions of life, people derive the sum of perceptions that make up the basis of their experience from different sources. Because of this, the content of concepts that are signified by the same words turns out to be more or less different, and this is true as well of the entire course of the thinking that connects and systematises these concepts.

All this is completely applicable to the circle of ideas that are inseparably linked together and that are signified by the words 'idealism', 'ideals', 'progress' ... These concepts have immense significance. They have to do with the most vital interests of the individual human, a group, society; they summarise the most important aspects of the human experience. It is, consequently, perfectly natural that these concepts are especially debatable and that they excite an especially large number of ideological differences and contradictions. What represents regression for bourgeois thinkers is precisely what their ideological opponents see as a most progressive phenomenon. For a rentier, the ideal of human life is the diametrical opposite of the ideal formed in the psyche of a producer. A refined aesthete and an unsophisticated ideologist of the class struggle apply the term 'idealism' to completely different things. And between extremes like these, one can find an endless number of intermediary forms, inflections, and combinations ...

Should this diversity and these contradictions be the end to the question? Should this individual and group subjectivism be accepted as unavoidable for all human thought and be submitted to without a murmur? Or is it possible to establish an 'objective truth' for the given circle of ideas? Scientific knowledge must provide the answer.

As science develops, it strives to express the life experience of all humanity and not of a separate group. It must, therefore, rise above the one-sidedness and contradictions of particular views – both of individuals and of groups – and replace them with a unifying idea that provides a point of view from which it would be possible both to explain these particular views and to assess them objectively. This is the task of scientific research.

The course of this research must be the same as the one that scientific knowledge always follows. First, a simple description of the facts, i.e. in the given case, an empirical explanation of the question of what exactly people call 'idealism', 'ideals', and 'progress' and under what conditions they do so. Then an 'explanation' that issues from this description – in other words, a unifying and simplifying classification of those facts on the basis of established scientific forms of thought. If this process of treating experience can grasp everything that is typical and repetitive in the phenomena without any contradictions or important gaps, then the goal of scientific knowledge has been attained.

And what if this attempt fails? What if the description must surrender in the face of extremely complex and diverse facts, and what if the explanation is tangled up in hopeless contradictions? Then those who so desire can be granted a certain right to give free rein to their imaginations and seek an explanation of the baffling facts beyond the bounds of any possible experience and any possible scientific knowledge. But it goes without saying that this right will not be taken advantage of by people of the most rigorous frame of mind, by people who are predominantly critical. They would prefer to wait for the development of science to elucidate unresolved questions.

II

We will begin our analysis with the idea of 'progress'.

This idea is applied in the most varied domains of life. The simplest case is its application to biological facts proper – to the life of animals and plants.

People use the term 'progress' or 'progressive development' to refer to the entire period in the life of an organism when it passes from an embryonic state to maturity, gradually increasing its energy and the diversity of its vital functions. Just the opposite, the process of transition from maturity to old age and death – from the greatest fullness of vital activity to its lowest level and then to its end – is designated by the word 'regression' or 'degradation'. In the history of species, the development of multi-cellular forms from one-celled forms, of complex forms from simple forms, and of forms with intense and many-sided vital activity from forms in which vital processes are weak and undifferentiated is recognised as progressive development. Just the opposite, if freely living forms with developed organs of feeling and movement turn into parasitical forms whose organs of feeling and movement atrophy because they are not needed and in which almost all life is reduced to immediate nourishment and reproduction, then such a transformation is characterised as 'regressive development'.

All such facts can easily be summarised in one generalisation: in biology *the growth of the scope of life*, in regard to both its intensity and the variety of its manifestations, *is called progress*. And any diminishment of that scope of life is designated as regression.

But is such a purely biological definition sufficient where the matter at hand is the human psyche, conscious life? This must be examined. And what first catches our attention is the fact that people do not always agree regarding the progress or regression of psychical life.

In quite a few cases, however, there are no disagreements. If a person's activity expands, experience accumulates, and knowledge increases, and if, in general, one directly observes a quantitative growth of conscious life everywhere, people would unanimously characterise this as 'progress'. In exactly the same way, people agree without argument that 'progressive' should also be applied to such changes in the psyche as when its internal contradictions are lessened or removed and its unity and harmony grows – for example, when a disharmonious mass of heterogeneous, disorderly scattered data take shape in a scientific system or when an indecisive, vacillating form of action is replaced by a definite and confident one. In general, people completely agree in using the term 'progress' when it all boils down to the *growth of the fullness of harmony of conscious life*.

Disagreement arises in those cases where the manifestations of psychical life are viewed by people from the perspective of the 'quality' of those manifestations – whether they are higher or lower. Everyone, of course, recognises that the passage from what is lower to what is higher is progress and change in the opposite direction is regression, but, from the perspective of psychological life, what exactly is considered 'lower' and what is 'higher'? In this there is very little meeting of the minds.

Imagine, for example, an artist who has lived to this point mainly in the world of art and who begins to study science. This person sacrifices a life of aesthetic sensations and artistic creativity for the sake of a life of knowledge. There can be no doubt that people committed to pure knowledge look on such a transition as a progressive phenomenon, while people committed to pure art will say that this is an extremely pitiful degradation. Imagine that a scientist or philosopher begins to give up pure theory for the sake of practical activity. Their comrades in their new walk of life see progress in this – the passage to a superior manifestation of life. But their former comrades see regression, the lowering of the quality of life.

It is clear that all such judgements proceed from a certain one-sidedness of development. If people live predominantly in the world of art, if they draw the greatest sum of life from the sphere of aesthetic perceptions, then they will be inclined to consider exactly that aspect of the psyche to be superior. If they attain the greatest fullness and harmony of existence in acquiring knowledge, then it is precisely knowledge that will seem to them to be the superior manifestation of life ... The subjectivism and disagreement here essentially proceed from the fact that people transfer the results of their own narrow, one-sided experience to the lives of other people, and they cannot imagine that it is possible to attain the fullest and most harmonious development of life on a path other than their own. It is obvious that regardless of the contradictions of their views people unconsciously proceed from the same point of view: they see 'progress' or 'the superior' in what is subjectively linked for them with the maximum harmony and fullness of life.

We thus arrive at the following conclusion: both where people agree in their opinions and where they disagree, the basic meaning of the idea of progress remains the same: *the growth of the fullness and harmony of conscious life*. This is the objective content of the concept of 'progress'. The subjectivism that appears in the judgements of separate people with their mutual contradictions is a result of the narrowness of personal and group experience. This narrowness leads to one-sided and contradictory evaluation of the phenomena of psychical life, even though the principle of evaluation is applied, consciously or unconsciously, without any contradictions, and it is completely 'objective', i.e. the same for everyone.

If we now compare the psychological expression of the idea of progress that we have obtained with the biological expression that was explained earlier, it is easy to see that the first completely coincides with the second and can be inferred from it. The scope of life grows both when the fullness of life increases and when life becomes more harmonious. The first is understandable in itself; the second, perhaps, needs explanation. The increase in the harmony of a process of life signifies the weakening of its internal contradictions; it signifies a decrease of the mutual unadaptedness of its elements that causes them to harm each other to one degree or another. It is obvious that even though the harm elements cause each other is only partial, it diminishes the scope of life, and so the removal of that harm elevates the scope of life.

Since social life boils down to the psychical life of members of society, the content of the idea of progress remains the same in both cases – an increase in the fullness and harmony of life. It is only necessary to add – of the *social* life of people. And, of course, there has never been any other meaning of the idea of social progress, and there can be no other.

III

The concept of 'idealism' is closely connected with the idea of social progress. In order to explain the true nature and meaning of this connection, let us investigate what exactly people have in mind when they use the word 'idealism'.

The term 'idealism' is applied not only *to active conscious life* but to the most varied manifestations of it. People speak of 'idealistic feelings', of an 'idealistic attitude toward knowledge', and of 'idealism in practical activity'. Let us take a series of concrete examples.

An acquaintance comes up to you and begins to complain about some misfortune that has befallen them. Their account summons up various emotions in you. The first to appear is boredom and irritation at the uninteresting narration that is imposing on your time. Later on, you feel sympathy for the suffering person. We are inclined to characterise this latter feeling as 'idealistic' in comparison with the former one.

But here is another case: you see a very evil and dangerous person whom you could turn in to the authorities, which would, of course, cause them great suffering. A feeling of immediate sympathy springs up in you, but it is subsequently displaced by a feeling of sympathy toward all the many victims of this person – those whom they had already harmed and those whom they could still harm in the future. Of the two conflicting feelings, it is not the feeling of immediate sympathy that would be characterised as idealistic, but the other feeling – a feeling that is broader in its sense of sociality.

Up until a certain moment, a man has lived exclusively for himself, not caring about anyone else in the world. But suddenly he begins to work energetically for his family, sacrificing his health and happiness. You find that his activity has become more idealistic. Later on, he begins to sacrifice the interests of his country for the sake of the interests of his family. You are inclined to admit that this is now absolutely not idealistic and that an idealist would of course sacrifice the interests of his family for the interests of his country. However, when you see that some kind of Tamerlane or Chamberlain[3] is prepared to trample on the rights and happiness of all other peoples in order to exalt their country, then it seems to you that this is not particularly idealistic and that it would be more idealistic to strive for the benefit of all humanity.

---

3 Joseph Chamberlain (1836–1914) was a British politician considered by the left to be the epitome of rapacious imperialism [trans.].

All such cases can be packed into one simple generalisation: the term 'idealism' is applicable where the feelings, desires, and actions of people are directed more with society in mind, where psychical activity develops toward greater social consciousness. But there is a series of cases in which this generalisation is obviously inappropriate.

A person sacrifices the interests of many people for the sake of 'honour', 'duty', 'justice', and this is accepted as idealism. A person is not satisfied with approximate and hypothetical explanations of nature's secrets but wants to know 'pure truth', and this is also idealism. What do these examples have in common with the preceding ones?

'Honour' expresses an obligatory relationship that has taken shape within some kind of group, either an estate or a class. These obligatory relationships appeared in the course of the development of the given group – in the course of its struggle for power and well-being – and have no other content besides the desire to maintain and increase that power and well-being. Thus, if 'honour' requires a feudal lord to fight a duel over an insult, this expresses the historical dependence of the supremacy and well-being of feudal lords on their personal bravery and pitilessness toward enemies. If 'honour' forbids a feudal lord from marrying a plebeian, this expresses the historical dependence of the social power of feudal lords on their aloofness and their solidarity. Thus, 'honour' is a fetishistic form behind which the interests of a social group are hidden, and the idealism of honour, just like any other idealism, boils down to people's socially directed activity. In any given case, it makes no difference whether idealists understand the true content of their desires, cannot discern that content behind its fetishistic exterior, or, finally, do not give it any thought at all.

The same thing relates to the idealism of 'abstract duty' and 'justice', except that here the social basis of idealism is considerably broader and the vital interests of a broad class, of a whole society, or even of humanity are hidden behind an abstract, fetishised idea. (It was because of this that the idea of 'duty' as being absolute and universally obligatory – Kant's idea, for example – was able to arise). Those who give up their lives in the name of 'duty' sacrifice themselves not for the sake of an empty abstraction but for the sake of the life and development of their social whole, even though they are not clearly conscious of it or are not conscious of it at all.

But what is the idealism of knowledge, the idealism of 'pure truth'? The essential feature of 'pure truth' is its universal obligatoriness: pure truth must give cognitive satisfaction to any thinking being. Truth in general can exist only in human thought, and its universal obligatoriness signifies the necessity of its governing not only individual thought but the thought of all humanity. To strive toward pure truth is the same as to strive toward truth for all thinking beings, for all humanity in its development. The striving for partial, practical truth is considered to be much less idealistic – for example, when a technician calculates the maximum load for a steamship or when a land surveyor figures out the distance between two villages. In both cases people seek truth, but we do not find any particular ideals here, even if those who pursue this truth do not have any personal interests in mind. The truth that they arrive at can be relevant only to a limited circle of people.

We can now formulate our conclusions with precision: *the characterisation of 'idealism' is applied to the manifestation of active psychical life; feelings, desires, and deeds are considered to be idealistic the more they are socially directed.*[4] At the same time, this characterisation always presupposes a real or only a conceptual *clash* between attitudes that are more social and attitudes that are less social whereby the first is victorious. The term 'idealism' does not in general apply where there is no such clash of feelings and desires of a different order. People can act for the benefit of many millions of people, but if we know that they do not have to sacrifice either their own interests or the interests of those close to them to achieve this and that, on the contrary, the given form of action is most beneficial to them and gives them great profit, rank, etc., then we are not inclined to expatiate on the 'idealism' of those people. Idealism signifies a victorious struggle of more social elements of the psyche with less social elements.

IV

The concept of the 'ideal' is the connecting link between the ideas of 'progress' and 'idealism', and an examination of this concept allows us to provide a full and definite correlation of these ideas.

In our times, the word 'ideal' is often thoughtlessly employed to designate everything a person strives toward or dreams about. One often has to hear such expressions as, 'the ideal of a Muslim is an afterlife with *houris*', 'the ideal of the artist is eternal renown', and so forth. But such a vague concept is useless, and we can be interested only in a stricter and more precise conception of 'ideal' that corresponds to the fundamental meaning of the word: 'ideal' in the meaning of an *idealistic goal*. People always strive toward some kind of good. If they

---

4 Even aesthetic emotions can acquire the colouration of idealism. But as Guyau has explained, this colouration appears only to the extent that social feelings and desires also participate in them. [Jean-Marie Guyau (1854–1888) was a French poet and philosopher who was particularly interested in moral philosophy (trans.).]

consciously strive to conceive of this good in a specific form, then it is their goal. And if this goal does not lie entirely within the bounds of a purely personal struggle for life and happiness, if people strive for the good not only for themselves but for a certain broader whole of which they are a part, then their goal can be called an 'ideal'.

In so doing, one is not always conscious of the social nature of the goal; sometimes it is masked by various fetishes, as has been partly shown in the preceding. Idealists can set 'pure truth' or 'pure art', for example, as their goal and represent these things as something completely separate and completely independent from human existence. The fact that people do not always clearly understand the essence of their strivings does not change things in the least.

Thus, idealists always strive not for a narrowly personal good but for the social good, and, of course, the attainment of this good – what they call their 'ideal' – seems to them to be 'progress'. In so doing, idealists can be mistaken. Their ideal can in reality be reactionary, i.e. such that if it is realised it does not increase but diminishes the fullness and harmony of life. Nevertheless, subjectively – for idealists themselves – the ideal necessarily must be progressive and express *what is superior* to what is. The ideals of de Maistre, Bonald, and Chateaubriand[5] were reactionary; their preaching strove to return humanity to lower forms of existence. But these idealists themselves were completely convinced that the return of the old authorities would make life incomparably more harmonious and perhaps fuller for people than the rule of revolutionary principles.[6]

In general, an ideal that is not progressive from the point of view of the person who supports it is a flat contradiction. If any idealist summons people back toward the past, then they consequently see regression and degradation in the present, so for them going backwards in time means to go forward on the path

---

5   Joseph de Maistre (1753–1821), Louis de Bonald (1754–1840), and François-René de Chateaubriand (1768–1848) were leading lights of the 'counter-Enlightenment'. They endorsed the restoration of the Bourbons after the French Revolution, and they supported theocracy, aristocracy, and tradition [trans.].

6   The ascetic idea consists in the absolute harmony of life achieved at the expense of its fullness. This, at first glance, contradicts our understanding of progress altogether (the growth in the sum of life). But, in reality, for an ascetic, the fullness of life is not at all what we mean by this term. The ascetic apprehends the contradictions of life with painful sensitivity, and a growing number of external impressions means a growing sum of suffering. Suffering is a negative value of life, and if this value grows then the sum of life diminishes. To 'renounce the world' for an ascetic does not mean to sacrifice the fullness of life, but, on the contrary, to escape from the excruciating contradictions that undermine life. The fullness of life is its positive magnitude; it is what is called 'happiness'.

of progress. Idealism is, in any event, a *socially progressive mood*, and an ideal is the stated, concrete goal that this mood attracts people toward.

Since we know that a socially progressive mood is far from always expressed in socially progressive activity and since idealism can turn out to be reactionary in practice, then it becomes self-evident that ideals must be evaluated.

At first glance, the question of the progressiveness of ideals is resolved very simply. Since the essence of progress consists in the increase of the fullness and harmony of people's conscious life, then an ideal is recognised as socially progressive if its realisation must lead to the growth of fullness and harmony in the life of society. But such a resolution of the question would be far from sufficient.

Bellamy's ideal of a future society, as depicted in his novel,[7] would seem to correspond to the idea of 'progressiveness'. But progress remains progress only as long as the harmony and fullness of life continue to grow without interruption. Bellamy's society is a society that is frozen in contentment and self-satisfaction, serenely resting on its laurels after victories over social nature and external nature won by preceding generations. Such a society does not contain stimuli for further development; it is not progressive in itself. Therefore, in the final analysis, Bellamy's utopia is not a progressive idea at all, and contemporary idealists are repelled by it, seeing in it a philistine caricature of their own ideals.

The ultimate resolution of the question of how progressive an ideal is depends on the extent to which the attainment of this ideal creates the possibility for further progress. We must treat an ideal as 'higher' (the most progressive in a series of particular, concrete ideals) if it has the greatest capability of becoming the starting point for subsequent development.

This point of view leads to conclusions that are rather uncommon for the kind of everyday thinking that is inclined to differentiate 'material' ideals from 'spiritual' ideals and to consider the first to be lower and the second to be higher.

Let us suppose that some society, class, or group lives in the sort of material conditions that severely impede all progress: there is a great deal of work, a low standard of living, and people do not have enough time or energy for physical, intellectual, or moral development. Two idealists come to these people and try to instil their (very different) ideals into these people's consciousness. One of the idealists proves to these people that they are utterly bogged down with material cares and that such an existence is unworthy of a human being and convinces them to be filled with the higher moral ideas that the idealist

---

7 Edward Bellamy, *Looking Backward: 2000–1887*, first published in 1888 [trans.].

expounds to them. The other idealist explains to them how truly impossible human life is for them under the given material conditions and proposes that they strive for the improvement of their material situation. It would seem unarguable that the ideals of the first are as high as the ideals of the second are low. One offers the development of moral ideas; the other offers a 'five-kopeck raise', etc. But, from a historical point of view, it does not turn out this way at all. The first idealist wants suffering, exhausted people to spend the last of their energy on moral self-perfection, but if they do this, where will they get the energy for further progress? The second idealist sets a goal that, if it is attained, will free part of their vital energy for the further development of life. The realisation of the first ideal leads to stagnation; the realisation of the second opens up the possibility of continuous progress. The second ideal is clearly more progressive – *historically higher* – even though it is only a 'material' ideal.[8]

The evaluation of the breadth and depth of ideals is inseparably connected with the assessment of how progressive they are – I would say, of how idealistic they are.

Since the essence of idealism consists in the social nature of its frame of mind, the more social the ideals are, the more idealistic they are. In this sense, an ideal that does not go beyond the confines of the relationships of life of a limited group of people is lower than an ideal whose content embraces the life of a whole class, and a class-focused ideal is lower than one that embraces the life of all society. Such are the distinctions regarding the 'breadth' of ideals.[9]

Further, people are inclined to accept as more idealistic those ideals that are more distant from the present, from immediate reality. And this makes complete sense. People consciously struggle for that ideal whose full realisation seems to them to be possible only for distant descendants; this means that

---

8   In Mr Berdiaev's article *'Bor'ba za idealizm'* ['The Struggle for Idealism'] (*Mir bozhii*, 1901, issue 4) one can detect a disdainful attitude toward 'material' ideals ('five-kopeck improvements', etc.) from a 'spiritually' idealistic perspective that is devoid of any analysis and is obviously based on the usual prejudices. Meanwhile, Mr Berdiaev knows that the most progressive idealists of our time have quite consciously set as their *basic* (but not, of course, their exclusive) goal a change in the life of society that Mr Berdiaev would call 'material' – like the reorganisation of production.

9   Speaking of group-focused, class-focused, or broadly social ideals, we have in mind here only the content of the ideals themselves, and we are definitely not yet dealing with the question of *who* bears those ideals. In this sense, a 'class' ideal – i.e. one that consists in the striving to transform the life of a whole class – might be advanced by an insignificant group of people or by a separate individual, and a broadly-social ideal might rely on the striving of a separate class, if the development of this class is directed toward the transformation of all social life as a whole. This proviso is necessary since the expression 'class ideals' is usually employed to signify the ideals of a *specific class* regardless of their content.

idealistic desires connect those people to many generations of society – both those who will continue that struggle for the ideal and those who will have the pleasure of making use of the fruits of the whole struggle. Such an attitude is more idealistic because it is more social; it expresses the social interconnectedness of all society as it successively develops. That idealism whose tasks are all confined to the life of one generation is not a profound idealism.

Assessment of the idealism and progressive nature of ideals still far from resolves the question of how to assess the idealism of activity directed toward realising those ideals. More than once in historical memory the highest ideals have led to socially fruitless or even harmful activity because they were *unrealisable*.

The study of whether ideals can be realised has meaning and becomes possible only when one is convinced of the strict regularity – the conditioned nature – of social life. Without question, such a conviction has already begun to prevail in our times, and the very posing of the question of whether ideals are realisable hardly ever encounters a protest anymore. But this still does not say anything about the means of examining the question.

Here we enter the sphere of the struggle of mutually exclusive sociological theories. It is necessary to choose from among them: what seems completely realisable under one understanding of the regularity of social life must be accepted as unrealisable under another. Fortunately, the choice is not particularly difficult. Of all the contemporary social scientific theories, one – historical monism – is dramatically distinguished by its positive nature, its concreteness, and, what is more important, the correspondence of its conclusions with observed reality. The principles of historical monism not only allow the possibility of setting forth the interconnectedness of phenomena of the past life of society with the greatest clarity and convincingness, but these principles have more than once been used to assess the probable fate and social significance of various emerging or developing social currents, and subsequent experience has validated these assessments. The ability to predict is the most convincing proof of scientific truth.

Historical monism provides methods for the fullest explanation of the historical fate of any ideal. It indicates the course for investigating where a given ideal came from, what social forces stand behind it, if one should expect these forces to develop and grow or to decline and collapse, what is the possible extent of its influence in the historically given circumstances ... The question of the feasibility of an ideal and the question of the possible means of realising it are answered simultaneously. Reliable criteria are thus obtained for judging how productive, in the final analysis, the idealistic activity must turn out to be in its given concrete form.

V

Until now our examination of the idea of progress has been aimed at establishing its *objective content*. In so doing, we have already touched on the subjective colouring that comes from the one-sided development of many people and that creates disagreements when the question concerns the progressive nature of changes that would realise progress. We will now turn to another more profound subjectivism that arises from people's very *means of thinking* and that obscures the *basic meaning* of the idea of progress.

In order to act with certainty and confidence that their activities are conscious and progressive, people must constantly keep in mind a definite, concretely conceived goal that they call their 'ideal'. Thus, the ideal directly guides their progressive activity, and the idealists themselves are so accustomed to concentrate their attention on the ideal in this activity that they think of progress as *drawing nearer to the ideal*.

This is the subjective understanding of the idea of progress. In the great majority of cases it utterly conceals its real, objective content. Such concealment of the idea of progress is especially unavoidable when cognition is dominated by *stasis*. Static thinking is characterised by the fact that it is alien to the idea of development, that it seeks only stationary, unchanging essences in the phenomena of nature, and that it finds satisfaction only in the *absolute*.[10] When encountering progressive phenomena, such static thinking cannot conceive of those phenomena historically – as an ongoing process without a beginning or an end – because it cannot find anything in this conception on which it can come to a stop. It seeks a stable, stationary point of support, and a concretely conceived ideal serves as such a point of support. In this conception, every step on the path of progress can be made dependent on the ideal, while the ideal itself does not depend on anything. An ideal is something absolute and unchanging that static thinking can settle on, like a sailor who reaches dry land. Static thinking does not ask the question of where to go further after the ideal has been attained, and so it takes shape on the basis of stagnant forms of life. It does not find anything strange in the idea that progress will end it after it arrives

---

10   We bring up static thinking here simply as a given fact, not going into a direct investigation of it and not touching on questions either of its origin or its historical significance. In our work, *Poznanie s istoricheskoi tochki zreniia* [*Cognition from the Historical Point of View*] (St. Petersburg, 1901), we attempted, among other things, to explain that static thinking is a necessary adaptation to specific forms of social life, to a specific type of social labour.

at the 'final goal'. The static constitution of mind is completely satisfied with the idea that movement exists for the sake of the immovable and that progress exists for the sake of an ideal.

The objective and subjective understandings of progress diverge so much that they can be considered utterly incommensurable. The first is historical. It provides the idea of continual, unlimited progress, because it is impossible to imagine a kind of growth of fullness and harmony of life that would not allow new growth to follow from it. The second understanding, as we have seen, is static. It provides the idea of limited progress, because movement toward the ideal comes to an end when the goal is attained. The first has an absolutely positive nature – for it, progress signifies a good in itself. The second has a more negative colouration – approach to the ideal signifies, properly, only the *lessening of the distance* between 'is' and 'ought'; in this case the ideal of 'ought' – and not progress, itself – is the good.

Regardless of such essential differences, in many cases the objective and subjective understandings of progress can be reconciled in practice. If the ideal is really progressive, then approaching it is, obviously, real progress, and, as long as the ideal is not attained, it is utterly unimportant in practical terms how distinctly idealists envision it – whether they realise that this ideal is only a partial expression of the historical tendency of development or whether they attach absolute meaning to it. The latter way of understanding it even has a certain advantage. Someone who thinks concretely – someone in whose consciousness sharply delineated, specific, and firm images predominate – might be considerably more attracted to a vivid conception of one unchanging 'final goal' than the idea of continual transition from some ideals to other, higher ones.

But under some conditions the subjective understanding inevitably comes into conflict with the objective understanding of progress. An ideal often turns out in reality to be reactionary, and the idealist considers to be progress everything in which an approach toward that ideal can be seen. This frequently happens with the ideals of the obsolete classes and in just this way. For example, many times the worst forms of economic oppression have been idealised in our Russian literature. An ideal that is completely progressive might ultimately be attained, and then yesterday's progressive figure becomes an enemy of any further movement, since such further movement must inevitably appear to be moving away from the ideal that has been attained, i.e. it appears to be 'regression'. This is approximately what has happened, for example, with many liberals in contemporary France.

Those classes whose potential to develop is not limited by a narrow field of vision necessarily work out for themselves over the course of time a historical, objective understanding of progress. This is revealed in their very means of conceiving of ideals; they are not only conscious of the historicity of their ideals but that historicity often appears plainly in the very formulation of those ideals. Such is the ideal expressed by one prominent European thinker in the words: universal cooperation for universal development.[11]

VI

The broader the field of people's historical experience becomes, the more they are conscious of the obviousness and the necessity of the idea of continuous, unlimited progress. This idea absolutely contradicts static thinking. Static thinking finds no point of support in the idea of unlimited progress, it can find no conception of the fixed and the unchanging, and it cannot manage without one. But static thinking cannot admit that it is untenable, and it cannot surrender without a struggle. Types of thinking are in general the most conservative aspect of the human psyche, and static thinking, in particular, is particularly tenacious and is held on to long after its basis in life has disappeared. It adapts to what is unavoidable and creates new forms in which it tries to reconcile the irreconcilable – the idea of continual movement with the idea of the stationary.

How can one combine the limitlessness of progress with the idea that progress is the approach toward an ideal? For this it is necessary to move the ideal away to an infinite distance, to make it unattainable. In place of finite, particular ideals, universal and infinite ideals appear that are absolutely perfect in their forms – absolute goodness, truth, and beauty, for example. All progress is directed toward these absolutes. Every step of progress brings one nearer to them, but arriving at them is impossible because they are infinitely far away. Absolutes are unattainable.

When this idea becomes the basis of a worldview, the entire world process is viewed teleologically, as eternal movement toward eternal goals. But such a conception has nothing in common with the usual, practical teleology of people; it has absolutely nothing to do with the kind of particular, relative, subjective goals that people set themselves. The goals of the world process are universal, absolute, and superhuman, and, at the same time, they exist objectively (and not only in the consciousness of separate people). They are continually realised to a greater and greater extent, but their full realisation is inconceivable in any time or any place. They lie outside space and time. All 'provisional

---

11   Bogdanov is referring to Petr Lavrov (1823–1900), a Russian radical publicist and philosopher who emigrated to Europe in order to write freely [trans.].

values' have meaning only in relation to 'eternal values'; everything that is relative, including progress, receives it value only in its relation to these absolute goods.[12]

If words serve to express concepts, then what concept is concealed behind the words 'absolute goal'?

The content of an idea is made up of concepts, but it is obvious that no concrete particular goals can provide the material for an 'absolute goal'. Any particular goal that is conceived of is relative, and the primary characteristic of the absolute is that it is the opposite of relative. Any content that is conceived for the goal is finite, and no kind of finite content is conceivable for absolute goals. All goals that are conceived of belong to the psyches of specific conscious beings. Absolute goals pertain to the world process in its whole, and that whole is not given to us in either perceptions or conceptions.

In general, since a concept presents an abstraction whose content arises out of the facts of human experience, it is impossible to find any content for the concept of absolute goals. There is no place for the absolute in the sphere of human experience; everything there is relative. Absolute goals are *abstractions from non-existent experience*; they are *words* behind which no kind of cognitive content is concealed. But this is not how those words stand out in the psyches of people who accept that absolute goals have value for thinking.

Empty abstractions are composed of vague and unclear content instead of content that can be specifically and clearly conceived. The material of empty abstractions consists in conceptions that are psychologically close to but that do not correspond to the intrinsic meaning of the abstraction. Thus, conceptions of particular, relative truths, combining and diffusing in consciousness, form fictitious, imaginary content for the idea of absolute truth. And when an intense, satisfying, sublime mood is combined with this, then no room remains for doubting the reality of the absolute. An empty abstraction thus acquires flesh and blood and becomes the object of faith.

The more often a given psychical state is repeated the more one gets used to it and the more its content acquires subjective validity. It is precisely in this way that various products of fantasy acquire supreme, immediate obviousness in people's psyches. Appearing thousands and millions of times in experiences, many objects of faith attain incomparably greater certainty than the most established truths of empirical knowledge.

---

12   I have taken most of the expressions which characterise the 'absolute theory of progress' from Mr Berdiaev's article, 'The Struggle for Idealism', to which I have already referred.

One can find a great many examples like this in the history of mystical and metaphysical views, and it was in this way that the subjective certainty of 'absolute ideas' developed. Faith in such ideas becomes an incontestable belief, and the feeling that is caused by contemplating them turns into passionate worship. At that point any logic is powerless against them.

This is how ideals are made into idols. Pre-civilised fetishists imagine there to be sacred content behind the rough, material exterior of the unsightly idol that they worship. But there is no god in the idol; there is nothing but matter. Contemporary fetishists imagine an absolutely ideal content behind the delicate, ethereal exterior of the beautiful words that they also worship. But there is no absolute idea in the empty abstractions; there is no reality other than words.

VII

If we have correctly understood the origin of the idolistic theory of progress, if it really emerged from the desire to reconcile the irreconcilable (the idea of continual movement and the idea of something that is immovable), then the theory itself must turn out to be contradictory: a contradiction in principles inevitably causes contradictions in conclusions.

In reality, what kind of progress is there in the idolistic understanding of something? Drawing nearer to an absolute, decreasing the distance between 'is' and 'ought'. And how great is the distance? It is infinite, and it will always be infinite. What does this mean?

An infinite distance is one which it is inconceivable that you can really draw near the end of – no finite movement can 'draw nearer' to the absolute.[13]

What lies at an infinite distance lies *outside of distance* so that, in regard to the absolute, the term 'drawing nearer' has altogether no meaning. The idolists themselves admit that 'eternal value' exists outside time and space and that the concept of quantity is incompatible with it. Meanwhile, the concept of 'drawing nearer' has an *exclusively* quantitative spatial and temporal meaning. Thus, joining the concept of 'drawing nearer' with the idea of 'absolutism' logically boils down to a blatant contradiction.

---

13   In mathematics, two infinitely large magnitudes remain equal even if *unequal finite magnitudes* are added to or subtracted from them. This is possible, of course, only because the mathematical symbol ∞, like 0, is a symbol with a negative meaning and is not at all a real magnitude, so that the laws of magnitude are incompatible with it. Such symbols do not exist only in mathematics.

One must inevitably draw the following conclusions: if the absolute lies outside distance and no real drawing nearer to it is possible, then 'progress' is the purest *illusion*. It is running in place and not movement forward. If idolists continue to believe in progress, then they unquestionably do it at the expense of logic. There is nothing strange here: as soon as people take a concept that has been formed on the basis of real experience and then apply it beyond the bounds of any possible experience, they have thereby liberated themselves from the rule of logic.

This emancipation from logic is closely tied with a distinctive *dualism of knowledge* that is inevitable for all idolistic views. Since the relative and the absolute are essentially different from one another, it is evident that they involve two different types of knowledge. Relative knowledge is usually called scientific, and absolute knowledge is usually called metaphysical. Sometimes these two types of knowledge are contrasted under the terms 'reason' and 'mind', and sometimes – and this is more to the point – they are spoken of as ordinary knowledge, on the one hand, and as mystical meditation, etc., on the other. In reality, as we have shown, the second type of knowledge boils down to faith.

In any event, from the point of view of contemporary scientific thinking, a sharp dualism of reason and mind is no more understandable and valid than the dualism of spirit and matter. It is hard to say which of them makes an integral worldview more impossible. Dualism in knowledge cannot be refuted because the proof of dualism is meaningless. By contradicting the unity of knowledge, dualism eliminates beforehand the necessary foundation of any proof: it insists that arguments from scientific cognition have no power over a kind of knowledge that is above science.

The true meaning of this dualism – and of idolistic views in general – is illuminated to a considerable degree if we turn our attention to its connection with intellectual aristocratism. Since absolute and relative knowledge differs not in quantity but in essence, a person who takes the point of view of absolute knowledge cannot view people who take the point of view of relative knowledge as anything other than lower beings. At best they do so with the majestic condescension of a truly developed human toward an undeveloped foetus and, at worst, with the icy disdain of a feudal lord toward contemptible rabble.[14]

---

14   It is approximately in such a tone as this that Mr Berdiaev discusses evolutionists, positivists, etc. As long as 70 years ago, Herzen wrote, '... Idealism (i.e. *idolism*, A.B.) always has something intolerably insolent about it. People who believe that everything that is provisional is not worth their attention, become proud and relentless in their one-sidedness

VIII

Now we can sum up the results. In the preceding, we have tried to explain the positive content and the mutual interrelationships of the ideas of 'progress', 'idealism', and 'ideal' from an historical point of view. We found that progress means the growth of the fullness and harmony of conscious human life, that idealism expresses the victory of more social over less social sentiments in the human heart, and that a progressive ideal is the reflection of a socially progressive tendency in an idealistic psyche. We asserted that this is the only possible explanation of these ideas.

Along the way, we presented a critique of the idealistic understanding of the same ideas. We explained that such an understanding suffers from profound, inescapable inner contradictions – that it is logically unviable.

But here we run up against the view expressed by a poet in the words, 'A delusion that exalts us is dearer to me than a myriad of base truths'.[15] They tell us that idolism is illogical but that it alone raises aloft the banner of the ideal. For idolism, the ideal is an unapproachable sacred object, and analysis of it tries to break it down, to reduce the higher to the lower, to degrade eternal truth, and to undermine the foundation of idealism – the passionate worship of absolute ideals. The ideas of goodness, truth, and beauty thus lose their absolute meaning, and progress itself is turned into an illusion. All this is really said in our times, and the defenders of idolism – calling it theoretical idealism – believe that it alone can provide the philosophical foundation for practical idealism.[16]

---

and absolutely impervious to the truth. Idealism was utterly certain that it would take only one contemptuous phrase to cause empiricism to scatter like dust. The celestial spirits of the metaphysicians were mistaken' ... It would seem that this could have been written just today.

15   The line comes from Alexander Pushkin's poem 'Hero' (1830) [trans.].

16   In the article cited above, Mr Berdiaev says much more even than this. He asserts that evolutionists prove that human ideals are illusory by making a reference to the moral ideals of fish and molluscs (p. 13). I do not know what to call this. In the best case, it is a bad joke. In the worst case, it is ignorance of the subject. In any event it is a false description. And, incidentally, many such false descriptions are to be found in Mr Berdiaev's work, and they touch on quite important things. Such, for example, is his assertion that the ideals of the 'students' [of Marx] are narrowly materialistic, 'bourgeois', i.e. that for them the entire essence of progress boils down to purely material improvements. Where did Mr Berdiaev find this? On what basis does he speak in this way of people whose entire activity is intellectual? Further, presenting *Zusammenbruchstheorie* in the vulgarly utopian form such as it has been presented by Bernstein, Mr Berdiaev calls it 'an attempt at the evolutionary-scientific substantiation of idealism' (p. 17), and he tries to attribute it to evolutionism. Meanwhile, it is well-known that such a utopian understanding of this theory has exposed

At this point, we must first and foremost ask the question: since when does 'explain' mean to 'debase'? Why does to scientifically understand the content of idealism mean to turn it into an illusion? Did Darwinism debase human dignity with the theory of the origin of human beings? Was heat turned into an illusion because of the mechanical theory of heat? Was sunlight turned into an illusion because of the theory of wave-like vibrations of the ether? What is higher does not become less high because it developed from what is lower, and what is real does not become less real because it is reduced to a simpler reality.

Evolutionism, of course, cannot create ideals for anyone, because idealism is a matter of feeling and not of knowledge. But like any definite knowledge, evolutionism provides a solid, reliable basis for idealistic activity. It shows how to evaluate the progressiveness and feasibility of ideals and how to figure out the means of realising them. It is true that one gains only progressive and feasible ideals in this way and not reactionary and utopian ones, but there is no need to be disappointed by this.

The same is not true of idolism. Idolism cannot point out the means of calculating whether given ideals are realisable or how to realise them, and it does not even think that this is its task. Idolism also cannot provide convincing and clear criteria for progressive ideals. After all, progress is defined as drawing near to the absolute, but it is not subject to definition since it cannot be expressed in words. Thus, if some people were to assert that their activity is progressive because it brings us nearer to absolute goodness, truth, and beauty, and other people were of the opposite mind, then it is impossible to even talk about any kind of proof or verification of them. Both groups of people can cite only their own immediate conviction – i.e. their faith – and at this point a vast space opens up for capriciousness. Everyone fills up the empty idea of the absolute with the content that is most convenient for them. Any conservative or reactionary class can use absolute goodness, truth, and beauty advance their interests just as well as the bourgeoisie and bourgeois politicians can use the ideas of freedom and equality to advance theirs.

Sooner or later, logic will assert itself, and then idolists will be compelled to conclude that the ideal always remains infinitely distant. The result is neither comforting nor useful for idealistic activity. It will then be clear that only understanding the true nature of progress in an evolutionary way can save idealists from despair. But, having become enamoured of the idea of the absolute, they cannot easily give it up; it is difficult for them to understand that, at each step

---

itself to critique precisely because it is non-evolutionary, because it sharply contradicts the historical point of view. Is all this really a way to engage in polemics?

forward on the path of the increasing fullness and harmony of life, the ideals of beauty, truth, and goodness are continually realised in people's mutual relationships, in their knowledge, and in their perception of nature. And the less idolists are able to understand all this, the more painful and harmful the crisis will turn out to be.

Thus, idolism prepares the idealist for unnecessary internal struggle and useless suffering. This is why the struggle against idolism is a necessary phase in the struggle for idealism.

CHAPTER 3

The Development of Life in Nature and Society

It is unarguable that the most vital of all the questions of science is the question of the laws of social development. All human individuals who are aware of their living, indissoluble tie with a specific group, nation, class, and all humanity cannot but strive to know these laws. It is necessary for such individuals to know what they can expect, what can be hoped for both for the collectivity they belong to and for themselves as active members of that collectivity. To find any reliable answer to these questions without a clear understanding of the basic laws of the life of society is inconceivable.

But here the difficulties of investigation are extraordinarily great. Its subject is so close to the vital interests of the researcher that it is not easy to avoid a subjectivism that distorts the truth. People involuntarily imbue the reality that they are studying with the colours of their own inclinations and desires; they involuntarily combine – if only in part – what they hope for with what is possible and what is necessary. And, at the same time, the object of study is so infinitely complicated that it is very easy to become entangled in the intertwined links of the chain of cause and effect and to conceive of the relationships of things inaccurately. These conditions have long held back scientific knowledge of the laws of social development.

In 1859, a decisive step was made in this direction. In the introduction to one of his works on economics, a great sociologist of that time concisely and clearly formulated a series of guiding ideas on which, since that time, scientific research of the life of society can successfully be based. We will cite here the most substantive part of that formulation.

> In the performance of their social life, people enter into definite, inevitable relationships that are independent of their will – relations of production – that correspond to a definite level of the development of material, productive forces. The sum of these relations of production constitutes the economic structure of society, the real foundation on which a legal and political superstructure rises and to which definite forms of social consciousness correspond. The means of production of material life conditions the social, political, and spiritual phenomena of the life process. A person's consciousness does not determine the form of their being, but, on the contrary, social being determines the forms of their consciousness. At a certain level of their development, the material productive forces of

society come into contradiction with the existing relations of production, or, to use a juridical expression, with property relations, among which they have so far operated. These relationships are transformed from forms of the development of productive forces into fetters of those forces. Then an era of crises begins. With the change of the economic foundation, the entire former edifice that was built upon it sooner or later collapses ...[1]

Since the time these words were written, the theory they expressed has spread ever more widely and has become firmly established as a science. Many historical events have been explained from the perspective of this theory, and no facts have been found that would contradict it. It has even happened that many writers have, in the process of rejecting this theory, involuntarily been influenced by it, and, in labouring over it, they have produced new arguments in its favour. For a little more than four decades no historical theory has been created that can in any way compete with it.

However, a great deal has changed since that time. All fields of science have developed with the greatest speed. The evolutionary worldview has attained considerably greater fullness and clarity to the extent that individual doctrines, having merged with that worldview, have unfolded more broadly and have become more precise. They have become ever more firmly established, and their mutual interconnection and tight unity have become more obvious. In these circumstances, it has become possible to present certain new claims on historical-philosophical theory.

The old formulation of historical monism, without ceasing to be true in its foundation, is no longer fully satisfying. There is a certain incompleteness in

---

1   *Zur Kritik der politischen Oekonomie*, Preface, Russian translation, page x.

'Material productive forces' signifies the sum total of the means of production plus the sum of technological techniques, the abilities of people to use these means. The concept is obviously quite complex.

'Relations of production' is an even more complex concept. It is made up, first, of the relationships of people in the process of labour itself – simple collaboration, division of labour, and so forth – and, second, of ownership relations – 'property relations' as Marx says. This includes possession of land and capital in a specific amount on the one hand and the absence of such possession on the other, etc. All this is combined in the concept of the 'economic structure' of society or simply its 'economics'. The expression 'forms of people's social being' means the same thing.

'Forms of people's consciousness' here signifies the worldview of people, their presuppositions and their knowledge, their science, philosophy, etc. All this, together with the legal and political relationships of people, is explained in the general concept of 'ideological forms' that form the 'superstructure' on the 'economic foundation'. These architectural terms must be understood simply to mean that 'economics' determines 'ideology'.

it. It does not explain the immediate vital significance of a whole, vast realm of social phenomena – ideology. It does not explain *why* society needs ideology, *what social purpose* ideology serves, and *to what degree* it is necessary.[2] At the same time, the tangential question remains of whether ideology is essentially *the same sort of thing* as 'economics' or whether it is *different*. Further, the old formulation suffers from a certain inexactness of its basic concepts. This especially relates to the concept of the 'economic structure' of society, in which are included, among other things, 'property relations' – i.e. essentially the *legal* relationships of ownership – while the 'legal superstructure' is generally counted as one of the forms of ideology.[3] Finally, a logical link between this theory and the theory of development in other realms of life was not established – could not be established – in the old formulation, and in our times the need for a unified, scientific worldview persistently reminds us of the necessity of clarifying this link. A series of questions arise whose answers will change the appearance of this theory more or less significantly.

To attain the goals we outlined above, we choose the path that science has followed many times in such cases. The contemporary development of psychology – to the point of its being a comparatively precise science – is based on introducing into it a physiological point of view and physiological methods. The perspective and methods of physical chemistry have served to make psychology a more precise science, and mathematics has done the same for chemistry and physics. The techniques and governing ideas of a more developed and elaborated science are applied to a less developed and less elaborated science. The former investigates phenomena that are essentially of the same kind as the latter but are simpler and more general. This is exactly how biology (the science of life in general) relates to sociology (the science of social life). So, we are attempting to explain what social life and development looks like from the point of view of the laws of life and development in general.[4]

---

2 In our literature one can encounter a point of view that understands ideology as something not essentially necessary in the life of society – a decoration, an amusement, something that finds its purest and most typical expression in metaphysical 'castles in the air'.

3 As we will subsequently see, the concept of 'productive forces' must be changed for the sake of scientific precision.

4 Many theorists of historical materialism have tried to establish a link between this theory and the ideas of contemporary biology, but almost all attempts have suffered from one general shortcoming – prejudiced eclecticism. They presuppose that general laws of life are somehow limited in the social sphere of life, and they work toward determining these limits and their consequences. This would be the same sort of abortive method as if a physiologist were to propose – before doing any research – that the laws of physical-chemistry could be partly

Of course, any such application of the ideas of one science to the sphere of another science must still justify itself. Its validity must be proven factually – to be exact, in such a way that the conclusions obtained with the help of this method not only do not turn out to contradict reality but also to permit a deeper, clearer, and fuller understanding of reality. To find out the true value of a method, it must be tested in practice. While illuminating facts with the theory, we must constantly verify the theory with facts, and the absence of contradictions between both these aspects will guarantee the truth.

But first and foremost, we must formulate as precisely as possible the general concepts of the science of life that serve as the starting point for the discovery of the laws of social development. Only the most precise understanding can serve as a reliable tool for investigating such a complex, difficult, and important question as the one we are now taking up.

I

Cognition finds that all the infinitely varied manifestations of life – plant and animal life, physiological and mental life, individual and social life – have a great deal in common. It is precisely what they have in common that serves as the basis for the idea that will direct our investigation – the *idea of adaptation*. In explaining the meaning of this idea, we will begin first and foremost with the question of what it is that adapts.

Observing the various processes of life, we find that each of them issues from a certain uniformity and permanency, according to a specific type. In each separate case, this uniformity, constancy, and trueness to type allows a series of phenomena of life to be combined in the concept of a specific *form of life*. A given organic cell, a given organism, society, species, etc. are all particular forms of life. The same form of life – let us say a human organism – can be composed of a multitude of mutually interconnected forms of simple (in this case cellular) elements and can become part of the composition of more complex forms – a given society or a given species, for example.

A form of life is something that has adapted. What does it mean to 'adapt'?

Any form of life is situated in a specific *environment* that exerts various forces on it and that produces various 'impacts' on it. If the form of life changes, if the course of its life process deviates from the normal, then we look for transform-

---

violated in the sphere of physiological processes and then especially looked for such violations.

ative influences on the part of the environment that would have caused this deviation. For example, when relationships of the human organism change – some of its elements degrade, others develop unusually, a third group completely disappears – we try to find the starting point for these transformations in the various external conditions of life of the organism – in the actions of the atmosphere, diet, or social surroundings, in mechanical influences, etc.[5] Changes of a form of life are constantly dependent on the influence of its environment, and this dependence is a particular expression of the *universal causality of phenomena*.

Of all the manifestations of a form's dependence on its environment, two are especially important for biology: the survival and the destruction of forms. In a given environment, forms of a specific type (or specific types) survive; forms of other types fail. Lapland moss, reindeer, and Inuits survive the natural environment of polar lands, but the date palm, the camel, and Arabs would inevitably perish if they were to be moved there. And the situation is the exact opposite in regard to the natural environment of tropical lands. Some forms of life are *adapted* to one environment; other forms of life are adapted to another.

All that 'adapted to a given environment' means is that a form of life survives in a given environment, and nothing more. Thus, the words 'survival of the adapted' would be a simple redundancy if they did not mean something more than is directly said in them. It means precisely the *strict regularity* by virtue of which under given conditions of the environment forms of a given structure or a given type survives, and, also because of their dependence on the environment, some forms fail. This is the essence of the 'natural selection' of forms of life.[6]

---

5   But could heredity not be a cause of a deviation of life? No. Heredity only transmits deviations from one generation to another, and the causes of these deviations then lies in the external environment that influenced the organisms of the ancestors. But what if 'harmful' deviations are encountered that ancestors did not have? They depend on some kind of external influence on the embryo during its development. Even if the transformative influences come from the parent organism – if, for example, those influences are caused by impairment of the parent organism – then, after all, the parent organism is the *environment* for the new organism that is gestating in it.

6   The conception of the competition of organisms is inseparably linked with the idea of natural selection. And this is perfectly understandable since competition is in reality one of the most important and widespread cases of the manifestation of natural selection. The relationship of the organism with other organisms of the same type that exist in its external environment is expressed in competition. For each organism, the other organisms that are competing with it represent one of the hostile, destructive influences of the environment. But natural selection also acts apart from any competition. For example, if the climate of a land becomes more severe, then many organisms and whole species can perish – i.e. be eliminated by selection –

In reality, *perfectly* adapted forms do not exist; they would have to survive forever, something that has never been seen. There are only forms that are more or less adapted, i.e. those that survive more often and live longer and those that fail more easily and die sooner. The first constitute the minority, and the second constitute the huge majority. But the first reproduce, and the second disappear after a short, incomplete life cycle, leaving no descendants. In this way, the more adapted forms become predominant and are continually transformed from the minority into the majority. But reproduction always creates more new forms than can survive in the limited space on earth that is available for them to live. Therefore, a more adapted minority must again be separated out from any new majority, and that minority, in its turn, becomes the majority. Thus, nature continually chooses the most adapted and puts them in the forefront.

Like everything in nature, forms of life are continually changing under the multifarious actions of the environment. In each succeeding phase a cell or an organism is not completely what it was previously. With each new generation a society or a species is not made up of the same individuals or the completely same kind of individuals as before. Not only does the matter and energy that make up the forms of life continually change, but the structure and characteristics of these forms also changes. The majority of these transformations occur so slowly and gradually that we are unaware of them; some take place so quickly and abruptly that we are amazed at their suddenness.

All changes in forms of life have some kind of influence on the level of their adaptedness – they either diminish it or enhance it. In the first case, there is a greater chance that the given forms will lose the struggle of life and tend to become extinct; in the second case, they win ever greater space in the economy of nature, replacing and pushing out forms that are dying out. In this way, although enhanced adaptedness occurs only in the minority of cases, it is precisely these cases that play the most important role in the general system of life. From all changed forms, life chooses those that increase adaptability, that possess the quality of *adaptation*.

Forms of adaptation are infinitely varied. Nature utilises the most varied means for increasing the sum total of life, for the victory of life in its struggle with the inorganic world. Change in the construction of claws or teeth, change

---

not at all because other organisms and species complete with them but simply because it turns out that they are not constituted to bear the severe climate. In exactly the same way, one may not speak of competition if, let us say, newly migrated birds destroy whole species of local insects – after all, the birds and insects do not share the same food supply, in which case there would be competition.

in the size of the body or the colour of fur, the production of new reflexes, the transformation of previous instincts, the variation of previous habits, new combinations of forms of an organism's consciousness and external movements – any of these can turn out to be an adaptation if it enhances the viability of a given form. There is no difference in meaning between physical and psychical changes; both are equally suitable as tools for the survival and expansion of life. What is attained in one case by a physical adaption is attained in another case by psychical adaptation. A change in the colouring of the covering or the elaboration of an appropriate instinct can equally serve to defend a given species of organisms from the same enemies. *In all its endlessly varied manifestations, life is uniformly a process of adaptation.*

II

In order to clarify the basic features of the process of adaptation, we will examine its interconnectedness and logicality with a rather concrete example.

A specific country with a specific climate, flora, and fauna is inhabited by a breed of birds that is sufficiently adapted to the external conditions of its life so that it does not go extinct, but it is not so well adapted that it supplants another competing breed. Provided the conditions of the environment do not change, such a stable existence can continue for many thousands of years, but there is nothing unchanging in nature. Any given environment changes more or less quickly, and sooner or later this will have an influence on the fate of forms of life.

Let us imagine one of the simplest changes of the environment: the climate becomes colder and more continental, and winters become more severe. In winter, many of the local species turn out to be comparatively unadapted, and the breed of bird that we chose for our example is one of them. There is very little food in the winter, and severe cold tends to kill off organisms weakened by hunger. Unadaptedness means the need for adaptation.

In times like these, the mutability of forms of life increases; the changing external environment engenders a great number of diverse changes in their structure, both physical and psychical.[7] Natural selection seizes the most beneficial of these changes, while eliminating those forms that change in a less beneficial way. In our case, let us suppose that a particular instinct develops

---

7 The structure of organic forms is so complex and so subtle that comparatively uniform and simple external influences cause a series of complex and diverse changes in them.

that, with the approach of autumn, prompts the birds to fly to a warmer land where they are not threatened to such a degree by cold and hunger and to return only in the spring. This is a new *form of adaptation* that corresponds to new conditions of the environment.

We thus see that *the motive force that creates new adaptations lies in the relationships of an organic form to its environment.*

But now another question arises: where does the material come from that these new adaptations consist of?

In our example, the instinct of winter migration could have developed gradually from the instinct that is expressed in ordinary, short flights of birds from one place to another in search of food. As the climate worsened, when it became cold such flights must have taken on an ever more particular trend toward warmth and light, and they would get continually longer ... Any other similar material of life can also serve for the development of a new instinct. In any event, consistent with the law of causality, this adaptation did not arise from nothing; it arose from elements that were already present – *from the elements of old adaptations with which it is more or less similar*. In this sense life does not create anything essentially new; what is new is always of the same sort as the old material from which it came.

Observing the development of life, we see how newer combinations are created from former elements, how countless complex adaptations arise from a few simple adaptations. The higher organisms with their huge number of adaptations came from some kind of one-celled organisms like present-day amoebae. Human beings with their psychical life developed from simple embryonic cells with the most elementary functions ... Going back from highly organised forms to the extremely simple forms from which they came, we see how huge differences came from ever greater uniformity. This leads us to the idea of the *single origin of life* ... But if there is one beginning to life and all new life is of the same sort of thing as the old one from which it originated, then *all manifestations of life are essentially similar*. This is the monistic view of development.

However, let us return to our example. No new adaptation is perfect. In changing the previous relationships of the organic form to its environment, it also commonly causes some new unadaptedness that can be more or less significant. This also relates to the migratory instinct of birds. Long journeys through the air are accompanied by great fatigue and innumerable dangers. This unadaptedness might turn out to be very serious; it might greatly undermine the viability of the species. In that case, new adaptations would be necessary, and, if conditions are sufficiently favourable, they appear. To be precise, a herd instinct develops, and birds travel in large flocks instead of flying singly. In so doing, the danger from enemies – predatory birds, for example – significantly diminishes. The degree of fatigue also diminishes because the mechanical conditions of flight are more favourable for a flock than for a separate bird – there is less resistance from the air.

In this way, a *secondary* adaptation arises due to a new unadaptedness or 'need' produced by a previous primary adaptation. And here, of course, any kind of previous adaptation can serve as the material for development. For example, flock instincts can be formed from family instincts (even though family instincts are considerably narrower) because they are similar.

In their turn, secondary adaptations can also cause a new adaptation, can cause the necessity of further adaptations of a third sort, etc. For example, travel in flocks creates the need for a system of signals. For a large flock, a great deal of food is needed along the way, and it is therefore necessary that when any bird sees a valuable source of food it can inform the others of this in one way or another. In exactly the same way, when danger arises there must be other signals so that enemies are not able to catch the flock unaware, and so on. The starting point for these adaptations might be nothing more than already existing summoning signals between males and females or 'sympathetic' movements of muscles associated with the breathing apparatus.[8]

Our example could be developed further, and many other examples could be cited as well, but what has already been presented is sufficient to explain three fundamental characteristics of adaptation that are important here:

(1) The process of adaptation begins with *changing relationships of forms of life to their environment. The motive force of development* arises from the realm of these relationships.

(2) By giving rise to new forms of unadaptedness, new adaptations can cause the need for still other adaptations. *Primary* forms of adaptation provide an impetus for the development of *secondary* forms, etc.

(3) Elements of the life process that are already present serve as the material for new adaptations, so that development *never creates anything that is essentially new.*

---

8 'Sympathetic movements' are those contractions of muscles that in a physiological sense are of no direct use but are the inevitable consequence of the very structure of nerve centres. These movements appear because the process of the first stimulus spreads from the nerve centres that carry out the work that is necessary under the circumstances to other centres that are associated with them. This includes, for example, the involuntary cry that accompanies certain abrupt movements, the clenching of teeth when lifting heavy weights, and so on.

It still remains for us to note the existence of two clearly different types of development. One of them was presented in our example: new adaptations are added to a previous adaptation whereby the sum total of adaptions of organic forms grows ever more complex and varied, and, since these adaptations are the material for further adaptations, it is obvious that *the possibility of adaptation in general also grows*. This is the *progressive* type of development. But there are cases of another kind, which essentially consist in the fact that a form of life simply loses certain adaptations that have become superfluous or even harmful due to a change in the environment. Thus, for animals that live in the depths of dark caves, the organ of sight becomes not only unnecessary because of its uselessness but also an extremely undesirable source of injuries, since it is an adaptation that has an extremely fine and delicate organisation. It therefore atrophies and disappears. In this case, a form of life *adapts* because this change is useful for its survival, but the *possibility of further development obviously decreases* so that we see more of a minus than a plus in the development of life. This is the *regressive* type of adaptation.

Since regressive development creates its own limits, it does not play a predominant role in the system of life. But all the same, regressive development is quite a frequent phenomenon in nature. It is particularly characteristic of *parasitic* organisms. The process of adaptation sometimes takes away almost all the organs of feeling and movement from parasitic animals that spend their lives adhering to some other independent organism, transforming such parasites into living sacks with the functions of feeding and reproduction.[9]

Both types of development – progressive and regressive – are also encountered in social life.

III

Moving on to the phenomena of social development, we first and foremost encounter this question: is it altogether possible to compare social forms of adaptation with biological forms of adaptation? Are we justified in considering a social whole, like any other form of life, as a specific complex of *adaptations* that emerge in the struggle for life?

---

9 Regressive development should not be confused with the simple degradation that occurs when maladaptation gradually destroys a form of life, and adaptations are absolutely not created. For example, if an organism is weakened by illness, when it needs strength for living, this is degradation and not regressive development. But if a parasite loses muscular strength that it does not need, this is regressive development.

If we attentively examine the various elements of people's social being, we will be easily convinced that they *factually represent nothing other than precisely the adaptations of people in the struggle for life*. This idea is irrefutable, because countless facts speak in its favour, and there are no other facts that would contradict it.

The validity of such a view stands out even more obviously in the sphere of the *direct struggle* of human beings with external nature – in the realm of the 'technological' process. The essence of 'technological forms' consists in the techniques produced by human beings in order to influence nature for the benefit of humanity's own survival and development. This means the skill to utilise one or another tools, the skill to find and process one or another material ... It is clear that the ability to use an axe or a machine in the struggle with external nature is just as much an adaptation as, let us say, the ability to possess teeth or claws, and the ability to build a house is just as much an adaptation as the ability to make a nest, and so on.

The same is true both of the entire realm of technological knowledge and subsequently the realm of scientific knowledge. An engineer *calculates* the line of least resistance (or of greatest force), an animal determines it *instinctively*, and even a plant – as far as can be judged according to the most recent observations – follows the line of least resistance reflexively (through the movements of its roots, for example). Nevertheless, the difference in these cases is only in the means by which the adaptation arrives at the line of least resistance and not in the general biological meaning of the fact. Geometry is a 'pure science' and is extremely abstract, but its significance for life consists in its countless practical applications – for the goals of mechanics, architecture, and so on, for example. For these practical applications the abstract ideas of geometry serve, on the one hand, as a starting point and, on the other hand, as a unifying link. If one pulls an individual idea of this science away from its interrelationship with other ideas, then it can seem that one simply cannot speak of it as any kind of 'adaptation' in the struggle with external nature. But if geometry, as a whole, turns out to be a powerful tool in this struggle, then all the separate ideas that are necessarily interrelated elements of it are also, if not whole adaptations, then *parts of adaptations*. In exactly the same way, the philosophical concepts that are the furthest from life serve to link and unify many other concepts that are more closely related to the struggle for life and are an adaptation together with them and through them.[10]

---

10   My work, *Poznanie s istoricheskoi tochki zreniia* (all of Part I) is devoted to a more substantive explanation of the question of knowledge as an adaptation.

Further, as far as the forms of custom, law, and morality are concerned, it is most obvious that they have the characteristics of *adaptation*. The meaning that these forms have for life is that they adapt people to social labour life, making relationships expedient in the process of people's joint struggle with external nature. Such, for example, is the custom of patriarchal hospitality. By providing people the help of other people during the difficulties and dangers of travel, by making it possible for people to learn from one another, by facilitating people's mutual relationships, and by generally expanding the realm of cooperation at early levels of development, patriarchal hospitality made a huge contribution to the victory of humanity over spontaneous nature. The law of property is another example. By protecting producers from attacks that could deprive them of the tools and the products of their labour and by guaranteeing them the continued possibility of working successfully, the law of property represented an extremely useful adaptation in the struggle for life of a society with independent petty producers. The moral aspirations of altruism and justice establish relationships of mutual aid and limit relationships of mutual hostility among members of society, and this would obviously lead to the increase of social labour energy, in general, and to the increase of the usefulness of individual expenditures of that energy, in particular.

In all these cases one biological stipulation must obviously be made. Just as in organisms, various 'rudimentary' organs survive that were previously useful adaptations but in the present are now useless or even harmful (for humans: the vermiform appendix, nipples on men, wisdom teeth), so also in social life one can observe alongside effective adaptations relics of the past that are in part useless and in part harmful. In our times, an especially great number of such relics can be found in the sphere of legal and moral life. But they are indeed adaptations in their genesis and their original role.

Further, what serves as a useful adaptation for one part of society often turns out to be not at useful for another part and can sometimes even be the source of unadaptedness. Thus, legal and moral forms that were expedient from the point of view of feudal lords at the end of the middle ages, absolutely did not seem that way from the point of view of the peasantry and of the bourgeoisie, which was taking shape in cities. But the only thing that follows from this is that the life of society does not possess absolute organic unity: in a great many cases society is a complicated complex of relatively independent forms of life that very often have adapted not only independently of one another but even to the detriment of one another. And, yet again, the same thing also altogether applies – to a greater or lesser degree – to all complex forms of life. Leaving aside for now the struggle and competition between individuals that make up one species, even within an organism – the form of life with the most unity and interconnectedness of its elements – separate tissues and cells complete for nourishment, and it often happens that some of them supplant others, to the detriment or benefit of the whole organism.

Yet one more question remains. Is there a material difference between social and biological forms *in the manner of their development, their elaboration*? No. Here, as well, there is not a single case in which it is necessary to recognise such a difference. The essence of the matter remains the same. Changes of old forms under the influence of the environment continuously generate a huge amount of new variant forms, but the majority of them turn out to be unadapted to the environment. Selection eliminates them and allows a minority to survive as adaptations, and therefore this selection is identically 'natural' whether in nature or in society.

Two objections could be made to this. First, as regards the selection of social forms, the *social environment* in which they spring up plays the main role and the 'natural environment' – i.e. external nature – is of less importance. Any new social form – a new idea, let us say – could easily disappear because it is unadapted to social conditions, even though it might be completely compatible with 'natural' conditions, or it could survive because it is adapted to social relationships, even though it is contradictory to relationships with nature outside of society. Second, the elimination of unadapted social forms frequently occurs without the death of the organisms it is associated with. For example, for any legal norm to be eliminated, it is not necessary that everyone who accepts that norm dies, while with biological selection the removal of unsuccessful adaptations usually occurs through the death of organisms. But these are not essential differences, and with purely biological selection the *immediate* environment in which it is situated has the most significance for each form. Consequently, the cells of an organism depend first and foremost on other elements of that form – on other cells and their mutual relationships – and thus altogether on the *internal environment* of a given form. Society is also a complex form of life and, consequently, selection of its elements must also be determined by its immediate internal environment – i.e. the social environment. Further, the elimination of elements without the whole perishing is often observed in the development of complex biological forms – for example, when many cells are destroyed in the course of the survival of the whole organism, or the atrophy of separate reflexes and instincts in the course of the survival of the psychical whole. It is therefore impossible to see anything supra-biological in the fact that social forms can be eliminated without the direct destruction of entire human individuals.[11]

11　I have discussed the processes of the selection of social forms more substantively in my

In general, no matter how one looks at it, social forms are adaptations in the same sense and to the same degree as any other biological forms.

IV

We have shown that social forms belong to a broad *genus* – biological adapt-ations. But by this we still have not defined the realm of social forms. For a definition it is necessary to establish not only the *genus* but also the *species*; it is necessary not only to ascertain the traits that given forms have in common with others they are related to but also to ascertain the distinguishing features that set them apart from these other forms. A precise *characterisation* of social forms is needed.

In their struggle for existence, people cannot unite in any other way than through *consciousness*. Without consciousness there is no communication. Therefore, *social life in all its manifestations is consciously psychical*. This idea needs no special proof: it is sufficient that it is simply impossible to imagine a kind of social fact that could occur without the participation of conscious-ness. It is true that particular expressions are used that seem to contradict this – 'physical labour', 'the unconscious actions of crowds', etc., for example – but it is clear that such expressions are not to be understood literally. Physical labour is made up of perceptible – i.e. conscious – movements that are direc-ted toward conceived – i.e. conscious – goals. They are only distinguished by the fact that they produce 'physical' changes in the external environment. And the unconscious actions of a crowd do not occur beyond the bounds of the con-sciousness of the participants. It is only that they do not find clear motivation in this consciousness. In general, sociality is inseparable from consciousness.[12]

---

previously cited work, *Poznanie s istoricheskoi tochki zreniia*. (See the sections on 'Selec-tion of Psychical Forms' and on 'Social Selection', pp. 40–7 and 115–18.)

12   In the collection, *Problems of Idealism*, prince E. Trubetskoi tries to provide a critique of historical materialism based on the idea that not only the 'economic factor' but also the 'mental factor' have meaning for people's social life. It is obvious that such a critique is fundamentally mistaken, since it proposes that the 'economic' is something that is com-pletely *non-psychical*. But 'economics' means the *labour relationships of people* and not the physical relations of bodies. People are *psychical* beings, and labour is a *consciously-purposeful* activity. Prince Trubetskoi makes a quite common, but, all the same, quite flagrant error here of confusing 'ideology' with 'psychology'. Ideology, as we shall see, is the realm of concepts that organise social experience – i.e. it is a specific, particular sphere of social psychology. 'Economics' is another realm of the same social psychology. The critic has not gone beyond the surface of the words 'the social being of people determ-ines the forms of their consciousness', and he understands them in the sense that 'social

Social being and social consciousness, in the precise meaning of these words, is identical.

It does not, of course, follow from this that everything in consciousness is social. The realm of consciousness is broader than the realm of the social, and it contains the social realm within it. But there remains a huge number of consciously psychical phenomena that is not at all social – for example, all the immediate sensations that are generated by physiological life, all feelings, emotions, and actions that are not socially directed or that are even anti-social, etc.

Now we must explain the nature of those consciously psychical phenomena which make up the social process. The social struggle of people for existence is activity of a completely specific type. In all its manifestations, this activity is directed toward the attainment of a *goal*. This general trait stands out in all the forms of people's activity that have a social content. In material production, in verbal communication, in research, and in legal and moral life a person continually acts for the sake of some conceived goal. This kind of activity is called *labour*. Thus, the social process is a process of *labour*.

Here, again, an explanation is necessary. Any manifestation of social life has the nature of labour, but not all manifestations of labour life have a social nature. There is labour that is not social and that is even anti-social. Examples include the labour of parasitic consumption or the labour of useless killing and destruction – in general, labour that does not enter the social struggle of people for life or that even contradicts it. The realm of labour is broader than the realm of social being, and it includes the realm of social being as a part of the whole.

Labour, then, is social activity when it is aimed – directly or indirectly – toward the survival and development of *not only the labourer but other people as well*, when the labourer is useful not only individually but also socially. Through

---

being' is something absolutely different from the 'consciousness of people' – something 'material' in the *physical* meaning of the word. But for Marx the point had to do with various formations of what is socially experienced – with more elementary and more complex formations, lower and higher. It would be interesting to know how the critic understands the term 'material interests'? Does he consider them a non-psychological fact?

Addition in 1906. Unfortunately, comrade Ortodoks has displayed the same level of ignorance as prince E. Trubetskoy in regard to the concepts of 'psychology' and 'ideology' (see his article in *Iskra*, no. 77). This is how certain inferior theorists create the basis for a 'solid' bourgeois polemic against Marxism. ['Ortodoks' was the pseudonym of Liubov Akselrod (1868–1946). She was a close associate of G. Plekhanov and was second only to Plekhanov among Menshevik philosophers of Marxism. Because she wrote under a masculine pseudonym, Bogdanov refers to her with the masculine personal pronoun. For Bogdanov's refutation of her critique, see Bogdanov 2019, p. 298n (trans.)]

their actions, producers, researchers, those who implement moral norms, etc., create adaptedness not for themselves alone but also for other members of society, and therefore their actions enter the sphere of social life. These are social labour adaptations.

An individual social labour adaptation is useful sometimes for broader and sometimes for narrower circles of people – for all society, for a class, for a group, for a family. In this adaptation, the breadth or narrowness of social interconnectedness is expressed in one or another of its particular manifestations. An adaptation that is useful for some members of society can be harmful for others, as evidenced by the struggle of classes, by competition, and so on. This reveals the incomplete unity of society as a complex combination of comparatively separate groups that are not adapted to one another in everything.

To summarise the conclusions of this section: social adaptations represent forms of the labour activity of human beings in their struggle for existence, and, moreover, activity that is directed toward the good not only of the labourer but of other people as well. In sum: social adaptations are *forms of labour collectivity*, and society as a whole is a *system of collaboration* in the broadest meaning of the word.

v

We now turn to an examination of individual types of social adaptation. We must clarify their differences and establish their mutual interrelationships in regard to their origin and their significance for life, and we must therefore begin with the broadest subdivisions.

We have previously noted, although only in passing, two broad groups of social adaptations: technological adaptations, which are directed toward the *immediate* struggle of society with external nature – toward *direct* action upon it – and ideological adaptations, which have a more *indirect* significance for this struggle, although, as we have seen, indirect significance is frequently no less important than direct. People who fell trees carry out a technological process; people who consider how to more effectively fell trees carry out an ideological process. For the first, the object of action consists in objects of external nature: a tree, an axe. For the second, the object of action consists in concepts and judgements that take shape on the basis of past labour. It is most convenient to fell such and such a tree by such and such a method; one should begin from such and such a place, one must meanwhile be on guard against such and such, etc. Both processes of labour can flow together so closely that it is difficult to distinguish them even abstractly, but the type of labour to which any act of labour belongs is always clearly indicated by whether it is more or less immediately related to external nature.

Let us dwell for a while on technological adaptations. This is a very broad group in which things are brought together that at first glance are quite heterogeneous. Compare, for example, technological life at the early stages of the development of culture with the technological life of contemporary capitalist society. Back then people foraged in the forest for fruit, collected shellfish on the shore, pulled roots from the earth with their hands, hunted for small animals with stones. Now people carry out complex actions upon endlessly varied means of production, from virgin soil to automatic mechanisms and everything in between. But, all the same, we are fully justified in bringing together such different adaptations under the general concept of 'technology', because their significance for life is really the same. They all represent forms of the immediate relationships of people to the environment, of the immediate struggle of society with external nature.

At this point, we must remove one of the usual misunderstandings. The term 'technological adaptation' is often applied to the means of production – tools, machines, etc. – but this is an imprecise, figurative use of the word that is not suitable for our goals. Only living things adapt; only forms of life can be forms of adaptation. Tools, machines, materials of labour are *elements of external nature* that humanity, in the process of adapting, disposes in ways that are most beneficial to itself. Here 'adaptation' consists in the skill of people to act on external objects in such a way that they obtain the most expedient combination of them – in the form, for example, of an axe or motorised machine – and, further, in the skill to use that combination. Consequently, 'technological adaptations' are located *in people's psyches* and not outside them. It goes without saying that if the tools of labour are taken away from someone, that person will be 'technologically incapable', as if the actual adaptations had been taken from them. But these adaptations essentially remain with them. That is, they will be capable of using tools just as they were before, and what would be taken away would only be the external conditions necessary for manifesting this capability. In exactly the same way, farmers would seem unadapted if the land that they plough were taken from them, but no one would call that land an 'adaptation'. The technological adaptations of farmers (that is, the skill to plough, to sow, etc.) continue to survive in their psyches, but they are not applied because they do not possess one necessary external condition – land. If this condition once again comes into being – i.e. the farmers obtain land again – then their technological adaptations are again in business. Otherwise, over the course of time, those technological adaptations will be lost like an organ that atrophies because it has not functioned for a long time.

Such a painstaking explanation of concepts might seem rather tiresome for the reader, but nothing can be done about it. Precision is the most important thing, and at least we can now step forward with greater confidence.

In the preceding, by the way, it was established that the changing relationships of living forms toward their environment in the process of the struggle for existence is the starting point of any development of life. If this is so, then one must then accept a priori that of all social adaptations *it is precisely technological adaptations that must initially spring up and develop*, since they have the closest and most immediate relationship to the external environment of society. This is so far a theoretical conclusion, but it is fully affirmed by observations of actual social development.

In the life of contemporary cultured society, we are struck by the extreme profusion of ideological forms in it. A huge number of cognitive adaptations – the endless complexity and variety of manifestations of legal and ethical life – occupy a very significant part of the social process, and it is very significant even in comparison with the colossal development of technological life, of immediate production. But if one looks back on the course of development of culture, down to its increasingly lower levels, then the relationship changes. Ideological life becomes continually narrower, and, moreover, narrows more rapidly than technological life. The lower the culture, the more the *immediate* struggle of humanity with nature – the *direct* struggle with nature – comes to the fore. At these stages of development, people are comparatively much less thoughtful, deliberative, and evaluative; they react comparatively much more spontaneously to the external environment. To the extent that one approaches the conjectural, unknown beginning of social life, the content of labour boils down to the simple struggle for existence, uncomplicated by abstract ideas and norms. Ideological life disappears in comparison with technological life.

This correlation is so constant in what is known of human history that we are fully justified in conceiving of it as continuing to earlier periods of social development that are still inaccessible to scholarship. In so doing, it turns out that in its most primitive form, which can only be logically surmised, social life must entirely boil down to the *technological* process. The technological process must consequently be recognised as the *historically primary realm of people's social being*.

But at all later stages of development the primary nature of technological adaptations is still well confirmed. To be precise, in cases where ideological life undergoes material transformations and revolutions, it is always possible, with sufficient investigation, to find changes in the realm of technology that preceded it, and it is possible to show that these technological changes can and must serve as the *starting point* of changes in ideology. Thus, the Reformation was preceded by a rapid broadening of production and improvement of the methods of production and also by the development of trade. (The *technological* process of the movement of goods was fundamental to commerce). And in historical literature it has frequently been shown how this progress in productive life has caused ideological consciousness to progress.[13] In the same way, the revolutions at the end of the eighteenth and beginning of the nineteenth centuries were connected with the development of capitalist technology, and this connection is recognised to a significant degree even by historians who are definitely not of a monistic bent. Many more examples could be presented. In general, it should be recognised that everywhere that the interrelationships of the facts of social development are uncovered with appropriate fullness and clarity, the motor force of this development turns out to issue precisely from the realm of immediate production, from the sphere of the technological process.[14]

Thus, in the series of social adaptations, technological adaptations are primary in origin and development. Having acknowledged this, we thereby set ourselves this task: to show how the complex system of social being with its varied elements and unified whole develops on the basis of the technological process. It goes without saying that the attempt to resolve this task can be given only in the most general and most basic outlines.

VI

We begin with a minor digression into the realm of biology, but, as will become evident, the digression is only apparent.

Of all complex forms of life (the organism, the family, the species, society, etc.) none possesses *perfect* internal unity. The higher organisms are distinguished by the greatest wholeness of the life process, the greatest intercon-

---

13   This is presented particularly well in the works of K. Kautsky. There is a Russian translation of 'The Age of Humanism and Reformation' (a selection from a work on Thomas More) in Kautsky's *Essays and Studies*, and his 'Social Movements in the Middle Ages and the Era of Reformation' is part of a large, collected work translated under the editorship of V. Bazarov and I. Stepanov.

14   The reader will see that we have carefully avoided the term 'productive forces' and prefer to speak of 'technological adaptations'. The concept of 'productive forces' is too imprecise and ambivalent, since it embraces both the material means of production and the psychical adaptations of producers. Such a concept is appropriate only for the early stages of analysis. For our goals a more rigorous discrimination is necessary in which elements of the social psyche are not mixed up with elements of the material environment of society.

nectedness of their parts and harmony of their mutual relationships. However, even they are not devoid of certain 'internal contradictions', sometimes insignificant and barely noticeable, sometimes significant and a threat to the life of the whole. The performance of various organs, tissues, and cells is never *completely* mutually adapted, and at times they seriously impede one another. For example, under normal conditions, increased activity of the digestive system hampers and limits the work of the psyche by diverting some nourishment away from the higher neural centres. Similarly, excessive development of sexual life leads to constraint and even impairment of the vital functions of other systems of the organism. Cells of connective tissue constantly take advantage of the diminishment of the vital capacity of other tissues in order to supplant and replace them – this is a partial cause of the degradation of organisms during illness and one of the basic causes of physiological 'old age'. In psychical life some forms, desires, and ideas continually struggle with others for predominance, the less stable of these elements are ousted by the more stable, and this is far from always of benefit to the organism.

It is obvious that the more complex any form of life is and the more numerous, varied, and independent its elements are, the easier it is for vital contradictions to spring up between them, and the more often it must occur that some of these elements will undermine the viability of others and consequently also the viability of the whole. Development must eliminate such unadaptedness. This is achieved by means of special *organising adaptations*.

For higher organisms, neural centres serve as such adaptations. Neural centres harmoniously unify the vital activity of various organs and tissues of the whole; nourishment is expediently distributed so that some elements (trophic and vasculomotor centres) do not take nourishment away from others, and the most beneficial combinations of separate muscular contractions and perceptions (sensory and motor centres) are produced, etc. An adaptation, of course, is never perfect in this regard. Within certain limits, the struggle for nourishment between parts of the organism continues, and some – even if very few – persistently develop excessively at the expense of others. The contraction of separate muscle fibres far from always combine harmoniously, and therefore movement of the organism does not achieve the greatest conceivable force and expediency, etc. But, all the same, only the organising activity of neural centres gives the complex structure of the organism a high level of vital unity and wholeness.

Organising adaptations of another type are seen in more complex forms of life. For families, flocks, and herds of animals such a role is played by specific family and herd instincts that unite them into a collective whole. Additionally, these instincts are supplemented by a system of signals that allow individuals to unite their actions in the struggle for existence in the most harmonious way. All such adaptations are psychical, and they consequently develop from adaptations of the same system that serves as the organising form for the life of individuals. This is perfectly natural, since collective forms like a family, a herd, etc., are always made up precisely of individuals.

Human society is one of the most – if not *the* most – complex form of such a construction. We must obviously expect to find especially complex organising adaptations here, and this is exactly what turns out in reality.

Individual people, even taken in the aggregate, still do not make up a society. The concept of 'society' contains the idea of organisation, the unification of the vital commonality of individuals. Thus, in order for the very use of the word 'society' to have any meaning, it is necessary for a specific organising adaptation to be present. This adaptation is the social instinct.

The social instinct is not something that is constant, unchanging, and identical in all manifestations of social life. It develops over time and appears in various forms. There is no need to go into the origin of the social instinct here; only the most general features of its place in the biological world need be pointed out. There is no doubt that the direct predecessors of the social instinct are herd and family instincts that are so widespread in the kingdom of life. There is also no doubt that in its first manifestations it was not exclusive to human beings but is also encountered in a great many other social animals. But this instinct attains its greatest development for people both in terms of its breadth – in our times it unites all of humanity to a certain degree – and in the sense of the complexity and variety of its manifestations. The most heterogeneous elements of the social labour process are coloured by it to various degrees. People are social beings first and foremost.

In its primary form the social instinct represents quite a complex vital phenomenon. Its essence consists in the *desire of people to keep together with other people and to act together with them and the same as them.*[15] This desire makes up the psychical basis of all sociability.

Technological forms, the content of which consists in the action of humanity upon nature, obviously could not be the least bit social if they were not inseparably connected with the social instinct. What is social about a person picking fruit from a tree? It is social if it arises from imitation (i.e. the desire to act *the same as other people*) or if it is done *for other people* (in the latter case,

---

15 I thus take *imitation* to be a primary manifestation of the social instinct, and, in reality, it is already ubiquitous at the earliest levels of sociality – for example, among social animals. Regarding the biological and psychological bases of imitation, see my work *Poznanie s istericheskoi tochki zreniia* (pp. 109–13).

however, we see a more developed form of the social instinct about which it will be necessary to speak later on). Technological adaptations become social to the extent that they are imbued with the social instinct, which enters them as an inseparable element of their psychical content.

The same applies also to ideological forms, but, as we shall see, with the difference that the very appearance of ideological forms already presupposes the existence both of technological forms and of social instinct. Let us now turn to ideology.

VII

The significance of the social instinct is that it ties together and unites people as members of society. But this is still insufficient for the harmonious life and harmonious development of the social whole. Simple unification does not eliminate the possibility of contradiction, and even closely connected elements can be mutually unadapted. Hence, still other organising adaptations are needed, and ideological forms are precisely such adaptations. Such forms can be broken down into several basic types, and we will examine them, beginning with the least complex.

The individual organisms that make up a society are quite independent as far as their vital processes are concerned, and this is the first source of unadaptedness in people's actions.

People's activities in the struggle with nature depend above all on the influences of the environment that they experience at a given moment – on the perceptions that those influences provide them. If someone sees a wolf or feels its teeth, they try to run away; if they see fruit, they try to pluck it, etc. Specific perceptions elicit specific actions. But imagine the following state of affairs: one person sees a wild animal and another person, located at a distance, does not see it. The actions of both people can then seem mutually unadapted. One, in running away, exposes the other to danger, allowing that person to be unexpectedly attacked by the predator, or even both people could die, one after the other. Whereas, by acting together, they could cope with their enemy and save themselves. In exactly the same way, if one found a tree with fruit and the other did not notice it, then the first might not be able to eat all the fruit, while the second might waste a lot of labour searching for food and remain hungry. In general, if what is seen, heard, or felt (in a word, *experienced*) by some people is not seen, heard, or felt (experienced) by others, then one can always expect that their actions will turn out to be mutually harmful or unhelpful (i.e. mutually unadapted) and, in any event, not optimally adapted.

From this the need arose that gave rise to the first series of ideological adaptations – forms of gestures and speech, forms of expression. Gestures and speech represent a system of signs by which means what is experienced by some people is transferred to others – so that people's 'experiences' are *socialised*. No kind of joint labour can proceed successfully and develop if people are unable to communicate to others what they see, hear, feel, and want. Mutual help would in many cases be impossible, and quite often people's actions would only interfere with those of others. Just try to imagine production organised without words, or at least without gestures.

Thus, speech and gestures serve as tools for mutual adaptation for a system of social labour. This adaptation, it goes without saying, is far from completely perfected. Communicating their experiences to one another is usually still not enough to provide for mutual harmony in the actions of different people, but, all the same, it is the first and necessary condition of such harmony. Later on, we will examine the further conditions for mutual harmony in connection with other forms of ideology.

Since the primary realm of social being is the technological process then, obviously, that process first and foremost provides the content for forms of speech and gestures. At the very lowest levels of social development that are known to us, almost all the lexicon boils down to a small number of words that signify first technological actions and then the external conditions for those actions – materials, tools of labour, and, in general, elements of the external environment that are important in the struggle for life.[16]

As ideological life develops above technological life, the same organising adaptations – words, gesturing signals – are also created for it. For example, it is through speech that acquired knowledge is relayed (organising social experi-

---

16   The brilliant philological theory of Ludwig Noiré reduces the origin of words to techno-
      logical processes. According to his theory, primary root words are the involuntary sounds
      that accompany the joint, uniform labour activities of people. These sounds perfectly nat-
      urally became 'signs' of the social labour acts connected with them because they were
      'understandable' by each member of the group, and because each of them, due to con-
      tinuous association, evoked the conception of the corresponding action. We know that
      such sounds spring up due to the fact that motor stimulation spreads ('irradiates') from
      some neural centres to others, according to a definite path, the path of least resistance.
      Thus, the primary roots can be viewed as separated, differentiated parts of real labour
      complexes.
          Russian readers can get to know Noiré's theory in greater detail through the present-
      ation of it by one of his followers, Max Muller (*The Science of Thought*). [Ludwig Noiré
      (1829–1889) was a German philosopher of language; Max Müller (1823–1900) was a Ger-
      man philologist and orientalist (trans.).]

ence into a system) and established customs are relayed (organising customary law into a system), etc. Ideological experiences must be relayed from some
people to others in exactly the same way as technological experiences are,
because, generally speaking, the former are no less significant than the latter;
they only have a *different* significance for the social struggle for life.

Speech thus serves as an organising form for the whole system of social
labour in all its forms. Naturally, the development of speech proceeds in correspondence with the general development of this system. It is easiest to
see such correspondence from the perspective of the quantitative development of speech. As the realm of social labour becomes broader, the manifestations of speech become more varied and the lexicon of words and other
signs that are employed becomes larger. There are a whole range of transitional stages from such dialects as those of the San or Papuans that have
several hundred words, to languages like contemporary English and German
that have many tens and even hundreds of thousands of denotations. These
levels approximately correspond to the levels of development of the activity
of labour, from the simplest techniques of the hunter-gatherer era to the most
complex and colossally developed technology and ideology of capitalist society.

The connection between forms of speech and forms of labour is no less clear
in yet another regard. At the earliest stages of the life of humanity, people's
labour life consisted almost entirely of *habitual* actions – i.e. of actions that
were constantly repeated in approximately the same, unchanging form. New
techniques of labour and new combinations and variations of previous actions
were created very rarely and slowly. It appears that language that consists of
unchanging words (roots) alone, such as all the least developed dialects, completely corresponds to this and under these conditions is completely satisfact-
ory. But to the extent that forms of labour become changeable and plastic,
new, derivative words are easily formed with prefixes, suffixes, and inflections.
Thus, we can suppose that forms of declension and conjugation were initially produced precisely by the changing, increasingly complex relationships
of people to external nature and to one another during labour. For example,
what does the imperative (and in the more ancient languages also the optative mood[17]) express, if not an incompletely defined type of relationship of
labour in which one person directs or desires to direct the activities of another?
What does the accusative case mean other than the relationship of people to

---

17   The optative mood is a grammatical feature of verbs that indicates a wish, hope, or desire
      [trans.].

the external object of their activity, primarily the material of their labour? In certain grammatical terms such a connection is expressed with complete clarity, for example in such terms as 'instrumental implement' (Latin and Russian), 'attentive relationship' (Greek), and so on.

All these, it goes without saying, are only illustrations. It is impossible to provide more here, but we think they are sufficient to make our idea clear. This idea is, after all, not particularly complicated: speech is an organising adaptation for social labour in all its manifestations, and its development must therefore follow after the development of social labour, adapting to its requirements.

With the development of gestures and speech – and subject to it – a new phase in the development of social instinct began. Social instinct took the form of a desire to impart one's own experiences to other people and to apprehend what other people experience – to live together in common with other people in the broadest meaning of the word. This exchange of what is experienced leads to where people begin to relate to the experiences of other people to a significant degree as they relate to their own. In many cases, people act *because of* other people and *for* other people – for example, protecting others as they would protect themselves. *Altruism* springs up in desires and actions.[18]

Thus, due to the integration of human experiences that is achieved through gestures and speech, the social instinct is transformed from the simplest primitive form to the higher form of altruism. Without gestures and speech, it would be inconceivable that someone could *understand* someone else's soul and struggle for that person's life and development the same as for their own.

VIII

The mutual exchange from some people to other people of what they immediately experience is still far from sufficient for the complete, harmonious unification of human activities. These activities depend not only on what people immediately experience at a given moment, but also on what they have experienced previously. People's actions are based on their previous experience of labour. In people's experience of life, they work out expedient techniques of labour and then they apply them. The broader, the more varied, and the more thorough this experience, the more successfully people will adapt in the future and the more 'productive' their labour will be.

---

18   There is no need to especially explain that higher forms of the social instinct do not exclude lower ones – both are constantly observed together.

No matter what social forms it occurs in, the experience of labour of different people is always different to a certain degree. Some possess a greater amount of experience or more successful experience than others, or they are more capable of mastering and utilising it. Finally, the experience of some simply unfolds a little differently and in different directions from the experience of others, especially with the division of labour when people have different jobs.

With such heterogeneity of experience, it is inevitable that there is a need to harmoniously unify it. First and foremost, in the difficult conditions of the primeval struggle for life, when all of a society as a whole could hardly sustain its existence, insufficient experience and lack of skill of some members of such a society must have placed an oppressive burden on the life of the others. The more capable and skilful members would have been forced to expend a huge amount of unnecessary labour for the sake of the survival of the lives of less capable and skilful. It would have turned out that the progress of the most vital elements was held back by the least vital elements. Additionally, because of the multiplicity of experience, people could have utilised the same conditions in such different ways that it would be easy for them to conflict and interfere with one another. For example, some members of a primitive society might, on the basis of their experience, consider it useful to conserve a given tree because good fruit grows on it, but others, on the basis of *their* experience, consider it expedient to use the wood of the tree for heating. Clearly, a huge mutual unadaptedness would result from their actions.

Finally – and what is most important and most obvious – the greatest adaptedness of people cannot be achieved if their work experience remains un-unified – if what is acquired by some people in this sphere is utterly missing for others and if individual people must learn everything by themselves and for themselves.

All this together makes necessary an adaptation that would unite people's different labour experiences and would remove the contradictions that issue from this heterogeneity. In short, there is a necessity for organising forms for social labour experience. *Knowledge* serves as such an organising form.

The labour experiences of separate human individuals, crystallising in their psyches, form their *individual experience*. This is still not knowledge, but people express their personal experience and convey it to other people through words, and they apprehend the expressions of the experience of those other people, also in the form of speech. Then *experience is socialised* and becomes *knowledge*. The only products of experience that enter the realm of knowledge are those that can be expressed in words and that are therefore transmitted from some people to others. What cannot be expressed in words does not belong to knowledge. The element of knowledge is a *concept* that is signified by a word and that cannot exist without this sign. Knowledge is socialised experience, and the tool of this socialisation is speech.[19]

It is obvious that the realm of knowledge, with all its content, is *completely determined* by the realm of social experience, and this latter corresponds to the realm of people's social labour.[20] Therefore, the development of knowledge necessarily must *follow after* the development of social labour, and must *correspond* to it.

The knowledge of primitive society was just as narrow, limited, imperfect, and unreliable as its labour. The technological process is of predominant importance in life, and, correspondingly, their knowledge boiled down to a small quantity of data of an immediately practical nature. This does not exclude so-called 'superstitions' of primitive humans. Superstitions were also usually purely practical data, and their basic content boiled down to the conditions for success or failure at hunting, fishing, sowing crops – in general, one productive process or another. 'Superstition' is distinct from true practical knowledge in that the former represents *unsuccessful* knowledge. The boundary of successful labour experience is always also the boundary of successful knowledge. Unadaptedness of labour causes knowledge to be unadapted; the dominion of the elemental environment over humanity gives rise to error.

Each step in the development of social labour broadens the realm of knowledge. Contemporary knowledge, with its infinitely varied material, with its specialisation, with its broad but still not completely unified generalisations is a true reflection of the contemporary labour life of society with its colossal development of technology, its infinitely varied means of production, the specialisation of its various divisions, the tight interconnectedness of all the elements of this system, and, at the same time, its overall lack of organisation. Just like production, knowledge in our day develops in the direction of tighter and tighter unification of heterogeneous elements, in the direction of increasing organisation, of increasingly full 'monism'.

---

19   At this point it is not necessary to present detailed proof of this idea. It so happens that it is currently accepted by a majority of authoritative thinkers, including philosophers with such different views as A. Riehl (*The Philosophy of Criticism*) and R. Avenarius (*Critique of Pure Experience*).

20   In regard to the question of the boundaries of knowledge, A. Labriola (in one of his 'Letters to Sorel') says: 'One cannot establish the boundaries of knowledge either a priori or a posteriori, since *in the process of labour that is experience and the process of experience that is labour* humanity knows everything that it is necessary and useful to know' (my italics, A.B.). [Antonio Labriola (1843–1904) was an Italian Marxist theorist. The book referred to was translated into English under the title *Socialism and Philosophy* (trans.).]

Changes in the very nature of knowledge depend strictly on the nature of social labour. Thus, in those eras when forms of labour were stable and conservative, when labour life fit almost entirely within the confines of habitual activity, knowledge was *static* – i.e. all concepts and ideas were conceived of as *immovable* and *unchanging*. Nature appeared to the human mind as a system of independent, solid, conservative *things*. Just the opposite, when forms of labour became variable and changeable, when the techniques of labour began to quickly develop and change, when people's activities became plastic – then knowledge began to change in the direction of *the historical point of view*. The conception of progress, development, and change began to imbue all elements of knowledge. Nature was transformed in people's consciousness into a continuous series of *processes*. Knowledge was adapted to the new type of labour and took shape according to that new type.[21]

The more that ideological and organisational forms spring up alongside technological forms, the more knowledge is also directed toward ideological life and its relationships. In knowledge, itself, higher concepts that are more abstract or broader and more general serve as 'organising adaptations' for lower concepts that are more concrete and for ideas that are narrower and more particular; they give them interconnectedness and harmonious unity. Manifestations of custom and legal and moral life constitute a vast realm of knowledge and provide material for a huge number of concepts, judgements, opinions, and theories for a great many disciplines. But it is completely natural and understandable that knowledge that deals with ideological life (the sphere of secondary adaptations) lags behind knowledge that deals with technological life (which is based on primary adaptations). So far, the 'exact sciences' only include technological sciences and the natural sciences that derive from them.

And in both the technological realm and the ideological realm the role of knowledge as an organising adaptation is materially the same: the harmonious unification of social labour experience.

Cognitive activity is tied just as inseparably to social instinct – just as imbued with it – as any other process of social labour. But this instinct transforms into yet a new form: the form of a desire to pass one's labour experience on to other people and to receive their experience. Such a desire is always present in any knowledge, although it is far from always precisely realised. There is no kind

---

21   There is no need to review the link between forms of labour and forms of knowledge in more detail. I did this to a significant extent in my work *Poznanie s istericheskoi tochki zreniia* (pp. 194–213). A large specialised work would be needed in order to thoroughly analyse this question. In this chapter the matter has to do only with the *basic point of view* regarding various realms of the social process, one of which is the realm of knowledge.

of 'pure' knowledge – and there never has been any – that can be completely devoid of this social element. Such knowledge is even altogether inconceivable. In investigating phenomena and broadening their experience, people always strive toward truth, and truth signifies precisely what is *socially obligatory in knowledge* – what is obligatory for any 'knower' and not only for the given person. Consequently, the desire for truth is essentially a desire for knowledge for everyone, even if the 'knower' is not aware of it. It is not accidental that anyone who thinks and investigates feels the insurmountable need to *express* in one way or other the results of their knowledge – i.e. to give it social form. *The idealism of truth is one of the transmutations of the social instinct.*

IX

Speech and knowledge, in unifying both people's immediate experiences and their established labour experience, are powerful organising adaptations in the life of a society. But they themselves still cannot create full, perfect organisation. They remove defects in the interconnectedness of people in their labour life, but they do not remove imperfections that could be inherent in the very *form* – the *structure* – of this interconnectedness. Even with the closest communication among people in their labour life, it is possible that their mutual relationships could turn out to be fundamentally contradictory and disharmonious.

Suppose that several primitive people, members of the same clan group, hunt in the same forest. One of them spots a live prey and is stalking it, and another one of them, seeing this from the side, rushes to seize the prey themselves, so that all the labour of the first obviously goes for naught. Or suppose that the same people together come up against a powerful, dangerous beast and are forced to defend themselves from it, but some of them turn and run, and so the others find it much more difficult to fight with the beast and flee from it. Finally, suppose that at the conclusion of hunting, some of them take so much of the common catch that not enough remains for the others ... In all such cases we observe mutual unadaptedness in labour life, but this unadaptedness is not caused by a simple defect in the interconnectedness of people but from an imperfect form – inexpedient organisation – of that interconnectedness.

A third series of this kind of adaptation has arisen to eliminate such unadaptedness – *custom*. For example, the custom arose of not interfering with one another while hunting, to help one another to the bitter end when in danger, to take no more than necessary from the common catch, etc. If individuals tried to violate the custom, the other members of the group tried to prevent them from doing so or even banished them. Consequently, the essence of custom consists in that people become accustomed to recognising certain relationships as normal, and wherever they see a deviation from these normal relationships to try to prevent it or stop it. This results in great harmony and expediency in the relationships of the labour process.

The ideological form of customs presupposes knowledge and includes elements of knowledge. To be precise, a custom is not conceivable without a *conception* and a *judgement* regarding people's relationships. To accept one or another relationship as normal means first of all to know those relationships and then to judge them appropriately. Both are accomplished with the help of cognitive acts, although, of course, they are not the only things that form the content of custom, and later on we will need to say more about this.[22]

Because the technological process is the basic process in the social struggle of people for life and development, relationships in the technological process must provide the primary material for customs. In reality, the principal and greatest part of the customs of primitive people are of this sort, and the customs that figured in our previous illustrations can serve as examples. As ideological life develops, custom also begins to regulate its relationships. For example, custom prescribes specific opinions for people in the sphere of religion and of knowledge in general and also in the sphere of moral beliefs, and it persecutes anyone who departs from these opinions and contradicts them. At the earliest stages of culture this 'secondary' realm of the development of customs is, of course, comparatively very narrow.

It is extremely difficult, by the way, to draw a strict line between customs that organise the relationships of people in technological labour and those that organise the ideological process. Thus, for example, at first glance one might be inclined to attribute to ideology the 'superstitious' custom of pre-civilised tribes to liberally share food with dead ancestors, but in reality this is one of the same series of customs that organises the distribution of products among living members of the group. Primitive people had not yet worked out special relationships toward dead co-workers and shared with them as with the living.

Custom is the source of a great number of the same sort of ideological adaptations, such as customary law, the law of cultured peoples, and morality. In

---

22   The word 'custom' is often used in another sense – in the sense of spontaneous *habit* that
       determines the actions of people so directly that they cannot even imagine the possibility
       of acting differently. This is true of many 'customs' of uncultured people. But custom in
       this sense is not 'ideology' at all.

regard to their vital significance these are not distinguishable from custom. They are also directed toward the harmonious organisation of mutual relationships among people in the social process, and their essence also consists in the recognition of certain relationships as norms and in the desire to suppress everyone who diverges from these norms. What is meant, for example, by the law of property? It is the social acknowledgment that a specific person can freely and exclusively make use of certain things and the social desire to prevent anyone from violating this relationship. What is meant by the moral duty of the powerful to help the weak? It is the acceptance as a norm of the kind of relationship in which the strong support the weak and the desire to resist relationships of a different sort.

Customary law is distinguished from primitive 'custom' in that it is realised less spontaneously and has a special organ for it, one or another 'authority'. In the primeval group, the violation of custom causes an immediate, purely spontaneous influence upon the violator by the entire group just as pain causes a reflexive movement by an organism. Meanwhile, in a patriarchal clan group or in a federally organised tribe, for example, the violator of customary law is first 'judged' and then the law is put into effect by a specific person – the patriarch of the clan, a council of elders of the tribe, etc.

'Law', proper, that arises in large state organisations is distinguished from customary law by still less spontaneity; it has the character of social custom to a considerably lesser degree, in that writing – written law – is necessary for it to be strictly and exactly maintained, and it is realised by means of a whole series of specially created organs: judicial and executive powers. Usually such law is established by the governing groups of society and supports precisely those relationships that these groups recognise as normal – i.e. generally speaking, relationships that are advantageous for them.

In contradistinction to law, morality is closer to primitive custom. Like primitive custom, it also takes shape on the basis of habitual relationships, it also does not have special, separate organs in society, and it also is spontaneous and immediate. Moral assessment is reflexive, so to say, whereas legal assessment is based on deliberation. But in a developed society, where a system of law exists, morality is limited in its manifestations and cannot be expressed by direct, spontaneous action on the violator of norms, otherwise it would continually come into conflict with the coercive action of the law. Therefore, involuntary action on the violator of moral norms is weakened to the level of simple censure. What is immoral for a given group or class is what summons censure on the part of the 'social opinion' of that class or group. Precisely the absence of direct, brute force on those who violate norms endows the moral tendency with the character of special 'spirituality'.

From this it is clear that it is possible for moral norms to transform into legal norms and for legal norms to transform into moral norms. When a moral idea – for example, the idea that usury is evil – gains the support of the coercive power of the state, it becomes a legal statute (the prohibition of usury). When a legal norm – let us say the right of blood vengeance by relatives – loses its coercive support, but it has become so habitual that it still survives in people's consciousness, it can still acquire the character of a moral norm. (This is observed in regard to blood vengeance among certain backward tribes that have come under the jurisdiction of a cultured government – for example, to a certain extent down to the present day with Corsicans, Calabrians, and so on).[23]

Many so-called 'economic relationships' have to do with the realm of custom and law, to be precise, with relationships of ownership – forms of property and the distribution of property in society. As we have already pointed out in passing, the essence of any property consists in the fact that it is socially recognised and supported by the coercive force of the social organisation. The reader can see that we have avoided the very term 'economics' in our presentation. Actually, the concept that 'economics' expresses cannot be considered satisfactory for precise historical analysis. It combines, on the one hand, such relationships of the *technological* process as the division of labour, cooperation, and forms of collaboration, in general, and, on the other hand, such *ideological* relationships as property relationships. In the specialised research of the economist this duality of a basic concept might not present any difficulties, in view of the particularly close vital connection that exists between these two elements of 'economics'. But when both laws of historical development must be explained, particular conceptual precision – especially strict discrimination of what is heterogeneous – is necessary.

But we have digressed somewhat. Returning to the topic of our presentation, we will summarise in a few words the vital significance of the ideological forms we have just examined. Custom, law, and morality represent a particular series of organising adaptations directed towards attaining the most harmonious mutual relationships among people in the process of social labour.

---

23   When a moral idea takes the form of a legal institution, it still, of course, does not lose its 'moral character'. The application of coercive force toward the violator of the norm can go hand in hand with social opprobrium of the violation. The majority of violations of the law are simultaneously 'immoral'. But when a legal institution loses the support of coercive force, it obviously ceases to be a 'law' in the strict sense of the word, and, at the very most, it retains the significance of 'moral law'.

Social instinct in the sphere of what are regarded as 'normal' adaptations is subject to a new transformation. It is expressed here in the desire to realise and defend normal relationships in which, as we know, the vital interests of a society or group are embodied. But this desire, in light of its deeply social nature, can and must be directed against individual members of society who violate social norms. It not infrequently occurs that when people violate a norm that they believe in, they even apply that norm to themselves. The human psyche does not possess absolute unity, and, like any complex form of life, it often contains internal contradictions. The 'struggle of duty and feeling' and subsequently a 'guilty conscience' on the occasion of violating a duty signifies precisely the desire of people to prevent the violation of norms that they themselves accept. (In a 'guilty conscience', this desire is combined with the consciousness that it is impossible to realise it, and this increases the intensity of the internal contradiction still more.)

Thus, a peculiar phenomenon results: the social instinct engenders a struggle of some people against other people and even against themselves, and this is possible precisely because specific normative relationships – and not the people who are concealed behind those relationships – represent the immediate goal of social aspiration. Hence a special kind of fetishism appears. In social consciousness, 'norms' or 'principles' of law and morality stand apart from people themselves and are represented as something independent. They include such fetishes as 'sacred tradition', 'class honour', 'absolute duty', 'pure justice' for the sake of which the world could end, etc. There is less of this kind of fetishism in forms of custom that correspond to still quite uncomplicated – and therefore understandable – relationships among people, and there is more of it in the 'absolute' morals of modern times.

In any event, this fetishism is unavoidable only where normative adaptations are really insufficient and do not eliminate vital contradictions in society and where, as a result of this, the social instinct engenders struggle among people. Where this struggle is eliminated, there is no place for fetishism. Where this struggle is eliminated, the idealism of law and justice – the highest form of social instinct that we know of – must be transformed into in another form, still more perfected but crystal clear to human consciousness ...

X

We have examined the vital significance of the basic forms of ideology, and it turned out that ideology is an *organising adaptation* in the social labour struggle for existence. Such a characterisation turned out to be applicable to all basic types of ideological forms, regardless of their significant differences.[24] Now we must plainly clarify the question of what precisely is organised by means of individual ideological adaptations.

Since the primary series of social forms are technological, they must also represent the initially organised material for ideological forms. In reality, as we have seen, at early stages of development a huge number of words, concepts, and customs relate precisely to the technological process. They serve precisely as an instrument for that process, and it is with their help that the unity and cohesion of 'that which is organised' is attained. Subsequently, the realm of ideology broadened, and ideological life consolidated itself in new words and concepts and produced social norms of customs and morals for itself. Organising forms developed in which ideology was 'that which is organised'.

But the ideological forms that are *organised* in this way by other ideological forms, became, in their turn, *organising* forms for still other adaptations, whether technological or, yet again, ideological. In the latter case, organised ideological forms of a lower series must also be organising forms for others, etc. As in the army, moving from the highest organiser (the commander-in-chief) to their subordinates (generals), from the generals to *their* direct subordinates, etc., we end up at the last 'things that are organised' – the soldiers who directly engage with the enemy. Thus, in any chain of ideological forms, in moving from what does the organising to what is organised by them, we sooner or later arrive at the final thing that is organised – technological adaptations that appear in society's immediate struggle with nature. For example, the most general and

---

24 I have not touched on one realm of ideological phenomena – the realm of art. But art is not a special type of adaptation that can be separated from what we are discussing. The social content of art boils down partly to the transmittal of immediate experiences from one person to another and partly to the communication of accumulated experiences to others. Songs, music, the rhythmical movement of dance, etc. – like speech and gestures – serve as means of 'expression'. They transmit experienced moods to others, only in a less specific form. Many primitive and pre-civilised tribes use music and especially dance in order to achieve a unified mood prior to the joint undertaking of some important matter (a council of tribes, going out to war or to hunt, and so on). In certain events in life, singing and music have a similar meaning even with cultured people (in military marches, for example). Additionally, a song or a drawing are – especially at early stages of development – the means of transmitting accumulated experience. One need only recall what huge cognitive significance the poems of Homer and Hesiod and works of art and sculpture in temples and town squares, etc. had for the education of the ancient Greeks. Singing and poetry undoubtedly have a common origin with speech and dances, the plastic arts have a common origin with gestures, and music originates with gestures and speech. In a word, art is a series of ideological adaptations of a rather distinct kind (it contains quite a few technological elements, especially architecture, for example).

abstract judgements in a system connect more particular and less abstract judgements, and these latter are the same kind of connecting links for even more particular and even less abstract judgements, etc., right down to concrete judgements that summarise a series of immediate experiences that spring up in the sphere of the technological process. In exactly the same way, any legal principle can serve as the harmonising consolidation of several more specific legal norms. They might, for example, regulate contradictions between old customs and new moral tendencies, etc. But, descending further and further down this series, we without fail must end up at the vital relationships among people that emerge out of their immediate labour activity.

Our conclusion is this: if one follows the derivation of any ideological form back far enough, it is possible to find its starting point of development in the realm of the technological process. In other words, *in the final analysis, every ideology develops on the basis of the technological life for which it is an organising adaptation.* In this sense, the 'basis' of ideological development consists in technological development.

A quite specific relationship to historical facts – a quite specific line of advance in regard to historical investigation – follows from this. In studying any ideological form whatsoever, we must conceive of it as a derivative adaptation that arises on the basis of other adaptations that it regulates and unifies – in general, 'organises' – one way or another. If these other adaptations turn out also to be ideological – i.e. derivative – then the analysis must go further, moving down the chain of development from one to another until we arrive at a primary adaptation, at the sphere of labour where the social individual comes face to face with external nature. This is the 'final analysis' of social science, since further investigation would take us beyond the confines of social science. Further causes of social phenomena lie in the extra-social environment and are studied by the methods of other sciences.

Suppose, for example, that we need to investigate the moral principle of absolute duty. It is perfectly obvious that this principle is a unifying form for a great many moral norms with more specific meanings. Historical investigation must therefore be directed at these latter norms in order to explain their vital content. We cannot do this here, but let us say that it has been done and that we have figured out certain general traits of relationships in life that reflect the particular norms that are included in the system of duty. It turns out that the idea of what is required by duty combines various demands imposed by social consciousness on individual people in the most varied realms of life. It turns out, further, that in all these demands at least three basic ideas equally stand out. First, the ideal of the *independence* of the human individual. The principle of duty everywhere presupposes a free, autonomous will for which moral demands are absolute and that can realise them utterly independently of any other will and independently of external circumstances. Second, the idea of *equivalence*. The demand that is expressed by the idea of duty always applies neither more nor less in relation to one person than in relation to others; each person is conceived of as equal to everyone else in regard to this duty. Third, the idea of *reciprocity*. The duty of one person in regard to others presupposes the identical, same, and equal duty to that person. Finally, the very form of the idea of pure duty – an *imperative* and, at the same time, an *impersonal, abstract* form – speaks to us of the psychology of *subordination*. This is not the simple subordination of one person to another, however, but subordination to some impersonal force that does not appear to that person in the form of living, concrete images.

It is obvious that the relationships of labour that ideologically organise the principle of duty must be characterised as the independence of human individuals, the equivalence and reciprocity of their actions, plus the subordination of individuals to some kind of impersonal forces that their imagination cannot grasp. Where do we find such relationships? They must be sought, of course, where we find the principle of duty elaborated, since these relationships must be its basis in life. And these relationships must be distinguished by breadth and universality, so that they could be the basis for the elaboration of a principle that acquired such a broad universal meaning in moral life in a certain era. These are the relationships of petty commodity production. They are based on the independence of the labourer – since the petty commodity producer possesses complete external independence – and on the equivalence and reciprocity of labour activities – since individual labourers, in reality, work for others just as others work for them. And all commodity producers provide the same amount of their labour for the benefit of others as the others do for their benefit – as is expressed in exchange according to the value of labour. At the same time, these relationships, as is well known, entirely subordinate the fate of humankind to the spontaneously impersonal forces of 'people's economic being' – the forces of the market, the forces of the supply and demand of commodities.

But petty commodity production means, as economists have ascertained, a specific stage of technological development; it is precisely that level of technological specialisation in which the individual producer still creates an entire product. Here, therefore, is the starting point for the development of the principle of 'duty'. Investigation has brought us, through a whole series of immediate links, from this extremely abstract idea to the realm of technological life, to a particular form of specialisation. In stands to reason that the more such intermediary links there are, the more time is necessary for a given ideological 'superstructure' to develop on a given technological 'basis' and, in the event that this 'basis' changes, the more time that is necessary for the 'superstructure' to disappear, because before it disappears all the intermediary links between it and its 'basis' must disappear. In general, the entire adaptation, having become unnecessary, does not disappear immediately but dies out only gradually.[25]

XI

Thus, we consider it possible to connect all social forms in one unbroken chain of development in which technological adaptations represent the basic series, and above them, one series after another, rise ideological forms that are derivative but, at the same time, are of considerable organisational importance. Of course, all the links of this chain are interwoven in the tightest way, but the model that has been outlined permits us, when investigating individual cases, to gradually disentangle the thread of development to arrive at its starting point that is accessible to a sociologist's view.

However, we would only have the right to connect all these different forms in one really unbroken chain if we had previously acknowledged them to be homogenous to a certain degree *and not different in essence*. And can we suppose such homogeneity when the matter has to do with technological adaptations, on the one hand, and ideological adaptations, on the other? Are not these two types so different that a strict continuity in the transition from one to another is impossible? This brings us to the question of the content and structure of individual social forms.

First of all, let us recall that any social adaptation is a psychical adaptation. Only the psychical activity of a person can have a social character, only by means of consciousness does a person become an element of the social whole. Forms of ideology and forms of technology both have an identically psychical nature. Let us examine what kind of psychical elements they are composed of.

Let us begin with technological forms. Their content boils down to the immediate struggle of humanity with nature, and at all stages of development it represents identical combinations of psychical phenomena. Pre-civilised people see fruit and pluck it. First there is *perception*, then an act of will that

---

25   We remind the reader that our example is intended only as an illustration and elucidation of our understanding of the historical interconnectedness of development. It was therefore possible to be limited to a concise, schematic indication, whereas the question that is touched on in this example is extremely important in itself and deserves a separate investigation.

is expressed in *external action*. Workers on machines observe the movement of the machine and act on it as necessary with their own movements; a series of *perceptions* are combined with a series of sequential *actions*. This is true of any technological process; its psychical elements are the immediate perception of phenomena of the external environment and immediate action upon them.

The social instinct is a universal organising adaptation that permeates people's entire social life; it is inseparably connected with both technological and ideological forms, endowing them with the character of social adaptations. What are the psychical elements of this instinct? In its basic form it boils down to the desire to act together with other people, and it is clear that this already presupposes the presence of a mental image of these other people. Here, consequently, we have the combination of a certain *mental image* (of other people) and a certain *desire* (to act together with them). Keeping the higher, transformed forms of social instinct in mind, we find that they can be broken down in the same way into elements of mental image and desire, only with a somewhat different content. It might appear that what we see here are elements other than those in technological adaptations, but in reality this is not so.

Psychology teaches that a mental image originates in a perception and is its 'psychical residue', the incomplete reproduction of it in the psyche. Thus, a mental image is the same sort of thing as a perception – this is why it is possible to point out all the transitional forms between them.[26] Analogously, a desire is – according to contemporary views – the psychical residue of an action. It is the uncompleted, weak reproduction of that action in the psyche; it is an incomplete act of will. This is why a desire, as it intensifies, turns into action.[27] Consequently, desire is the same sort of thing as action.

Thus, as far as their psychical composition and structure are concerned, the phenomena of the social instinct are essentially the same sort of thing as the phenomena of the technological process. It then follows from this that, to the

---

26   There are weak and pale mental images, there are sharper and more vivid mental images, and there are mental images so bright that they are easily confused with perceptions and even transform into them (as happens in dreams or hallucinations). Certain previous mental images participate in any perception, forming one indivisible whole for consciousness. Those previous mental images usually correspond closely to the perceived subject and provide specificity and fullness to the perception; but sometimes they far from coincide with what is perceived and then an illusion results – the person perceives something that does not exist or takes one object to be another.

27   Observations have revealed that when a person wants to do something, the very same muscles contract (although weakly and insignificantly) that participate in carrying out that action. This means that the neural current goes from neural centres to muscles as it does with real action only it is too weak and cannot cause sufficient muscle contraction.

extent that the social instinct permeates all ideological adaptations, these ideo-logical adaptations also turn out to be the same sort of thing as technological adaptations. But, could it be that there are still some elements in ideological forms that materially distinguish them from technological forms? It is easy to be see that, in reality, this is not so.

The psychical content of forms of speech or body language is quite uncom-plicated. A specific perception or conception is combined with a specific word or gesture. But what is a word or gesture? It is a specific combination of muscle movements. A word is pronounced by means of the habitual contraction of the muscles of the chest and throat and the cavities of the pharynx and mouth; a gesture is carried out by means of the habitual contraction of the muscles of arms, neck, torso, etc. The matter thus boils down to a perception (or concep-tion), on the one hand, and muscle action, on the other hand – elements that are essentially the same sort of thing as elements of technological adaptations.

Of course, the particular regions of the neural centres and the particular groups of muscles used in speech (and, in part, in body language) are not the ones that participate in technological activity. Indeed, in technological activity different elements of the neural-muscular system become specialised for dif-ferent processes of labour, but this still does not create an *essential* difference between technological forms.

Things are a little more complicated when it comes to forms of cognition. These forms consist of *concepts*, and a concept, itself, is far from a simple technological formation. Take, for example, 'person'. This concept combines in the psyche a whole long series – a vast 'association' – of concepts about one, two, three, etc. people – about every person that a given individual encoun-ters in their perceptions (or in their derivatives – forms of imagination). The word 'person' incorporates this entire association. A word, of course, is not always pronounced and is often only 'thought' – i.e. the conception of the word appears and is inseparably connected with the desire (sometimes very weak) to reproduce it. But there is nothing in all this that would *in essence* distinguish forms of knowledge from technological forms. The conceptions that constitute the basic material of a concept have the same origin as perceptions, and, as we have seen, a word does not contain anything materially different from what technological forms contain. In a word, the elements here are all the same.[28]

---

28   The psychological picture of a concept must be supplemented by one more trait: in all the particular conceptions that are incorporated in a given concept – let us say the concept of a 'person' – consciousness strives to sort out *common* elements and connect precisely them in the given word – 'person' – whereas elements of *difference* that express what is discordant in individual people who are perceived are obliterated and disappear from

Normative adaptations – custom, law, morality – remain. But their structure, even though it is even more complex, nevertheless does not add anything substantially new. They are formed from a *concept* that expresses one or another norm of human relationships and from the *desire* to oppose anything that contradicts it. This is only a new combination of elements that we have already examined.

Thus, all social adaptations – primary technological adaptations, the universal organising adaptation of social instinct, and secondary organising and ideological adaptations – are made up of essentially the same sort of elements and belong to one continuous vital series.

XII

We take the technological process to be the primary realm of social development; it is precisely in it, as we have tried to show, that any progressive change of social forms has its start. If this is so, then the question arises of what role the ideological process plays in social development.

To acknowledge that ideological forms are of secondary derivation and, in the final analysis, are determined by technological forms, still does not require the assumption that ideology has no significance for social development. On the contrary, the significance of ideology is huge – only it is *of a different nature* from the significance of technology.

Any new step in the development of a vital form depends on all its previous development; any new adaptations of a vital form appear on the basis of all previous adaptations. This also applies to the development of society – to technological development just as much as ideological development. For example, a new technological form, being created and perfected, is constantly and vitally dependent not only on the technology that has formed before it but also on existing ideology. Let us examine this more concretely, with regard to a particular case.

In our day, a new technological adaptation appears most often in the form of an 'invention'. An invention is prompted by some kind of 'unadaptedness' in

consciousness. But this kind of process occurs with any common perception: some parts of the perceived image appear more sharply and 'attention turns' to them while others recede to the background, hardly noticed in consciousness. What is vitally most important occupies the most space in consciousness, and what is less important is hardly noticed. This occurs equally with ideological and technological processes, and it also occurs with conceptions that enter the system of 'concepts'.

the process of labour. It is realised *by means of the entire sum of technological and abstract knowledge at the disposal of the inventor*. Inventors conceive, ponder, calculate; in general, they apply cognitive material and cognitive methods to the matter. They frequently employ the most varied data of science in their reckoning, and that data influences the final form of their inventions. In the great majority of cases, an invention could not have appeared without all these 'ideological' prerequisites, and the degree of its perfection is determined by the quantity and quality of these prerequisites.

Such interconnectedness is completely understandable in itself; after all, cognition is the organised labour experience of society; it sums up and systematises adaptations that have been achieved by people's previous labour activity. It is natural that cognition provides the basic material for further adaptations and serves as a point of support for further movement. But does this not contradict the idea that technological development is primary, that technology is the basis of social life?

No, it does not contradict it and precisely because of the following. Forms of cognition – and all other ideological forms as well – serve as the *material* and the *conditions* of social development, but the *motive force* of this development does not lie in their sphere. The impetus toward the formation of new forms proceeds from the realm of technology, and it is there that all progress of social transformation *begins*. This is one important difference. Another difference proceeds from the very meaning of ideology in general. Ideology is an organising form and, in the final analysis, what it organises is the technological process. Thus, ideology is entirely limited to the bounds of the technological process, and the content of ideology is entirely determined by it. Therefore, after sufficient analysis one finds that the influence that ideology has on technological development has its basis in technological life. For example, a new invention immediately depends on the technological and natural sciences – but these very sciences draw their content from the realm of labour's immediate struggle with nature (the realm of technology), and this is their real basis.

We have said that ideology lies entirely within the bounds laid down by technology. Ideology cannot serve as the starting point for the change of social forms, and it cannot provide the motive force for their transformation. But is this always true? In our times, frequently some *scientific* discovery made by a specialist researcher immediately leads to the appearance of new technological forms. For example, a new chemical reaction or a new compound is discovered, and significant changes occur in the means of dying textiles, extracting metals, etc. Is not ideology primary here and technology a secondary adaptation? In order to answer this question, it is necessary to take a look at how scientific discoveries are made and upon what they are based.

In many cases a discovery is the result of new labour experience obtained in the sphere of technological life proper. In less cultured societies where there are no specialist researchers, discoveries are *always* accomplished in exactly this way. But in civilised societies this also happens frequently. For example, air pressure was discovered and measured because when it was necessary to lift water during construction, suction pumps could not raise it higher than 34 feet. These purely technological facts served as the basis for a scientific theory that, in its turn, significantly influenced the development of certain realms of technology.

More often, however, the interrelationship of facts is not as direct and obvious as in the example just given. A new discovery appears on the basis of an endless series of small, repeated experiments in the technological process, and, in its final form, the discovery is not directly connected with them even in the psyche of the discoverer. Thus, the law of the conservation of energy was undoubtedly prepared by machine production, on the one hand, and by the lack of success in the technological realisation of a perpetual motion machine, on the other hand. Working with machines, people continually ran into a definite limit to their working capacity. And the results of attempts to construct a motor that would run continuously forever by itself led to a definite understanding of these boundaries – to the idea that a machine does not create work but only transforms and transmits it. But it took so much time and labour to elaborate that idea that its scientific creators had already lost sight of the 'technological basis' that planted the germ of the idea in their psyche, and they connected it pre-eminently with certain experiments of a 'purely scientific' character (which was easy, since the idea appeared all the clearer in such experiments).

But in contemporary societies scientific research has become a particular speciality, and often a scientist, striving toward purely cognitive goals, attains results that have important, direct significance for the progress of technology (recent discoveries can serve as examples – Roentgen's x-rays, radium, etc.). How can these cases be understood?

Scientific research that leads to technologically important conclusions is not a process that is only ideological; it based on *technological* labour. It begins with immediate experience and immediate observation – the same immediate relationship toward external nature as in any other technological process. Here the activity of people is made up of the same elements: direct perception and direct action. Here, also, various means of production are applied: instruments and machines that are often even more complex than with usual technological processes – microscopes, telescopes, recording equipment, etc. Is there any essential difference between the chemical laboratory of a scientific researcher and the chemical laboratory of a factory technician? The immediate content of the activities of both people is completely the same, and the social results of their activities also have the same kind of social utility. Their goals are different, but in manufacturing in a society with many members, there can be an altogether endless variety of goals, and those goals often do not correspond in the least to the objective historical results of their activities.[29] From an objective point of view, the technological labour of research plays the same kind of role in a system with the social division of labour as the role played by the technological process in any other struggle with external nature.

We note that in social development the labour of research, as far as it is possible to judge, is acquiring ever greater significance compared with other forms of technological labour, and the time is probably not far away when research will play the leading role in conditioning and determining the course of the progress of social forms. In essence, this is what Engels had in mind when he said that in the society of the future the 'production of ideas' will acquire the same basic, determinative significance for social life as the 'production of things' has in the contemporary world. Except that Engels did not pay attention to the fact that right now the 'production of ideas' already plays such a role to a certain, limited extent. In addition, Engels also apparently overlooked the fact that the labour of scientific research, in its social and psychical content, *has the same basis as other psychical processes* and (to the extent that it includes elements of immediate experience and observation) must be considered as part of the technological series of social phenomena.

Thus, nothing really contradicts the proposition that the starting point of any social development is the technological process, i.e. the process of the immediate adaptation of people to the external environment. It is only in the technological process that society enters into direct contact with external nature. It is in the technological process that society acquires new forces. It is in the technological process that the vital renewal of society continually occurs that floods throughout its entire organism.

Our previous conclusions are thus confirmed. No matter how huge the vital significance of ideology, it does *not* play an *independent* role in social development. These 'organising' adaptations cannot in themselves be primary developments; all of their progressive changes have their staring points outside ideo-

---

29   For example, in our time, the personal goal of someone engaged in technological labour might not be to create one or another product for society at all but might be to acquire 'crystallised value' in the form of money – a goal that is, properly speaking, not technological in the least.

logy in the sphere of technological process and can be traced through a series –
sometimes long and sometimes short – of intermediary links.

But besides the positive significance that we have pointed out, ideology also
has another (and, to a significant degree, negative) significance for the process
of development. It sometimes turns out that, despite its usefulness, an emerging technological form is materially maladapted to the existing ideology of
society, does not find a place in the social system, and perishes without issue.
Thus, Catholicism destroyed many inventions along with their inventors, and
guild law and guild privileges held back the development of many technological adaptations. Machines were especially victimised.

Here we run into a very important phenomenon of social life – ideological
anachronisms. Well-established worldviews and well-established legal norms
are conservative; they fight for their lives against anything that threatens them
directly or indirectly, and hence they struggle against any new ideology and the
new technology that engenders it if they are incompatible with the old. Such a
struggle often holds back the progressive movement of society.

Old concepts formed on the basis of former labour experience can turn out
to be insufficient and even outright unsuitable from the point of view of new
labour experience. Thus, concepts that arise under conservative, stable technology – 'static' concepts that are thought of as thoroughly *immovable* and
unchanging – become unsuitable in an era of rapid technological progress
and rapid change in the forms of life. Old legal norms that fully correspond to
former labour relationships turn into vital contradictions for new labour relationships – for example, feudal law when an exchange economy and capitalism
appear. However, such obsolete forms do not immediately disappear and are
not immediately replaced by new ones. Forms of ideology are in general very
conservative; many of them display striking vitality even long after they have
lost their positive meaning in the life of society. They are therefore, of course,
not so much organising adaptations as disorganising influences on the social
process.

In a class society that is broken up into groups with different organisation and different tendencies of development, the question of ideological anachronisms becomes rather complex. Often when the content of life changes,
the ideological forms that were formerly useful adaptations for all society turn
into outright anachronisms for certain progressive groups of society, while they
continue to remain vitally expedient for other more conservative groups. For
example, feudal law was socially useful under the technology of the Middle
Ages when the feudal lord was the necessary organiser of the kinds of undertakings that separate peasant households could not arrange by their own efforts –
military defence, communication routes, coinage of money, community ovens,

etc. – and was the means by which such undertakings were organised. But with the passage of time, as a result of the development of the organising activity of other groups of society, the role of the feudal lord in social production was reduced to zero. At the same time, feudal laws, while remaining, of course, useful adaptations for the feudal lords, became not only useless for society, as a whole, but even a harmful remnant of the past. Naturally, the power of the feudal class aimed to defend the 'anachronisms' of feudal law, and the degree of the tenacity of these anachronisms depended on the extent of that power.

The negative significance of obsolete ideology sometimes reaches a level where ideology becomes the starting point of social regression and technological and all sorts of other kinds of degradation. The system of slavery of the ancient world created in the governing classes an ideology full of disdain for productive labour, and because of this there came a time when society lacked the strength for development. Its principal groups began to degenerate. One group – the slaves – degenerated due to excessive oppression, and the other group – the lords – degenerated due to parasitic living. The flourishing of the classical era was replaced by the barbarism of the middle ages. Feudal-Catholic ideology had the same significance for Spain in recent centuries; it was one of the immediate causes of the fall of the Spanish nation.

Facts like these do not contradict our basic point of view in the least. No matter what the kinds of social forms, they only survive if they turn out to be adapted to the social environment in which they arise. And ideology makes up a part – and a very important part – of this environment, so that a newly born social form can easily perish if it turns out to be contradicted by ideology.[30] When *all or a majority* of progressive forms are eliminated in this way, it is possible not only for stagnation but for regression to occur. This is because the continual expenditure of social forces as the result of the destruction of new useful adaptations must diminish the sum of life of society, the sum of its energy.

On the other hand, the ideology that holds back development or causes degradation itself took shape on the basis of a historically given technology. Consequently, the primary conditions that engender stagnation or regression lie in technology. Thus, the ideology of the ancient world, with its negative attitude toward productive labour, was itself the result of a specific technology – precisely the technology in which a human slave is used for production just

---

30   We consider it unnecessary to add that existing technology is a still more important part of the social environment and a still more influential factor of social selection, and it is even more certain that those emergent forms of life that are not adapted to technology will perish.

like a tool or domesticated animal. Consequently, stagnation or degradation of social life here, as in other cases of social development, has its starting point in the technological process and, in the final analysis, is determined by it.

XIII

In explaining the correlation and interconnection of ideology with other elements of social life, we have for the most part considered society as an indivisible, unified whole. Nevertheless, we have already found it necessary to note in passing that the unity of a society is not absolute and has limits. In investigating the question further, we must keep these limits in mind.

Only primordial clan groups possessed the kind of solid bond and internal cohesion that allows us to consider them to be almost perfectly integral societies. All cultured societies that we know of – and particularly the one in which we live – present an utterly different picture. They are broken down, as we know, into various classes and social groups that in some cases are united by the bond of collaboration and that in other cases are separated by an existential struggle. For example, in contemporary society, capitalists and farmers are connected collaboratively to the extent that they mutually deliver to each other the products of their enterprises by means of exchange and are thus useful and even necessary for one another. But they are enemies of one another to the extent that they divide the very same amount of surplus product between them in the form of profit and rent in such a way that an increase of the share of one class means a decrease of the share of the other. In the first case both classes appear as inseparably connected elements of a single society; in the second case they appear as two separate 'societies' standing against one another.

Thus, the concept of 'society' is relative and conditional. The life of social groups is not entirely embraced by social instinct and social collaboration; society also remains a site of hostility and vital contradictions. Depending on what aspect of the matter we turn our attention to, we will find either one social whole or a series of comparatively isolated social units. What causes this duality?

The starting point of the isolating out of social groups consists in the division of labour among them, differences in their productive activity. The content of technological life for one, another, or a third group is different, and the form of the ideology that organises this content naturally develops in different ways. The labour activities of peasants and artisans, for example, are extremely different both in material and in methods, and the ideologies of the two classes are no less different. This technological divergence is intensified even more by ideological divergence. Accordingly, the difference in vital aspirations grows to the point where it turns into a direct contradiction and leads to strife. Consequently, the system of social labour as a whole turns out to be unorganised, as is observed in all modern societies.[31] In the final analysis, the 'anarchy of production' – a term economists use to characterise the structure of contemporary society – is caused by the division of labour among groups, and the division of labour, in turn, causes struggle between the divided groups.

Under such conditions, the need for organising adaptations is particularly great, and it is because of this that the anarchical society of modern times creates a huge number of ideological forms that far surpasses anything that was created by the more integral and less atomised societies of earlier times. Science and philosophy develop that strive to harmoniously interconnect the infinite diversity of labour experience. A system of legal institutions develops that strives to provide coherent unity to the infinite diversity of labour relationships, etc. But the lack of organisation of social labour as a whole remains the predominant fact and limits the organising significance of ideological forms.

In this case it is easy to point out the direction of possible development. It must tend to organise the social whole in a way that eliminates vital contradictions among its parts. Differences of social groups must be submerged in the organised unity of society. This is not impossible. First, if the division of labour is on-going, the differences between its individual forms can be increasingly smoothed over if increasingly similar techniques take shape in the different realms of production, if *general methods* of acting upon nature appear. For example, in machine production – especially in the case of automatic mechanisms – the labour of workers on the most varied machines and the most varied materials turns out to be extremely similar in its psychical content, which boils down predominantly to oversight of the machine, to supervision of its operations. Second, even quite significant differences in the elements of the whole still do not at all mean that contradictions are inevitable. Generally speak-

---

31   In exchange society, each separate business of a small or a major producer can be considered, to a significant degree, as a particular social group. Each is separated from other such groups technologically (by their independence from the others in the conduct of production) and also ideologically (by a specific understanding of the benefit and interests of that group as being contradictory to the interests of all others that buy from it, that sell to it, or that compete with it). Broader groups are formed from such minor groups or from their elements (if these groups disintegrate internally into different elements – entrepreneurs and workers, for example) that are, for all that, still connected by the commonality of their technological role and the commonality of their ideology. And even broader groups form from them, right up to such groups as the great social classes of our times or the estates of the Middle Ages.

ing, contradictions result only when these elements, besides being different, *develop in different directions*. However, even in this case the possibility does not completely disappear that contradictions could be eliminated by organising adaptations. After all, tissues in a complex organism develop in different directions, but their vital activity is still brought to the greatest unity by the organising activity of neural-psychical tissue.

There is only one case in which differences of elements of the social whole must transform into a hopeless contradiction. This is when social groups develop in *contradictory directions* – one in a progressive direction toward a broadening of the struggle with external nature and the enhancement of the methods of productive labour and the other in a regressive direction toward parasitism and the consumption of the products of the labour of others. In this case it is biologically inconceivable that any organising adaptations could harmoniously tie together the life of the two groups. In this case the vital contradiction must continually grow, and the idea of 'blunting the contradictions' is utopian. As one part of society concentrates in itself the whole sum of socially necessary adaptations, the other loses its function and turns into a useless organ.[32] What happens in this case?

History shows that such cases have their own particular type of adaptation. For example, when the feudal estate in France gradually lost its significance for social labour and was ultimately transformed into a parasitic group, the productive classes eliminated it from the social organism like a foreign body. It is true that it was still possible for individual members of that estate, having lost their former place in social life, to adapt to the new relationships and take on new roles – as bourgeois entrepreneurs, for example – but feudal lords ceased to exist as feudal lords. This was simultaneously the *'Zusammenbruch'* (collapse) of feudally organised society and the liberation of bourgeois society.

But such an outcome is possible only if the productive classes have developed progressively and have actually succeeded in becoming proficient in all the useful functions of the parasitic class, as in the example we just provided. Things turned out differently in the ancient world. The parasitic development

---

32   But could not the parasitic development of an obsolete group once again be replaced by productive development, whereby the vital contradiction between it and other groups loses its sharp and hopeless nature and be 'blunted'? This, of course, is conceivable, but only in exceptional cases and rather for separate individuals than for broad groups. New adaptations spring up from specific material – from previous adaptations that are similar to the new ones – and in the case of parasitic, regressive development the former useful adaptations continue to be lost. Consequently, material for progressive, productive development disappears, and the further this goes, the less possible progressive development becomes.

of the class of slave-owners was not accompanied by sufficient productive development of other classes. The burden of directing the vast system of production fell from the weak hands of the degenerating group, but there was no class that was able to take that task upon itself. As a result, there was a *Zusammenbruch* of a completely particular kind – the collapse of a higher culture and the transition to a lower one.

All this results in a specific point of view regarding any *Zusammenbruch* in social life. In no case can such a collapse be a moment of direct creation of new technology and a new ideology; both must be ready-made in the productively developed class. At the moment of the French *Zusammenbruch*, at the end of the last era, the bourgeois worldview – new bourgeois legal and moral norms – already existed in various strata of the bourgeoisie and the classes associated with it, except that the whole ideology was *prevented from being manifested* by the ideology of the ruling, feudal estate. All adaptations of the new society were already prepared within the confines of the old; it was only that the vital activity of the new forms was fettered by the domination of the old and they were not able to freely unfold in life as long as that domination was not eliminated.[33] Before birth, a baby does not breathe or cry but possesses all that is necessary for these adaptations; the act of birth does not create them but only liberates them. This comparison is not completely apposite, however, since there is no reason to think that a baby wants to breathe and cry before birth and that it actively strives to do so. The birth of a new society is more reminiscent of a case of paedogenesis – reproduction in which the larval child having formed inside the larval mother bursts through its mother's shell and crawls out (as with the insects *Cecidomyiae*).

The idea that new social forms are created in the moment of crisis – the collapse of the old forms – harshly contradicts the evolutionary worldview.[34] In essence, this contradiction is not at all that new forms must develop 'gradually'. Evolutionism is not a matter of 'gradualness', since that is not altogether a scientific concept. 'Gradually' means not very quickly, and what one calls 'very quickly' depends on one's frame of mind. Evolutionism knows only the idea of *continuity* in which any kind of speed – from the smallest to the greatest – is

---

33 Thus, for example, a certain legal norm prevailed in the psyche of the lower classes, but it was not manifested externally in life. It was not expressed in social-legal actions but remained at the stage of social-legal desire because maximum social force fiercely suppressed it and prevented it from being applied.

34 The reader should recall that Bogdanov had replaced the idea of dialectical change (abrupt, qualitative change through contradiction) with the idea of dynamic equilibrium of forces [trans.].

logically possible. If the solar system was formed in one second, this would still not contradict the idea of evolution. No, the essence of the matter in the case we are talking about is completely different. The concepts of 'crisis' and 'Zusammenbruch' are applied where the speed of the processes that occur is so great that the usual measure applied by people – that measure being the normal flow of psychical processes in people themselves – is not appropriate. But since new forms of ideology and technology are formed precisely in people's psyches and the creation of them is a psychical process, then the speed of this creation can in no way surpass the constant measure of speed of psychical life, and it therefore cannot be perceived in the form of a 'crisis' or 'Zusammenbruch'. Only the removal, the destruction, of obsolete forms can have the appearance of a crisis, just as the death of an organism is usually seen in the form of a crisis.

We see that even in such complex and difficult questions as the question of the development and transformation of societies, the idea of adaptation can serve as a reliable guiding thread for investigation and can provide a general point of view that has no internal contradictions and is consistent with external reality. The idea of adaptation cannot, of course, provide more, precisely because of its breadth, generality, and abstractness. Everything else is a matter of concrete investigation.

∵

Starting from the idea of the essential unity of life in nature and in society, we attempted to explain in general traits the laws of social development. In so doing, it was necessary to depict the basic types of social forms in their vital correlations, explaining them from the perspective of the basic evolutionary idea – the idea of adaptation.[35] A series of conclusions were derived that coincides in essential traits with the usual theory of historical monism but that is dis-

---

35   In studying the question of the laws of social development, we consciously removed from analysis those psychical adaptations that have no inherent social labour nature, such as, for example, the sexual instinct. Manifestations of the sexual instinct relate solely to species and not to social life, and, therefore, they do not appear as an independent factor in social development but as passive material. Such manifestations change under the influence of changing labour relationships but themselves serve neither as a starting point for the change of social forms nor as the defining moment of that change. Social development transforms the whole psychical organism of a person, it embraces and subordinates its non-social and pre-social adaptations, but in so doing the progress of those adaptations turns out to be not of a primary but of a secondary character. The progress of non-social and pre-social adaptations is determined and conditioned by technological and ideological progress.

tinguished from it, as we suggested, by greater specificity and greater monism in its understanding of the social process. We attempted to sharply differentiate among the various categories of social phenomena according to their real vital meaning, and we found it especially important to establish the huge social role of ideology as a system of organising adaptations of the social process. Going further, we attempted to show that all social forms are fundamentally homogenous in regard both to their origin and their content; they are made of similar psychical elements. In this way, we established the continuity of the whole endless series of social phenomena. We considered social life as a whole as a process of adaptation, and this allowed us to conceive of social life as an individual link in the unbroken chain of biological development.

We believe that it is in precisely such a form that the theory of historical monism must become an inseparable part of a clear and coherent, harmoniously whole worldview that is capable of providing the greatest sum of truth to people of our times.

CHAPTER 4

Authoritarian Thinking

The social life of human beings is the most complex phenomenon that cognition has to deal with. Understanding social life is the most difficult task that science takes on, but it is also the most important. To understand means to master, and accurate knowledge of phenomena is the necessary basis for real dominion over them. Primeval society did not possess precise knowledge of external nature. It understood nature fetishistically, and this meant that primeval society did not rule over nature, but nature ruled over it. Exchange society does not understand nature properly. It knows its own internal relationships fetishistically, and as long as this is so, it cannot break free from their iron rule. The spontaneous, blind power of these relationships causes a great deal of senseless, hopeless suffering. 'Know yourself' is a demand that history places on contemporary society with ever greater insistence.

Society is gradually beginning to know itself. In its most vital elements, it is gradually arriving at an understanding of its own nature and is becoming victorious over it. So far these have been small victories, but they are clearing the way for further, more significant ones. The growing self-knowledge by the most progressive and most productive elements of society signifies their growing influence on the course of social life, and this influence is such that the social process is becoming increasingly expedient, increasingly 'rational'. Although basic contradictions still remain in social life, their destructive influence on the forces of social development are becoming ever weaker. The acquisitions of progress are becoming more reliable; the speed of progress is growing.

This progress is *active*: it springs up from *people's labour activity* and represents the historical outcome of millions of human *actions* consciously or unconsciously directed toward development. But human activity is far from always progressive. In a great many cases, its direction is neutral regarding the tendency to progress, and in a great many cases it stands in the way of progress. The basic task for knowledge of social nature consists precisely in clearly distinguishing phenomena of progressive activity from phenomena of neutral or regressive activity. Such a distinction creates a point of support for progress that is not only 'active' but is simultaneously more *conscious*.

This task must be resolved for every era individually. What is progressive for some historical conditions becomes neutral under others and reactionary under a third set of conditions. Thus, the task turns out to be very complex. It is necessary to simplify it enough so that it can be resolved, and the sole reliable means of doing so consists in placing it not in relation to individual facts but in relation to a great many similar facts, in relation to whole *types* of social phenomena. As is now clear, the question of types of social phenomena turns out to be of very great practical importance. Social phenomena must be correctly grouped in series that have the same vital significance; we will then be able to know them sufficiently in order to properly deal with them in life itself.

It is precisely from this point of view that we will now examine one extremely broad series of socio-psychological facts – the elements of *authority* in social thinking, to be precise. The elucidation of this question requires us to begin, of course, with the origin and development of these elements, because it is only in this way that we can establish their real vital significance.

The facts of authoritarian thinking lie in the sphere of ideology, in the realm of the understanding and evaluation of phenomena. These facts are characterised by the idea that certain elements of life are essentially inferior and are subordinated to others that are essentially superior. Authoritarian thinking appears in an understanding of social nature in which some people are considered to have been specially created for dominion and freedom and others have been created for subordination and slavery. Authoritarian thinking appears in conceptions of human individuality in which the individual is seen as the combination of an active, creative, higher principle – spirit – with a passive, inert, lower principle – matter. Authoritarian thinking appears in explanations of nature in general that divide the world into secret, superior forces, which act independently and freely, and ordinary, inferior objects, which move and change only under the influence of these forces and which are entirely determined from the outside. In practice, authoritarian thinking is expressed in people's absolute subordination to and worship of other people or some elements of nature – of both social nature and external nature.

Having established the concept of authoritarian thinking – the reader will see that we take it in the broadest scope and meaning – we now move on to an investigation of the genesis of authoritarian psychology. The idea of historical monism will serve as our guiding thread in this investigation. Taking the perspective of historical monism, we must first of all explain the objective labour relationships on the basis of which the authoritarian type of thinking arises and to which it is adapted.

I

The labour relationships in primeval clan groups were far simpler than those of contemporary society. Social life was still almost undifferentiated in them; people's labour activities were identical to a high degree. Almost every member of the primeval group possessed all of the group's technology and was able to carry out all the work that was necessary for the life of the group. Primeval tools – stones, sticks and their immediate derivatives such as axes, spears, etc. – were attainable by all members of the group, and it did not take them very long to learn how to use these tools. In addition, the paltry practical knowledge that had been acquired by people at this stage was also stored without much effort in every primeval brain. Any member of the group could hardly be distinguished from any other in regard to the content of psychical life.

At this stage of development there existed only trifling seeds of the division of labour, seeds that had their basis in purely physiological differences between individuals. Children cannot accomplish the kinds of labour processes that require the power of adults, women cannot always exert great physical effort, and it makes sense that both women and children specialise to a certain degree in forms of labour that they are most capable of carrying out. Dragging heavy loads, difficult construction work, and serious hunting fell mainly to the lot of men. Women and children predominantly hunted for small animals, gathered fruit and roots, sewed clothing, etc. But this minor specialisation was only temporarily significant in the life of the individual. Children grew into adults who were capable of any work; women, except at times of pregnancy, nursing, and menstruation, could also do almost everything that a man could. People's labour psychology was therefore almost entirely uniform.

Under such conditions, the labour activities of individual people were comparatively independent. Whether making an axe from a sharp stone or a spear from a pointed stick, obtaining food in the form of fruit, roots, grain, and small animals, or making clothing from leaves, each person managed without the help of other people in the majority of cases. Only rarely did the necessity of the direct collective combining of labour activities arise, and this was precisely in those cases when it was necessary to undertake work that exceeded the power of an individual person – defence from a powerful enemy, construction of dwellings, etc. Thus, generally speaking, labour in primeval clan groups was *not organised*. Socially organised actions were virtually non-existent.

Sociologists and psychologists established long ago that the division of labour is at the same time the disintegration of human individuality, that specialisation means one-sidedness and an incomplete life for individuals. If this is so, then primeval people, who were virtually unaffected by the division of labour, had one undoubted advantage over people of a more advanced culture, and that was a great wholeness of life. To be precise, the fullness of existence that their group possessed was reflected in the psyche of each member. But this wholeness came with a certain cost; the sum of conscious life for them was in general so insignificant that it was immeasurably small in comparison with contemporary life (despite how one-sided and disharmonious the manifestations of contemporary life are). It was the wholeness of an undifferentiated embryo of a lower organism. It was only simplicity and not harmony; it was the result of weakness and not of power.

The progress of primeval life was accomplished through the loss of its simplicity. Development engendered specialisation. The wider that the labour activity of the group unfolded and the more varied its manifestations became, the less it was possible for each human individual to carry out all aspects of labour activities that were present in the group's production. Embryonic forms of the division of labour developed further and became more permanent. Individual members of the group gradually concentrated their activity on certain specific aspects of socially necessary labour and left the remainder of the work to other members. Thus, the primeval wholeness of the psyche was destroyed; the individual ceased to be a universal being. As life broadened, individuals lost their former many-sidedness, and, losing their completeness, they reflected the growing diversity of the process of social labour in their psyches.

But along with specialisation there developed the need for greater organisation of labour. The more varied the activities of different people, the more necessary it was for them to adapt to one another and also the more difficult it was to do so. It was necessary to spend precisely the quantity of human power on each separate aspect of social labour that corresponded to the needs of society. If all members of the group independently chose their own occupation, then a great deal of unnecessary labour power might be wasted in one sphere of production, while in another sphere considerably less might be utilised than was appropriate. For example, the group might produce more clothing than necessary but not enough food to feed itself. A deliberately rationalised distribution of workers' forces in production was necessary. Labour had to become *organised.*

As long as a group was still small and the work of organising labour was not very complex, organising activity could be carried out by all members of the group jointly. They could discuss together and resolve the question of how to distribute the available forces of the group and the available products of its labour. But, as production became broader and more complex, this became less and less possible. For average members of the group who were not distinguished by great experience or particular talents questions of the division of labour and produce were too complex; they were unable to provide anything of use to the discussion and resolution of them. In these cases, their voices were usually useless and often even directly harmful, since they could tip the scales in favour of an unfortunate outcome. Organisational activity was gradually isolated out and became the specialty of one member of the group – if not the most capable then the most experienced and oldest in the clan. Patriarchal clan organisation was the result.[1]

The head of the patriarchal group was the overall organiser of production and distribution, and the other members of the group were implementers of the head's will. In accordance with the existent sum of labour forces and the existent dimensions of the needs of the group, the head told each of the members what work they must undertake and what share of the common product they could take for their personal consumption, and everyone carried out these directions. This is the *authoritarian* type of labour organisation that apparently governed all peoples at a certain stage of their development, and, at the present time, it also predominates among the majority of savage and barbarous tribes.

Leadership by a patriarch is only the primary and simplest form of authoritarian relationships. Considerably more complex forms and considerably broader organisations developed from this. Within the patriarchal group, as it grew, a partial division of organisational labour occurred. To a certain extent family groups were isolated out in which the elder member was a special, particular organiser, even though he was subordinate to the overall organiser, the patriarch. As time went on, the family increasingly began to live an autonomous life within the confines of the clan, but this occurred, of course, only in the fields of labour in which a family could carry out its productive activity without the help of other families of the clan. What resulted was a system of relationships in which the highest organiser had a few implementers who, in their turn, were organisers for the rest of the members of the clan.

Later on, through the further isolating out of small groups in the old clan organisation, the monogamous family was decisively separated out, and in contemporary society it stands out as a direct remainder of patriarchal relationships. The father plays the same authoritarian role in the family as the patriarch did in an old clan group. The father is the same omnicompetent organiser of his small enterprise and, free from external supervision, he directs the application of the labour forces of his wife and children and the distribution of the objects

---

1 Matriarchal organisations, with the oldest women at the head, might have arisen in a similar way, but very little that is reliable is known about them.

of consumption. This is a patriarchal group of a diminished size and weakened by the disintegrating force of new relationships.

From another perspective, a patriarchal group serves as the starting point for the development of widely ramified feudal organisations. Here the chain of organisers, each standing above another, lengthens still more – especially if one keeps in mind the lord-vassal relationships between lesser and greater feudal lords. At the same time, the higher the organiser stands in the chain of these relationships, the broader the circles of their subordinates, but, at the same time, the narrower the sphere of the labour activities that the organiser in fact organises. In a peasant economy, all productive activity is accomplished under the direct oversight and supervision of the head of the family. The stewards of the feudal lord only deal with the part of peasant labour that is immediately connected with the enterprise of the feudal lord himself, and it is mainly in the form of corvée and quitrent. Feudal lords themselves, besides supervising their stewards, are predominantly occupied with organising military defence and also such broad enterprises as the construction of roads, bridges, etc. and adjudication and punishment – i.e. the organisation of the juridical relationships of their subjects. As far as they are concerned, their suzerains are almost exclusively military organisers (commanders in campaigns and battles), and organisers in the sphere of law (a higher judiciary when he has conflicts with other of their vassals). In this unwinding chain, human individuals who stand at the very bottom and play absolutely implementational roles are utterly crushed under the mass of authorities who weigh upon them.

Despotic monarchies of the Eastern type are a considerably more perfected form of authoritarian organisation. The same chain of rulers and ruled runs through them, but the connection between the links of the chain are tighter, the supervision of higher links over lower links runs deeper, and people's lives are more completely embraced by power and subordination. Here the ruler is everything and his subordinates are nothing. And if any of the ruler's subordinates have subordinates of their own, they are the same kind of absolute lord toward their subordinates. In such despotic monarchies, all life is completely in the thrall of authoritarian relationships, and human individuality is utterly insignificant in the face of them.

Significant but greatly modified remnants of complex authoritarian forms still survive in contemporary society. Hierarchies of priests developed from ramified patriarchal relationships and military organisation and bureaucracy developed from feudal and Eastern autocratic relationships. What we see in these cases is precisely an unwinding chain of organisers and implementers. Authority and subordination are expressed very powerfully, except that the sphere of these relationships is comparatively limited and completely defined:

command and submission occur only within the confines of 'service'. Nevertheless, the sphere of authority and subordination remains in these old authoritarian forms and, though comparatively indefinite, can always come to light in any area. For example, although feudal lords usually did not in fact interfere in the family affairs of their subordinates, they nevertheless always could interfere and considered it their right to do so. This sort of distinction, by the way, does not completely disappear even in the most recent authoritarian relationships. The limited potentates of the bureaucratic, hierarchical, or military type very often display the tendency of so-called 'exceeding their authority' – interfering in the private affairs of their subordinates, etc.

Slave economies and serfdom must also be considered to be modified authoritarian forms. Both forms arise from patriarchal clan or, more frequently, feudal relationships that are under the influence of monetary exchange, and they are distinguished from these latter because of the extreme development of domination and subordination. It is well known that monetary exchange engenders an unlimited desire for acquisition, and, as a result of this, the organiser begins to use the implementers exclusively as tools for acquiring money, as means for obtaining profit. Organisers then become not so much the organisers of group production as organisers of exploitation, and their actions consequently do not predominantly guide the interests of group production but the interests of exploitation. Naturally, the phenomena of domination and subordination stand out here in particularly sharp, crude, severe, and oppressive forms. The connection between master and slave, lord and serf almost loses its *social* character (that is, *collaboration* among people) and acquires the character of the relationship between a person and a tool of production (for example, livestock). This is actually not the development but the degradation of authoritarian collaboration; it is not without reason that the prolonged survival of such forms leads to full or partial social degradation, to the degeneration of both classes – masters and slaves.

Conversely, the *conditional subordination* that prevails in contemporary capitalist society represents a comparatively highly developed and progressive form of authoritarian relationship. In hiring workers, an entrepreneur acquires authority over their labour power. The worker is subject to the orders of the entrepreneur, but both the authority of the entrepreneur and the obedience of the worker are limited by the conditions of the agreement. The worker fulfils the organisational directives of the capitalist, but only within the confines of a previous agreement regarding the working day, the work, and the conditions of labour. Outside these conditions, the authority and the obedience come to an end; the entrepreneur ceases to be an organiser and the worker ceases to be an implementer. This, properly speaking, is not a purely authoritarian type of collaboration but is mixed with another type – what type exactly we will explain later.

We find an even more divergent form of authoritarian collaboration in relationships between 'ideologists' and the 'masses' – between 'heroes' and 'the crowd', in general. Just as in the previous examples, there is organisational behaviour on the one hand and implementational behaviour on the other. The ideologist tells the masses where to go and what to do and the masses go and do it. But obedience in this case is both limited to a specific, narrow sphere and is also 'voluntary'. In other authoritarian organisations, authority has coercive social powers at its disposal, and they are powers that are usually so significant that for a human individual they are simply overwhelming. The member of a clan group cannot but obey a feudal lord because lords are supported by both custom and the material power of armed force. Workers cannot but obey entrepreneurs because entrepreneurs have custom, law, the material power of the state, and the no less material power of hunger on their side. But in regard to the behaviour of the masses, individual people can follow the orders of the ideologist or not follow them, and, generally speaking, can follow them only to the extent that they wish. Ideologists have no socially compulsory power behind their organisational directives; they persuade and do not coerce. And the followers of ideologists can, in turn, persuade those ideologists to act in a certain way, can give them orders and make demands on them in regard to their ideological work but still without any external compulsion. Thus, readers who learn from writers – i.e. who submit to them in certain realms of thought and practice – often 'teach' writers, in their turn. They explain to writers exactly what the readers demand of them and how the writers should change their behaviour. In a word, such readers in their turn behave as organisers in regard to the work of their ideologists.

Here also the authoritarian type of relationship is mixed with another higher type that we still have to speak about.

We have, of course, far from exhausted all the forms of authoritarian collaboration that are encountered in reality, but in our view their essence is sufficiently elucidated even in the cursory, schematic, and incomplete description that we have provided. Concisely put, authoritarian collaboration is the kind of labour relationship in which organisational behaviour is distinguished from implementational behaviour in such a way that the one and the other are embodied in different individuals.

The basic vital characteristic of authoritarian relationships is their profound conservatism. Authoritarian forms are rarely reconciled with any changes in the course of social life, and this is easily explained, provided one keeps in mind a distinctive feature of the social role of the organiser.

Under all conditions, organisational work is, in general, extremely difficult and complex compared with implementational work. Even in normal times it demands that the organisers apply their powers to their fullest extent. It presupposes a great number of psychical adaptations that embrace the whole system of the group's labour relationships and that constantly operate in close interconnection and harmony. It is understandable that for the elaboration – and even the simple maintenance – of so many adaptations a very great and moreover unremitting expenditure of psychical energy is necessary. But with almost any change in the means of production, this system must undergo certain transformations in many, if not all, of its parts. A new technique of production usually means the elevation of productive labour, and, in so doing, a certain part of the energy of social labour is freed up, and labour forces must be redistributed. This occurs especially in the case when a new technological technique requires that new tools and new materials must be produced specifically for this goal. It is necessary to adapt all the 'economics' of the group – all the existent relations of production and distribution – to that technological change, and this means a huge amount of work for the psyche of the organiser. Many of the existing adaptations of their psyche are immediately made inadequate, and some of them turn out even to be directly harmful. Naturally, there must be some extraordinary causes for the organiser to decide to subject their psyche to such a wrenching change, and they are inclined to be averse to all 'novelties' that make the execution of their vital task so much more difficult and more complex.

We thus see that the conservative attitude is unavoidable for an organiser, at least in regard to the sphere of production. And if this is so then it is also unavoidable in the sphere of ideology. After all, the realm of ideological life is derivative from people's social being. It is an organising phase of productive life, so it is entirely defined by productive life. And, in general, ideological life is characterised by considerably greater conservatism than technological life, since all changes in ideological life originate in technological life. Technological conservatism is incompatible with ideological progressiveness, and it is more likely for it to be the other way around.

It goes without saying that due to the conservative attitude of organisers, society as a whole must turn out to be a very conservative system. Because the psychology of implementers is limited and automatic, it cannot, of course, serve as the basis for progressive social changes.

In reality, the conservatism of authoritarian relationships is very obvious and clear. This trait is powerfully revealed in the life of patriarchal and feudal governments (to say nothing of despotic governments), as history quite clearly shows. But, in addition to this, history also reveals the extent to which elements of higher authoritarian organisations – priestly, bureaucratic, military – become a conservative force as soon as these organisations take shape and become firmly established. They often turn out to be extremely powerful restraints on progress, and they have often come down with the greatest destructiveness on any germs of new life in society.

It is an indisputable and highly significant fact that progressive changes are frequently directed against the material rule of old authorities-organisers causing them to become conservative and reactionary by virtue of blatantly material interests. But their conservatism cannot be entirely reduced to this one cause, since the hostile relationship of authorities toward innovation is also observed when innovation does not directly affect the vital bases of the rule of those authorities. It is obvious that there is a general conservative attitude that takes shape on the basis of authoritarian forms.

In modified, mixed authoritarian forms it appears that the case is somewhat different. It is well known that capitalism is distinguished by conditional subordination and a highly progressive tendency in all realms of life. At least, progressive tendencies decisively predominate over conservative tendencies. However, if one attentively examines the conditions under which this progressiveness is revealed to the greatest extent with those in which it is revealed to the least extent, then it becomes obvious that it is definitely not the authoritarian elements that are progressive in capitalism but completely different ones. The technological progressiveness of capital is caused – as all economists admit – precisely by *competition* and the desire for accumulation, i.e. by precisely those aspects of capitalistic life in which there is nothing authoritarian. On the contrary, when these aspects are minimally expressed, and authoritarian elements proper are in the forefront, then progressiveness is manifested considerably more weakly. At the early stages of capitalism, when competition among enterprises is insignificant, when the subordination of workers to the entrepreneur within enterprises is almost unconditional, and when the patriarchal tone predominates in capitalism, the technological progressiveness of capital turns out to be comparatively extremely low. Improvements are introduced slowly and reluctantly and only when they promise very large and immediate benefits. It is exactly the same way at rather higher levels of capitalism. If protectionist policies limit and weaken competition and if class struggle is poorly developed, then a comparatively great stagnation of technology results; capitalists do not bother themselves with any reforms but prefer to obtain a decent profit under the old means of production and not to pursue new methods, even if those methods present the prospect of even greater profit. If the progressive tendencies of capital still ultimately predominate, this occurs, obviously, not *due to* authoritarian elements of capitalism but only *despite* the presence of these elements.

In a similar manner, a profound conservative tendency is seen in the relationships between ideologists and masses precisely to the extent that purely authoritarian elements predominate and to the extent that people blindly obey their ideological leaders. This characteristic appears even more clearly in the history of religion. Religious leaders usually demand absolute ideological obedience from their followers, and those followers really do obey absolutely, since the authoritarian nature of the relationships approaches the highest possible degree, and a conservative tendency – the basic trait of religious thinking in general – is revealed to the same degree. In the world of scientific knowledge, it is just the opposite. The role of the authority is incomparably less important, and there is much less room for blind obedience. There is a much greater space for progressive tendencies, and development encounters many fewer obstacles.

The profound conservatism that is characteristic of the *psychology* of authoritarian relationships in no way precludes a progressive *social role* of these relationships under certain conditions. Sometimes new authoritarian forms appear on the scene of social life, and they carry on a struggle against old forms that are also of an authoritarian – or other, lower – type. It is self-evident that these new forms will turn out to be objectively progressive; they strive to change what exists in the direction of greater perfection. But in themselves and in relation to themselves they are then just as conservative. They strive to change what contradicts them, but they exert the greatest resistance to any germs of transformation within themselves. Where the patriarchate eliminated more primitive communistic forms, it was, of course, a progressive force, but its psychology was not any less conservative because of it. Religious reformers act progressively, carrying on a struggle against obsolete religions, but no sooner do new progressive tendencies appear among their followers than the reformers turn into inquisitors and begin to burn and drown such people no less than their predecessors. This is just how Luther and Calvin, for example, related to religious currents that were more radical than their own. Even here, authority here remained authority.

III

The conservatism that is characteristic of authoritarian relationships, as has been shown, is weakened and retreats where these relationships are combined with elements of other forms of a higher type. What exactly are these other forms, and why are they capable of counteracting the conservative tendency of authoritarian relationships?

It is above all necessary to make special mention of anarchical labour relationships. These are the relationships that constitute the distinctive trait of any commodity society. Their essence consists in separate groups or even separate individuals carrying out their social labour functions on their own, independently of other people or groups. Without following the directive of any organiser, all commodity producers produce in their businesses the product they choose in the quantity and quality that they think is appropriate. Thus, the system of social labour as a whole turns out to be unorganised and anarchical. Distribution in this system is accomplished through exchange. That is, distribution also has an unorganised nature, and is even inevitably connected with struggle – struggle between buyer and seller, between competing buyers, or between competing sellers. Everywhere that anarchical labour relations exist, intra-social struggle also exists, primarily in the form of competition and subsequently in other forms.

Anarchical relations of labour appear where a system of social production becomes very large and expands to cover so huge an area that it is simply impossible for individual people to consolidate and organise it. Thus, the lack of organisation here is the result of the breadth of the social union, and struggle is caused by the development of collaboration.

This lack of organisation and this struggle represents not only the deficiency of anarchical collaboration in comparison with authoritarian collaboration but also its advantage. To be precise, it is lack of organisation and struggle that make anarchical relationships so very progressive; they engender chronic unadaptedness but also the constant striving to adapt. Competing producers constantly try to expand their production and improve their methods of production in order to sustain their struggle and defeat their rivals. Thus, competition leads to constant technological and economic progress, and this also means the need for ideological progress. The psychology of anarchical labour relationships cannot be conservative because immobility and stagnation in these relationships would mean inability to struggle and death.

The conditional subordination of the hired worker to the entrepreneur combines authoritarian and anarchical relationships. The limited nature of the power of the entrepreneur and the conditional character of the subordination

of the worker proceeds precisely from the circumstance that workers possess
the formal freedom of independent producers, and they sell their labour power
in the same market and in the same way that independent producers sell their
goods. In the sphere of their personal household, hired workers enjoy the same
independence as any other member of a mercantile society. They are different
from other members only because, due to the vagaries of fate, they have lost a
very important part of their household economy – the means of production,
to be precise. Peasants lost land and artisans lost tools, and, because of this,
they both became proletarians and were forced to work for wages. Formally,
however, they remain in the same relationships to other members of society as
previously – in relationships of anarchical collaboration. Under suitable conditions, proletarians can even become independent producers again; they need
only acquire the means of production (the objective, historical possibility of
such a thing is, by the way, almost non-existent). And to the extent that hired
workers are situated in an anarchical interrelationship with other members of
a mercantile society – in particular with an entrepreneur – they compete and
struggle with them. For example, as sellers of labour power they struggle in the
market with the purchasers of labour power, and this is what constitutes the
basis of the chief class antagonism. It is precisely from struggle that progress
emerges, since the progressiveness of the psychology of conditional subordination is determined by its anarchical labour elements.

The relationships that we call synthetic are of a still higher and more progressive type than anarchical forms of production. Their essence boils down
to one in which the labour system is organised but without a division into
organisers and implementers. Imagine a tightly cohesive group of people of
a homogenous, highly developed psychical type; the group does not consist of
a leader and a crowd, but its members all jointly consider and decide all matters and jointly carry out the decision. All members of the group are organisers
when they participate with their opinions and their votes in the elaboration
of the common will, and they are implementers when they actively participate in the realisation of the common will. Thus, both organisational activity
and implementational activity belong to the same human individual in equal
measure, and both are realised in all their wholeness and fullness only in the
life of the entire group. This type of labour relationship develops predominantly in the most recent historical eras and appears to a greater or lesser degree
in all organisations that are called democratic.

The synthetic type of labour relationship possesses the basic advantage of
the authoritarian relationship – organisation – while not suffering from its
deficiency – narrowness of individual psyches (especially the psyches of the
implementers, the masses). At the same time, the synthetic type is also even

more progressive than the anarchical type of labour relationship, and, in addition, this progressiveness is not bought at the cost of internal struggle and contradictions. Its progressiveness is based on broad, continuous communication among many human individuals who, although similar in the eminence of their psychical type, are nevertheless naturally different in the material of their lives so that as they mutually adapt to one another they continuously enrich one another's psyches with new elements. As a consequence of this, the wider the circle of synthetic labour relationships the more progressive is the psychology that is created. Any narrow circle of comrades constructed according to this type can easily solidify into the stationary conservatism of a well-established form – into complacency, laziness, and dogmatism. Small communities that are founded by utopians also usually turn out to be incapable of prolonged development, while, just the opposite, a broad democratically organised party – and especially a whole society whose diverse collective experiences are synthetically organised – cannot but continually draw on more and more stimuli for movement forward.

The 'voluntary obedience' of the masses to ideologists – just like the voluntary service to the masses by ideologists – is different from the simple authoritarian relationship precisely due to the fact that many elements of synthetic collaboration enter into them. Individuals that make up the masses both consider and determine the bounds within which they will follow an ideologist. They 'implement' the organisational directives of the ideologist only to the extent that those directives express the desires and wishes of the individuals who make up the masses; in various ways these individuals themselves show the ideologist what the ideologist must provide them. They not only *subordinate themselves* to the ideologist but to a significant extent *subordinate* the ideologist to themselves. And the more that there are synthetic elements in these relationships, the livelier is the communication of ideologists with their followers, the more their mutual interrelationship acquires a comradely nature, the more both sides acquire a progressive psychology, and the more vital their work is. On the contrary, the more that blind obedience predominates, the higher the ideologist is raised above the masses, and the less the masses are able to influence the ideologist's organisational work, the more inevitable it is that their common life freezes into elemental conservatism. This has occurred in many movements that were cast in a religious-sectarian form, with the inevitable predominance of authoritarian elements.

IV

We have depicted the authoritarian type of labour relationships among people and contrasted it with other types that are both more and less progressive than it, but in so doing we have essentially dealt not with real, concrete facts but with their more or less abstract cognitive characteristics. In actuality, types do not exist; they are created by cognition in order to understand phenomena. Pure authoritarian forms probably do not exist anywhere; in the life of any society in history, all types of relationships of labour are inseparably interwoven and form an unbroken chain of transitions, nuances, and combinations. Life is infinitely complex, and any phenomenon bears the traces of all preceding facts of the world process. How can we distinguish out of this solid chaotic mass those elements that we want to investigate in all their specific distinctiveness?

The power of abstraction must help us here. We can use definitions worked out by abstraction to isolate what we need out of the concreteness of phenomena. Thus, definitions play the role of boundaries or empty forms into which we fit reality, choosing and keeping what fits into these boundaries or forms. Thus, authoritarian relationships can be reduced to the following abstract formula: relationships in which the actions of one person are directly determined by the expressed will of another. To the extent that this formula is applicable to one or another concrete phenomenon, we move such phenomena into the series that we are investigating. To the extent that there are elements in phenomena that do not fit the formula, we strive to single out the effect of these elements on the general course of the process and remove them from our analysis.

A concrete example will provide some clarity. Suppose that you are the head of your own family circle, and, under normal circumstances, your wish is the equivalent of law. This aspect of your life therefore falls into the category of authoritarian relationships. You are the organiser; all the others are implementers. But in some cases, your wife decides to object to your organisational directives and gives advice that from her perspective seems like a better way to do things. Your children, as they grow up, also display the same propensity. These are the seeds of the synthetic type of relationships, a type in which the organiser and the implementer continually change roles. It is not a matter of lord and slaves but of comrades. It is necessary to clearly distinguish those elements in your psychology that adapt you to the first order of relationships, on the one hand, and those elements that arise on the basis of the second order of relationships, on the other hand. But you do not just live in a family; let us assume that you also have a job. At work you are subordinated to some people and you command others, but your subordination and your authority are relative to a significant degree. They do not carry over beyond the bounds of your contract with the bureaucratic collectivity that has hired you. And here there is an element, however weak, of anarchical relationships – to the extent that you can choose whether or not to work or where to work, to the extent that you negotiate your pay, and to the extent that your labour acquires the kind of formal freedom that is characteristic of the anarchical type. It is nevertheless necessary to clearly distinguish your psychical adaptations to a given realm – those that are connected with one series of your relationships to people and those that are connected with another series of relationships. Further, let us say that you are involved in commerce. In that capacity, you are surrounded on all sides by the atmosphere of competition, i.e. relationships of an anarchical type. Still, the 'relative subordination' of your salesclerks and agents introduces certain adaptations of an authoritarian nature. It is necessary to investigate and separate both groups of facts. Suppose also that you read a book. In much of it you accept the ideas of the author – you are subordinated to the author – but sharply oppose many other things – your relationship to the author is now not a relationship of social labour. It is not a form of collaboration but a form of struggle, a manifestation of direct antagonism that again gives rise to particular, specific adaptations in your psyche. All this is subject to analysis.

V

It is obvious that authoritarian relationships can exist only under specific psychological conditions and only when certain psychical adaptations are present. The division between organisational and implementational activity would be utterly inconceivable if the desire of the organiser to give orders were not inextricably connected with the understanding that other people would carry them out and if orders from the organiser were not also inextricably linked with the desire of the implementers to carry them out. The constant association of the psychical forms of 'command' and 'implementation' is an utterly necessary adaptation everywhere that human life is organised according to the authoritarian type.

Let us imagine a society in which authoritarian relationships embrace the entire system of production so that every action of social labour breaks down into actively organisational and passively implementational elements. Thus, a whole huge realm of experience – the sphere of immediate production – is inevitably cognised by members of society *according to a specific type, the type of homogenous duality* in which organisational and implementational elements are constantly combined. Generation after generation, the association of the idea of command with the idea of subordination must be solidified and must become ever more inseparable in the social psyche.

The development of life everywhere is accomplished in such a way that the greatest possible adaptedness is achieved with the least possible number of adaptations. This also relates to social life and to social thinking. People always strive to cognise activity in the same – or at least in similar – forms. They are always inclined to conceive of what is distant in terms of what is near, of what is less understood in terms of what is more understood, and of the unusual in terms of the usual. Any new phenomenon only ceases to be a mystery to people when they are convinced that it is 'the same' as certain other phenomena that they are familiar with. To create completely original adaptations for new facts of life that are dissimilar from previous ones is altogether difficult work, and it is especially distressful for the crude, unsteady psyche of less developed tribes. The painfulness of the emotion of 'bewilderment' in such a case can acquire very serious dimensions. Just the opposite, when a formerly separate and dissimilar series of impressions are successfully combined so that they appear as similar and homogenous, a person experiences deep satisfaction – a feeling which expresses an elevation of vitality. Such a feeling is experienced by each of us when, for example, we learn for the first time that the movement of planets and comets in their orbits is a phenomenon that is basically and essentially the same as the movement of a rock that we throw either horizontally or at an angle. This relates in general to any *monistic* advance of cognition, to any act of thinking that brings unity into the diversity of experience. The fragmentation of the elements of the psyche is diminished, its orderliness and inner harmony grows, and its whole becomes more organised and more cohesive for the struggle of life. This is the significance of the *monist tendency* in psychical development.

In the sphere of the relations of production of authoritarian society, as we have seen, a specific means of conceiving of facts, a specific type of unification of facts in the psyche must inevitably take shape, and it is expressed in the inseparable connection of the idea of the organisational act with the idea of the implementational act. But once such a form of thinking takes shape and becomes solidified as a necessary element of the structure of the psyche, the development that leads to homogeneity in cognition – to cognise the whole sum of facts with the least sum of adaptations – must gradually extend this form to all of cognition, *to make it universal*. People become accustomed to understanding their labour relationships toward the external world as a manifestation of an active organising will exerting influence on a passive implementing force, and they begin to find the same thing in all phenomena. They see the movement of the sun and the flow of water, they hear the rustling of leaves, they feel the rain and wind, and it becomes all the easier for them to conceive of all this in the same way as they conceive of the social labour aspect of their life. Behind the external force that acts on them directly they presume a personal will that guides it. And although this will is invisible to them, it is nevertheless immediately authentic, because without it the phenomenon is not understandable. This is how the idea that 'things have souls' originates.

People also apply the same point of view to all human actions. Even in a society that is structured in the most authoritarian way, many human actions are carried out by people independently of any kind of external organisational will. People satisfy their personal needs mostly without any kind of command, and in social labour implementers must sometimes act independently. In that case, by virtue of the monist tendency, by virtue of the desire to conceive of everything in the same forms, a person is mentally divided into an organiser and an implementer, into an active and a passive principle. The implementer is accessible to external senses (this is the physiological organism, the body), and the organiser is inaccessible to them. The organiser is assumed to be inside the body (this is a human individual's spirit). An invisible being is 'introjected' (inserted) into a visible being.

It is in this way that animism, a specific and distinctive worldview, is obtained. In animism, nature appears to the human outlook as uniformly dualistic; every subject stands out as an indivisible combination of two elements, and the relationship of these elements is the same as the relationship of the elements of an authoritarian group. Here is the starting point of all dualistic conceptions of the world.

What is the basic, original difference between the two principles? Why, precisely that the manifestations of one of them are completely determined by the other in such a way that the latter is not dependent upon the former in any manner. The actions of an implementer depend utterly on the will of the organiser – and this relationship is continuous – while it is impossible to see what determines the will of the organiser. Once you know the will of the organiser, it is completely possible to predict the actions of an implementer. But what about the organiser? Generally speaking, it is impossible to anticipate the actions of an organiser, and it is especially impossible for a regular implementer whose psyche is incomparably cruder and less complex than the psyche of an organiser, so that the implementer is utterly incapable of conceiving of the motives of the organiser with any kind of completeness. People's thinking must adapt itself to such a difference, and it does adapt. The bodily principle stands out as something that is inert – something that is *determined from without*. The spiritual principle stands out as something that is *free* – something that is not determined from without. The conception of a 'free' will quite simply means that it is impossible to predict the manifestations of this will and that there is no desire even to find the conditions of such manifestations. The idea of 'free will' appears in an abstract formulation comparatively later, but, as a *form of thinking*, it originates along with animism.

Animism contains the first germs of causal thinking: the cause of a phenomenon turns out to be the spiritual essence that is concealed behind it. But it stops at this consciousness. The chain of causality is broken at the second link and there is no need to go further. The spiritual cause is 'free', i.e. it needs no further causes. However, this relates only to the initial, simplest authoritarian forms. We shall subsequently see how the situation changes as authoritarian forms change and become more complex.

Animism serves as the starting point of the development not only of causal thinking but also of the teleological worldview. The principle of 'freedom' acts in conformity with its *goals*, just as organisers direct the work of implementers in conformity with their goals. And here, at the early stages of authoritarian life, thinking is not capable of going further than the first goal – the immediate goal of the given directive of a spiritual essence. It is only subsequently, as authoritarian forms become more complex, that the 'final causes' or goals, in their turn, become more complex.

A purely animistic worldview is as much an ideal case – as much an abstraction – as a purely authoritarian society is. In the actual worldview of one or another society, social group, or human individual, animism is one of the elements that predominates under specific conditions but that is less significant under others. It is intertwined with other elements; it combines with them in a specific vital whole that is sometimes more and sometimes less harmonious.

VI

We must make a slight digression here. The views we have presented on the origin of animism do not agree with the most widespread theories regarding this question, and it is necessary to explain why we do not consider it possible to be satisfied with the old views.

Most cultural historians tend to explain the appearance of animism as due to causes that are not of a social but of a more general psychological nature. They present the matter approximately as follows. After the destruction of something or other, after the death of an animal or human, the *image* of the object that has disappeared is preserved by other people for a little longer. For primeval people, this image is characterised by a particular clarity and vividness that is considerably greater than with contemporary people, so that it hardly differs from an immediate perception, from 'reality'. In dreams it even appears to be something completely real. Thus, the conviction is created that the object that has disappeared or has been destroyed has not in reality been completely destroyed. Something remains from it, and it is something that is completely like it. Connected with this is the observation of a sleeping person, of someone who has fainted, or of a corpse. The organism in these cases, apparently, preserves its reality, but it is as if something is missing – it does not display the active manifestations of life. In dreams a person often visits various places that are very distant; the body lies in one place, meanwhile the person travels and looks around. So there must be something in a person that is invisible, that is capable of surviving after the death of the body, and that can temporarily leave it during life, and it is on this 'something' that all the most complex manifestations of life depend. This invisible vital principle is what the animist calls the 'spirit'.

There is no need to utterly reject this explanation of the sources of animism. It can accurately indicate the psychical *material* that served, at least in part, for the construction of animistic views. But the question remains: why did a form of thinking that appears to be *basic* and *universal* spring up from this material at a certain level of development. First and foremost, we know that the whole series of observations mentioned above play a comparatively unimportant role in the human struggle for existence; it is obvious that it remains to be explained precisely why it lay at the basis of the whole worldview of animists. Next, we know that among the least developed tribes, animism – the conception of the spiritual principle – is completely absent, while all the psychical material that the old theory uses to try to explain the origin of animism is present. The question arises: why does this material acquire such a special significance precisely at a later stage of development and not earlier? Further, history shows that a special kind of connection exists between animistic dualism and authoritarian social forms. It accompanies organisations of this type everywhere: patriarchal, feudal, slave-owning, despotic. Dualism is also supported by authoritarian elements in contemporary society: first of all, the monogamous family, then the aristocracy and church, state, and military bureaucracy. It begins to subside only where authoritarian forms and authoritarian classes break down and fall into decline and where new groups and organisations arrive to replace them. The question arises of what can lie at the basis of such a permanent connection between dualism and authoritarian social forms. In the end, comparing the relationship of body and soul, it is not difficult to see that in all basic features it corresponds to the social relationship of the organiser and implementer. What causes such a correspondence must be explained.

In our opinion, only the point of view we have adopted provides a satisfact-ory answer to all these questions. One cannot but recognise that social forms of thinking are adaptations to forms of labour, and they are therefore determined by labour relationships. It then becomes clear that animism is inevitable for authoritarian relationships; it is the mode of thinking that corresponds most closely to them.

Richard Avenarius has provided the most harmonious and perfected philo-sophical picture of the development of the dualism of body and spirit. The essence of his 'theory of introjection' consists in the following. You immediately observe other people only as physical bodies that move around, emit sounds, etc., but those other people cannot remain *only* physical bodies for you. It is possible to explain and predict the movements of other people only when, in thinking about them, you attach various thoughts, feelings, and desires to their movements that are similar to the thoughts, feelings, and desires that you immediately experience yourself. You assume that other people think, feel, and desire, and, although it is impossible to directly prove that this hypothesis is true (it is impossible to see, hear, or touch the experiences of other people), the hypothesis is completely justified in experience, since it explains a great deal and does not encounter any contradictions.

But the hypothesis causes complications, since experiences of other people *are placed inside their bodies* – are inserted (introjected) into their organisms. This hypothesis is unnecessary and even gives rise to many contradictions, and Avenarius systematically notes these contradictions and describes a successive series of historical phases in the development of dualism and subsequently of philosophical idealism. But there is no need here to continue following Aven-arius's account.[2] What is important is that introjection is an *explanation* of the dualism of mind and body.

And here the question arises: where are the forces that cause introjection? If introjection is a logical error, then what made this error universal and necessary for a whole vast period of the life of humanity? The model of introjection as a logical development cannot provide an answer to this question. It is necessary to explain the profound *practical* bases of introjection in the life of humanity; it is necessary to establish the general *objective* conditions to which introjection is an adaptation. This is precisely what our outlook can provide, and it explains the act of introjection as follows. Under authoritarian relationships of labour, the organiser and implementer are *two separate real people*. When, from the

---

2 The ideas about the origin of animism that we have just examined and found unsatisfactory constitute one of the phases in this system of the development of dualism.

same point of view and in accordance with the type of thinking that has taken shape, individual actions are considered in which there is no separate organiser then such an organiser *is constructed* by the creative activity of the imagination. To consciousness, the organiser is real but invisible, and at these levels of culture invisible means hidden, since the conception that invisibility is the result of immateriality cannot arise from primeval experience. Thus, the invisible organiser must be introjected, located inside the implementer. Avenarius himself very accurately pointed out that originally the introjected 'soul' was in no way distinguished from the body; it was a simple *doubling of the human being*. And we explain this doubling by the fact that the person was conceived of both as an organiser and as an implementer, and in their social experience people were accustomed to apprehending both of those roles as separate concrete individuals.

Animism is a worldview that is a whole system that embraced the entire sphere of social experience over the course of many centuries and that left its imprint on the entire psychical life of human beings. The genesis of such a system cannot be reduced to a particular, vitally unimportant group of psychological facts or to a huge logical error. But if we recall that cognition is social and that it is generalised experience, then we will start to seek the basis of such a universal (though impermanent) form of cognition as animism in the fundamental but historically changing relationships of the social struggle of people for existence. Then the objective dualism of society will explain to us the subjective dualism of human individuality.

VII

We have examined one of the forms of thinking – an extremely general form – that was generated by authoritarian relationships: dualistic fetishism in cognition. Let us now move on to another form that has a more particular meaning but that is also very important for ideological development.

The qualitative and then the quantitative differentiation of the elements of experience is what constitutes the basis of conscious life. At the very earliest stages of psychical life, people distinguish pleasant from unpleasant, light from dark, red from green, high pitch from low pitch, etc. They also distinguish more pleasant from less pleasant, stronger light from weaker light, a clear tone from a less clear tone, etc. Later on, yet another kind of distinction appears: people begin to accept that some people are qualitatively superior, others are qualitatively inferior – lords and slaves, for example. In the same way, when making evaluations people differentiate the manifestations of life of an individual person – considering spirit to be essentially superior to body, good deeds superior to neutral ones, for example. Here the matter has to do not with quantitative differences of more or less – even a million bodies cannot form one soul. Nor does it have to do with simple qualitative differences, such as the difference between red and green – this distinction is expressed by the word 'different' and not by the words 'superior' or 'inferior'. The matter has to do with a new, distinctive relationship of the psyche to various facts of experience. Where does this come from?

To the extent that organisational activity becomes ever more isolated from implementational activity and to the extent that organisational activity is ever more concentrated in the hands of individual people or specific groups in society, a real chasm is formed between the two in human consciousness, and it grows ever wider and deeper. The implementer cannot become an organiser and cannot conceive of the psyche of the organiser with all its complexity and activity; the organiser can do everything that the implementer can do and knows that the implementer's psyche is simpler and weaker. From the weakness and subordination of the one and the domination and power of the other there arises reverence from the former and contempt from the latter. This is how the fetishism of a superior being originates.[3]

This fetishism presupposes authoritarian relationships that have already developed sufficiently; we do not find it where these relationships are still not expressed too sharply, where they have not solidified and petrified into real differences between people. In the old clan group, the patriarch still stands too closely to the rest of its members. He is in too close communication with them, and he is insufficiently distinguished from them in habits and thinking for him to be transformed into a being that is superior to them. Just the opposite, the relationship of master and slaves in a slaveholding group, the relationship of lords and peasants in a feudal group, and the relationship of monarchs and their subjects in Asian despotisms are all conceived of in the same way – the relationship of superior beings to inferior ones. Patrimonial aristocracy is in general imbued with this sort of fetishisation of relationships between people.

A similar psychology also appears in the intellectual and artistic aristocracy. The relationships of the ideologist to the masses, as we have seen, are partly authoritarian, in general, and this is even clearer in the relationships of ideologist leaders to their political followers. It is also the case with ideologist thinkers

---

3   We use the word 'fetishism' in general in those cases when an object is ascribed special qualities connected with people's mystical sentiments.

or ideologist artists who are intellectual organisers of various groups of society to whom they provide unity of thought and mood. And here the organisers usually so greatly surpass the power of thought and creativity of other people that their followers are incapable of imagining their leaders' psyches and consider them to be qualitatively superior beings while the simple, alien, insubstantial psyches of the followers can seem to the leaders to be qualitatively inferior.

In a dualistic worldview, the spiritual principle is precisely an organisational principle. It is therefore natural that it becomes qualitatively superior in comparison with the passive, 'implementational' – bodily – principle. The further such dualism develops, the deeper the chasm between the two sides of nature becomes and the sharper the fetishism of superior-inferior in the views of people regarding spirit and body.

VIII

Another distinctive feature of authoritarian thinking – the juxtaposing of the mysterious to the ordinary, to be precise – is inseparably connected with the fetishism of superior-inferior.

Nothing in nature is mysterious for the primeval psyche. A great deal is unknown, and a great deal is unexpected, but this is still not 'mysterious', since that idea can take shape only at higher levels of development. Travellers have frequently noticed what is at first glance a puzzling fact: the absence of a feeling of wonder among unadvanced pre-civilised peoples. The unknown or the new does not cause any observable emotion in them, provided that it does not seem important or dangerous. If it does so, then it excites alarm or fear, and that is all. Everything is 'natural' for them because there are no antecedents in their thinking for the idea of the supernatural.

In the basic meaning of the word, 'mysterious' is not something that is unknown or not comprehensible; it is something that is *hidden* from people, precisely from people with ordinary intelligence. It is something that is not comprehensible or accessible to their own weak cognition but that is comprehensible and accessible to a superior intellect. Any 'mystery' presupposes a majority who do not know it, and a few who do know it; anything 'mysterious' presupposes ordinary minds that cannot grasp it and special, superior minds than can grasp it. Without this, only the unknown or the incomprehensible can exist, while the mysterious, with its mystical colouring, cannot.

Thus, the idea of the mysterious is conceivable only in connection with the idea of superior and inferior intellects. Where does the latter come from? The answer is easy to derive from the preceding.

To the extent that the activities of the organiser and the activities of the implementer become isolated from one another, the psyche of each becomes, as we have seen, increasingly different from one another, whereby one emerges as 'superior' and the other as 'inferior'. Everything that is accessible to the intellect of the implementer is also accessible to the intellect of the organiser; but much that is accessible to the latter is not accessible to the former. The more sharply both groups of society are isolated from one another, the deeper the chasm between the two types of psyche becomes, the broader the realm that the unprivileged mind cannot access grows, and the more natural and unavoidable it is that the antithesis of mysterious versus ordinary takes shape in people's thinking. The mysterious is a cognitive privilege, the object of superior cognition.

Overall, the development of the idea of the mysterious was facilitated to the greatest degree by priests, and this makes perfect sense. In ancient times, priests were usually the actual organisers of production, especially of those realms that required broad unification of the working forces of society. Priests, for example, were in charge of regulating rivers in the countries of the great river civilisations such as Egypt and Mesopotamia. They set the times for carrying out various jobs in the fields. For the most part it was they who directed such collective undertakings as digging canals, building roads, and so forth. In all these cases, priests utilised special knowledge that had taken shape among them in regard to astronomy, meteorology, engineering, architecture, etc. This knowledge was completely inaccessible to the broad masses, to the people who carried out implementational labour. It was natural that, in their own interests and in order to elevate and consolidate their position, priests concealed this knowledge behind a shroud of mystery. Various synonyms of 'the mysterious' indicate the connection between this idea and the role of priests in society: 'magic' (the magi were Chaldean priests), 'mystical' (mystery), and so forth. The idea of the mysterious developed wherever and approximately to the same extent that a caste of priests separated itself out and became dominant.

In general, wherever knowledge becomes an implement of rule and ignorance the condition of subordination, the idea of the mysterious will appear and will be strenuously cultivated. This is the historical basis of the development of all mysticism, no matter how far its individual, particular manifestations subsequently deviate from it.

IX

Earlier we noted the deep *conservatism* that is characteristic of the authoritarian relationship both in the sphere of production and in the sphere of ideology. This conservatism proceeds, as we have seen, from the huge growth in the complexity and difficulty of the organisational role that occurs with any change in the technology of social labour; thus, technology inevitably turns out to be conservative and, in its turn, causes a conservative ideology. Forms of people's consciousness take shapes that correspond to forms of social being: the conservatism of life corresponds to static thinking.

When the actions of people in practical life are constantly directed toward the same goals and along the same paths, when any change of these goals and paths is felt to be something that is unhealthy, thinking then inevitably strives toward stable, fixed forms and phenomena with as solid and as immovable boundaries as possible. These boundaries are static concepts. Nature is reduced to an infinite mass of separate 'things' of which each thing in itself is fixed and unchanging and separated from others by sharp, unchanging borders. A stone is stone. It is always a stone, and it is completely separate from everything that is not this stone. The idea of continuity, the idea of process, the idea of development is utterly alien to this type of thinking. Any movement, any change in the external world appears as a certain force, as the manifestation of a 'free' will, i.e. a force that acts outside causes and lawfulness, a force that is the embodiment of the unexpected. In ancient mythology, some kind of creative act – uncaused and unmotivated, an act of caprice from on high – is the basis of all movement and even of all interconnectedness among things. By taking such acts as the ultimate explanation, static thinking *is reconciled* with the fact of movement and the subsequent interaction of things, but it always *seeks* what is fixed and separate and is only satisfied with that. Static thinking constantly creates the fixed and the separate in its conceptions and ideas. This is all the more likely to result since cognition that is comparatively less developed does not detect either gradual, slow processes of change or transitions and nuances that connect what is heterogeneous. Static cognition strives toward *absolute* ideas that are conservative and that express what is conservative in life. The absolute is that which is unconditional and fixed, that which exists in itself and is constantly the same as itself.

This is how static thinking comprehends every thing, taken separately, and every force that causes things to move. But this trait is most characteristic of the highest concepts that broadly unify experience, and that is why the features of the authoritarian psychological type would be concentrated in it. As we will subsequently see, this is exactly what the highest religious concepts are like in authoritarian thinking.

Static thinking extends far beyond the bounds of authoritarian forms of life, but it is tied to them most closely, and it finds them to be its most solid support. Static thinking and authoritarian forms are so interlocked that everything that is hostile to stasis usually encounters the bitterest opposition of the authoritarian classes. One need only recall the hatred feudal lords and clerics still have in our day for the idea of progress and the hatred they had in the past for the idea that the earth is in motion. The anathemas against Darwin and the fate of Giordano Bruno and Galileo express the same tendency of authoritarian elements – the tendency to defend stasis, the underpinning of all conservatism.

x

In our times, it is usual to consider the traits of thinking that we call fetishism and stasis to be delusions of the human mind. However, over the course of a number of centuries, humanity lived by these delusions; they were truth – the most unquestionable truth – for humanity. What does this mean? How was this possible?

It would be highly mistaken, having arrived at the height of truth achieved through the development of culture, to be limited only to contempt for the mistaken views of people of the past. First, what guarantee is there that our truths will not suffer the same fate – will not become delusions in the eyes of the people of the future? And, second, is it sufficient to reject delusions or should we not, in addition to that, understand and explain their vital necessity?

Our point of view provides a clear and definite answer to both questions. Cognition is one of the processes of adaptation in people's social labour struggle, and truth is a form of adaptation that is worked out by these processes – the most expedient, progressive, and vital form. Like any adaptation, truth is determined by the sum of conditions amidst which it springs up, and it is truth to the extent that it is a real adaptation to these conditions. What is truth for us today will be a 'delusion' in the relationships of life of the distant future, because it will not then be the most suitable adaptation. The same thing happens in our times with the truth of the past.

Fetishism and stasis are, in reality, the most adapted forms of cognition in authoritarian relationships.

It is obvious, first and foremost, that a static worldview is completely sufficient for conservative forms of life and is therefore the best adaptation. The idea of unchanging and detached 'things' is considerably less complex than the idea of the changing and the interconnected. Therefore, it is considerably easier for the former idea to be worked out, and it requires considerably less expenditure of energy for it to survive in the psyche. And when it runs into any significant contradictions in regard to practical life, the idea of unchanging and detached 'things' inevitably turns out to be the most adaptive. This is precisely how it is in all conservatively organised societies where life constantly produces the very same forms, when generation after generation always experiences the same, identical series of impressions, and, if noticeable changes are encountered in the course of life, they usually appear in the form of the destructive action of external forces (war, famine, pestilence) and not in the form of continual progress that brings ever more life and power over nature. Stasis in authoritarian relationships is a necessary adaptation to their elemental conservatism.

The dualism of free spirit and inert body is also an optimal adaptation for all the conditions of cognition that the authoritarian world provides. To be precise, two series of phenomena are provided. Some phenomena (implementational actions and also many usual facts of external nature) *can be anticipated* by people according to their interrelationship with other phenomena, and some phenomena (organisational actions and also unusual processes of external nature) not only *cannot be anticipated* by people with a certain amount of significant reliability, but people cannot even hope to ever achieve such knowledge. It is precisely dualistic fetishism that is capable of unifying and connecting these two extremely heterogeneous series in the psyche with the minimum contradiction and consequently with the greatest economy of expenditure of energy. At the same time, the duality of dualistic fetishism appears as universal homogeneity, and freedom of the spirit serves as the necessary complement to the inertness of matter.

The categories of superior and inferior and also of mysterious and ordinary have generally the same significance. It is the significance of forms that reconcile the contradiction of different series of experience to the greatest extent by uniting them in a homogenous duality. But besides this, the fetishism that is connected with these categories is an important condition for the durability and stability of the authoritarian relationships, themselves. The more that the organisational groups of society are surrounded by the aura of the 'superior' and the 'mysterious' in the eyes of the masses, the more reliable and unassailable their position is and the more they are protected from any movement in society that is capable of undermining their social significance, their organisational role. This is why these groups sometimes even display a direct conscious striving to develop such fetishism in the other groups of society.

Stasis and fetishism are also historically vital and therefore are also historically true for the social relationships that correspond to them, just as the evolutionary-monistic worldview is true for contemporary social relationships. Old forms of thinking become delusions and lies when new relationships and new social tendencies appear to which those old forms are not adapted.

XI

Now let us dwell a little on the concrete forms that authoritarian thinking has adopted in the process of its development. We will begin with its simplest and historically earliest manifestations.

The patriarchal clan commune was the ground on which the very first foundations of authoritarian thinking took shape. All of the elements of authoritarian thinking that we have noted already appeared there in their first, still rough, incomplete, and unfinished forms.

At the beginning of this phase of development, stasis was infinitely more dominant than at any subsequent time, because no germs of a higher type of thinking existed. But stasis still did not have the finished form that we have depicted above. The conceptions of fixed *things* were still far from having taken shape, and the world presented itself to people predominantly as a combination of various *actions*. The primeval conception of the world was precisely like this because action is the basic element of experience; it was of the greatest vital importance and was originally the most familiar element of experience. But in the conceptions of these fixed things, there was no of sense of the historical point of view or 'primeval dialectics' of any kind, since an action did not appear in the consciousness of primeval people as anything like a developing process that was connected with others but as a *completely isolated* act that was repeated without any change. Consequently, both basic features of stasis – the complete separateness and the complete conservatism of the elements of experience – are present. Later on, with the development of language, conceptions of 'things' took shape that acquired ever greater significance in the general system of understanding the world. Thus, stasis took on an ever fuller and more finished form.

Along with the psychology of domination and subordination, all the forms of fetishism that issue from that psychology appear on the scene. Since a sharp, caste-like separation of rulers and the ruled did not occur in the clan group, the manifestations of fetishism were still comparatively undeveloped. The chasm between spirit and body, between superior and inferior, between mysterious and ordinary still had not become wide and deep enough to prevent the continuous blending of the phenomena of both worlds in the crude thinking of this era. But already at this stage the complex system that is known as natural religion and that occupied such a broad and important place in the worldview of people of that time took shape from the elements of fetishism.

Under the deep conservatism of authoritarian psychology, the force of tradition gave rise to one very important transformation in that psychology – to be precise, the transformation of certain deceased people into divinities. It might seem strange and even unbelievable that conservatism and tradition could be capable of engendering psychological transformations and especially such significant ones. The idea seems to contain an inner contradiction, but it is only apparent.

The organiser of the economy of the group – the patriarch, let us say – enjoys particular respect from his kinfolk because of his particular role in the group's life. However, due to the closeness and constant communication between the patriarch and rest of his kinfolk, this respect still does not make him a superior and mysterious being in their eyes. A fetishistic relationship toward him has as yet only begun to be created. But the germs of such a relationship undergo a peculiar process over a number of generations that can be compared with accumulation.

The patriarch, as the oldest in the clan, is the preserver of the past experience of the group, the preserver of its history. Before he became the organiser, he was one of the ordinary members of the group, one of the implementers, and he was subordinate to the previous organiser whom he later replaced. While he was subordinate to this predecessor, he was accustomed, of course, to relate to him with special respect and was accustomed to considering his predecessor to be superior to himself. Due to psychical conservatism, he continued to maintain this view even after he himself became the head of the group, and he not only continued to maintain this view, but he also transmitted it to all the other members of the group. Thus, in the eyes of the other members of the group, the previous organiser stood higher than the patriarch and was more highly respected. But this predecessor stood in the same relationship in regard to the organiser whose place *he* had taken, and, in the same way, the predecessor's predecessor stood even higher in the eyes of the group higher than the predecessor himself, etc. Thus, in the tradition of the clan, the further that the era of the activity of previous organisers receded into the depths of the past, the greater that respect for them grew. And, in regard to the most distant of those who still survived in memory, the growing sum of respect reached the level of deification. The ancestor was fetishised and became the object of worship.

It goes without saying that the deified ancestor, being deceased, appeared as a 'spirit' – to the extent that the concept of spirit had taken shape. He was a 'superior' and 'mysterious' being in the highest degree, and the vagueness and fragmented nature of the memories about him that survived surrounded him with a mystical haze and stimulated the creative activity of fantasy. Fantasy supplemented what was missing in such a way that the picture of the life of the deified ancestor corresponded to the level of the reverence toward him: gradually a mythology of his deeds, miracles, etc. was created.

Thus, at the basis of natural religion lies a 'cult of ancestors', as it is usually expressed by cultural historians, but it would be more accurate to say 'cult of previous organisers'. In reality, the matter always has to do precisely with organisers – patriarchs, leaders – and not at all with ancestors in general. Regular members of the group are not deified, and their spirits do not usually enjoy real immortality but die as memories of them disappear.

This is not the place to review the further development of religion, but, in any event, it is unquestionable not only that religion originated in authoritarian thinking but also that it was continually and inseparably connected with authoritarian thinking in the subsequent stages of humanity's development. Everywhere we encounter a religious worldview, we also find all the basic features of authoritarian thinking. The central point of such a system always consists in the static idea of the absolute and the unchanging; its content is continuously pervaded by the dualism of spirit vs. matter and the categories of superior vs. inferior and mysterious vs. ordinary. On the other hand, everywhere that authoritarian relationships play any significant role in life, ideologies are clothed in religious forms. The entire history of antiquity and the middle ages exemplifies this.

In subsequent eras when authoritarian forms were gradually forced out by new relationships, the religious shell of ideology also retreated to the side lines and gradually disappeared. However, even there the religious shell still survived among those classes that, being comparatively more conservative, still continued to live to a significant degree under authoritarian forms. This is the case in our times with the remnants of the feudal estate, the peasantry, and the backward part of the petty bourgeoisie with their patriarchal family structure. It can be said in general of the contemporary monogamous family that to the extent that it maintains the features of the patriarchal clan, of which it is a remnant, it represents the main bastion of authoritarian psychology, in general, and of religious forms of worldview, in particular.

XII

Sophisticated and advanced forms of authoritarian relationships engender sophisticated and advanced forms of authoritarian thinking. Unfortunately, any kind of full description of them would take up too much space, and we will therefore only briefly indicate the especially characteristic traits of several stages of the development of such relationships.

Feudal society is a complexly organised authoritarian system, and its ideological forms are correspondingly complex. Technology was already comparatively quite developed and led to the knowledge of many causal relationships between phenomena, but the understanding of causality, itself, remained absolutely fetishistic. Philosophers who have noted this fetishism of causality usually depict it in the following way: in this conception, they say, the relationship of cause and effect is completely analogous to the relationship between an act of will and the movement of the human body. Just as the impulse of will causes a corresponding movement of the body, so an active cause brings into being a corresponding effect. We can accept this description, but we must cast the issue in a somewhat different light. As we have seen, the general separation of the will and the body reflects the division in society into organisational and implementational activity. Consequently, in the final analysis, it is this latter that lies at the basis of the fetishism of causality.

The religious exterior of the feudal worldview at this stage developed magnificently, and religion emerged as the basic organising foundation of social life. One need only recall the role of Catholicism in the medieval world. The broadest organisational activity was concentrated in the hands of the hierarchy, something that was possible only in feudal society with its notably atomistic character, with the rather dysfunctional independence of its individual parts. All relationships between people were under the direct control of religion and the church. The papacy used papal bulls and bishops to direct the course of the life of vast social units – states and their federations – and used confessions and monks to extend its supervision of individual people down to their pettiest activities and even their thinking. And all this colossal work was conducted in one direction and was imbued with one spirit – a tendency toward the greatest possible strength and stability of the authoritarian system and toward the mutual harmony of its countless individual elements. Everything was sacrificed to the elemental conservatism of this system; everything that did not bow down to it was condemned to death. Subordination, stasis, and fetishism were utterly dominant.

The organising activity of the secular feudal lord was incomparably narrower and more limited. On the one hand, organising activity, as we have seen, did not extend beyond the bounds of their estate, and, on the other hand, even within those bounds it included only a specific realm of social labour – mostly military affairs, means of communication, justice, and so on. All remaining economic activity was carried on independently by units of small-scale production – families under the immediate direction of their own individual organisers.

On the basis of the unifying activity of the feudal lord, shallower and less substantial forms of fetishism took shape that corresponded to the comparative narrowness of that activity. This had mainly to do with the principles of hereditary aristocracy – ideas of the origin of the superior and the inferior. Conceptions of the nobility of blood drew a sharp boundary between the governing and the subject classes. It was not only the feudal lord who sincerely considered himself to be a superior being in comparison with those who were subject to him, but his subjects believed this no less sincerely. For feudal thinking, nobility of blood was something exquisitely fine, something mysterious, and something that could not be replaced or equalled by any physical or mental perfection. A knight worshiped a fair lady; she represented an ethereal ideal essence to him. But if it suddenly turned out that she was of 'common origins', it was all over. Even though she had not changed at all, nevertheless the same knight would consider marriage to her as degrading and shameful for him. Why? She was not from the *organisational* class.

Curiously, the degree of nobility was measured by the number of ancestors of the feudal lord, i.e. the length of time during which a given family had belonged to the organisational group of society. A feudal lord with thirty ancestors would consider another feudal lord who had only ten ancestors as comparatively inferior and less noble. And the former, in his turn, would regard a representative of an even more ancient family with involuntary awe. Thus, the real organisational role of a person in society became more fetishised with every generation. The founder of the family, who had been elevated from among the commoners to be consecrated as a knight was an organiser only in fact, and he was respected only for his personal qualities that stood out in his activity. But his distant descendant appeared in the eyes of society as provided with some kind of special organisational essence that elevated him above everyone else, even though this essence was not expressed in any particular actions.

It is well known that eastern despotism is distinguished from feudalism by a more profound development of authoritarian relationships and by highly centralised organisational activity. Under such conditions, the fetishism of the superior position in society naturally takes on even cruder forms, where it often extends to the direct deification of the despot, as can be seen in the examples of the ancient Egyptian pharaohs, contemporary Chinese emperors, and so on.

Present-day remnants of the authoritarian system – various forms of bureaucracy – are also connected with certain elements of authoritarian fetishism.
One need only note the psychology of an old bureaucrat: the respectfully rever-
ential feelings that he displays in regard to higher ranks and the truly mystical
mood that overcomes him when he attains a high title – the post of general,
let us say. It then seems to him that some kind of change has taken place in
him, that some kind of new essence has been implanted in him that changes
his entire relationship with the external world. He thus perceives as mystical
what is merely a broadening of the sphere of organisational activity.

But in addition to such particular varieties of fetishism, we find more important general traits of thinking in all authoritarian forms, both old and new: a profound inclination toward stasis, cognitive dualism, and a religious understanding of the world. Authoritarian groups and organisations everywhere invariably
provide support for these forms of social consciousness.

XIII

Let us turn to modified labour relationships that contain other elements besides authoritarian ones.

We have already noted the extreme harshness of the forms of rule and subordination in classical slavery where worker-implementers and the products
of their labour are equally merchandise and where anarchical (exchange) relationships exist among slave-owning groups. Corresponding to this, all the traits
of dualism – the contraposition of spirit and body, superior and inferior, mysterious and ordinary – are expressed with extreme harshness in the ideology of
the era. But at the same time elements of the anarchical system of relationships
put their particular stamp upon these ideologies and modify them to a greater
or lesser degree.

First and foremost, anarchical relationships bring many internal contradictions into social life and cause many kinds of struggle. The struggle between
buyer and seller, competition among buyers, competition among sellers, and
the mutual inadaptability of people in the face of these conflicts do not allow
conservatism to become as absolutely entrenched in the human psyche as is
the case in a society with a purely authoritarian structure. Therefore, although
stasis is the governing feature of this kind of thinking, certain elements of the
historical point of view appear along with it in various cases and to various
degrees. Thus, for example, Greek philosophy, which summed up the worldview of the most developed slave-owning nation, is far from alien to the concept of 'process' and even 'development', and especially the concept of the

universal interconnectedness and continuity of phenomena. Heraclitus's idea about the flow of being, about the constancy of change of everything in nature, is, it is true, only an isolated fact in the history of Greek thought, but even the kind of static philosophy, deeply imbued with the conception of the absolute, such as Plato's, was not devoid of the idea of the improvement of forms, for example. For the Eleatic philosophers, the conception of the immutability of real being was combined with ideas of universal unity that profoundly contradicted stasis, etc.

As far as dualistic ideas are concerned, they are utterly dominant in slave-owning societies. The influence of anarchical relationships is revealed only in the significant abstractness of these ideas – the striving toward the abstract form of thinking is an obvious characteristic of the anarchic construction of society in general. It is worthwhile to compare, for example, the feudal-Catholic conception of the soul, in which the soul is blatantly material and capable of physical suffering, with Plato's conception of the soul as a pure idea. Apart from philosophy, even in the purely religious conceptions of the Greeks the soul appears as comparatively quite abstracted from reality – a pale, spectral essence, that does not possess real life but only a phantom of life.

It would be very interesting to follow the changing varieties of religious and philosophical thinking of the ancient world in relation to the various cultural-historical conditions that engendered them – but we obviously are not able to do this here.

The ideologies that arise on the basis of a capitalist system represent a considerably greater deviation from authoritarian thinking. Here, first and foremost, stasis generally retreats in the face of the historical point of view, and the more the contradictions between labour and capital develop, the more stasis retreats. Life that is full of struggle and striving – life that is full of changes in people's internal and external world that have complex causes and are intricately interwoven – is not reconcilable with stasis, and it bursts the boundaries of the fixed and absolute. The principle of change and relativity becomes ever more victorious, and there is ever less room for the absolute in ideology, even though the ghost of the absolute, ever paler and more bloodless, still continues for a long time to weigh on people's minds.

As far as authoritarian fetishism is concerned, although it still survives to a significant degree, its viability continues to diminish. It cannot completely disappear, since the relationships of both domination and subordination that engender it still exists, but the particular nature of these relationships quickly weakens it.

To be precise, for authoritarian fetishism to develop, an integral homogenously dualistic society in which there is no struggle between organisational and implementational groups is necessary. Wherever there is such a struggle, there already actually exist not one society but two societies with different conditions of life and different tendencies of development. Each society works out its *own* ideology that is adapted to its vital relationships and desires, and one common ideology does not appear, as it does in patriarchal or feudal society. Instead, two whole ideologies appear that contradict each other in many respects. In so doing, it stands to reason that the inseparability of the conceptions of the organisational and implementational basis that provides such solidity to authoritarian dualism is destroyed. Fetishism of the superior and the mysterious also disappears, since it would be an utterly unfit adaptation for the struggle of the implementational groups of society against the organisational groups, i.e. against precisely those groups with which this fetishism is linked and whose social role is made impervious and inviolable by this fetishism.

In this light, it is completely understandable that elements of stasis and fetishism are retained with considerably more strength among groups of the rulers who need conservatism to preserve their social position than they are among the subordinate groups. Often the rulers do this completely consciously, keeping their direct interests in mind, and they preserve in society authoritarian forms of thinking that ensure the survival of a social structure that is desirable and advantageous for them.

The relationships between ideologists and the masses presents the most modified of the authoritarian forms.

These relationships are characterised, as we know, by *voluntary* subordination, the limits of which are determined by the wish of the people who subordinate themselves. In addition, there are elements of reciprocity between organisational and implementational activity to a greater or lesser extent. The masses not only follow ideologists, they also present significant demands regarding their activity that ideologists must satisfy. Consequently, the masses, in their turn, determine the field of activity, and, within certain limits, 'organise' it.

In explaining the psychology of these relationships, we run up against one circumstance that significantly complicates things. Ideology is created by the life of a specific class and is an adaptation to its external and internal conditions. Consequently, both the psychology of the masses and the psychology of the ideologist – the person who expresses its spiritual life – depend all the more on the basic conditions of the life of this class – on its internal and external relationships. As far as the relationship between ideologists and masses is concerned, it is derivative and not based in class life and cannot have a predominant influence on the psychology of either side; the influence of basic relationships is considerably stronger. Therefore, in the psychology of the mutual relationships between ideologists and masses it is difficult to single out what precisely is caused by these ideological relationships and what is caused by other economic or technological relationships. One can, in any event, note several general types of authoritarian thinking connected with ideological 'subordination'.

In the period when a new class is struggling for social power, its ideology has few characteristics of conservatism and stasis. This makes perfect sense: its whole point is to change what exists, and therefore its forms of thinking cannot be completely rationalised and adapted and thoroughly imbued with the spirit of immobility and the idea of the immutable. Some elements of development must be found in the ideology of struggle. But once victory is attained, all ideologies aspire to congeal into set forms, and 'dogmatism' replaces 'critique'. Just like economic organisers, ideological organisers try to make their labour easier by means of routines and traditions, and so elements of stasis arise with considerably greater strength and intensity. Thus, static ideas occupy a considerably greater place in the ideology of the present-day bourgeoisie that is striving to hold on to its dominance, than they did in the ideology of the young bourgeoisie of the eighteenth century that was struggling against feudalism. The religious reformers of the seventeenth century began with ideas of freedom and tolerance – ideas that were hostile to stasis, that were closely associated with the idea of development, and that were directed toward removing obstacles to ideological progress – but those same reformers ended up exemplifying the victory of dogmatism and intolerance, and they burned their 'heretics' at the stake.

Authoritarian ideological relationships are also characterised by various varieties of dualism and fetishism to a very considerable degree. We can point, first and foremost, to the huge role of authority in the activity of professional ideologists. Everyone knows how in ideological struggle criticism and arguments are often countered by simple appeals to the opinion of one or another celebrated thinker, and this is most characteristic precisely of frozen and reactionary ideologies.[4]

---

4 It is interesting that the distinctive process that lies at the basis of the 'cult of ancestors' occurs in the sphere of ideological life, and here respect for authority seems to accumulate to the same degree that it recedes into the realm of the past.

As one generation follows another in unbroken succession, great thinkers, great poets, and great artists of the past grow in the eyes of the people into something like titanic figures, and any attempt to compare them with great ideological organisers of the present seems strange and even absurd. Of course, in this case the matter does not involve real deification of ideological leaders of the past. Their names began to be preserved in people's memory only at the higher levels of culture and at a time when new non-authoritarian relationships began

Fetishism of the superior and the mysterious is manifested with particular force in conceptions of talent and genius. The aura of greatness and mystique that surrounds the psychical life of these elite beings can be explained due to the fact that talent and genius – genius, in particular – seem to be what organises ideological life. What, for example, does the expression 'head of a school' mean if not the fact that a given person seems to be the organiser of a specific ideological tendency? A distinctive cult of genius often springs up even on the ground of ideological subordination. Carlisle's idea of heroes as the sole movers of progress represents the clearest example of such a cult, but a somewhat mystical relationship to one or another great mind is found in our time even among the most critically minded people.

Finally, the dualism of 'spirit and matter' also has a basis to a certain degree in ideological subordination. This dualism is revealed in the customary usage of the terms 'spiritual and material life of society' in place of 'ideology and economics'. The fact is that the economic life of society belongs just as much to the sphere of the psyche as ideological life does, but crude materiality is ascribed to the former and pure spirituality is ascribed to the latter. Customary usage creates a sharp boundary between them that cannot exist for contemporary scientific thinking.

In any event, the psychology of the relationships between ideologists and the masses contains, besides authoritarian elements, still other elements of a higher type that are less developed in some cases and more developed in others but that in the most progressive classes can rise to the first importance, removing the basis for any stasis and any fetishism.

XIV

To this point, history has not known the kind of society in which there are no elements of an authoritarian structure. But at a certain level of development these elements cease to play a predominant role in the life of society, and other forms rise to the fore. The first and foremost of these are the relationships of anarchical labour.

Anarchical relationships are characterised by the fact that individual people or groups carry out their activity of social labour independently of one another so that production as a whole is not organised; there is no single will that

---

to develop along with criticism that does not permit extreme veneration. However, as far as religious reformers go, after a series of generations in which their ideas develop and solidify, outright deification occurs (the Buddha, for example).

controls and directs it. It is only in the process of exchange that the mutual dependence of producers is revealed. Only the spontaneous force of the market with its fluctuating prices regulates social labour and makes one or another of its sectors profitable or unprofitable by turns. Individual producers must adapt to the demands of this spontaneous force, otherwise they are threatened with ruin. They must produce what there is a demand for, and they must not exceed this demand, otherwise they will lose income and will be deprived in general of the ability to produce.

But the spontaneous forces that replace the conscious activity of a general organiser never speak in the kind of clear and understandable language of a human organiser. The market is full of surprises and dangers for producers. At any moment they might be ruined, regardless of any of their efforts and through no fault of their own. It is sufficient that other producers have brought to the market too much of the same merchandise that they produce, and they cannot find buyers. They are then ruined, or at least have to sell their merchandise too cheaply, i.e. they suffer greatly as a result of the insufficient satisfaction of their needs.

Thus, a mass of vital contradictions springs up from the lack of organisation of labour, and they engender a bitter struggle among producers. Antagonism between seller and buyer, competition between sellers or between buyers – these are constant external manifestations of the mutual maladaptation of people in the process of labour. At subsequent stages a harsh struggle between classes is added to this that is based on the antagonism between the buyers and sellers of labour power in the labour market.

Where the lack of organisation of society causes it to be internally maladapted, the need of *organising adaptations* arises. An anarchical social system creates a huge number of such adaptations. Instead of an organising human individual who regulates and oversees the labour relationships of members of society, impersonal *ideological forms* appear that have a completely analogous significance. These are especially normative forms: customs, law, morality.

In a society built on struggle, any social connection becomes impossible if definite boundaries to that struggle have not been established, and if, at the same time, cooperative relationships are not established that contradict it. Buyers and sellers struggle with one another, and if this struggle were to freely unfold and become aggravated and if obligatory forms of peaceful dealings between both sides were not created by custom, then the situation would inevitably be reduced to mutual thievery or destruction instead of exchange. If manifestations of competition and class struggle were not regulated by the legal and moral consciousness of members of society, they would also just turn into constant bloody warfare. In all cases where a customary, legal, or moral norm appears on the scene, its role boils down to *organising* the relationships between people, i.e. mutually accommodating them, weakening or eliminating vital contradictions between them, and creating the greatest possible unity and harmony.

It goes without saying that organising adaptations, like all other adaptations, do not always achieve their goal and do not always diminish the mutual disharmony of elements of society that are not organised into one whole. We know too well from experience that contradictory results are often attained and that, for example, obsolete norms of law are often themselves the cause of the greatest unadaptedness for society and the greatest suffering for its members. But only one thing follows from this: that organising adaptations, like all other adaptations, have only relative and not absolute significance and that, having been established under specific circumstances, they can easily turn out to be disadvantageous outside of those circumstances. They then cause the lowering and not the elevation of the sum total of life. This continues until, in one way or another, these adaptations are destroyed or are changed to correspond to new circumstances. In order to understand the vital meaning of one or another adaptation, it is necessary to examine it in the very conditions that created it.

XV

The anarchical type of relationship has never conclusively ousted the authoritarian type from any society that we know of. In petty bourgeois society each separate enterprise is run on its own by a family that is organised in an authoritarian fashion under the rule of the father or the eldest member of the family in general. In capitalist society, the authoritarian family is dissolving to a significant degree but still partially survives, and, in addition, relative subordination springs up, as we know, in accordance with modified authoritarian forms. Nevertheless, the division between the organisational role and the implementational role remains.

It is evident that the explanation of this fact is that anarchical relationships are not unconditionally higher than authoritarian relationships. Although the former are considerably more progressive, they do not possess the organisation and internal unity that distinguish the latter. Therefore, the former cannot biologically replace the latter completely and without leftovers.

In any event, the old type of thinking cannot but survive along with the old form of collaboration, and it cannot but leave its imprint on the worldview of anarchically organised society. In particular, that imprint must be powerfully evident in the *organisational adaptations* that play a role in anarchical society, a role that is analogous to the former authoritarian organiser. Impersonal norms of custom, law, and morality are understood in an authoritarian manner and appear in social consciousness with all the characteristic traits of authoritarian thinking.

Above all, these ideological forms are totally dominated by conservatism and stasis. It is hardly necessary to prove that custom is pre-eminently a realm of conservatism. In the history of cultures, one continually observes the supreme durability – one might say petrification – that is characteristic of old customs and how incredibly resistant they are to the penetration into the life of society of new elements that contradict them.

The same thing, but to a lesser degree, also applies to legal phenomena. While a legal norm exists, it presents itself to social consciousness as something immutable and absolute. Even if the forces of development in fact produce changes in it, there is still absolutely no element of change in the idea of the law. Any established system of law is a powerful conservative factor in the life of society. Having crystallised from the past, it constantly strives to cram both the present and the future into its unchanging bounds, and it makes a crime out of any vital fact that does not fit within these bounds. It is worthwhile to recall the iron system of Roman law with its unassailable definitions, a system that is shot through with the idea of immobility and with the idea of the absolute perfection of its logical, dry, and cold formulas. The idea that Roman law can develop is unthinkable.

Forms of morality are approximately as conservative as forms of customs, and they lack any hint of the idea of development to an even greater degree than legal forms do. The deeply static and absolute nature of moral consciousness is manifested all the more clearly in the fact that, regardless of the growing mutual acquaintance of peoples with the most varied types and levels of development and the most varied manifestations of moral life, so far the huge majority of people of even the most cultured nations consider moral laws to be unchanging in their foundations and universal in their significance. The absolute finds the last but also the most durable of its supports in the world of moral ideas. A morality that discards the conception of the absolute and bases itself exclusively on the idea of development no longer essentially corresponds in any way to the concept of morality. This is a phenomenon of a completely different, utterly new type. The logical conclusion of evolutionary thought must inevitably be amoralism. Amoralism does not, of course, mean villainy, baseness, or crude egoism; it rather means the rejection of morality in general as a static, conservative form.

It is also easy to detect all the traits of authoritarian fetishism in the organisational adaptations that we have examined. First, they all appear in people's thinking as an independent, active principle to which people subordinate themselves just as people would subordinate themselves to an organiser. 'Custom does not permit', 'the law forbids', 'morality demands' – these expressions are not simple comparisons; they are tied up with the idea of some kind of external force that exists independently from people and that governs their actions. Norms are *objectivised* and obtain independent life just like real organisers of human activities. At the same time, the characteristic of special 'spirituality' is peculiar to all organisational adaptations – they all relate to the sphere of so-called spiritual culture that is juxtaposed to material culture, the immediate struggle of people with external nature. They are all conceived by social consciousness as something higher in comparison with other manifestations of life and especially those that oppose it. The demands of custom, law, and morality stand higher than any individual demands. They are even higher than social interests, and any violation of these demands places a person lower than the rest of society and even degrades society. Further, normative adaptations are surrounded by a customary aura of mysteriousness to various degrees. Their origins are attributed to a higher reason, and it is accepted that their essence is inaccessible to the understanding and critique of ordinary reason. Any attempt to draw the mystical veil away from them appears as something that is stupidly insolent and transgressive. This applies in the greatest degree to the forms of morality and custom, which are the most conservative forms. Even now it is possible to find 'philosophers' for whom the attempt to explain the genesis of morality in historical terms is thought to be an outrage to its dignity. Analogously, in ancient times priests persecuted people who tried to portray the establishment of customs as the work of human hands. Such an outlook is less associated with legal life, probably because law is the product of more advanced and developing cultures in which there is a strong influence of higher, non-authoritarian elements of life. However, there is also plenty of mysticism in legal life. One need only recall the close tie between Roman legal institutions and Roman religion or the variation of the theory of 'natural law' that still has advocates among us, which treats the bases of this law as lying outside the empirical world – i.e. as supernatural.

   In authoritarian societies, people create idols for themselves in the form of individual beings according to the form and likeness of human organisers. In anarchical society, in which there are still strong authoritarian elements, impersonal idols are created according to the form and likeness of the socially spontaneous forces that rule over the internal life of that society. These idols demand the same absolute worship and devotion as their ancient predecessors. They similarly do not permit any free manifestations of personal human will, they similarly rule out the possibility of any higher instance, and they similarly rule 'categorically'. The idol of absolute justice expresses the challenge that, if necessary, the whole world should be sacrificed for its demands. The idol of order has often used its power to destroy the most noble manifestations of social development. The idol of honour – personal and national – has often seen thousands and tens of thousands human beings lying dead at its feet. The idol of pure duty demands that the human individual sacrifice to it, if necessary, what is best in life – the possibility of happiness for oneself and for others ...

In our time, the stasis and fetishism that is embodied in these idols often turns out to contradict the most vital strivings of humanity, but this was not their original role. They sprang up as social adaptations, and at the early stages of the life of anarchically organised society they were useful for its survival and development. Here stasis was the condition providing strength and solidity to established social forms, and the fetishism of the superior and the mysterious elevated this strength and solidity even more, sanctifying the established forms and making them inviolable. In addition, dualism, which is characteristic of fetishistic ideas, was cognitively useful, permitting heterogeneous series of experiences to be interconnected with the least contradiction. Thus, for example, people can find two sharply heterogeneous series of desires in their own psyche: some completely correspond to traditional forms of social life, others are directed toward the development of individual life, and sometimes this development can be accomplished only at the expense of these traditional forms. Dualism creates a kind of relationship between both series so that their contradiction does not destroy the unity of human individuality. Some desires enter the system of 'duty' and are considered to be superior, the others are placed in a subordinate and inferior position, and manifestations of the latter are suppressed everywhere they contradict the former. Thus, an internal bifurcation remains at a specific level of development and does not intensify to the point of becoming a destructive inner struggle and so does not lead to an external conflict of human individuality with the society in which it lives.

XVI

Although authoritarian psychological elements still continue to survive in anarchical society, they nevertheless can no longer remain predominant. Anarchical labour relationships create their own forms of thinking, forms that are completely distinctive. To investigate these forms of thinking in detail would mean to go beyond the bounds of our topic, and we must therefore outline their general features only to the extent that it is necessary to understand their influence on the fate of authoritarian forms.

The anarchical system of production is based on broad specialisation. Producers not only work *independently* of one another, but they also perform *different* work. The manifestations of social life turn out to be qualitatively heterogeneous – so heterogeneous that it is impossible at first glance to distinguish any common elements in the activities of different people. Indeed, to take an example, what psychical content do the jobs of a farmer and a goldsmith, a cobbler and a scholar have in common? Only one thing: the social nature of all these types of labour, the social purpose of their products, which workers mainly produce not for themselves personally but for other members of society. The producers, however, are entirely unconscious of this social nature of their labour, because it is unavoidably masked from them and made invisible to them by the manifestations of the *struggle* between people that issues from the unorganised nature of the social process. The psychology of struggle leaves no space for understanding the relationships among people that unite them in the struggle with nature. Consequently, all the material for cognition that is provided by the system of production appears to contain no immediately visible elements of unity; it appears that it contains nothing that can be *generalised*. At least, this is what the material of ordinary mass consciousness is like, and, after all, it is in mass consciousness that social types of thinking are established.

But as consciousness develops, it necessarily strives to organise its material and to unify all its data, and this unification is accomplished through generalisation. Phenomena are necessarily grouped into series and summed up into concepts, concepts form new series that are organised with the aid of new, more general concepts, and so on. This process provides organisation for the psyche, without which the vital stability of the psyche – its ability to harmoniously react to the influence of the exterior world – would be inconceivable.

Thus, under anarchical relationships, in what form can the entire realm of experience that is production – social labour – be unified and generalised? Since at this stage thinking cannot find universal elements in the various manifestations of anarchical labour, it is obvious that this realm of experience can ultimately be unified only in *content-free generalisations*. It is precisely in this way that the idea of 'sociality' appears to psyches that develop in an anarchical system. The basic content of sociality – the collaboration of people in the struggle with external nature – is absent from the consciousness of commodity producers. For them sociality is simply a connection between people, i.e. sociality and nothing more. We never find a commodity ideologist who understands 'society' as a system of collaboration. Instead of that, we usually encounter a reference to 'psychical association' that unifies people or to common norms that tie people together, and this is essentially only a tautological reference to the same social connection among people. It turns out that society is society and nothing more.[5]

As we have pointed out, any established form of thinking strives to become universal: this is the 'monistic tendency' of the development of cognition. Thus, the cognising psyche, in becoming accustomed to the fundamental sphere of experience – the realm of production – unites various series of phenomena into content-free concepts and inevitably also transfers this habit to all the remaining content of experience. The content-free concept becomes the universal organising form of thinking.

This phenomenon is utterly clear and obvious in petty bourgeois and bourgeois ideologies – classes that are anarchically organised.

In the sphere of economic intercourse, the concept of exchange value completely predominates. For the commodity producer, the content of this concept is determined in the following way: the exchange value of a commodity is what is paid for it. But this is essentially the same thing as saying that the value of a commodity is its value. The real content of value, as is well known, is the socially useful labour that is crystallised in the commodity. This content eludes the consciousness of the producer since the social nature of labour is concealed behind an apparent struggle among people, behind the individualistic tenor of their actions and desires. What remains is an empty form of value that commodity thinking is completely satisfied with.

In the moral life of exchange society, all values are based on the idea of duty. Philosophical criticism has repeatedly and for a long time explained how empty and content-free this idea is. Duty is what a person should do. In other words, duty is duty; this, in the end, is how the content of this idea is defined. The real meaning of duty consists in the fact that specific relationships between people are placed under it: to be precise, those relationships that lead to the greatest solidity and stability of the social whole. Nevertheless, the social essence of the moral idea eludes petty bourgeois or bourgeois consciousness.

---

5   At the same time, one can encounter less content-free definitions of sociality. In some of them a connection with the state and in others a connection with the nation appear as the essence of sociality. But these concepts are not at all related to anarchical forms of production. This is obvious if only because exchange relations – and consequently also anarchical collaboration – are not organised within the bounds of the state or the nation but continually go beyond them, striving to embrace all of humanity. Confusing the social connection in general with the governmental connection or the national connection is based on completely different relationships – in part on simply authoritarian relationships and in part on more complex tribal relationships. But there is no need to go into this question here.

It is masked by the vital juxtaposition of human individuals as independent units that often come into conflict and fight among themselves. The result is that a content-free idea remains as the ultimate generalisation of moral life. The emptiness of this idea, however, does not cause any contradiction in the consciousness of anarchically organised societies or classes.

In the realm of cognition, the ultimate unifying idea is 'truth'. But for petty bourgeois or bourgeois consciousness, this idea is transformed into the same kind of abstraction as duty or value. For such consciousness, the criterion of truth is that it is universally obligatory. In other words, truth is what everyone must accept, or, even more concisely, truth is truth. According to its real vital meaning, truth is a social adaptation – a cognitive adaptation that can serve as a reliable basis for expedient activity. It is harmoniously socialised experience. But for a psyche that is brought up on anarchical forms of labour, the social content of truth is inaccessible. For such a psyche, cognition – like labour – is conceived of as an individual process and a process that is isolated in itself, independent of practice. And once the social content of the idea of truth is removed, the only thing that remains is an empty form.

Metaphysics is pre-eminently the product of exchange society. Its countless empty abstractions – like the essence of being, of reality – are the purest manifestations of the psychological type that arises from anarchical relations of labour. It is characteristic of this particular type that it is satisfied with such hopelessly content-free abstractions.

However, it is possible to find in the psychology of exchange society not only a tendency to empty abstractions but also other traits of a less negative nature. The most important of all is that this psychology does not reconcile itself with stasis. Stasis cannot be a suitable adaptation for anarchically organised society, with its comparatively rapid development and with the progressiveness that issues from its inner struggle. Thus, the idea of change – the idea of progress – must necessarily win an increasingly predominant position in people's views on life and the world. Gradually the historical point of view must take the place of stasis. In this, the thinking of anarchically organised society diverges especially sharply from authoritarian thinking.

The history of ideas shows that the birth of the historical point of view and the first stages of its development are really connected with anarchical labour relationships, and in ancient and modern European culture the historical point of view appeared on the scene after trade appeared, and it progressed to approximately the same degree as trade developed. The feudal world was thoroughly imbued with stasis. Ideas that were hostile to stasis were first born in the merchant republics of Italy in the great era of the Renaissance. Capitalist society, with its huge development of anarchical relationships, first gave the historical point of view decisive preponderance over stasis. But the final destruction of stasis lies in the future, beyond the bounds of anarchical forms of production.

XVII

We have seen that, as the psyche develops, it strives to cognise everything in the same forms and according to the same type. Therefore, when the anarchical type of thinking encounters the authoritarian type in the same society and in the same consciousness, a struggle between them inevitably arises, and one would think that the anarchical type, as the higher type, must gradually force out and replace the authoritarian type. This would not be hindered even if the circumstances are such that authoritarian relationships continue to survive. If the new type were really the higher type in all relationships, then it would turn out to be an adequate adaptation for lower forms of social labour as well. There would be nothing in these forms that could not be contained within the bounds of anarchical relationships. But this does not happen in reality, and it does not happen precisely because anarchical relationships of production and the forms of cognition that issue from them are not absolutely and entirely higher; they do not provide everything that is present in authoritarian forms.

To the extent that the issue has to do with replacing conservative relationships with progressive ones and replacing stasis with the historical point of view, the new type of thinking is completely capable of replacing the old type. In the process of change, the stability of forms signifies the phase when opposite changes that are equal to one another occur simultaneously. What is conservative *is contained* in what is changing as one of its phases. In exactly the same way, the static conception of *things* can be completely eliminated by the historical concept of *process* because the perception of process can remain unchanging just like the perception of things. For this it is only necessary that the different sides of the process are in equilibrium. In general, the historical point of view has everything that stasis can provide and a great deal more in addition to that.

Things are different when it comes to dualism and fetishism. They issue from the very form of authoritarian organisation.

Authoritarian collaboration is organised; anarchical collaboration is unorganised. In this regard, the latter is not at all a vitally higher form; it does not have the very important element of vital strength and stability. Compared with authoritarian collaboration, anarchical collaboration is disharmonious and contradictory. From its disharmonious and contradictory elements, anarchical thinking can create only content-free generalisations, only empty abstractions, whereas authoritarian thinking produces concepts that, although they are fetishistic, are not empty but have a certain content (dualism of spirit and body, antithesis of superior and inferior, mysterious and ordinary). The *organisational* significance of fetishism is that it cannot be replaced by empty abstractions. Therefore, the anarchical type of thinking can force out the authoritarian type only to the extent that the anarchical organisation of labour forces out the authoritarian organisation of labour. And since, as they develop, ideological forms inevitably lag behind the forms of production that lie at their base, authoritarian thinking always survives to an even greater degree than authoritarian labour relations.

In undermining the old forms of social organisation, anarchical labour relations destroy, one after another, the old authorities that are connected with those forms. This process is observed in modern history on a large scale, and it constitutes the clearest distinctive feature of the merchant capitalist world. However, the fall of authorities of one kind or another does not prevent authoritarianism from surviving. A great many of its manifestations remain, except that its nuances change, becoming increasingly colourless. Minor concretely conceived personal authorities are replaced by broad, abstract, impersonal authorities. The old type of thinking is given a distinctive, abstract colouration by the new type of thinking, but it does not disappear, and it is not destroyed. Exchange society is incapable of achieving this.

XVIII

Synthetic relationships of production and cognition are higher than anarchical relationships. Their basic distinctive feature is that they organise the relationships of labour not by setting the organiser and implementer individually apart but, just the opposite, by the joint execution of both organisational and implementational activity by the whole collectivity. All members of the group are thereby both organisers and implementers by turns, and they alternately participate in discussing and resolving issues and in putting into effect the decisions that have been made. Thus, the labour activity of separate individuals turns out to be homogenous to a significant degree.

This homogeneity grows even more with the further development of synthetic forms of labour. Common and uniform means of struggle with nature are worked out; production of the most varied products begins to be carried out with the aid of the same basic techniques with only small additions and variations. This is how it is with machine production, especially when automatic machines are employed. Here, whether we are dealing with the manufacture of a match, a pin, or a cartridge, the psychical work of the labourer boils down to directing and managing the operation of a machine. The psychical work remains the same in essential details; it is only certain particulars that change. The tendency toward such unity of methods of production appears along with the use of machines, and it is strengthened to the degree that those methods are perfected and to the degree that they approach the ideal of an automatic worker made out of iron. Specialisation continues survive in the sense that different people or groups continue to produce different products, but it loses its former significance and ceases to create sharp differences between people by narrowing their horizons, crippling their psyches, and making them abnormally one-sided. The development of new forms creates the continually growing possibility for the harmoniously integral existence of people in society.

Because the synthetic type of organisation of labour is a combination of both progressiveness and organisation, it is a higher type than authoritarian organisation of labour. In exactly the same way, it is also obviously higher than the anarchical type. This is why we can think that synthetic forms are capable of completely removing and replacing both of the preceding types of relationships. It is precisely here, obviously, that the historical role of stasis and fetishism must come to an end.

As noted earlier, synthetic relationships are not characterised by conservatism; they are, generally speaking, progressive. At the same time, the broader the group that is organised according to the synthetic type, the greater the progressiveness will be, since progressiveness is based on the broad mutual communication of human individuals who are approximately equal in their level of cultural development but nevertheless have considerable differences in regard to the content of their experience. Thus, the more the synthetic organisation of relationships develops and the further it spreads, the less compatible it will be with conservatism in people's social life. Corresponding to this, there is increasingly less room for stasis in social thinking. As synthetic forms develop, the process of pushing out stasis, which had begun under the influence of anarchical forms, will continue, and for the first time the complete elimination of stasis will become possible. Anarchical collaboration, as we have shown, cannot serve as the starting point of such complete elimination, and it cannot do so precisely because it is not capable of putting an end to the authoritarian forms of labour that inevitably bring stasis along with them. It goes without saying, however, that even when a higher type of life predominates, remnants of lower types of life will take a long time to disappear.

The elimination of dualism and fetishism by new forms of cognition is a process that is somewhat more complex.

First and foremost, due to the ever more homogenous nature of the labour activity of different individuals, the tendency to cognise all phenomena of social life as homogenous – as not differing in essence – necessarily arises. And because the human psyche strives toward the maximum harmony – toward the orderly unification of all the material of experiences in the same forms – this homogenising tendency subsequently spreads to the entire realm of experience in general. Thus, the elimination of qualitative differences in people's social roles – as subordinates or rulers – leads to the elimination of any fundamental dualism from the entire worldview. The need to perceive and understand all phenomena as homogenous engenders corresponding methods of cognition, and monism – acceptance of the idea that nature is unitary *in essence* – arises. As a matter of fact, this is monism with very little content – not much more than the denial of dualism. However, such a denial has huge vital significance. In order to understand this significance, one need only consider how the whole sum of a person's relationships in life would change if the categories of essentially superior/essentially inferior, mysterious/ordinary were destroyed.

But in synthetic forms there are also conditions for working out a more substantive monism. Of primary importance here is the elimination of the former type of specialisation. With the predominance of the former type of specialisation, human psyches appear to be heterogeneous. One person behaves utterly differently from the way another person would behave in the same conditions, and neither one of them is at all capable of predicting the actions of the other. In the synthetic type of relationships, due to the growing psychical homogeneity of people, such prediction becomes ever more possible. In this way, the idea of strict *regularity* spreads through the psychical life of people and becomes entirely predominant, and because of it the idea of free will, which expresses precisely the impossibility of predicting the actions of other people, is decisively silenced. The idea of regularity already presents a certain unifying content for a synthetic worldview, but such content is as yet very insignificant.

As we have said, the greatest homogeneity of the psychical make-up of the human individual is attained when *common methods* of production are worked out, when similar methods of labour appear in different realms of the struggle of society with nature that are only supplemented and modified in various cases by other, more particular techniques. These common methods obviously must also constitute the basis of the unifying ideas around which social experience is monistically organised, and it is possible to show that this is exactly what happens in reality.

Machine production works out common methods of struggle with nature that gradually remove the sharp differences of specialties. What do these common methods consist in?

They consist in *the transformation of the forces of nature from some forms into other forms* that correspond more to the goals of labour and in which there will be the least expenditure and loss of those forces. Chemical reactions and then heat in a steam engine is transformed into mechanical work, mechanical work in a dynamo is transformed into electricity, and electricity is transformed in the filament of light bulbs into light, and so on. How is this common method manifested when it is transferred into cognition and is converted into an idea? *The principle of the transformation of energy from some forms into others.* The idea of the conservation of energy in all of these transformations expresses the basic general condition of machine production. This, to be precise, is the constant need to draw the energy that is subject to transformation from any available source. Thus, the law of conservation of energy appears. It is the broadest generalisation of contemporary cognition, the only generalisation that is capable of lying at the basis of the logical unification of scientific methods. We thus see that this law is the cognitive expression of the objective unity of the methods of labour activity that have arisen in machine production.[6]

There is every reason to think that the development of common methods of struggle with nature not only has not yet been completed but is at the very beginning and that in the future these methods will be elaborated ever further, ever more broadly, and ever more perfectly.

Then, corresponding to these methods – since science is altogether nothing other than the process of organising the experience of social labour – the unifying ideas of a scientific worldview will become ever more substantive and

---

6 The historical link between the law of the conservation of energy and machine production becomes clearly evident if one recalls how and when science arrived at this law. Energetics developed from thermodynamics, which studied the relationship between thermal and mechanical processes involved in the expansion and compression of bodies. Carnot, the great founder of thermodynamics, was the first to clearly formulate the idea of the transformation of thermal into mechanical energy and back again and who calculated the approximate magnitude of the mechanical equivalent of heat. Carnot did this ten years before Robert Mayer, and it was only a historical accident that his discovery was missed by his contemporaries. But the very task of thermodynamics arose from the desire to find the conditions for the maximum output of steam engines. This is exactly how Carnot himself understood his task. Thus, the use of steam engines created the atmosphere in which the supreme monistic idea of science grew and matured. [Lazare Marguerite, Count Carnot (1753–1823) was a French mathematician, physicist, and politician; Julius Robert Mayer (1814–1878) was a German chemist and physicist (trans.)]

precise. The *unity of cognitive methods* (the highest form of monism) that is developing will make human thinking an ever more systematic and harmonious system.

The unity of scientific methods decisively eliminates the possibility of any kind of dualism whatever. If we use the same techniques in the cognition of 'material' and 'spiritual' phenomena, if we explain both with the very same laws, if our thinking is not required to change its norms and habits while switching from the one to the other, then how can a sharp discrimination between these two realms of experience make any sense at all? It falls away like an unnecessary complication of life, like an adaptation that has been outlived.

Fetishistic ideas of the qualitatively superior and the qualitatively inferior disappear along with dualism. In their place, a scientific conception appears for which life is homogenous in its essence but is more intense, varied, and harmonious in some of its manifestations and is poorer and more disharmonious in others. This conception reflects a picture of real progress that has been accomplished in the life of society.

The fetishism of the mysterious also disappears. For the developing human mind there is nothing that is unknowable in all of nature. There is only the known and the unknown. What is unknown does not appear with any halo. It is an enemy that must be overcome and not a secret of a higher intellect that must be worshipped.

⋰

We have examined the distinctive forms of social being and social consciousness that are the basis of the fact of domination and subordination. We have seen that a specific type of psychology inevitably proceeds from these forms – a type that is conservative, dualistic, and fetishistic. We have pointed out that this type is historically necessary, and under the particular social conditions of the past it was completely reasonable. But we also explained that it is historically necessary that this type of psychology be eliminated in the process of social development; it is necessary that it be supplanted by other, higher forms.

Such a change of form is being accomplished along a far from trouble-free path; it proceeds in the form of a bitter struggle in the form of countless collisions between groups in the same society, between human individuals in the same group, and between conceptions in the same individual. Progress is being purchased here at the price of great suffering, destruction, and death.

The struggle of authoritarian norms with the highest types of life has appeared with special force during the most recent centuries of the history of humanity. To the extent that the old psychology retreated in the face of the new, this struggle lost a little of his former cruel, destructive nature, but it did not become less intense. Our time is full of its manifestations.

In order to accurately assess these manifestations, it is necessary to know how to detect them. Often the old life drapes itself in the accoutrements of a new costume and so holds its ground by deception. Whoever cannot penetrate through this surface appearance can do harm to their cause, and this often happens nowadays. It is necessary to clearly keep in mind the basic traits of obsolete principles in order to discern them in any disguise and under any presentation of them. It is especially where we encounter people who tell us that it is impossible to live without idols and fetishes – without the absolute and the unknowable – that we must firmly keep in mind that these are people who want to be slaves or to own slaves.

A New Middle Ages: On *Problems of Idealism*

The less a person knows, the greater their disdain for the ordinary, for what surrounds them. Unwind the history of all the sciences: without fail they begin not with observations but with magic, with abnormal, distorted facts, expressed hieroglyphically, and they end with what reveals the essence of these secrets, these difficult truths. They end with truths that are so extremely simple and ordinary that at first no one wants to think them. In our times, the prejudice has still not been completely eradicated that forces one to expect something out of the ordinary in the truths of science, something that is *inaccessible to the crowd* and that is not applicable to the vale of tears that is our life. Before Bacon, everyone thought this way ...

ALEXANDER HERZEN

•••

The middle ages were an era of the greatest development and flourishing of *authoritarian* forms of life in the history of humanity. Authority ruled in all realms of people's social being; the system of feudal-aristocratic relationships embraced all the 'worldly' life of society, and the system of Catholicism ruled all 'spiritual' life. Both systems put a deep imprint on all human thinking, both theoretical and practical. Every law took the form of *privilege*; every truth had to be placed within the bounds of *revelation*. The extreme conservatism of existing relationships gave them an absolute and unchanging character in the eyes of the people. There was no conception even of the possibility of other forms of life.

But, despite the fact that life sometimes flows slowly, it nevertheless moves. Gradually, in a long and difficult struggle, its current changed. The era of stagnation gave way to an era of headlong development; a period of authority was replaced by an era of all-embracing criticism. This process, however, is still far from finished. The current of evolution carries with it a great deal of debris from the past that restrains and retards the movement of progress. Along with development and criticism, practical and intellectual life retains a huge quantity of elements of stagnation and authority.

These remnants of the past are so numerous and their weight lies so heav-
ily on all that is vital and progressive that it is neither possible nor necessary
for us to provide a general description of them here. At the present moment
we are occupied specifically with those cases where these anachronisms try to
smuggle their contraband into the future under the flag of the most vital tendencies and in the guise of the most progressive currents of modernity. To the
extent that the fundamental victory of the new principles becomes more evident and the inevitable death of the old forms more certain, cases like this are
becoming more frequent and are acquiring ever greater significance. However,
such types of phenomena are too numerous and varied, and the attempt to
completely embrace them all in a generalised description would be too ambitious. We intend to dwell on one particular extremely contemporary and, in our
opinion, extremely *typical* fact.

In order that there be no misunderstanding, we will make one important
stipulation beforehand. In striving to expose the 'objective falsehood' of reactionary ideas and attitudes that appear behind the mask of progressiveness,
we do not in the least intend to call into question the 'subjective uprightness'
of those who bear that falsehood (we employ the felicitous expression of Mr
Struve, which he used in a polemic with Mr Mikhailovsky). In intellectual life,
because the spirit of the past is just as cunning as the spirit of the future and
people can easily become the playthings of its spontaneous will, deceivers are
often deceived. It is especially important here not to be annoyed but to understand.

We have before us new articles by two writers who possess an undoubted
and rather distinctive renown – Mr N. Berdiaev and Mr S. Bulgakov. The first
article bears the pompous title, 'The Ethical Problem in the Light of Philosophical Idealism',[1] and the second bears the weighty title 'Basic Problems of the
Theory of Progress'.[2] The matter at hand is the posing and resolution of two
of the most serious and at the same time most vital philosophical problems –
the problem of the goal of human life and the problem of the real meaning of
human life in the general course of the world process. Conscientious thinkers
put all their soul into the investigation of such problems, and therefore the
forms of this investigation express to us very precisely the forms of thinking of
those thinkers. The content of their conclusions expresses their basic, practical
thoughts. From this point of view, the articles by Mr Berdiaev and Mr Bulgakov
are of great interest, not only as characterisations of their own psychology but

---

1   The collection *Problemy idealizma* [*Problems of Idealism*], pp. 91–136. [See Poole 2003, pp. 161–
    97 (trans).]
2   The same collection, pp. 1–47. [See Poole 2003, pp. 85–123 (trans).]

as typical phenomena of a certain part of society. The task we now take up is to elucidate and critique the forms of thinking and the practical desires that appear in these articles.

The problem of the goal of human existence is resolved for Mr Berdiaev by the morality of absolute duty. This is the morality that is based on the 'critique of practical reason'.[3] It is the voice of conscience that speaks in a person's soul; it is the internal voice that, with no ulterior motive, commands a person 'you must do this' or 'you must not do that'. Absolute duty is acknowledged as the sole and universal source of morality, its highest sanction. The morality of absolute duty ascribes a super-experiential origin to a person's internal voice, and it rejects in principle any scientific posing of the question of its origin. Accepting and propagating this morality, Berdiaev considers it possible to reject all the criticism that it has undergone without any analysis.

Let us summarise the basic results of that criticism. On the one hand, it showed and explained that the idea of pure 'duty' is hopelessly empty, that it is a naked form in which the most varied content can be packed, and that, in itself, it does not indicate a specific direction for moral life. Duty means that it must be done. Logically this doctrine is incapable of going any further than this tautology, and nothing is added by such derivative formulations as the proposition that 'humans are ends in themselves', the idea of 'value in itself', and so on. These formulations conceive of people exclusively as moral beings, i.e. yet again as advocates of 'duty'.[4] One is left to insert one's own content into the empty form, which is what Kant did. But, since the inner voice does not say the same thing to everyone, this content appears different to different people. And the fact that, for example, one person could in the name of duty send others to be executed for their beliefs and that the latter, also in the name of duty, could calmly die for their beliefs, could not be more natural and legitimate. The inquisitors considered it their 'duty' to burn heretics, and, in so doing, they considered the soul of a heretic to be a 'goal in itself' or a 'value in itself' and that to save the souls of heretics it was necessary to sacrifice their bodies. The idea of 'duty' does not give a *specific* answer to the vital question of ethics – the question 'what is to be done?' It is only through scholastical games using unclear concepts that it is possible to 'infer' from the idea of duty one answer or another.

---

3   That is, Immanuel Kant's *Critique of Practical Reason* [trans].
4   The formulation (in *The Critique of Practical Reason*) that says, 'behave in such a way that the maxim of your will can always also be the principle of universal law', is no less content-free. What is being talked about here is only ideal, universal, absolute duty, and this obviously relates to its form and not its content.

But criticism is not limited to this. The investigation of socio-psychical life from an evolutionary point of view has led to a new and important conclusion. It turns out that any 'normative' socio-psychological form – customary, legal, moral – strives to strengthen and solidify certain *completely specific* relationships among people that are well-established or are being established, so that from the point of view of these specific relationships it is inevitably *conservative*. Such is the moral idea of 'duty'. Once it achieves a definite content: 'it must be this way', then, having arrived at 'it is proper', any further movement is halted. Each new step is now 'it is not proper', and the idea of duty remains hostile to it until the moral consciousness of the people itself evolves and its content changes. Thus, criticism unmasked the conservative nature of the morality of duty and the way it contradicts the striving for continuous development. As a result, an energetic struggle against that morality began on the part of the most progressive thinkers in the name of the most active forms of idealism.

Where does the morality of absolute duty that Mr Berdiaev preaches stand in relation to the basic ideas of the criticism of 'absolute duty' that we have pointed out? How does he eliminate the formal emptiness of the 'categorical imperative' and its fundamental conservatism?

It is achieved by a quite simple method: packing specific content into an empty form that would exclude all conservatism as far as possible or at least would contradict it superficially. The following formulas result:

... '"Ought" is not "is" ... we take it as the starting point of our ethical frame of mind' (p. 97, *passim*).

... 'The pure idea of the obligatory is a revolutionary idea, it is a symbol of rising up against reality in the name of an ideal and against existing morality in the name of a higher morality. It is against evil in the name of the good' (p. 94).

'Absolute obligatoriness cannot be made to coincide with any fixed form of empirical being. The "obligatory" that any spiritualist worthy of the name speaks about is a summons to eternal struggle with what exists in the name of ever higher forms of life, and this idea does not ever permit one to come to a stop on anything' (p. 119).

All this is very, very good, but ...

... 'for us the world "duty" does not have an unpleasant historical flavour' (p. 129).

'Too often in history the moral tastes and demands of the given reality were considered to be obligatory, and rebellion against it was considered to be a violation of duty' (pp. 93–4).

'It is only by the complete obfuscation of thought that the radical idea of absolute obligatoriness, as it is understood spiritualistically, can be linked with the strengthening of the most outrageous and reactionary forms of things' (p. 119).

Additionally, Kant – that Columbus of 'absolute duty' – put content into duty that was far different from what Mr Berdiaev did. This could still be justified by the fact that Kant did not understand the idea of duty 'spiritualistically', even though a 'spiritualistic' understanding of duty is often connected with 'the strengthening of the most reactionary forms of things' that in general are encountered down to the present time in the accompaniment of an 'unpleasant historical flavour'.

From this it is obviously and definitely possible to infer the following dilemma: either the 'categorical imperative' is often confused and provides the most unsuitable commands, or it is really an empty form in which those who so desire can insert any content that they want.

But Mr Berdiaev points to a third way out: an 'obfuscation of thought' that confuses the commands that are obtained and transforms them into something that is their diametrical opposite. This way out is not terrible, but ... it must be substantiated. It is necessary to show, first, that the idea can be obfuscated and that it can obfuscate moral desires, and, second, that any other understanding of 'absolute duty' than Mr Berdiaev's is really an 'obfuscation'. To prove this, since the 'obfuscation of thought' is a fact from the realm of cognition, arguments of a factual and logical nature are necessary. What kind of proof does Mr Berdiaev present to those arguments?

To demand scientifically logical demonstrability for ethical propositions means to fail to understand the essence of ethical problems. These propositions have specifically ethical demonstrability. They draw their value not from the cognitive activity of consciousness but from purely moral activity (p. 97).

In light of all this, any adherent of a reactionary – albeit a 'spiritualistic' – understanding of the morality of duty, can dare to self-confidently declare that: 'only the extreme obfuscation of thought can explain how the most conservative idea of absolute obligation – understood spiritualistically – could be connected with a protest against the most sacred, the most inviolable bases of being'. And if such adherents are asked to prove this, they answer that it is absurd to require scientifically logical demonstrability for ethical propositions; their demonstrability issues from the purely moral activity that had brought them (reactionaries) to the aforesaid conviction. How can you refute this, Mr Berdiaev? Even millions of flowery and passionate phrases cannot change the fact that people with opposing ethical principles will be in an equal position, and both sides have an equal right to put their own content – no matter what it smacks of – into an empty formula. If one admits that Mr Berdiaev is indeed competent by virtue of his 'specifically moral' activity to answer the question of what absolute duty 'must' be for everyone, then it is clear that this 'duty' will now not be absolute. One higher authority, in the person of Mr Berdiaev, will tower over it, and, on top of everything else, it will have a certain 'empirical' character.

In any event, the process of filling an empty form with arbitrary content cannot proceed in a strictly logical manner. Indeed, it is easy to observe this in Mr Berdiaev's constructions where he tries to define the content of his 'absolute duty' more concretely. Proceeding from the idea that duty is an expression of the moral autonomy of the human 'I', Mr Berdiaev draws the following conclusion: 'The demand for absolute moral law is a demand for the absolute freedom of the human "I"' (p. 133).

But in this transformation of 'absolute law' into 'absolute freedom', the 'I' should not at all be understood in the sense of a terrifying leap from the legalistic Kant to the anarchist Stirner.[5] No, here the matter boils down to an ingenuous play on words. By 'human individuality' or 'I', Berdiaev has in mind only 'norm-governed I', and for 'morally rational nature' he has in mind only 'normative consciousness', that is, exactly what corresponds to the demands of absolute duty. It is understandable that for Berdiaev the freedom of 'I' seems to be identical with the 'freedom of absolute duty'; one might say that it is identical with the absolute rule of the categorical imperative. The result is that 'the human individual' is capable only of wanting 'what is absolutely obligatory'. Through such usage of terms, the transformation of 'duty' into 'freedom' becomes a simple tautology.

But this does not make it any easier for 'empirical human individuality' – the concrete human individual for whom 'duty' is too often a bitter enemy of their most cherished and essentially best desires and a harsh master who mercilessly batters and breaks their lives? It is true that Mr Berdiaev denies the very existence of empirical human individuality: 'unfortunately' the concept of empirical human individuality is not only indefinable but is not even conceivable … To be a human individual … means to single out one's 'norm-governed' ideal 'I' from the chaos of the fortuitous empirical cohesion of facts, and this empirical chaos is still not in itself 'human individuality' and the category of freedom is not applicable to it (p. 138, *passim*).

---

5 Max Stirner (1806–1856) was a German philosopher who contributed to individualist anarchism and ethical egoism [trans.].

'Unfortunately' this argumentation is difficult to consider as anything other than a clever philosophical joke. The complex organised unity of the facts of consciousness that is called psychical individual personhood is not at all simple 'chaos' but is a definite system, albeit possessing only relative and not absolute actuality. This real psychical system contains extremely varied tendencies and desires that struggle among themselves, and the absolute suppression of some of these tendencies and desires by others is an absolute constraint on the 'freedom' of those that are suppressed. For people who have experienced the painful struggle of 'feeling' and 'duty', a discussion with Mr Berdiaev would seem like the most malicious mockery. Such people know very well that to suppress a feeling does not mean to give it 'freedom' and that after the victory of the 'norm-governed I' – i.e. of duty – they frequently do not feel themselves to be 'free' but would put a bullet in their brain in order not to undergo any more slavery. And there is no way Mr Berdiaev can dissuade such people from thinking that their 'feeling' is *their* feeling and at the same time their 'duty' is *their* duty. There is no way Mr Berdiaev can convince them that freedom of feeling and subordination to duty are the same thing. Mr Berdiaev suggests to them, of course, that they ascribe either of the two not to their own 'I', but to 'empirical chaos', but ... we would prefer not to witness the kind of answer that Mr Berdiaev would receive.

In further developing the concrete content of his morality, Mr Berdiaev poses the question: 'What is the relationship of inner freedom to external freedom and of moral freedom to social freedom?' (p. 133). He answers this way:

Is it possible to reconcile the inner self-determination of the human individual – its moral freedom and the recognition of absolute value behind it – with external oppression, with the exploitation of it by other people and by whole groups, and with the desecration of its human dignity by social institutions? Can those people and groups, who, in the end, are conscious of the dignity of human beings and of the inalienable 'natural' rights of the human individual endure arbitrary rule and coercion? There cannot be two answers to these questions; any vacillation here would be shameful (p. 134).

This is very beautiful and appealing, but, alas, far from convincing, or, more accurately, convincing only to the extent that it has no relation to the morality of absolute duty. The absolute 'I' that figures in this morality can concern itself perfectly 'freely' with 'internal self-determination' and with 'recognition of itself as having absolute value' no matter what the 'external oppression'. It is the *concrete* human individuals who embody not one 'absolute duty' but countless and various experiences, and who are gifted with the thirst for life, strength, and happiness – it is they who cannot put up with outrage and exploitation in reality, because it is precisely on them that the outrage and exploitation falls. Let Mr Berdiaev, if he pleases, accuse us of 'outrage' against the absolute 'I', but all the same we cannot refrain from asking the question of where he saw a capitalist capable of 'exploiting' this pure abstraction? Perhaps the abstraction received wages and created surplus value? No, if anyone has been able to exploit the absolute 'I', it is Mr Berdiaev himself, extracting from it a whole system of morality, including the liberal programme.

The logical leap from an ideal 'I' to a real, empirical human individual – such is the method by which Mr Berdiaev bases the necessity of 'external freedom' on 'internal freedom'. This is no better than to base people's need of air and light on the substantiality of the soul, and it is of dubious service to the problem of 'internal freedom'.

We see that the emptiness of the formula 'absolute duty' is specifically reflected in Mr Berdiaev's constructions, making them extremely capricious and illogical. Let us see how another trait of this formula – its fundamental conservatism – is reflected.

'The idea of *moral development* is inconceivable without the idea of a supreme *goal* that must be realised by this development' (p. 112).

'Ethical norms themselves can no more evolve than logical laws can. Morality is unchanging; what changes is the level of proximity to it' (p. 104).

We can clearly see that the desire to stubbornly think in *conservative* forms reduces the real movement of life to something stationary and unchanging. Why must the development of life inevitably be presented in a naively teleological form like a journey to some final station, the so-called 'supreme goal'? The boundless growth of the fullness and harmony of life that is the real content of progress logically excludes any idea of a 'final goal', an unchanging ideal. It is true that for fainthearted types, the picture of infinite progress without any fixed substratum, without any reassuringly solid basis in which a weary imagination can always find true and safe respite is unbearable, and they are prepared to sacrifice both logic and experience if only they can escape from the agonising vertigo. But faintheartedness has always been a bitter enemy of rigorous truth.[6]

---

6   In the era when stasis ruled, even strong minds could not reconcile themselves with the idea of infinite progress, since it contradicted their conservative forms of thinking. This is why the Greeks considered a finite magnitude to be 'more perfect' than an infinite magnitude, and Hegel called unclosed endlessness 'stupid'. But when in the era of evolutionary thinking Mr Bulgakov calls the progress of science 'stupid endlessness' and finds that it really is not even progress, that science 'is no closer to its task' than it was several centuries ago ('Basic Prob-

'Morality is unchanging; what changes is the level of proximity to it'. Let us try to analyse this thought logically. It presents progress as a lessening of the distance that separates reality from 'morality', from an absolute moral norm. But this norm, as Mr Berdiaev subsequently explains, is a 'beacon that shines to us from eternity'. Thus, the distance is infinite and therefore progress can also be infinite – we do not risk approaching it completely since the very norm 'always is only a summons forward, ever forward' ... (p. 104). No matter how seemingly attractive this idea is, still ... 'scientifically logical' thinking cannot but recall its own 'natural law'.

'Infinite distance' is a symbol that repudiates all distances: one cannot draw near to what is infinitely distant by means of finite movement. Progress toward an infinitely distant goal is simply impossible because it is not progress at all. Is humanity any closer to the end of eternity now than it was 100,000 years ago? As it moves forward, is the solar system any closer to the border of limitless space? These are absurd question because infinity is not a station for travellers, but, just the opposite, the rejection of any station. 'Approaching the infinitely distant' is simply a flat contradiction, and this fact is not changed by any rhetoric.

A year and a half ago, we had the honour of explaining all of this in detail to Mr Berdiaev, on the occasion of his summons at that time 'to draw near to absolute truth, goodness, and beauty'. But we were not able either to convince Mr Berdiaev or to receive any response from him. We now strongly believe that we have been completely successful in this matter, since we can rest our case on the philosophical authority of the famous economist Mr Bulgakov, whose critical-mystical article adorns the first pages of *Problems of Idealism*. Mr Bulgakov, just like us and our logic, proposes that it is impossible to draw near to the infinitely distant, and, therefore, as we have pointed out, giving science an absolute, infinitely distant goal denies that science can progress. We personally, not having an intimate relationship with infinity and the absolute and acknowledging that knowledge can only have relative goals, do not vouch for the truth of this last conclusion but completely rely upon Mr Bulgakov to prove to Mr Berdiaev the utter impossibility of *his* 'ethical progress'.

In any event, once a mind is taken hold of by the idea of unchanging norms and absolute goals, there is no room left in it for consistent evolutionary thinking. In our time, however, it has become impossible to get rid of evolutionism completely, and the desire to curtail and discredit this unpleasant point of view

---

lems', p. 2), then how can this be explained except by faintheartedness? Is not this just atavism ...? In any event it is a decisive condemnation of either of two things: the scientific activity of all humanity or the philosophical practice of Mr Bulgakov himself.

consequently arises. It is necessary to curtail it in regard to what is most essential: to be precise, to exclude from its purview the most important question of the theory of ethical development, the question of the origin of ethics. This is done by repeating over and over again the unconditionally dogmatic assertion that evolution must not touch on this question.

'Evolutionary theory often successfully explains the historical development of morals and moral concepts and taste, but morality itself eludes it. Moral law is located outside its narrow cognitive horizon' (p. 103).

'Evolutionism ... has no right to derive morality from what is not morality, from the absence of morality. It must assume morality to be something given before any evolution. In its evolution, it only unfolds, and it is not created' (p. 103, *passim*).

'Moral law ... is given "for this world", but not "from this world"' (p. 104, *passim*).

'Moral law ... is given before any experience' ... (p. 117, *passim*).

But, for all that, where is the proof? We have reason to suspect that Mr Berdiaev considers the proof to be his own repeated assertion of the following formulation:

> All the arguments of the positivist evolutionists against the absolute idea of what is obligatory, independent of experience, usually miss the mark, since they turn moral law, which is inherent in a subject, into an object of scientific cognition, i.e. they situate it in the world of experience where everything is relative. We first and foremost set absolute moral law – as something that is obligatory – apart from the entire empirical world as it exists ... Positivism (empiricism) uses the scientific-cognitive function when it is not appropriate ... (pp. 96–7, *passim*).

So, what is being said here? That 'what is obligatory' lies outside experience, and, since it belongs to the kind of 'subject' that cannot be an object, it is therefore 'inappropriate' to use the 'scientific cognitive function' in regard to it ... But it is obvious that this is only one more repetition of the same stark dogma: what is obligatory is outside experience and it cannot be known scientifically. Perhaps the force of the argument consists in the words 'we first and foremost set apart', etc.? There is nothing objectionable about that; it is doubtful whether anyone would allow themselves to contradict Mr Berdiaev's 'inalienable natural right' to oppose whatever he wants, because of whatever he wants, and whenever he wants. But we can in no way figure out how this gives Mr Berdiaev the right to reprimand the 'scientific-cognitive function' for its 'inappropriate' behaviour.

'The special and grievous sin that is inherent in evolutionism is precisely the worship of the God of necessity instead of the God of freedom' – this is the grave accusation made by Mr Berdiaev against evolutionism. Fortunately for the accused, we can utterly reject the punishment it is threatened with by establishing a strong alibi for it. The reality is that evolutionism, as a 'scientific-cognitive function', is incapable in its very essence of engaging in 'worship' and always only investigates and explains ... Nevertheless, we do not venture to defend evolutionism unconditionally; we must admit with great sorrow another really 'grievous and special sin' on the part of evolutionism that constitutes the real basis of Mr Berdiaev's accusation. This is the sin of obstinate disobedience to Mr Berdiaev.

In our view, the most pitiable feature of the position of criminals in contemporary society consists in the fact that, when opportunity offers, no one restrains themselves from imputing to them in passing all sorts of vices and lawlessness, without taking the trouble to be guided by facts and to prove the accusation. Here, for example, regarding the evolutionary point of view, Mr Berdiaev talks to us as if in the realm of ethics evolutionism 'resorts to purely external criteria, assesses the sacred rights of human individuality from the point of view of social utility and adaptation, and *sees the moral ideal in a disciplined herd animal*' (p. 108, our italics). And this is not some kind of accidental slip of the tongue; unfortunately, Mr Berdiaev systematically spreads such unverified hearsay about the aforesaid socio-philosophical trend. Thus, two years ago, in an article 'The Struggle for Idealism', Mr Berdiaev announced that 'when you want to go forward[7] and serve the idea of the good', evolutionism 'calls us back to the investigation of molluscs', that evolutionism debunks the very idea of the good, portraying it as 'only a useful illusion in the struggle for existence', and that evolutionism wants to conclusively establish 'the level of the moral ideals of fish'. In general, evolutionism 'tries', by any means, 'to quench your idealistic summons toward the truth' (*Mir Bozhii*, 1901, 6, p. 15). We permit ourselves to assure Mr Berdiaev that, being personally familiar – and not at all only by hearsay – with the accused, we have never heard from it the kind of 'twisted words' that Mr Berdiaev relays to us from unknown sources.

As we have shown, Mr Berdiaev's bitter antipathy toward evolutionism is explained by the fundamental conservatism of the very form of 'absolute morality'. But this conservatism is also manifested in a more direct and immediate manner when it comes to the concrete content of 'absolute duty' in the life

---

7 This, evidently, is the same 'forward' that is otherwise known as 'back to Hegel and Fichte' and back to the 'traditions of the immortal Plato'.

of humanity. Incidentally, in depicting his ideals Mr Berdiaev describes them as follows:

> In regard to society, equality that is based on the moral equality of human beings cannot and must not go beyond equal rights and the elimination of classes as the condition of the actual realisation of equal rights, and in regard to psychology, such equality cannot and must not go beyond the similarity of the basic spiritual traits that make each person (p. 128).

So, here at last are the boundaries beyond which the progress of humanity 'cannot and must not' go – progress, which, however, 'can' and 'must' be infinite. We will not undertake to judge what new social needs might arise in society in which there are no classes, and we therefore are not going to especially dispute the part of Mr Berdiaev's assertion that applies to social equality. But, speaking candidly, it seems to us that what he says about 'psychological equality' is not a very high ideal. 'The similarity of those basic spiritual features that make each person' is too near to what exists in the present, and it would be no more than simple justice on the part of Mr Berdiaev if he would permit humanity to go a little further. It seems to us, personally, that what is utterly necessary is such a degree of psychical similarity that people can completely understand one another, that every mental movement of one is completely clear and regular and is not reflected in a distorted way in the psyches of other people when communicating with them. And for this much more is necessary besides a 'similarity of basic spiritual features' without which a person would not be a person. For this, it is necessary first and foremost that personal experience represents a real microcosm of collective experience, that all essential acquisitions of the colossal historical work of humanity are present in the psyche of each person, perhaps in a scaled-down version but one that is true and harmonious.

But Mr Berdiaev goes even further in his structures on progress: 'I think', he says,

> that a spiritual aristocracy is indeed possible in a democratic society, although it will not have anything in common with socio-political oppression. The first impetus to further progress must be the work precisely of such an aristocracy that rises above all social-class and group morality; without it, the reign of stagnation and herd behaviour would set in (p. 128).

Thus, there will be spiritual aristocrats and spiritual plebeians, active heroes and a passive crowd – the social categories of feudal thinking once again. The

issue has nothing to do with simple factual inequality of strength and ability – this kind of inequality still does not provide an active basis for such social
categories. No, the difference between 'initiating individuals' and a 'stagnant,
herd-like' mass is not at all a quantitative difference of strength and ability but
a fundamental, qualitative difference, and the issue obviously has to do with
real privileges and real subordination.

   Let us imagine a comradely circle of people who are consciously striving
toward one common goal that deeply permeates their entire life of feeling and
will and puts its imprint on all their thoughts and ideas. For whomever lived in
such a group – and who lived a real and not an illusory life in it (because there
can be illusory associations) – these relationships would forever remain the
best and most precious of all the things that gave those people living experience. These relationships would be the concrete form of the practical ideals
of our time and simultaneously the embryonic form of the realisation of those
ideals. And what does this mean? In such groups one usually encounters people
who are extremely unequal in mind and will, in psychical development, and in
their fund of experience. This inequality is clear to everyone as a fact, but no
one talks about 'aristocrats' and 'plebeians'. No one's attention is at all focused
on elevating themselves and determining the level of their 'aristocratism'. No
one bothers about whether they 'push' or 'are pushed' as long as they are moving forward. All people in the circle feel that in striving toward their cherished
goal it is only the collectivity that is powerful and that it is incomparably better
to feel oneself to be an integral element of a powerful progressive whole than
to take a superior position and to think of one's comrades as a 'stagnant' and
'herd-like' crowd that must be 'pushed'.

   And what a cruel injustice toward people of ordinary strength and ability
this baseless conviction of Mr Berdiaev's is! According to him even in the best
of circumstances such people are 'stagnant' and need 'aristocrats' to give them
a 'push toward development'! If Mr Berdiaev were familiar with the history
of technological progress, he would know how greatly indebted progress is to
the huge sum of small 'pushes' that are individually almost unnoticeable but
are completely real that are made by people of quite an average level of mind
and will – often even people who are not highly developed and are frequently
rank and file representatives of the army of industrial labour. Mr Berdiaev
would then know that 'aristocrats' – the inventors that are exalted by history –
depend in reality on these 'pushes', which the inventors supplement and sum
up.

   This is how technological progress is accomplished, and Mr Berdiaev knows
that, so far, the movement of all social life has originated in the realm of technology. In a society where 'ideology' will not be the privilege of the few, the

significance of the masses in the ideological sphere must turn out to be the same. And even now, in our opinion, sufficient analysis could reveal that this is partly the way things already are in reality.

Comradely democracy lies entirely beyond Mr Berdiaev's field of vision. He cannot think of democracy in any other way than in the form of a 'herd'. This is a characteristic feature of feudal thinking, for which the 'aristocratism' of the few, on the one hand, and the 'herd-like nature' of the masses, on the other hand, are necessary categories of social life. But how does this go together with Mr Berdiaev's 'moral equality' of all human individuals?

The ideal of the 'spiritual aristocrat' always hovers before Mr Berdiaev's mental gaze, and there is no doubt that the worthy author strives to realise it in life. In so doing, 'mentally aristocratic' manners automatically appear on the scene that, by the way, are evidently not entirely the same as manners that are purely aristocratic.

Pursuant, one can suppose, to the conception of 'mentally feudal' rights and privileges, Mr Berdiaev in his book *Individualism and Subjectivism*[8] revealed a strong propensity to decisively and severely judge (without explaining his motives) those thinkers who seem insufficiently aristocratic to him for some reason. Typical in this regard is his laconic judgement regarding Mr Lesevich.[9] Of this distinguished contributor to Russian philosophical literature, Mr Berdiaev remarks in passing that Mr Lesevich 'stands far from the peak of philosophical recognition' (*Individualism and Subjectivism*, p. 12).

In the article 'The Struggle for Idealism', Mr Berdiaev goes even further. He expresses his severe judgements in a distinctive form that we find difficult to characterise with any academic expression. Marxists, he says, are notable for the 'narrow materialism' of their desires; for them, everything boils down to 'looking for five more kopecks'. Marx's and Engels's 'spiritual horizon is limited'. Utilitarianism is a 'swinish philosophy', etc. But obviously this kind of progress cannot be infinite, and therefore in 'The Ethical Problem' the worthy author remains approximately at the level of the 'Struggle for Idealism'. Let us cite one typical point. Promising to explain the contemporary relationship of his point of view to the point of view of Mr Struve, Mr Berdiaev adds in passing: 'Most of my other critics hardly inspire an answer since their inability to pose philo-

---

8 The actual title of the book is *Subektivizm i individualism v obshchestvennoi filosofii: kriticheskii etiud N.K. Mikhailovskom* [*Subjectivism and Individualism in Social Philosophy: A Critical Study of N.K. Mikhailovsky*] (1901) [trans.].

9 Vladimir Lesevich (1837–1905) was a positivist philosopher who contributed to the popularity of Richard Avenarius and empiriocriticism in Russia [trans.].

sophical questions and their lack of philosophical training is too obvious. Our task in regard to the most important social problems is to replace superficial comment with philosophical treatment' (p. 95 note). In our view, the worthy author reveals here a tendency toward that mixing of 'ought' and 'is' of which he accuses his opponents; after all, the feudal privileges of 'spiritual aristocrats' so far apply only to the realm of 'ought' and not to the sphere of 'is'.[10]

However, let us return to Mr Berdiaev's theoretical views. His specific theory of social development – the main merit of which consists, in our opinion, in its extreme simplicity and lack of complexity – corresponds to the practical tendencies of 'spiritual aristocratism'. Here is how the worthy author formulates it in his article 'The Struggle for Idealism'.

> ... Ideology is not created automatically by economic development, it is created by the spiritual work of people, and ideological development is only the discovery of spiritual values that have eternal meaning independently of any kind of evolution whatsoever. But ideology is really conditioned by the state of productive forces, and economic development really creates the basis for ideological development. In a word, the ideal goals of life are attained only when material means are available. Thus, we recognise the spiritual independence of any ideology and that it is socially conditioned by productive forces and dependent on economic development (p. 20).

So economic development delivers 'material means' and when those means are present, ideology develops 'independently' – this is what Mr Berdiaev's historical philosophy boils down to. With the aid of this philosophy, all sorts of questions regarding the forms and types of ideological development are resolved with remarkable simplicity and ease. The question arises, for example, of why feudal lords had a feudal ideology and why the bourgeoisie had a bourgeois ideology – why the former 'discovered eternal spiritual values' in the form

---

10   We note, by the way, that, when expressing his fundamental agreement with the metaphysics of Hegel, Mr Berdiaev does not cite Hegel but Kuno Fisher's history of modern philosophy. We cannot but strongly doubt that it suits the dignity of a 'spiritual aristocrat' who is called upon to judge the level of 'philosophical training' of his critics to be a 'Hegelian according to Kuno Fisher'. What might the 'superficial' Beltov, one of the undoubted experts on the real Hegel, say about this? [Kuno Fischer (1824–1907) was a German academic philosopher. Beltov was the pseudonym used by G.V. Plekhanov (1856–1918), 'the "father" of Russian Marxism', when writing for the legal press (trans.).]

of the theory of authority and why the latter discovered them in the form of the theory of individualism. Obviously, the following answer is obtained: economic development provided sufficient 'material means' to both classes, and with the availability of these means, the ideologies of both classes took shape completely 'independently'; their 'spiritual content' was utterly independent of the social relationships of these classes. 'Material means' were available in a sufficient amount, but there was no fundamental obstacle preventing the content of the ideologies from developing in an opposite meaning: in the form of an individualist doctrine for feudal lords and in the form of an authoritarian doctrine for the bourgeoisie. There is no point in asking why the 'spiritual work' of these classes proceeded in the direction it did and not in another. One can resolve the question of why vulgar economists distorted science in defence of bourgeois relationships in the same way: they were able to discover 'eternal values', but they did not discover them very successfully. And economics has nothing to do with it, since 'all ideologies are spiritually independent' as long as 'material means' are present. But could not these means be insufficient? Perhaps the content of 'productive forces' in the era of the vulgar economists was lower than in the era of classical economists?

There is no need to explain how useful Mr Berdiaev's historiosophy is for all reactionary doctrines and for justifications of the world as it is. And in this regard, the metaphysical views of Mr Berdiaev on the essence and significance of evil in life is in remarkable harmony with his historiosophy. 'Kant still clung to the view that' ... and so on:

> I stand on the point of view of the metaphysical rejection of evil; I do not see anything absolute in it, and I consider evil to be only an empirical outward appearance, the insufficient realisation of the good. For me, human nature is neither sinful nor depraved. Evil is empirically negative, it is an 'abnormality', i.e. it does not sufficiently correspond to an ideal norm (p. 130).

So, 'evil is the insufficient realisation of the good', i.e. baseness, for example, is the insufficient realisation of the ideal of nobility, a lie is the insufficient realisation of truth, treachery is the insufficient realisation of loyalty, etc. As for reaction, it must be only the insufficient realisation of the idea of progress and no more ... There is no evil, but only good at various stages of realisation; bonfires, torture, the birch rods of executioners, the silver coins of Judas Iscariot – all these are only appearances, there is nothing absolute in them ... What a soothing doctrine! What a pity that those who undergo such an 'insufficient realisation' cannot find satisfaction in it ... But on the other hand, energetic representatives of this 'insufficient realisation', surely endorse Mr Berdiaev's theory with both hands. They say that they are realising the good, only insufficiently, and, all the same, this is better than not to realise it at all. As for the ugly 'appearance' of their deeds, that after all is 'empirical chaos' and no more ...

Mr Berdiaev would probably say that we did not understand him correctly and have confused the denial of 'metaphysical' evil with the denial of 'empirical' evil. But we do not think that reference to the 'Pickwickian' meaning of words changes the essence of the matter. If 'empirical appearance' is a form in which 'metaphysical' content is realised, how can one distinguish between them to the extent of acknowledging something empirically while denying it metaphysically? In any event, meta-logic would be necessary for this, and Mr Berdiaev has so far not been able to reveal its laws to us.[11]

The 'critical' frame of mind – or, better, the critical condition of Mr Berdiaev – can be summed up in the following: doctrines that are reactionary in practice that explain the essence of how the world and society works, feudal categories applied to democratic society, the conservatively-progressive morality of absolute duty, practically-progressive phrases that are arbitrarily interwoven into that morality, and masses of logical contradictions and dogmatic assertions. Let us now turn to his worthy comrade-in-arms, Mr Bulgakov.

Before embarking on an analysis and critique of the theory of progress, the worthy economist attempts to prove the complete validity and necessity of the points of view – metaphysical and mystical – from which he intends to proceed in his exposition. In Mr Bulgakov's opinion this is undeniably proven by the fact that in reality no one can manage without these points of view and, consciously or unconsciously, everyone arrives at them in the end. We will cite the Mr Bulgakov's basic formulation regarding the universality of metaphysical thinking.

All these (anti-metaphysical, A.B.) schools do not deny metaphysics in essence. They only deny certain conclusions and certain methods of metaphysical thinking, and they cannot thereby abolish metaphysical

---

11   About a year has gone by since Mr Berdiaev established forever the *goodness* of human nature in his classically modest antithesis ('Kant assumed ... I think' ...), and now Mr Berdiaev no less resolutely declares: 'Human nature in itself is dual – evil is hidden in its spiritual depths' ... (*Mir Bozhii* 1903, no. 10, 'Critique of Historical Materialism'). Thus, metaphysically intoxicated and 'thinking' in every which way, the contemporary idealist marches toward absolute truth.

questions in the same way that the development of science has abolished questions of woods goblins and house sprites, the elixir of life, the alchemical production of gold, etc.

On the contrary, all these schools, even those that deny metaphysics, have their own answers to its questions. As a matter of fact, if I pose the question of the existence of God, of the essence of things (*Ding an sich*), or of freedom of will, and then answer these questions negatively, I do not at all destroy metaphysics, but, on the contrary, I thereby accept it by accepting the validity and necessity of posing questions that are not accommodated within the bounds of positive knowledge (pp. 3–4).

Mr Bulgakov is probably not unaware that there is a doctrine called Spiritualism, a doctrine whose adepts consider it at the very least a science and even higher than a science. Applying the logic of Mr Bulgakov, these adepts could say approximately the following: 'Contemporary scholars and philosophers, when they have occasion to pose the questions of spirits and mediums usually answer these questions negatively. But by doing so, they do not in the least destroy Spiritualism. On the contrary, they accept it and admit the validity and necessary of posing questions that are not accommodated within the bounds of positive knowledge'.

In supposing that Mr Bulgakov has not yet arrived at this point of view, however, we are doubtful that he could raise any objection to such an argument, aside, perhaps, from pointing out that it is plagiarism of his article. To consider the historical presence of one or another question in people's heads to be sufficient proof that it is universally obligatory and historically universal seems to us to be unreasonable in the highest degree.

But here is yet another mistake. Mr Bulgakov ought to know that since the time of Kant it is not appropriate to consider every given philosophical question as a real question that must be answered. There are questions that appear to be questions only due to their grammatical form and not due to their logical and factual content – questions that are contradictory, content-free, or illusory. Mr Bulgakov also ought to know that modern anti-metaphysical schools view metaphysical questions in precisely this way – they consider them partly illusory, like demonological questions, and partly content-free and contradictory. Thus, in analysing the question of the 'essence of things', Ernst Mach adduced the following formulation: it is a question of what is left over when all the elements of which a real fact is made of are taken away one after another so that nothing remains. Mach's conclusion is this: the 'essence of things' is an expression without an idea. Is such an answer really an 'acceptance of the validity and necessity' of the question of substance?

As can be seen in the citations given above, metaphysical questions are associated in a mysterious way – even in the psyche of Mr Bulgakov, himself – with
questions of woods goblins and house sprites. We are inclined to think that this
fact is fraught with significance.

In preparing to undertake a metaphysical-mystical investigation of the theory of progress, Mr Bulgakov considers it necessary to depict the 'mechanical
worldview' that lies at its base.

> ... According to this view, mechanical causality rules the world. Having
> begun in an unknown time and place – and perhaps existing eternally –
> our world develops according to the law of causality that embraces liv-
> ing matter just as it does dead matter, psychical life just as it does phys-
> ical life. In this dead movement, which lacks any creative thought or
> rational meaning, there is no living principle but only a certain state of
> matter. There is no truth or error, but both are the equally necessary con-
> sequences of equally necessary causes; there is no good and evil, but only
> states of matter that correspond to them (p. 7).

What a truly monstrous worldview! For this worldview, there is 'no truth and
error', and, nevertheless, in violation of all logic, both truth and error exist for
it and are even necessary, as the 'consequences of necessary causes'. For this
worldview, 'there is no good and evil', and there are only 'states of matter' that
'correspond to them', i.e. to these non-existing facts. It is no wonder that after
this, on page eight, Mr Bulgakov becomes horrified: 'Even the most pessimistic
systems turn pale before the chilling horror of this view' ... What could be more
horrible!

But there is no reason for Mr Bulgakov to take fright. His nightmares are
caused by his own fantasy. The 'mechanical worldview' – even in the old and
quite primitive form in which the worthy economist expounds it to his reader
(he cites Holbach[12]) – never denies the existence of good and evil, truth and
error, but only denies that they have an absolute character. It does not see them
as independent elements but as combinations and correlations. In exactly the
same way, the 'mechanical worldview' does not sacrifice the world to 'absolute
chance', as Mr Bulgakov says on page eight, since it considers 'chance' to be no
more than a complex and unexplained causal combination, and it unconditionally rejects 'absolute' chance.

---

12   Baron Paul-Henri d' Holbach (1723–1789) was often cited in Marxist circles as a great 'pre-
      dialectical' materialist [trans.].

Having thus familiarised the reader with the essence of the 'mechanical worldview', Mr Bulgakov finds that he has prepared the ground sufficiently to be able to undertake the exposition of the theory of progress that is part of this worldview.

But it is curious that this mechanical philosophy turns out to be unable to completely sustain the logical development of its principles and ends up attempting to accommodate and embrace teleology and to accept the eventual triumph of reason over unreasoning causality in the same way that this is also done in philosophical systems that issue from the utterly opposite principle. This flight from its own philosophical foundations is expressed in tacit or open admission of the fact that at a certain stage of world development this same principle created human reason, which subsequently began to construct the world in conformity with its own rational goals. This victory of reason over the principle of unreason is accomplished not immediately but gradually, whereby the collective reason of people who are united in a society learn how to use dead nature for their own goals and to conquer nature to an ever greater extent. Thus, dead mechanism gradually yields to rational expediency, to its complete opposite. You already know that I am speaking of the theory of progress, which is a necessary part of all doctrines of the contemporary mechanical worldview.

If it is agreed, following Leibniz, that the appearance of higher reason, higher expediency in the world should be called theodicy, then one can say that the theory of progress is the theodicy for the mechanical worldview without which humanity, apparently, cannot manage. Along with the concept of evolution – goalless and insensate development – the concept of progress is created. Progress is a concept of teleological evolution in which causality and the gradual revelation of the goal of this evolution become completely identical, exactly the same as in the metaphysical systems that have been referred to. Thus, both doctrines (mechanical evolution and progress) – no matter how different their conclusions appear to be – are united by a necessary psychical, if not logical, connection (pp. 8–9).

Such is the theory that 'constitutes a necessary part of all contemporary doctrines of the mechanical worldview', and Mr Bulgakov dedicates his subsequent exposition to elucidating various of its defects. This elucidation, unfortunately, is not complete. Mr Bulgakov did not point out what in our opinion is its worst defect, which is that 'theory of progress' that he presents – the part that Mr

Bulgakov says is a necessary part of that worldview – *does not exist at all* in the 'contemporary mechanical worldview'.

Darwinism and Marxism – these 'contemporary doctrines of the mechanical worldview' – *never created and never acknowledged the kind of 'teleological evolution'* in which causality and the gradual revelation of the goal of this evolution become completely identical, 'exactly the same as' in the ethereal constructions of metaphysics. Scientific theories of progress investigate the question of the causes and courses by virtue of which progress is accomplished and in what direction progress can go, but they never permit themselves to assert that the causal chain of phenomena and the line of progress 'become completely identical'. They never confuse 'teleological evolution' with the real historical process 'just like' metaphysicians do. Noting the possible forms and the necessary conditions of progress, the scientific theory of progress never decides beforehand the question of whether this progress will inevitably be accomplished and whether these conditions must without fail turn out to exist. These are question of fact, questions of concrete historical relationships. Mr Bulgakov, obviously, confuses Darwin with Nägeli[13] and Marx with naïve optimists – of Mr Berdiaev's sort, for example. Darwinism says: if sufficient conditions are present, then natural selection produces an adaptation; if they are not then it removes the unadapted form. Marxism says: if sufficient social forces manage to take shape, then society will be transformed by such-and-such a means; if not, then society will deteriorate. Where, in these cases, is the revelation of the goal of revolution 'completely identical' with causality?

Both Darwinists and Marxists can propose on the basis of certain data – or they can even simply believe by virtue of what they feel – that progress, as they understand it, is being accomplished in reality, but they never confuse their suppositions with the objective regularity of facts or their faith with scientific theory. And if Mr Bulgakov triumphantly finds bad metaphysics in the scientific theory of progress, it is because he put it there himself.

We do not at all assert that Mr Bulgakov consciously distorts the view he is criticising. No, it is obvious that what is going on is that he cannot escape the confines of metaphysical-mystical forms of thinking. He even uses those forms to interrogate scientific theories, and it is therefore natural that these latter radically change their appearance and turn out to be 'just like' metaphysical theories. In this regard, the following passage is characteristic: ... 'Let us therefore concede that the theory of progress has all the attributes of science

---

13   Carl Wilhelm von Nägeli (1817–1891) was a Swiss-German botanist [trans.].

that it has pretentions to. All the same, is this theory capable of satisfying those who seek in it a solid refuge in the basic principles of faith and hope and love?' (p. 15).

We could provide Mr Bulgakov with millions of citations from ancient and modern poets to prove that love is a matter of feeling (and not of scientific theory), but it will hardly be possible for us to convince him, since he cannot but confuse science with religion, and he understands religion in the most Catholic and even super-Catholic spirit, as is evident, for example, in the following passage from his article: ... 'The entire life of a truly religious person, from the most important to the least important, is defined by that person's religion, and hence there is nothing that would be neutral in regard to religion' (p. 5).

If we were talking about a writer who was less Catholically inclined than Mr Bulgakov, we would try to explain to him that scientific theory really provides the basis *for practical activity* precisely in the sense that it points out the most expedient means for attaining goals, once people have set them. One can also think that scientific theory provides 'basic principles' for hope if it can establish the feasibility of these goals, but it has no direct relation to faith (in the religious sense) or to love (in all senses). This is not its realm.

The entire psychical life of a human being, in all of its manifestations, boils down to three basic phases: first of all immediate perceptions and feelings, then cognition, and, finally, action. People *perceive* certain harmful or useful influences, and the perception causes them to experience a *feeling* of pain or pleasure. This feeling draws them to *action*. But in conscious life an intermediary phase arises between feeling and action. This is *cognition*, a phase when the most expedient form of action under the given conditions is worked out on the basis of previous experience. People feel an immediate need and, having ascertained through cognitive activity the means of satisfying it, satisfy it through an act of will that is transmitted to muscular movement.

The process of development of the psyche leads to each of these three phases being increasingly more distinguished from one another and increasingly less confused with one another in consciousness, so that the power and vital significance of each of them grows. When an immediate sensation is admixed with the element of reflection and cognition, the sensation becomes vague, unclear, and less intense. When this outside element is removed, the immediate sensation attains the greatest possible intensity and clarity and leads more quickly and truly to the next phase. When the act of cognition is admixed with the element of immediate feeling or practical desire, cognition loses clarity and becomes unreliable; it is then 'illogical'. When the act of will is mixed with cognition – when people think about what they are doing and about whether what they are doing is expedient at the same time that they are doing it – then action becomes uncertain, indecisive, and falls considerably short of the goal or does not even come close. The greatest fullness and harmony of life is possible for people only when they wholly give themselves up to feeling when they are in the phase of feeling, wholly give themselves up to cognition when they are in the phase of cognition, and wholly give themselves up to action when they are in the phase of action. In this way, the energy of a strong feeling turns into the full energy of pure cognition and then turns into the energy of steadfast action. These phases can change in a fraction of a second but each of them must be whole, otherwise life does not unfold powerfully and harmoniously, and existence is poor and half-hearted.

But the complete differentiation of the three phases is only an *ideal* and up until the present in most cases people act like indecisive, inconsistent beings. Their feelings vacillate. They consider many things to be true because they like them and want them to be true. They act while having doubts. Hybrid, intermediate forms predominate in life. This is the nature of whole vast realms of the worldviews of various social groups and human individuals. *All mysticism and all metaphysics have precisely this significance*: they are undifferentiated forms in which cognition still has not completely freed itself from will and emotion and is coloured by them. In this situation, people accept something as truth not because it issues from their experience and is proven by experience but because they want it to be that way – because it is pleasant for them to believe it to be the truth.

The huge vital significance of criticism is that it consists mainly in liberating cognition from oppression by elements that are alien to it. It thereby facilitates not only the development of cognition but also the development of feeling and will, which suffer from the admixture to them of elements of cognition.[14]

In the actual scientific theory of progress, contrary to Mr Bulgakov's exposition, there is no place for elements of feeling – for faith or love. It is therefore

---

14   Kant's entire doctrine of practical reason, which lies at the basis of the morality of absolute duty, is the product of the invalid confusion of cognition and will. Schopenhauer has pointed out that 'practical reason' is a contradictory concept – something like wooden steel. In actuality, all cognition is *theoretical* in its form. One can, of course, call it 'practical' in its meaning for life because it points out the *means* for expedient activity, but Kant's practical reason is the ultimate authority that determines the very goals of activity. Meanwhile, in the final analysis, the choice of goals is always determined by *feeling*.

Schopenhauer pointed out that such confusion of reason and will corresponds to a level of development of society that has been outlived. He demonstrated the openly authoritarian-teleological nature of absolute duty. In his words, the imperative form of Kantian morality is rooted in the ten commandments of Moses, i.e. as we would say, in the bases of the life of the patriarchal world.

obvious that the analysis and criticism that Mr Bulgakov carries out on what he calls the 'theory of progress' cannot be of interest to us. It is a family affair between himself and his own mysticism-metaphysics. We will cite only one typical passage that is characteristic of the whole confusion that the worthy author arrives at when he operates with scientific-philosophical concepts that are foreign to him:

> The gratifying assurance that everything good and reasonable is invincible and will win out in the end is not supported by the mechanical worldview, since after all everything in it is pure chance. Why will that same chance that exalts reason today not do away with it tomorrow? Why will that chance that makes knowledge and truth expedient today not make ignorance and delusion just as expedient tomorrow? Does history not know of the collapse and death of whole civilisations, or does it testify only to regular and uninterrupted progress? ... (p. 16)

But the essence of the matter consists precisely in the fact that abstract scientific theories – the theory of progress among them – are not at all occupied with instilling 'gratifying assurance' in people as Mr Bulgakov says it does. Active people derive gratifying assurance of victory from the consciousness of their own powers and from the aesthetic perception of the picture of the unfolding struggle of life. People who have no connection with life at its most vital and who do not feel a solid support within themselves seek such 'gratifying assurance' in the 'quackery and charlatanism' of complaisant, optimistic metaphysics. Neither the 'collapse and death of civilisations' nor the absence of 'regular and uninterrupted progress' in the least contradicts the scientific theory of progress that addresses the direction and conditions of progress but that does address whether or not in any given case it is inevitable.

Therefore, Mr Bulgakov's idea that 'absolute chance' (by which he has in mind historical necessity, as we have seen) can make ignorance and delusion 'just as expedient' as truth and knowledge utterly contradicts the theory of progress. The point is that from the point of view of contemporary theories of progress the basic characteristic of truth and knowledge consists precisely in their *social expedience* (Mr Bulgakov should know Simmel,[15] for example). Therefore, ignorance and delusion can never become 'just as expedient' and must always turn out to be socially inexpedient, and if they in fact prevailed,

---

15   Georg Simmel (1858–1918) was a German neo-Kantian philosopher and sociologist [trans.].

it would signify the degradation of a society. And degradation is in its essence not 'expedient'.

Thus, all the contradictions in which Mr Bulgakov is entangled issue from the systematic confusion of scientific-philosophical forms of thinking, which are known by the worthy author but are alien to him, with mystical-metaphysical forms, to which he is accustomed and which he holds dear. The reader can already see how completely Mr Bulgakov is possessed by these mystical-metaphysical forms in the previous article[16] where the worthy author expresses the hope that knowledge will transform into theosophy, social life into theurgy, and social structure into theocracy. We will cite a few more examples from his article on the theory of progress. ... 'There are no unreligious people, but only people who are pious and people who are impious, righteous people and sinners' ... (p. 4) ... 'All the deceptive arguments of the positivists that represent morality as a fact of natural development (and that thereby undermine its holiness by equating it with all other natural needs such as hunger, sexual reproduction, etc.), have to do only with individual forms, particular expressions of morality, but' ... (and more of the same, A.B.) (p. 30).

We will not dwell on the logic expressed in the preceding dictum (to investigate development means to undermine holiness), but the tone ... It is the tone of an inquisitor looking into the hearts of heretics. What must an 'impious sinner', a 'positivist', feel while reading Mr Bulgakov's awful recriminations. Up to this point, Mr Bulgakov has limited himself in his persecution of sinners to quoting with pleasure from Dostoevsky's description of hellish torment,[17] but ... Will this satisfy the moral indignation of the worthy metaphysician for long? What will come next?

To answer this question means to make a prediction, but the question of predictions has been worked over in such detail by Mr Bulgakov in his most recent works, beginning with the book *Capitalism and Agriculture*, that we cannot but take into consideration his views in this area.

Mr Bulgakov divides predictions into three categories. When people of the camp that Mr Bulgakov dislikes 'precisely' determine the approach of future events' and indicate its 'point in space and time', this is 'quackery and charlatanism'.[18] (It would be interesting to know which of Marx's predictions Mr Bulgakov had in mind while applying these amiable expressions to him!) If the people of that same camp try to outline the probable results of tendencies emerging at a given time, then this is a 'platitude, a mental game devoid of

---

16   'Parallels', in the collection *Literaturnoe delo*.
17   'Parallels', *Literaturnoe delo*, p. 128.
18   *Capitalism and Agriculture*, the last page.

serious meaning' ('Theory of Progress', p. 12). But if, finally, Mr Bulgakov himself does the same thing then this is 'a sort of impressionism, not so much a
scientific synthesis as it is an artistic synthesis that is subjectively convincing
but that obviously cannot be convincingly proven' (p. 14).[19] We do not dare to
express an aspiration to an 'artistic synthesis' similar to the synthesis of the
worthy economist, and we do not doubt that Mr Bulgakov will dismiss our
prediction as second-rate, at best. But we suggest that to state tendencies that
are becoming factually manifest means to state facts and to make conclusions
about the future on the basis of these facts, and, to the extent that we have no
reason to expect the immediate cessation of the tendencies that we have discovered, it means to make plausible conclusions about the future. In addition,
for the reader who is inclined to classify predictions precisely from the point
of view of whether or not they are fulfilled, we remind the reader that more
than once the predictions of Russian 'students' have come true concerning the
development of one or another social class, concerning the appearance of one
or another ideological currents, and even concerning the evolution of one or
another ideologist (as was the case even in regard to a most serious and important writer of the ex-Marxist trend).[20]

But now that the topic has turned to predictions, we have no reason to limit
ourselves to Mr Bulgakov, alone. The probable evolution of his worthy comrade-
in-arms, Mr Berdiaev, is of no less interest.

First and foremost, in order that the reader cannot retain doubts concerning
our right to 'predict', we point out the clearly transitional nature of the present
mood or, more accurately, the present moods of both authors.

In fact, what do we find in the current psychical state of Mr Berdiaev – in his
'empirical I', as he expresses it?

Preaching faith in metaphysics but deliberately characterising the construction of metaphysics as 'building castles in the air',[21] accepting scientific evolutionism but also accepting unbelievable stories about evolutionists that are
similar to the naïve narratives of our ancestors about people with horses'
heads,[22] accepting the 'social dependence' of ideology on economics but at the

---

19   If readers find it necessary to verify our brief presentation of Mr Bulgakov's views on
      prediction, they can compare the conclusion of his aforementioned dissertation with
      pages 11–15 of the article we have analysed.
20   This is no doubt a reference to P.B. Struve, the first of the neo-Kantian Marxists to adopt
      idealism in philosophy and liberalism in politics. In polemics with Struve, while he was
      still a Marxist, both Lenin and Plekhanov predicted that Struve would abandon the Marx-
      ist camp [trans.].
21   'Struggle for Idealism', *Mir Bozhii*, 1901, p. 6.
22   Op. cit. and also in *Problemy idealizma*, pp. 103, 108, 112.

same accepting the 'spiritual independence' of ideology,[23] believing in limitless progress but striving to point out the boundaries beyond which progress
'cannot and must not go',[24] accepting the principle of democracy but conceiving of a 'spiritual aristocracy' as an eternal necessity,[25] and so on and so on. It
is clear that the situation cannot remain like this for long. A mutual reaction
must occur between the feudal static elements of Mr Berdiaev's psyche, on the
one hand, and its democratic evolutionary elements, on the other, in which
they mutually even out. What will be the result? Something in between, but
what precisely is clearly indicated by the following passages from Mr Berdiaev's
most recent article: 'The new idealist trend, of which I am proud to consider
myself a part, concludes that the spiritual hunger of the intelligentsia's soul
makes necessary a liberating struggle for "natural law"' (p. 135).

> Liberalism, according to its ideal essence, sets these goals: development
> of human individuality and the realisation of natural law, freedom, and
> equality. Collectivism only opens a new way to implement these eternal
> principles more consistently. The tendency to socio-economic collectiv-
> ism appears to be a useful and even necessary means, but ethical collect-
> ivism and spiritual collectivism is altogether not connected with it and in
> itself is a terrible evil (p. 118n).

This is the starting point of the whole confusion that characterises Mr Berdiaev's outlook, and this is an indication of the end point in which his views will
all come together. What we see here is an intellectual representative of a 'cultivated' class, and at the same time a person who is experiencing only 'spiritual
hunger' – obviously he is satisfied materially. This class is, as is well known, the
bourgeois intelligentsia. In contemporary society, this class is characterised by a
particular historical trend that is signified by the term 'liberalism'. What exactly
Mr Berdiaev's hungry heart is striving for becomes even clearer in the second
quotation in which liberalism appropriates 'ideal essence' as its exclusive and
hereditary privilege and firmly denies such an essence to other intellectual currents. At the same time, it is self-evident that the countless feudal elements of
Mr Berdiaev's psychology that we pointed out earlier cannot disappear without
a trace and define a certain tone that is characteristic precisely of the right wing
of the liberal trend.

---

23   'The Struggle for Idealism', see the citation above.
24   *Problemy idealizma*, see above.
25   *Problemy idealizma*, pp. 127–9, see the citation above.

But, asks the reader, what will become of the elements of Mr Berdiaev's psychology that are indicated by his remark regarding social and economic collectivism as a 'useful and even necessary means'? In our view, there is a misunderstanding in this observation. Mr Berdiaev (who, as we have seen, does not always understand himself with complete clarity) has a habit of using abstract forms of expression, and he talks about principles instead of the people who stand for these principles. Talking about the people who stand for these principles would produce a very insignificant change in his formulation: some groups 'set goals according to their own idealistic essence' and other groups are 'useful and even necessary tools for realising these goals'. Thus, the two ends come together, and harmony is established ...[26]

The situation is different with Mr Bulgakov. We have asserted that other elements of medieval psychology predominate with him – not worldly-feudal but Catholic elements. At the same time, his basic forms of thinking are considerably more definite, due to the fact that, regardless of a great many contradictions, one gets the impression of a certain relative wholeness. And this impression becomes even stronger as the result of a certain consistency of tone and style of his most recent articles – a tone that is generally reminiscent of something like an akathist.[27] It is necessary to add here that he expresses clearly nationalistic tendencies, which we cannot pay closer attention to since they are not allotted much space in the article we are analysing but which could not be clearer in the worthy author's previous articles.[28]

There are also many clearly progressive phrases in Mr Bulgakov's writing, but ... they are tied with a very fine thread to his basic fundamentally reactionary and mystical-metaphysical views. The entire part of his article that has a progressive tendency is substantiated in the following way.

> If we accept that history is no more than the revelation of the Absolute then we have thereby already accepted that history is not governed by chance or the dead determinism of the causal relationship; history is governed only by the determinism of the development of the Absolute. The

---

26   *1906 addition*. Because of censorship, our idea was not expressed clearly here. It is this: the bourgeois intelligentsia, as represented by the 'idealists', will 'set the goals', and the proletariat, and the people in general, will serve as the 'useful and even necessary means' for attaining them.

27   An akathist (*akathistos* in Greek) is a hymn dedicated to a saint, the Mother of God, or one of the persons of the Holy Trinity [trans.].

28   'Parallels' in the collection *Literaturnoe Delo* and 'Ivan Karamazov' in *Voprosy filosofii i psikhologii* for 1903. In general Mr Bulgakov's nationalism is rather accentuated by his reverence for Vladimir Solovev.

causal determinism of history acquires significance only as the auxiliary means toward the goal of the Absolute. And if the Absolute is a synonym for freedom, then the metaphysics of history is the revelation of the principle of freedom in history, the victory of freedom over mechanical causality (p. 35).

'If the Absolute is a synonym of freedom'. Everything related to 'freedom' in Mr Bulgakov's article depends on this 'if', but he makes no attempt whatever to substantiate this 'if' 'metaphysically' (i.e. purely verbally). In time, this thread will fray through, and because everything that is mechanically suspended on this thread from the 'Absolute' is not organically connected with neo-Catholic principles and even directly contradicts them, it will fall away of its own accord. Then Mr Bulgakov will be a welcome guest for that influential group in contemporary society to whom these 'principles' are dear, and, blossoming in a more favourable atmosphere, he will stand out as a glittering 'darling of the gods and the landed elite', as the Germans nicknamed their late minister Miquel,[29] who while an ardent youth found Marx himself to be too moderate. The worthy economist now occasionally displays a quite clearly and distinctively 'impartial' point of view on the class struggle for and against the bourgeoisie – the exact same point of view taken quite gladly by the landed elite when the class struggle does not affect them in an immediately unpleasant form. We will cite a passage that is particularly characteristic in this regard.

... Class struggle is a form of the assertion of one's right to share in the blessings of life. In the distribution of these blessing there are those who are deprived and those who do the depriving – the have-nots and the haves (the bourgeoisie), as our Herzen put it – but from the ethical point of view both the struggling parties are equal, inasmuch as they are not led by ethical and religious enthusiasm but by purely egoistical goals (pp. 25–6).

We will not take up an analysis of what this idea means in its essence, but we will pause to answer such questions as, for example, whether it is possible to accept the 'egoistic' struggle for development – even if without 'enthusiasm' – as being ethically equal with the struggle for parasitism – even if with great

---

29   Johann von Miquel (1828–1901) was a radical socialist as a young man but became a conservative government servant in later life. While serving as Prussian Minister of Finance from 1891–1901, he was sympathetic to landed interests and was reviled by the middle class and industrialists [trans.].

'enthusiasm' (since enthusiasm is possible in any class struggle – let us recall the aristocrats who died heroically in the days of the French Revolution). We only note that this is the point of view of a third class (for example the landowners), who often look from the side lines at the struggle of the first two classes – the bourgeoisie and proletariat – and who, serving their own interests, support sometimes one and sometimes the other. (There is no need to explain whom they mostly support.)

The reader can see that our 'prediction' boils down to stating the tendencies that are *factually* evident in the works of both authors but that have only so far not been brought to harmonious unity. We believe in the intellectual power of our worthy opponents and do not doubt that in the not-too-distant future they will be able achieve to attain this unity. By doing so, their theoretical and publicistic activity will profit greatly, not only in the sense of formal wholeness, but – we say this with utter sincerity – in the sense of objective value.

But, the reader asks us, if you have no doubts about this, then is it not all the same to you? Sooner or later the matter will clarify itself, and why take on such a risky thing as a 'prediction'? Ah, reader, but for a long time we and people who are close to us in spirit have found ourselves in the awkward position of someone who must repeat the same prayer day and night: 'Save us, Lord, from our friends, and we will deal with our enemies ourselves'. Our worthy opponents still continue to pass off as the newest Marxist criticism what long ago would have been considered old bourgeois dogma. They still are threatening to 'single out the healthy and living elements of Marxism', not understanding how unwise and hopeless such an operation is for a living and developing organism. While chiefly struggling against Marxism, they still call themselves critical Marxists. An extremely harmful confusion has issued from all this, which is all the more difficult to untangle, since, speaking objectively, the two sides have far from equal access[30] to the means of expressing themselves.[31]

Our goal will have been attained if it has become clear to the reader how fundamentally different the two worldviews are and how incompatible with

---

30   Under the conditions of censorship in Russia before the Revolution of 1905, revolutionary
      Marxists like Bogdanov, had greater difficulty than 'critical' Marxists in publishing their
      works [trans].

31   This was written in 1902. Since then, the ex-Marxists have ceased to interfere in other
      people's business.
      Addition in 1906. Mr Berdiaev now writes in the journals of the right wing of the
      liberal 'Kadets' and is predominantly engaged in a struggle against Social Democracy.
      Mr Bulgakov has not yet gone over to the side of the agrarian elite (the revolutionary
      era has slowed his movement to the right), but his clericalism is taking on an ever less
      'enlightened' and ever more *Eastern Orthodox* hue.

the bases of the contemporary ideological class movement are the medieval elements that they are trying to foist off on it from the outside. Our goal will be doubly gained if we succeed in speeding up the development of our worthy opponents' self-awareness and bringing that hoped-for moment closer when the pious neo-Catholics and the noble feudal lords of castles in the air finally understand themselves and decisively announce, 'What is Hecuba to us'?

CHAPTER 6

A New Middle Ages: On the Benefit of Knowledge

An article by Mr N. Berdiaev, 'Critique of Historical Materialism', was published last year in the October issue of *Mir bozhii*. The modest title far from adequately expresses the real wealth of content of the article, but, then on page three a precise plan is provided that immediately explains things for the reader. Here is the plan:

> ... I limit my task and will subject to examination *only* (my italics, A.B.) the following questions that seem to be to be particularly important. First and foremost, I begin with a critique of the methodological confusion of the economic materialists that immediately stands out and makes it difficult to determine exactly what scholarly discipline we are dealing with. Along with this, I will offer a critique of sociological monism – and scientific monism in general – which I thoroughly reject. I will then turn to a critique of quantitative, mechanical evolutionism and its application to sociology, and I will point out the necessity of a new theory of development. Having undermined (hm ... A.B.) the premises that monism and evolutionism (quantitative) provide to materialist sociology, I will then be able to turn to a critique of the central problem, the problem of the relationship between 'economics' and 'ideology'. Finally, I turn to the theory of class struggle and, in particular, to the theory of 'class ideology'. In conclusion I will speak of the supra-class nature of political ideology and the role of the intelligentsia.

Mr Berdiaev does this – and much else along the way – in the subsequent 27 pages of his article ...

The reader understands, of course, that under such conditions even the famous conciseness of the ancient Spartans would be insufficient for a 'critical' elucidation and resolution of the questions he has outlined. All that can be squeezed into an essay of this size is a series of corresponding theoretical *decrees* in which justification and reasoning are no more possible than in the well-known – and not at all theoretical – ukases of Peter the Great that begin with the expression 'inasmuch as'.

As regards Mr Berdiaev's decrees, it is obvious that neither a critique nor a polemic would be appropriate on our part. All that one can do is submit or rebel. For various reasons, however, we will refrain from either and limit ourselves to an attempt to provide the reader an idea of the nature and content of the aforesaid decrees.

The basic purport of these decrees is clearly expressed in the following words (p. 1): 'The materialist dogmatics that still infect too many people must be pulled up by the roots, and those roots are the dogmas of historical materialism that are taken on faith by the majority – and especially the so called "class" point of view' ...

So, the main object of Mr Berdiaev's administrative-theoretical attack is 'the class point of view'. He devotes many heated words to it. For example: 'The class point of view on ideology is the crowning false conclusion of a whole series of false premises: from false monism and evolutionism, from a false view of the relationship between economics and ideology, from a false understanding of the sociological theory of the struggle of groups' (p. 23).

Having rooted out the class point of view, however, it is necessary to provide something to replace it. This is not particularly difficult for Mr Berdiaev:

> ... We can further assert the following paradoxical proposition: that this very class struggle – the growth of its power and consciousness – is possible only because of the weakening of class antagonism, because of the merging of various natural groups. The human individuality of workers develops only to the extent that the group they belong to intersects with other groups and draws close to them, to the extent that their group narrow-mindedness weakens and individuals obtain impressions not only from their narrow group but from the entire totality of social relationships, from the most varied manifestations of culture. The same can be said about the human individuality of the members of the group of the third estate. It developed in the past to the extent that its sharp difference from the aristocracy was erased, and at the present time it can still develop only to the extent that its difference from representatives of the working class is erased (pp. 19–20).

But how narrow this 'class point of view' is! It turns out that it forbids the representatives of each class to obtain impressions not only from its own 'narrow group' but also from all social life. What a pity that we did not know this before now! Could there really be the kind of idiots who would give in to such unbearable despotism? We had naively supposed that, as a 'point of view', the 'class point of view' serves to elucidate and classify *all sorts* of impressions obtained from social life. But now Mr Berdiaev has defined it, and there is no room for any ambiguities.

And now, reader, you know your duty and can carry it out. If you are an honest bourgeois, then you must 'erase your sharp differences' first 'with the aristocracy' and then 'with the representatives of the working class'. If you are a proletarian, 'erase your differences with the bourgeoisie and the aristocracy', etc. There is only one thing here that is not clear: exactly which differences is it necessary to erase?

All differences? Apparently not ... But which exactly? After all, there are differences, and there are differences. It is a pity that Mr Berdiaev did not explain this to us. There is a risk of error here; it would not be good if you erase the ones that should not be erased ...

But no, Mr Berdiaev is prescient. He cannot leave us in such a hopeless situation. It is true that he has not pointed out to us precisely which 'features of difference' to 'erase' and which not to, but he has pointed out with sufficient specificity to whom one should properly turn for clarification. The point is to 'rise above the narrowness of class psychology'. Obviously, a certain 'supra-class' is needed that would have the power to do this for itself and then teach it to us. The intelligentsia is just such a supra class:

> ... The creator and bearer of political ideology is the inter-class, or, more accurately, the supra-class intelligentsia, i.e. that part of humanity in which the ideal side of the human spirit overcomes group narrow-mindedness. Members of the intelligentsia do not have an immediate tie with any economic group. They are people with the greatest inner freedom, they live first and foremost for the sake of reason and the intellect, and their predominating passion is spiritual hunger ... (p. 28)

One rarely meets people who are capable of providing such an impartial and unexaggerated evaluation of the very group to which they themselves belong. Of course, vulgar materialists will refer to history and assert that the intelligentsia was always one of the least independent groups of society, that it always vacillated between the ruling class and the class that was trying to overthrow it, that too often it did not turn up on the side of the progressive forces of society, that in June 1848 the uniformed supra-class university and polytechnic students turned up side-by-side with the uniformed soldiers of Cavaignac,[1] and that in May 1871 the greater part of the intelligentsia stood behind Ver-

---

1   The reference is to the 'June Days' uprising of Parisian workers during the Revolution of 1848. General Louis-Eugène Cavaignac was in charge of the military force that suppressed the uprising [trans.].

sailles,[2] and so on and so on ... But all these considerations are rooted, obviously, merely in class narrowness, and people who 'obtain impressions not only from their narrow group' need not bother themselves with examining such assertions.

Enjoying the benefits of the enlightened leadership of the intelligentsia that drags us from the swamp of class narrowness and elevates us to their supra-class heights, we must, in our turn, serve this same intelligentsia in some way. Simple justice demands it: 'The intelligentsia is elevated above the narrowness of each of the other social groups, understanding its liberalism in the actual, idealistic meaning of the word, but at the same time *making use of all these groups as its real basis*' (p. 29, my italics, A.B.).

Dear reader – bourgeois, proletarian, aristocrat – I see from this how flattered you are by this glittering prospect: to serve as the 'real basis' for the intelligentsia in the attainment of its 'idealistically understood' goals. What? You disagree? You find that you are a human being and not a pedestal, that you yourself understand your tasks with sufficient idealism? Oh, you ungrateful wretch! All right then, stagnate in your class narrowness! The idealistic intelligentsia will abandon you and depart into the transcendental spheres of metaphysics from whence it will look with contempt on all you vile slaves of 'group limitedness'.

But no! No matter how great your sin, the attempt to save you must be made. This class narrowness ... In order to pull it up 'by the roots', it is necessary to seek out and destroy all its 'roots and threads'. Let us take, for example, scientific evolutionism. There is no doubt that it is closely connected with the entire theory of historical materialism and also, consequently, with the 'class point of view': ... 'Quantitative, mechanical evolutionism is just as untenable and just as unscientific as monism. It must be opposed by another, new theory of development' (p. 9).

And Mr Berdiaev immediately 'opposes' it. The basic thought of the new theory is this: ... 'Development is precisely a disclosure and an unfolding. Something that is both fundamental and internal to it becomes external and attains its greatest possible expression' ... (p. 11).

Perhaps a reader who is familiar with biology will say that this is really not so new: it is simply the expression in a metaphysical form of a fragment of an embryological theory of evolution that has been rejected as fruitless and unscientific. (The term 'embryological theory' specifically refers to the idea that

---

2   Versailles was the headquarters of the anti-Communard forces during the Revolution of 1871. The Paris Commune was suppressed by the army in May 1871 [trans.].

everything that will later be realised in an adult organism and in all of its descendants already exists in an embryo). In the past, amusing debates based on this theory were carried on between the Spermatists and Ovulists.[3] Darwin himself vainly attempted to update it in his theory of pangenesis. The dying echoes of this embryological theory are heard in the Weissmannism[4] that is hopelessly living out its days. And now Mr Berdiaev, having dedicated himself to service in honour of such a decrepit beauty demands that we bow down to this Dulcinea ...

But now that Mr Berdiaev has decisively announced that this is a 'new' theory, we must agree. Except it is a new theory of an ancient sort, and Mr Berdiaev considers this to be such a great virtue that he announces with pride: 'This theory of development presupposes metaphysical pluralism (spiritualistic monadology) and originates in Plato's doctrine of ideas' (p. 11, note).

Many people would suppose that it is useless and wrong in the highest degree to support an idea that is extremely questionable – and that was even rejected long ago by developing human knowledge – by reference to its connection with another idea that is just as questionable and was rejected even longer ago ... But all these objections are obviously the obsolete prejudices of 'positivism'. However, the 'roots and threads' are still not exhausted. There remains one 'root' that is probably the most harmful: scientific monism.

> ... It is characteristic that much is said about monism only in regard to the sciences that are not developed and that have still not separated their tasks from the tasks of metaphysics. Nothing is heard about monistic astronomy and monistic physics, and comparatively little is said about monistic biology. More is said monistic psychology, and very much more is said about monistic sociology ... (p. 6).

Enough! At this point I am unable to joke anymore, and I will speak seriously. To be ignorant is the inalienable 'natural right' of everyone, but a *writer* should not abuse this right. Mr Berdiaev 'has not heard' of monistic physics and 'has heard little' of monistic biology! But if he were even a little acquainted with these sciences, whose name he takes in vain, then he would know that all con-

---

3 In the eighteenth century, Ovulists believed that the ovum was more important for embryonic development than the sperm, while the Spermatists believed it was the other way around [trans.].

4 August Weismann (1834–1914) was a German neo-Darwinist who held that the ovum and sperm are not affected by changes in the body, which meant that characteristics acquired during life could not be passed on to offspring [trans.].

temporary physics *is already strictly monistic*, since it treats all phenomena as fundamentally homogenous by considering them as energetical processes and by subordinating all particular laws to one universal law – the principle of the conservation of energy. Mr Berdiaev would also know that the predominant biological theory is also strictly monistic, treating all the phenomena of life as fundamentally homogenous – as processes of adaptation to the environment. And so on and so on.

Mr Berdiaev is abusing his right. Last year I had the honour of explaining to him that he *does not know* the modern positivists to whom he refers.[5]

This year a scholarly reviewer in a specialised journal – an idealist philosopher himself – felt compelled to direct Mr Berdiaev's attention to gaps in his education in another realm of philosophy and concluded his remarks about him with the words: 'it is necessary to study'.[6] Now readers can judge for themselves regarding Mr Berdiaev's *scientific* education. We are fully justified in liberating ourselves from further polemics with this worthy author.

Incidentally, such a polemic would be unproductive labour for yet another reason. Having decreed one or another 'truth', Mr Berdiaev often countermands it with a subsequent decree. Last year he said, for example, that only metaphysics is monistic,[7] and this year he announces that 'the future belongs to metaphysical monopluralism'.[8] Last year he declared that human nature 'is not sinful but is innocent' and evil is 'an empirical outward appearance',[9] and this year he has found that human nature is 'inherently dual and evil lies in its spiritual depths',[10] etc. What is there to carry on a polemic with, and what would be the purpose of doing so? Would it not be better to wait until Mr Berdiaev himself countermands what he decrees at any given moment?

But there is yet another thing in Mr Berdiaev's article that should be explained for his own good. Categorising his opponents as a '*quantité négligeable* in regard to ideology', he adds, 'I have in mind the polemic against me by orthodox writers[11] which I had no possibility of answering directly'. What does this

---

5 *Voprosy filosofii i psikhologii*, 1902, Nov.–Dec. [This was Bogdanov's response to Berdiaev's critical review of Bogdanov's *Poznanie s istoricheskoi tochki zreniia* (trans.).]

6 *Voprosy filosofii i psikhologii*, 1903, Mar.–Apr. [This is a reference to a review of *Problems of Idealism* by Iulii Eichenwald (1872–1928), a literary critic. The full quotation is, 'All the ideas that Mr Berdiaev has taken from German philosophers need further reasoning and deeper mastery. More study is necessary ...' (trans.)].

7 *Voprosy filosofii i psikhologii*, 1902, Sept.–Oct., an article by Mr Berdiaev.

8 *Mir bozhii*, 1903, 'Kritika istoricheskogo materializma', No. 10, p. 9.

9 *Problemy idealizma*, p. 130.

10 *Mir bozhii*, 1903, No. 10, p. 21.

11 Bogdanov wrote this article in 1904, when tsarist censorship made it difficult to discuss

passage mean? That there are so many incorrect 'orthodox' writers who began to engage in polemics with Mr Berdiaev under *conditions that are objectively inaccessible to him? This is not true. Mr Berdiaev has no such opponents.* No one published a polemic against him in a venue in which he 'had no possibility' of answering his opponents if he really wanted to.[12] There are two possibilities here: it is either an improper polemical ploy, or, what is more likely, Mr Berdiaev used the word 'impossibility' not in an objective but in a petty-minded meaning. This is his dilemma.

In bringing my remarks to a close, I cannot but express apprehension that previous critics of Mr Berdiaev, of whom the writer of these lines is one, have rather sinned against him. In treating with great seriousness everything that Mr Berdiaev has been pleased to write, they have greatly contributed to the growth in him of an extreme overestimation of his powers and knowledge. This obviously now prevents him from taking up the task that is most necessary for him – filling the gaps in his scientific and philosophical education.

---

radical politics. By 'orthodox', Berdiaev meant 'orthodox Marxists'. This also explains why the next footnote was added in the second edition when it was published in the 1906 edition, after censorship was greatly relaxed [trans.].

12   This is in regard to a polemic in *Zaria* [*Dawn*]. Mr Berdiaev wrote against the Marxists in legal journals, which at that time were all but inaccessible to the Marxists. *Later addition.*

CHAPTER 7

A New Middle Ages: Echoes of the Past

'Thou shalt not make unto thee any graven image' ...

∴

There is a huge fundamental difference between *theoretical conviction* and *faith*. When a person decides questions that arise by means of pure cognition, the answers that are obtained can be more or less certain – from simple 'opinion' or supposition to precise knowledge. But, as Kant explained long ago, among all these levels of confidence there is none that could be called 'faith'. The difference here is not simply quantitative but 'qualitative', and it consists in the fact that faith is not only a matter of knowledge but also of *will* – and even mainly will. Theoretical conviction says: on the basis of such and such facts and proof, I *think* such and such. Faith says: neither facts nor proof are important to me – I *feel* that it is so. Here 'I feel' simultaneously means both 'I think' and 'I want', or, more accurately, 'I think because I wish' that it were so.

People often attempt to theoretically substantiate and prove the truth of their faith, but those with strong and steadfast faith always reject such attempts. In fact, real faith has no need of theoretical supports. It is founded on a will that is uncompromising and true to itself, and arguments mean nothing to such a will. If faith begins to look for arguments, then it is obvious that the will is not steadfast, and faith has already been shaken. Living faith does not seek proof, and it does not even want it; it would be superfluous and useless ballast.

This does not alter the fact, however, that in life faith and theoretical conviction can both run in parallel and compete with one another. The same questions can be both stated and answered from the point of view of faith and from the point of view of theoretical knowledge. Sometimes there are even combinations in which a question is stated from one point of view and answered from another. Most often, however, both elements are combined or, more accurately, muddled up in the most varied proportions with the two criteria continually replacing one another. The intellectual result of this has nothing in common with either the virginal naiveté of faith or the cold purity of knowledge.

Various manifestations and traces of such confusion can be found in almost every realm of thought, but in the process of the development of humanity the reign of intellectual chaos has gradually narrowed and in our time for the most part extends only to the sphere of the so called 'ultimate' or, to put it differently, 'accursed' questions, such as the questions of the essence of the world, the meaning of life, the origin of good and evil, and so on.

Let us compare the different approaches to the same question taken from the point of view of pure knowledge, the point of view of faith, and the confused point of view that results from combining the two. Let us take one of the 'accursed questions' – the meaning of evil in life.

In order to pose this question clearly and precisely, a representative of scientific philosophy tries first and foremost to determine the entire sum of real facts from which the question and the need to resolve it arise. In so doing, we find that that the question has to do with the suffering that living beings must directly experience in the face of various conflicts with spontaneous nature and with other beings. Once this is established, the task becomes clear for the investigator, who expresses it in approximately the following way:

First it is necessary to determine under what real conditions suffering appears and under which conditions it increases, diminishes, and disappears.

Second, it is necessary to determine the results of suffering for the being that suffers – in the sense of the development or degradation of its life – and to determine under what conditions this occurs: how suffering influences that being in its subsequent relationship with external nature and with other living beings, in what sense and within what bounds suffering is a positive or negative condition for future suffering or pleasure, etc.

Thus, the point is to find the place of suffering in the vital chain of causes and effects. If the investigator resolves this task – even though approximately – they possess a definite *theoretical conviction* about the meaning of evil in life. How does the acquisition of this conviction relate to the *will* of the investigator?

On the one hand, the starting point for the investigation is, of course, the impetus on the part of the investigator's will, but this is only the *will to knowledge*. Later in the process of investigation, that will maintains neutrality and does not exhibit any demands or requirements in regard to the results of the investigation: cognition is 'pure cognition'. Once theoretical conviction is obtained, what does this have to do with the investigator's will? The will can *be guided by that conviction* in its striving toward particular goals. If, for example the immediate elimination of suffering is set as a goal, then the theoretical conviction that has been worked out shows what conditions must be realised in order to attain that goal and within what limits it is in general attainable. If the development of life in its fullness and harmony is set as the goal, then the theory explains to what degree and under what circumstances suffering can serve as a means to attain this goal, and when, just the opposite, suffering is an obstacle on the path toward it, etc. In a word, theory marks out for the will the means to *master* suffering – to remove it or to make it the means to achieve the goals that the will has established. And the more 'purely' cognition had created the theory and the less it was interfered with in its work by *practical* will, the better and the more completely the theory will fulfil its task.

Now let us see in what form the same question of the meaning of evil in life appears from the point of view of faith. In order not to distort the ideas of other people, we will take a ready-made formulation coming from the pen of a contemporary exponent of faith.

> This is the problem of theodicy (divine truth, A.B.) in the proper meaning of the word ... It is the greatest and most important problem not only of metaphysics and history but also of all moral philosophy. A 'justification of the good' must be provided here ... that must at the same time be a justification of evil – evil in nature, in humankind, in history. Philosophy must show the internal impotence of evil, its illusory nature, and – terrible to say – its ultimate rationality.[1]

The issue is completely clear: as this man of faith further points out, philosophy 'must', it stands to reason, resolve the question with complete 'honesty' but in such a way that without fail evil turns out to be 'impotent' and 'illusory', and, of course, 'rational'. Philosophy 'must' arrive at precisely this resolution and at no other. 'Why must it?' you ask. 'Well, because', answers this man of faith, 'with a different resolution it would not be faith and there would be no point in living'. In other words, it is necessary because it is desirable to me in the highest degree. The question is decided by the will, and 'philosophy' must 'freely subordinate itself and create suitable wording. If it does not do this, then' ... but we will subsequently see what will happen to it in the event of a conflict with the will.

Let us suppose that philosophy is subordinated to the 'primacy' of the will and answers the question in the sense demanded. What does philosophy give to this man of faith? Of course, it does not point out either new methods of struggle with evil or new means of transforming evil into a means toward the

---

1 S. Bulgakov, 'Osnovnye problemy teorii progressa' ['Basic Problems of the Theory of Progress'] in *Problemy idealizma*, p. 34. The passage cited was somewhat changed in the second edition of the article – in Mr Bulgakov's collection *Ot marksizma k idealizmu* [*From Marxism to Idealism*] – but the change did not affect its essence, and it was only put in a somewhat milder (less histrionic) form. We have chosen the more expressive formulation (cited *passim*). [For an English translation of Bulgakov's article see Poole 2003 (trans.).]

good. It cannot *really* subordinate evil to human will. It provides something different: 'gratifying conviction, the joy of which cannot be like anything on earth', as the same author explains a few lines later. There can be no question that with such a conviction life is considerably easier and more peaceful.

But here is a third, confused way of posing the question:

> Philosophy must honestly take all the dimensions of this question into consideration and not faint-heartedly evade and deprecate its difficulty; it must fearlessly look hope and despair in the eye. The philosophy that endures this struggle victoriously and travels this thorny and agonising path of doubts without losing any of its former conviction that existence is rational and that truth will triumph will be worthy of its name and will teach humankind ... Happy, oh thrice happy, are those who are able to honestly and piously suffer through to this gratifying conviction, since nothing on earth can be as joyous as this conviction.[2]

True steadfastness in faith is a very rare phenomenon in our times, and this explains the fact that after this author has given a comparatively straightforward statement of the question in the spirit of faith, we often find that he makes another statement that permits certain 'doubts' and 'difficulties', that permits the question 'in all its dimensions'. In other words, he does what is completely natural for an objective investigation in which the question is not answered in advance and but what is not natural for philosophical faith in which the possibility of a negative resolution was removed in advance from the 'dimensions' of the question of the meaning of evil, and all 'difficulties' and 'doubts' were removed along with it.[3]

What does a person gain by resolving the question on the basis of this third statement of it? Nothing more than the second method of resolving the question plus in addition perhaps remorse for former doubts that sinned against faith and joy that those doubts have been overcome. But until the appropriate resolution is achieved, the unpleasant risk still remains of resolving the question in the spirit of despair and of 'suffering through' to the loss of all hope. It is clear that this path is the worst.

---

2 *Problemy Idealizma*, pp. 34–5 *passim*.
3 This entire second statement of the question is completely thrown out by Mr Bulgakov in the second edition of his article. He also discards the words 'terrible to say' in the preceding citation – words that also indicate a certain doubt and uncertainty of faith (true faith can never find it 'terrible to say' something it agrees with). Obviously, Mr Bulgakov's hesitations are over and his faith has strengthened.

But, a knowledgeable reader observes, you have not depicted with complete accuracy how questions are resolved by means of faith in the sense that you overstate the subordination of thinking to practical will. The fact that thought enjoys a certain freedom in this regard is shown by the very fact that *different* answers to the same questions are given by different systems that think in terms of faith. Actually, for example, on the very question of the meaning of evil in life one metaphysician tells us one thing, another metaphysician tells us another thing, while a third tells us a third thing. A student of Plato tells us that evil is not truly real because true reality pertains only to 'ideas', and evil is the failure of empirical things to match their ideas – their ideas are incompletely realised. A student of Mani would talk about the struggle of two absolutely fundamental principles – good and evil – and of the inevitable ultimate victory of the former. Mr Bulgakov, a student of the contemporary gnostic, Vladimir Solovev, uses the words of his teacher to talk about the domestic relationships between the Absolute and the World Soul, and so on and so on.

Given all of this, what follows from it? If will predetermines both the statement of the question and the basic meaning of the answer that must be obtained, then thinking can naturally reward itself for its subordination to that will by being utterly capricious in the way in which it carries out what has been predetermined. But, no matter how subordination is combined with capriciousness, there will never be what is referred to as freedom. There will be only the manifestation of the two inseparably bound aspects of authoritarian psychology – the psychology of subordination and domination in which thinking takes on the role of the slave, which, taking advantage of moments of freedom, engages in licentious orgies.

Nevertheless, even this capriciousness in the means of carrying out what has been predetermined has quite narrow boundaries, or, more accurately, is associated with quite significant difficulties and discomforts. The fact is that different resolutions of the same questions, even if they agree in their basic meaning, still necessarily, because they all cannot be adopted simultaneously, come into conflict as they compete to dominate minds. What happens then? Let us begin with the facts of reality.

Here is what Mr Bulgakov has to say about the historical relationships of faith and reason:

> ... In living or 'concrete' consciousness ... three sources of knowledge – faith, reason, and experience – are all inseparably united. In the history of philosophy one of them at a time stands out, and the other two appear to be folly, even though living consciousness never gets rid of –

and cannot get rid of – them. In the era when theology – abstract clericalism – predominated, only the rights of blind faith were recognised
and not the enlightened 'whore' of reason, as Solovev has expressed it.
For the sake of faith, the bonfires of the Inquisition were lit against free
investigation. Centuries passed and faith befell the very same persecution from reason and science to which it, in its time, had subjected them:
the most legitimate and sacred demands of faith were ridiculed or simply
ignored.[4]

Let us make an important correction: 'the bonfires of the Inquisition' were considerably more impartial than Mr Bulgakov describes them. They 'were lit' not
only against free investigation but also – and even more so – against free faith,
against any creative work in matters of faith. 'Reason and science' also were not
so one-sided; they more often ridiculed and then ignored not 'sacred demands'
but poor theoretical constructs. And both reason and science were quite consistent and honest in their 'persecutions'. But here is the question: what has
possessed Mr Bulgakov that he can cold-bloodedly write the words 'the very
same persecution'? How can ridiculing and ignoring be 'very same persecution'
as bonfires. I, a partisan of 'reason and science', permit myself to discuss the
enlightened clericalism of Mr Bulgakov in a facetious tone and do not attach
great significance to his dogmatic propaganda. Am I 'the very same persecutor'
as the inquisitor who burned Giordano Bruno?! Well, Mr Bulgakov knows how
to put his position in the best light ...

Mr Bulgakov has not perceived the extremely profound fundamental difference – a moralist would call this an 'ethical' difference – between the methods
of struggle in both cases. And this difference proceeds from the basic content
of those principles whose struggle is under discussion.

When theoretical conviction struggles against other convictions, the essence
of the matter can be expressed in the following formula: 'I think this way, they
think differently, and it is therefore necessary to *refute* them'. To refute means
to show that a given idea is internally contradictory or that it is contradicted
by the facts. It is necessary to demonstrate this not only to an opponent but
also to anyone who might become acquainted with the opponent's ideas, and
for this it is necessary to describe the contradiction in a vivid, clear, accessible
form. This form is above all humorous, all the more so, since the essence of
the 'comic' consists precisely in the easy overcoming of contradictions by the
psyche. This is what 'ridicule' is. Sometimes contradictions are too obvious –

---

4 *Ot marksizma k idealizmu*, pp. 207–8, *passim*.

then there is no point in formally refuting them and it is better to ignore them. This is the logic of purely theoretical struggle.

The struggle of faith against faith is another matter, and here the formula that expresses the struggle between theoretical convictions does not work. Faith, as a primary undifferentiated form, contains elements of both thinking and will, with the latter being decisively predominant. 'I believe this and they believe something else' – this contradiction, if it is taken out of its embryonic form and unpacked, breaks down into two formulas: 'I think this way and they think something else' and 'I *want* this, and they *want* something else'. The conclusion from the first formula is the same as earlier: 'consequently, it is necessary to refute them', and hence there are theoretical arguments between people who believe differently. But the conclusion from the second formula is obviously utterly different. One will cannot 'refute' another will; it can only crush it or destroy it. Torture and bonfires proceed from this according to an inescapable logic. In *this*, the Inquisition did not err; it possessed excellent logic that was far from its contemporary mushy, sentimental descendants. And this makes complete sense: after all, the Inquisition had real power, and because of this there was no need for it to back away from the extreme practical conclusions of its own worldview.

Here is the factual boundary to 'freedom' – or, more accurately, capriciousness – in matters of faith.

II

From the preceding, it is obviously possible to draw the conclusion that with the transition from faith-based thinking to rigorous cognition, the content of life shrinks: after all, in so doing elements of will are *removed* from the sphere of thinking and consequently less remains than there was before. This is precisely Mr Bulgakov's opinion.

Due to the specific features that have been pointed out, the sphere that is accessible to faith is broader than the sphere that is accessible to discursive thinking. It is even possible to believe something that is not only utterly indemonstrable but that also cannot be made completely comprehensible to reason, and this realm properly constitutes the special possession of faith. Consequently, in examining the matter exclusively from its formal aspect, we must say that the knowledge (no matter, I repeat, how unsuitable this word is here) that faith provides is richer and broader than the knowledge that experiential science and metaphysics provide. If metaphysics bursts the boundaries of experiential knowledge, then faith destroys the boundaries of what is intelligible.[5]

We naturally leave the question of metaphysics to the side; this intermediary form does not concern us now since the question has to do with more particular and extreme types of thinking. It is important to explain how psychical life changes when the phase of cognition and the phase of faith are strictly differentiated from one another and cease to be combined together.

Cognition, having been liberated from the authoritarian interference of the will, obviously profits. It profits, first and foremost, in the sense that it becomes 'freer' in its creative work and gains the possibility of not shrinking from conclusions that previously were psychologically impossible because they were offensive to 'feeling' (the word 'feeling' in these cases is a loose definition of the general tenor of the will). Cognition also profits in the sense that new fields are opened for investigation that were previously utterly inaccessible to it – such as, for example, the objective nature and origin of the thinking of believers in all its various forms. (*In itself* faith-based thinking can, of course, only be considered as a given – and given from on high, to be precise – and therefore not subject to objective investigation). In general, when cognition is liberated from faith, it progresses both quantitatively and qualitatively.

And will? Will not will suffer a huge loss if it loses a whole vast realm over which its influence formerly extended? In order to make a judgement about this, it is necessary to keep in mind what kind of contribution it received from this realm.

Any kind of slavery depraves not only the slave owner but the master. The master becomes used to adulation and becomes effete. Faith-based thinking – in order to please its mistress-will – *postulates* what the will desires (the 'illusory nature and impotence of evil', for example) and thereby *satisfies* and *sooths* the will. If what is desired is now postulated and accepted as more real than reality itself, then why be concerned with its 'apparent' realisation? Vassal-like thinking brings opium and hashish in tribute to suzerain-will and, poisoning it with quietism, avenges its slavery.

Enlightened clericalism, however, does not want to admit this fact. Mr Bulgakov maintains:

> ... in accepting the rationality of the general plan of history, we are not at all freed from the obligation to love good and to hate evil and, if evil is

---

5   *Problemy idealizma*, p. 6; *Ot marksizma k idealizmu*, p. 118.

given a place in life and in history, to struggle against it. This acceptance can only strengthen confidence in the victory of good and thereby rouse the spirit for the struggle with evil.[6]

But if we compare this with what was said earlier about the meaning of evil in life, we see a clear inconsistency (more accurately, *one* of his inconsistencies). To use his own words, Mr Bulgakov 'bursts the boundaries of the intelligible' and 'even believes in what is not only utterly unproven but what also cannot be made completely comprehensible to reason'. After all, if evil is illusory and impotent, then how is it possible to relate to it seriously? 'To hate evil and struggle against it' while knowing that it is only apparent – does this not mean to throw oneself on a movie-screen villain or to challenge a phonograph recording of abusive language to a duel?

In this case, Mr Bulgakov's conclusions obviously do honour to his noble feelings but not at all to his logic.[7]

Thinking that is freed from subordination to the will, in turn, frees the will from the narcosis of comforting illusions, and the activity of the will can expand to its full measure. From this point on, the will finds cognition to be not an obliging flatterer but a reliable friend who conscientiously points out the best means of attaining the will's goals and explains the chances of realising those goals, how progressive they are, and how they are related to the general course of life overall.

Strict discrimination between the phase of cognition and the phase of will in psychical life removes obstacles to the development of both cognition and will. This creates the possibility for the free progress of the depth and clarity of cognition on the one hand and of the activity of the will on the other. The energy of psychical life grows.

III

In the introduction to his book *Ot marksizma k idealizmu* [*From Marxism to Idealism*], Mr Bulgakov recounts the story of his Canossa. The essence of the matter is this: Mr Bulgakov previously *believed* in Marxism, and then he discovered, quite properly, that Marxism is not a suitable object for faith and began

---

6 '*Ot marksizma k idealizmu*', p. 160.
7 The narcotic action of faith on an idealistic will is evident even in certain of our more modern opponents (see V. Kistiakovskii, *Problemy idealizma*, pp. 354–5). [Poole 2003, pp. 340–1 (trans.).]

to seek other objects. His search was crowned with victory only when Mr Bulgakov 'burst the boundaries of the intelligible' – boundaries which, as is well known, are determined by logic. Mr Bulgakov thereby completely shielded himself from substantive polemics from those who remained on this side of the border of logic, and our task in regard to him can be formulated in this way: to describe and, as far as possible, to explain, but not at all to refute.

Thus, Mr Bulgakov 'believed' in Marxism, and this was a big mistake not only from his point of view but from ours. 'The special property of faith', in the words of Mr Bulgakov, consists in 'what is not only completely unprovable but that cannot be made completely understandable to reason'. It is obvious that such a characterisation of Marxism goes far beyond anything that it justly deserves. In reality, could there possibly be room in Marxism for the kind of thinking that is based on will or belief?

Individual people and whole classes face a specific, practical task arising from various vital contradictions in people's social relationships, and this task is *to master those social relationships in the interests of humanity*. This task expresses a specific direction of an active will. The inexpediency of the first instinctive attempts of will in that direction (the utopianism of cultured people – appeals to the philanthropy of the ruling classes – and the utopianism of uncultured people – smashing machinery, etc.) aroused *the will to acquire knowledge*. The task was set to understand *how and under what conditions social relationships change*. This is a theoretical task, and if it is resolved, we will have a specific *theoretical conviction* relating to the nature of social relationships and the regularity of how they change. In relying on that conviction, a person will arrive at an explanation of such questions as the following. In what direction do the essential relationships of people change apart from the active interference of *conscious* will? What additional conditions for change can be created by such interference? Is the basic task of mastering social relationships in the interests of humanity realisable? Is it realisable given the present direction of spontaneous development of these relationships, and what additional conditions can make the realisation of this task easier, i.e. will they lessen the expenditure of human forces that will be required to realise this task? How can these conditions be created? Etc. As a result, we will have attained a harmonious system of conscious life in which an active will, striving toward a real vital goal, is governed by the free pursuit of the knowledge that will plan expedient means. Marxism is one such possible system – only not the Marxism that Mr Bulgakov 'believed in'.

The fact of the matter is that such a system has no room for thought that is based on belief. In this system, the direction of active will is determined by the demands of life, and the conclusions of theory are determined by the material of experience. These conclusions can be *hypotheses*, but they cannot be the object – and certainly not the result – of faith, since they are obtained through objective cognition and not subjective 'feeling'; they are motivated by the facts of experience and not the 'law-like demands' of a will that wishes things were one way and not another. In a system such as we have described, cognition and will are mutually differentiated and are not combined with one another.

However, it is often the case that a person, encountering such a system in life, makes it into an object of faith. This, as we know, is how it is with Mr Bulgakov, an educated economist, but it also occurs – and occurs more often – with backward, uneducated people who adopt a poorly understood worldview because of how it 'feels'. How is this possible?

The process unfolds differently in different cases, but it is not difficult to establish two main types of such phenomena. In some cases, because of a lack of knowledge and development, people apprehend a given system vaguely and unclearly. It is near and dear to their soul because it corresponds to the tenor of their will, but they are unable to evaluate the theoretical aspect of the system, and they usually do not even know it in its entirety. So, they take its conclusions 'on faith' and 'assume' them, because they *want* the whole system to be true. In this case, faith is the result of insufficient knowledge. With the course of time, it is replaced by knowledge or, speaking more generally, theoretical conviction. As soon as people acquire the knowledge and experience that are necessary to verify the theory, they pass to a higher phase of worldview. They consciously accept or reject the theory not because they instinctively want to but because the theory turns out either to correspond or to fail to correspond to the entire sum of their experience and knowledge. An embryonic form is replaced by a developed form; the 'instinctive' is replaced by the 'conscious'.

In other cases, the essence of the matter consists not in the lack of knowledge and experience but in the *type of thinking*. Imagine people whose point of view is that thinking is based on faith and who are fundamentally incapable of departing from it. They are believers because they live by faith. Their thinking cannot free itself from subordination to their will, and their will does not want to renounce the right to dictate thinking. Such people inevitably *apprehend* the system we have described in a perverse form – as a system of faith, to be precise. The theoretical propositions of the system do not appear to them as conclusions from experience – either precise or approximate – but as 'postulates'. They are true for them because they desire them, and nothing else is important. Therefore, what is conditional in theory they regard as unconditional. They see hypotheses as dogma, etc. It is clear that the system that they believe in is not the same as the system that the other type of thinking recognises; theirs is a system that has been made into a *fetish*. It is also clear that, being perverse in this way, the system must seem disharmonious and full of contradictions and confusion that flow entirely from conflating thinking that is based on belief with thinking that is free. A person ceases to be satisfied by such a poor faith and seeks a new one that would now be a real faith and not a perverse theory. It is of course not difficult to find one; one need only look back into the past.

This is what happened to Mr Bulgakov. The matter was even more complicated for him since he had, in his own words, two faiths: in Marx and in Kant. Mr Bulgakov believed in Kant even more than he did in Marx, since he 'used Kant to prove Marx'. But, it goes without saying, the two faiths are at variance and Mr Bulgakov chose ... a third.

IV

Mr Bulgakov's discussion of the scientific-philosophical theory of progress can serve as a vivid example of how a theoretical conviction is perverted when it is transformed into an object of faith. He proposes that this theory mandates belief in the unconditional necessity of progress, and he discovers, naturally, that in reality there are insufficient grounds to support this. However, this theory does explain what precisely the conditions of progress are and points out the means to master the spontaneous forces of life in such a way as to move them in a progressive direction. The theory of progress can also find – and with a certain degree of confidence confirm – whether the *given* reality includes sufficient conditions for further progress. It is precisely in this way that the contemporary theory of progress relates to the development of the capitalist system. But to 'postulate' progress as something that is necessary under all conditions, independently of conditions, is not the task of the theory of progress; it is the task of faith. And Mr Bulgakov himself is responsible for all the absurdity of the 'theory' that he criticises. He chose to fantasise and 'believe' what he should have investigated and understood.[8]

Having refuted *his own* theory of progress, Mr Bulgakov proposes replacing it with a new one – if it is possible to apply the word 'new' to a dogma in which 'there is not a word that is less than three thousand years old'. This is what he 'postulates':

---

8   I limit myself here to these few words, since I have explained Mr Bulgakov's misunderstanding in greater detail in the article 'On *Problems of Idealism*'.

Thus, the basic premises of the theory of progress are: moral freedom of the human individual (free will) as the condition of autonomous moral life, the absolute value of human individuality and the ideal nature of the human soul, which is capable of infinite development and perfection, absolute reason that governs the world and history, and a moral world order or the reign of moral goals – good not only as a subjective conception but also as an objective and powerful principle.[9]

Here is a series of 'unprovable' propositions that we must accept without question in order to 'base' a 'theory of progress' on them. Are you not demanding too much of us, Mr Bulgakov? And what if we are unable under any conditions to verify let us say even one of these propositions? It would then be useless to believe in the remaining propositions, and no kind of 'theory of progress' will be obtained. And would it not be better to not tire out faith with complex scholasticism and to simply and ingenuously 'postulate' only one 'presupposition' – progress, itself – and to say to oneself: 'I believe in progress because I very much want it to be' and be done with it? True, there would then be nothing to write long articles about, and, at the same time, the innocence of faith would be obvious to everyone. But all the same, what is easier: to believe in six complex and ponderous presuppositions or in one simple and easy presupposition – 'progress'.

Of course, if one has in mind the 'mortification of the flesh' (or, more accurately, of logic) then one must prefer the apparatus that Mr Bulgakov has proposed.

And Mr Bulgakov is merciless to the 'flesh' and is not shy about demanding from it what is quite impossible. 'Suppose for a moment', he says, 'that we have the most precise prognosis of the next decade and on the basis of this prognosis all our best desires are doomed to failure. Does it follow from this that they cease to be obligatory for us? In no way! You can because you must – this is the moral law'.[10] In other words, beating your head against the wall, deliberately wasting your strength without results, not daring to conserve your strength until it might be productive – 'you can because you must'. Destroy yourself now, so that when your 'best desires' become realisable in practice, you will have become an invalid, a harmful burden. All these considerations mean nothing – 'you can because you must'. 'This is a formidable formula', Mr Bulgakov suggests. Really? Is not another characterisation more appropriate for it? ...

---

9   From the article 'Osnovnye problemy teorii progressa' in *Ot marksizma k idealizmu*, p. 147.
10   Ibid., p. 146.

Here Mr Bulgakov obviously has in mind still another 'presupposition': credo, quia absurdum.[11]

V

As we have seen, in the days of what he called his 'atheistic faith', Mr Bulgakov distorted – unintentionally, of course – the scientific-philosophical theory of progress, attributing to it faith in the *absolute* necessity of progress. In so doing, that very theory naturally acquired the colouring of crude fatalism, and the role of progressive forces of history, the role of the progressive classes, appeared illusory: does it make any sense to occupy oneself with creating the conditions of progress when progress is *absolutely* inevitable anyway? The real theory of progress studies the general conditions for progress and accepts or rejects the objective probability of progress for a given society depending on whether conditions are sufficient or insufficient. Mr Bulgakov did not know this theory then, just as he does not know it now, because it does not fit in the confines of forms of 'faith' in general. And for his new 'theory of progress' the worthy economist significantly amplifies the tone of fatalism so that the 'theory' turns out to be fatalistic in the most precise and literal meaning of the word.

The original meaning of the word *fatum* is 'what is said', and the pure idea of predetermination consists in the concept of a *free will* that previously said – formulated and prescribed – what will happen. Now Mr Bulgakov accepts precisely such an individual will as the 'premise of the theory of progress', and he uses the expression 'absolute cunning' to refer to how this will makes a mockery of the 'absolute dignity of human individuality' so that an individual's 'free deeds and desires' turn out to be the 'means toward the goal of the absolute'. Which of the two forms of Mr Bulgakov's fatalism are more degrading to a human as a developing and active being? We think it is the latter: it is better to be the plaything of impersonal forces that 'do not know what they do' than the plaything of the 'cunning' of an individual will.

The terms that Mr Bulgakov uses for his critics who point out the fatalistic nature of his 'theory of progress' are amusing. First and foremost, he wards off critics who are positivists on the strange basis that they are fatalists themselves. But if this were so, then how would this justify Mr Bulgakov's fatalism or make his 'theory' less fatalistic? But he, as usual, transmits the views of his opponents inaccurately, distorting their *theory* into faith and their *principles of knowledge*

---

11   'I believe because it is absurd' [trans.].

into idols. In his opinion, by accepting the 'absolute rule of the law of causality', positivists thereby accept some kind of 'fate'. It is obvious that the law of causality appears to the worthy professor sometimes like an individual being that cunningly uses people's wills and sometimes like an independent spontaneously coercive force that governs them. He is certainly aware – though he does not *want* to know and see – that contemporary positivism considers the 'law of causality' only as a means of cognitively connecting phenomena in a continuous series; it is only a *form of the coordination of experience*. Positivism accepts this form as being historically produced, as universal by virtue of its expediency for cognition, and as subject to critique and further development. Mr Bulgakov prefers to end the history of positivism with the materialist Holbach, who lived approximately one and a half centuries ago. In general, Mr Bulgakov is adept at choosing the most favourable position for himself, and this, by the way, is a typical characteristic of enlightened clericalism.

Later on, Mr Bulgakov objects to being accused of being a fatalist himself, and, to be sure, his objections are very powerful from the point of view of 'faith'. But if one holds to the 'boundaries of the intelligible' – i.e. logic – then they produce a strange impression. Here are the objections:

> In any case in my article I did not give occasion to count myself among the adherents of metaphysical fatalism, since I speak in it about duty, about the categorical imperative, and about historical obligations. In a word, I speak about the kinds of things on which a fatalist should probably be silent. Just the opposite, I strove to reconcile necessity and freedom in my worldview, sacrificing neither freedom for the sake of all-devouring determinism nor objective determinism for the sake of absolute occasionalism and individual caprice. The world and the historical process can be thought of as a systematic process in which human freedom was included in its initial plan as a basic and necessary condition ... The existence of a general providential plan is possible without any sort of constraint whatever on human freedom. Of course, such a resolution of the question of freedom and necessity can be proposed only in connection with a whole metaphysical doctrine ... which I personally find in the philosophy of Vladimir Solovev, to whom I refer the reader.[12]

---

12   'Ot marksizma k idealizmu', p. 158. *We cite passim*. The omissions do not change the meaning.

Mr Bulgakov 'speaks about the kinds of things on which a fatalist should be silent: duty, historical obligation', etc. What does he prove with this? Evidently only his own inconsistency. And, by the way, does not all of this – duty, the categorical imperative, historical obligations – come under the purview of fatal 'cunning'? If freedom 'is included in the plan' and all its manifestations are provided for, then how is this 'freedom'? Here even Vladimir Solovev cannot be of any help ... And in this way, all the 'reconciliation of freedom and necessity' boils down to the fact that 'cunning' cruelly scoffs at both freedom and necessity. What a glorious reconciliation!

We repeat yet again: we do not at all intend to disprove Mr Bulgakov. This is *impossible*, since at any given moment he can completely defend from criticism any flat contradiction that he utters by declaring that it 'cannot be made completely understandable to reason'. Nevertheless, we have the right to *state* these contradictions, and it is up to the reader to judge them.

However, will the reader not find that there is too much argumentation and scholastic subterfuge in Mr Bulgakov's 'theory of progress' for it to be real faith and too many unprovable postulates for it to be a 'theory'?

It is hardly possible that this can be the end of it: it is an unstable combination.

VI

Mr Bulgakov's specialty is economics. Economic science is a science – so far not a particularly exact science – but in any event a *science*, and, as such, it of course acknowledges hypotheses and propositions but never postulates of faith. Here, however, Mr Bulgakov did not change his nature: he was and remains a *believing* economist; he changed only the objects of his 'true beliefs'. When he believed in his pseudo 'scientific theory of progress', he also believed in the economic doctrine of Marxism and introduced into it, it goes without saying, all the inevitable misunderstandings of faith-based thinking. When he began to believe in 'cunning', he found it necessary, accordingly, to move to another economic faith. It was to this latter that his articles 'On the Economic Ideal' and 'Tasks of Political Economy' were devoted.

This is what the new orthodoxy of the worthy economist is like:

> Political economy ... originated and exists, supported by the practical importance which economic questions have at the present time in the life of cultured humanity. It was born as the fruit of the search of contemporary consciousness and conscience for *truth* in economic life. It was

summoned not by the theoretical but by the ethical needs of temporal humanity. *Political economy*, according to this preliminary definition is *applied ethics*. To be precise, it is the ethics of economic life.[13]

From the point of view of 'the intelligible', one could find this to be a very strained interpretation. For example, it is somehow difficult to believe that only 'ethical' needs called forth the doctrines of 'financial balance' or 'trade balance', Adam Smith's doctrine of the economic principle of egoism that contradicts the ethical principle of altruism, various vulgar-self-serving theories, Senior's 'last hour',[14] etc. All this is explained by the fact that *any science arises from the practical needs of life* that rouses the will and directs it toward knowledge. Correspondingly, political economy appeared from *social-practical needs* so that from the point of view of 'free will' and 'cunning' there is no need to distinguish them from 'ethical' needs: in the light of the absolute, all human life is ethical practice.

An 'ethical economist' is, obviously, nothing other than a particular variety of 'subjective sociologist', and Mr Bulgakov himself recognises this perfectly well.

Subjectivism is necessarily inherent in any creative work – a creation from yourself or from your subjectivity – and, to the extent that political economy is not only a science but also a technique (it not only ascertains what exists but also postulates what is obligatory) subjectivism cannot be removed from it ... Thus, social science, in general, and political economy, in particular, cannot be understood without tears and laughter, and this is not only its right but its obligation ... And in this struggle with the pretensions of overweening objectivism – I repeat yet again – subjective sociology, no matter how badly grounded it is in philosophical terms, contains truth.[15]

'Bad philosophical grounding' – this, obviously, is the formal acknowledgement of the ideas of positivism by our old subjective sociologists. If they had considered departing from the 'boundaries of the intelligible' and 'grounding' their doctrine on 'cunning', nothing more would be required. True, Mr Bulgakov makes yet one more reservation – that 'sociological subjectivism must be as

---

13   *Ot Marksizma k idealizmu*, p. 264, *passim*.

14   In response to demands for shortening the working day in the early stages of the industrial revolution, the argument was made that it was only in the last hour that the factory owner earned a profit. See *Capital*, Volume 1, Chapter 9, Section 3, 'Senior's "Last Hour"' [trans.].

15   *Ot Marksizma k idealizmu*, pp. 332–3. Cited *passim* to avoid long extracts.

scientific as possible, regulated by means of scientific experience'.[16] 'Subjective sociology', of course, cannot object to such a reservation; on the contrary it must greatly appreciate the calm and confident repetition of its favourite flat contradiction, 'scientific subjectivism'. The repetition is particularly useful after its opponents explain and prove that, in regard to knowledge, 'objective' and 'scientific' are the same thing.

And, nevertheless, we permit ourselves to doubt that our subjectivists rejoice in their new ally. The path along which he came to this alliance does not cast a particularly flattering light on their own psychology: it underlines the confusion of the elements of faith and theoretical thinking than constitute the basis of their doctrine.

VII

Theoretical economics and its abstractive method is notable for its extreme objectivity, so that it is absolutely impossible to transform it into ethics – even applied ethics. Therefore, in order to sustain his point of view, there remains only one thing left for Mr Bulgakov: to completely do away with this science. And this is what he has done.

The worthy economist depicts theoretical economics in the following way:

> It sets itself approximately this question: how is it possible to abstractly conceive of the interrelationships among certain facts (the phenomena of price, profit, capital, rent) apart from the empirical interrelationships among those facts as they are established and explained in political economy? Based on these solid foundations, what kind of logical bridge can span them? It does not find this task directly in experience but invents the task, makes it up, and thereby invents theoretical economics itself.
>
> That theoretical economics in reality does not have experiential knowledge, study, and analysis as its goal is self-evident from its content. After all the logical efforts and constructions of theoretical economics, our empirical knowledge is not enriched at all, so that someone who wants to understand economic reality will lose nothing if they remain utterly ignorant of speculation regarding value, etc., as is well known from the history of economic science.[17]

16   Ibid., p. 334.
17   *Ot marksizma k idealizmu*, p. 342.

The most striking thing here is his reference to *the history of economic science*. In restraining myself from any polemic with Mr Bulgakov, which, as I have already pointed out, is essentially impossible, I cannot but point out to the reader how faith-based thinking distorts the facts without hesitation or doubt whenever it is necessary.

It is precisely the history of economic science that gives us an understanding of the huge significance that theoretical economics has had and has for knowledge and life. Questions regarding free trade and protectionism, questions regarding consumer and producer cooperatives for the general quality of life of the working class, the contemporary question of whether trusts can eliminate general crises, etc. have all been answered on the basis of economic science. Mr Bulgakov would propose to answer these questions on the basis of 'empirical facts', independently of general, necessary or, as he puts it, 'logical' correlations between capital and profit, between wages and the price of consumer goods, between enterprises in the same field and in different fields, etc. Enough! Mr Bulgakov obviously does not like the answers to all these questions that are obtained with the aid of theoretical economics, but for someone who thinks like a scientist and not like a believer this could never serve as the basis for asserting that such answers are altogether impossible and that theoretical economics is pure scholasticism, that it poses non-existent questions, and that it cannot contribute to the elucidation and understanding of the facts of reality.

The idealised and schematised representation of the facts of experience that characterises the abstractive method of theoretical economics is the general feature of *all sciences that establish general laws of phenomena*. Whoever is familiar with the natural sciences knows that any general scientific principle expresses a kind of ideal correlation that is never given in pure experience, no matter how rich that experience is. All these principles issue from ideal, *ultimately pure* conditions and express *ultimate* relationships between phenomena. No one has ever seen the interaction of only two bodies or the movement of a body entirely uninfluenced by its environment, and therefore the laws of motion established by Newton are only *ultimate abstractions*. But they provide us the means of analysing and understanding concrete phenomena. Such are the ultimate abstractions of theoretical economics, and such is their real significance.

VIII

There are many strikingly progressive phrases in Mr Bulgakov's latest articles that might seem to most readers as enough to compensate for the reactionary foundations of the worthy professor's worldview. In order to more precisely evaluate the mutual relations of these two sides of Mr Bulgakov's intellectual activity, we will make a few small comparisons.

Mr Bulgakov takes his ideas of equality and freedom from the world beyond, and for him this is their *supreme sanction*:

> People are unequal in nature, unequal in age, in sex, in talent, in education, in appearance, in the conditions of upbringing, in life success, in character, etc. and etc. As a result, we cannot derive the idea of equality from experience. In fact, experience is more likely to give us Greco-Roman or Nietzschean ideas. The equality of people is not only not a fact but cannot even become a fact; it is only a *norm* of human relationships, an ideal that directly contradicts empirical reality.[18]

Let us imagine a case such as this: Mr Bulgakov unexpectedly arrives at the conclusion that the idea of equality (and the idea of freedom, as well) has an *empirical* origin. The otherworldly sanction of the idea would then immediately disappear, and the idea would lose all significance as far as Mr Bulgakov is concerned. And meanwhile the notion of the empirical origin of the idea of equality is so simple and natural that even faith-based thinking cannot be secure from it. It is sufficient to reflect that people experience a great deal of hardship because of actual inequality, and, in their struggle with this inequality, they generalise their negative attitude toward it into an idea that turns out to be precisely the idea of equality. After all, people always strive for what they do not have, and, in consequence, they strive for what is still not given in their experience. But that very desire springs from the contradictions and discomforts of what is given in experience, and the generalising formula of this striving is only the generalised negation of those contradictions and discomforts – i.e. it does not include anything like the otherworldly. From Mr Bulgakov's point of view, one should assume that people altogether cannot make anything new on the basis of experience, since that new thing would be something that has not yet been given in experience. If Mr Bulgakov recoils from this conclusion, then

---

18   The article 'O sotsial'nom ideale [On the Social Ideal]', p. 300. [In *Ot marksizma k idealizmu* (trans.)].

the only thing remaining for him to do is to also admit that the idea of equality is not otherworldly in its origins. What value will he then consider it to have? In any event he will cease to *believe* in it – 'the "empirical" is too mundane an object for faith'.

'The ideal of equality', says Mr Bulgakov,

> has meaning and significance and corresponds to the supreme idea of justice only as a demand for the practicable equality of conditions for the development of human individuality with the purpose of its free self-determination and moral autonomy. In other words, the entire practical content of the idea of equality boils down to the idea of the freedom of human individuality. It boils down as well to the demand for social conditions that foster the development of the freedom of human individuality and to the demand for social conditions that are most favourable for fostering the development of this freedom.[19]

> Only concrete goals are attainable in historical conditions, while the ideal of justice is abstract and, according to its very meaning, it can be united with a variety of concrete contents ... Changing concrete conditions bring new potentialities for resolving the task of justice and for new discoveries of this world-wide historical goal ... Let us not forget that the ideal of equality and freedom is a rejection of these conditions and therefore cannot wholly be embodied in them.[20]

So, the ideal of equality is unattainable, although it expresses only the 'demand for the practicable equality of conditions for the development of human individuality'. Why is this ideal actually unattainable? Is it really impossible to admit the future possibility of social conditions in which *inequality of conditions for the development* of individual A and individual B can be made less that any given magnitude, i.e. lose any practical meaning? After all, this inequality is not *an infinite magnitude*. Like everything that is given in experience, it is limited and finite, and everything that is limited and finite lies fundamentally within the bounds of developing human forces. But faith *finds it necessary* to make the ideal unattainable, otherwise there is nothing to have faith in.

It is curious to compare the scientific-philosophical understanding of the ideal with the understanding of a believer. Scientific-philosophical understanding, finding that it is impossible to *actively* strive toward the unattain-

---

19   'O sotsial'nom ideale', p. 303.
20   Ibid., p. 307.

able, permits *only ideals that are attainable*. The unattainable is something one can only dream about; it is an idol and not an ideal. For faith-based thinking, because it is conservative and cannot create new ideals, the attainment of an ideal is 'the end of history, stasis'; its ideals come only from outside history. On the contrary, no sooner does free thinking combined with an active will attain some goals than it moves constructively on to others. Free thinking is not afraid to carry on.

Mr Bulgakov conceives of the ideal of freedom in this distinctive colouration:

> It is easy to distinguish internal or free dependence from external or compulsory dependence. We have the former in the relationships of student to teacher, a reader to writer, child to parent, etc. Such necessity not only does not destroy the spiritual freedom of human individuality but is truly a field for the manifestation of spiritual freedom, since freedom of human individuality is factually realised only in communication with other people.[21]

From all the forms of 'free' dependence, Mr Bulgakov does not point out precisely the *one* form that really deserves the name – the *comradely* from of mutual dependence. How 'free' a student is depends on the teacher; how free a reader is depends on the writer, etc. One is free to the extent that one person relates to another not as an authority but as a comrade and to the extent that students or readers do not consider themselves to be beneath a teacher or writer in principle but are able to relate to the latter completely consciously and critically and on occasion to teach them something in their turn. To Mr Bulgakov, *mild forms of authoritarian dependence* seem to be real 'spiritual freedom', while, from the point of view of contemporary thinking, this is far from the case. In its most strongly expressed manifestations, this 'free' authoritarian dependence transforms into the most real spiritual slavery – into blind obedience of one person to another in the manner of an inferior being to a superior one.

All this prevents us from having complete confidence in the vital validity of Mr Bulgakov's progressive desires. The same words mean something different to the enlightened cleric than to the representatives of really progressive forms of thinking.

---

21   'O sotsial'nom ideale', p. 304.

But this is still not the most important thing. The most important, pro-found, and irreparable contradiction is between the ideas that Mr Bulgakov talks about – no matter how uncertainly and unclearly he understands them – and the basic idea upon which he wants to construct his worldview. If one conceives of all of life as a whole – the entire world process – as a kind of 'obed-ience', if one views the ideal of life as full and unconditional subordination of each individual will to some other (but also personal) will, then how can one still speak of the ideals of freedom and equality or of ideals that exclude per-sonal subordination? Sooner or later they must be rejected.

At first glance, of course, it can seem quite natural and feasible that people, in satisfying their slavish instincts in one world – in the realm of the tran-scendental – will feel themselves all the more free from those instincts in another world – the sphere of experience. This would be conceivable if both worlds were absolutely separate, but this this is not the way it is. For faith-based thinking, the two worlds inseparably flow together and one of them is only a *manifestation* of the other. The authoritarian understanding of the basic inter-connectedness of the world order and the ideal of an autonomous will for the empirical manifestations of this interconnectedness are vitally incompatible with one another. This is why enlightened clericalism cannot constitute a solid system for a worldview; it is always only a temporary, unstable equilibrium of contradictory vital tendencies. Time will destroy it.

CHAPTER 8

A New Middle Ages: A Philosophical Nightmare

The title page of the book says: 'E. Boretskaya, *The Problem of the Objectivity of Knowledge*, Rostov-on-the-Don' ... etc. I learned from the introduction, which was modestly and reasonably written, that the author is a Kantian, but 'wherever there is a difficulty, she seeks her own path'. It is 'a short summary of the author's personal views, but perhaps a certain few of her views are rather original' – of which 'the publication of this book gives evidence'. And, finally, 'this pamphlet far from intends to be a popularisation' (p. ii). All in all, there was no reason to expect anything special from this little book. I expected to encounter a rather tedious epistemological discussion, utterly unhelpful but also quite harmless. It was recommended, compared with other similar works, by its small size (66 pages) and the absence of citations from which the author promised to spare the reader, since 'for the size and goal of this book they would be a vain affectation' (p. ii). Accepting all these preconditions and reserving a certain amount of patience and attention, I, blessing myself, followed after the author into the realm of the aforesaid 'problem', expecting in due time to make it happily to the end ... the end of the book, not the problem. But reality cruelly smashed all my calculations and expectations.

From the first pages I already began to notice that the wherewithal I had started out with began to disappear surprisingly quickly. By page 10, surprise was replaced by bewilderment, and all that was left of my wherewithal was the memory of it. Gathering my strength, I continued ... My bewilderment grew, and after page 15 it was aggravated by a feeling of a kind of oppression, not exactly physical and not exactly moral. By page 20 this feeling predominated, and by page 25 it was drowned by the wave of a severe headache. Nevertheless, a kind of incomprehensible, elemental stubbornness forced me to mechanically read on. On page 27, I semiconsciously read the following aloud:

> This path toward constructing a theory of objectivity is based on an interpretation of the epistemological subject that ascribes to its nature any kind of being as potential being, possible and realisable both in truth and in error. But from this it follows that such a hypothesis of objectivity proceeds from an a priori construction, and we said above that there is no need for the hypothesis of objectivity to be based on the a priori, just as there is no need for such a deductive project to be based on the naked

A NEW MIDDLE AGES: A PHILOSOPHICAL NIGHTMARE

psychologism of the factuality of states of consciousness. The seeming contradiction between these assertions ...

At this point letters of the alphabet began to dance before my eyes, a vague consciousness of a kind of danger took possession of my soul, and only after several glasses of cold water was I able to figure out what was going on. It became clear to me that decisive measures were necessary. Fortunately, large doses of narcotics take effect very quickly, and after ten to fifteen minutes the internal and external world mixed together and became chaotically indistinguishable for me.

This happy condition was very brief, however. Forms began to crystallise, now clear, now vague, but always changing and unstable. The world of dreams possessed me with its magic, but this time, alas, it was an evil magic. Worst of all, all distinction between idea and reality disappeared, and the highest abstractions appeared in sensuously concrete embodiments. I wandered through the dense forests of Subjectivity. I was chilled on the snowy heights of Objectivity. Pursued on my way by the terrible spectres of Solipsism and Scepticism, I vainly sought salvation on the Paths of Criticism and beseechingly asked every System that I encountered how to find the road to Absolute Truth. Directions were confused and contradictory. I walked in Vicious Circles and ran across my own footprints, until I was finally arrested for being philosophically illegal and was brought to trial in the court of the Transcendental Subject. There I was reminded of all my past and present crimes against the inviolable laws of Philosophy. I was accused of habitation without established a prioris, of offending the Absolute in thought and words, of armed resistance against the Categorical Imperative in the execution of its official duties. Attempts to defend myself were futile. Fear struck me dumb, and I was unable to utter a single epistemological term. After I mispronounced the title of the judge, I was immediately silenced. Kant, the counsel for the prosecution, was merciless and sentenced me to indefinite exile to the Transcendental in the furthest settlements of the realm of the Noumena. At this point, fortunately, I woke up.

While thinking things over, I came up with what seemed to be a good idea. In the nearest library I found an antique book, *Manual for the Reading of Cryptograms*. In one of the first paragraphs, I read this instruction: 'If any combination of signs is repeated in the cryptogram with disproportionate frequency, then one should try to simplify the cryptogram, underlining this combination everywhere it appears, since it might turn out that it was introduced to complicate the text of the cryptogram as happens with "naïve" methods of encryption'. On the first page I came across – a small page with quite large type – I found the combination 'subject' fourteen times and the combination 'object' fifteen times (p. 12), and I tried underlining them everywhere they appeared. The text, however, did not become clearer. I applied other methods of decryption, such as systematic transposition of letters, counting letters, etc., but they also did not produce at any positive results.

There was nothing for it but to accept that the book was written 'in earnest'. My professional pride was at stake and I read the book – little by little, of course – to the end. By rereading and making correlations I was able to figure out the following. The Kantianism of the author is of the least unsympathetic variety; it is positive and hostile to metaphysics. The author summarises her conclusions at the end of the work in these words:

> ... Neither the problem of the objectivity of cognition nor the problem of the cognition of objectivity opens up a perspective on the transcendental world. Even in accepting the objectivity of a particular being, we do not have the grounds for substantiating it, since the epistemological subject postulates its particularity and its immanence to an equal extent. Therefore, the values that we must realise in cognition issue from the idea of the sovereign rule of the epistemological subject in this realm, and to speak of transcendence means to accept the equivalence of the concepts of noumenality and transcendentality (p. 66). (I chose this as one of the *very easiest and clearest* formulations. A.B.)

Philosophy has to do predominantly with higher abstractions. But higher abstractions are at the same time the most content-free, the most lifeless, and the furthest from immediate activity. It is precisely this that makes *specialisation in philosophical questions* particularly dangerous.

People can become accustomed to abstractions and can work with them – but not as lifeless forms. No, people can live only with what is alive or with what they endow with life. The philosopher-specialist endows accustomed abstractions with life gradually, involuntarily, and without noticing it. For philosophers, such abstractions acquire distinctive, ethereally fine flesh and blood from the cognitive emotions that accompany them, from the mass of vague, indefinite experiences that are woven together with these emotions. Philosophers live with these animated abstractions, they enter into close and immediate relations with them, and the vitality of these abstractions – the subjective outcome of their narrow psyches – acquires the character of a higher objectivity. They now cannot conceive that these abstractions are completely different – different in content and relationships – for any other person. They do not understand that other people cannot live with them and weave them into their life *the same way* as they do. They do not understand that everything is different for other people. In recounting to other people the dramas that they experience in this realm of their own *special* thinking with its particular inhabitants, they do not realise that other people *cannot* understand them at all completely, and that if someone did understand them it would only be by virtue of the accidental coincidence of many individual particularities.

All this does not happen only with philosopher-metaphysicians, but it occurs much more easily with them; the 'supra-experiential' provides a wide expanse for the subjective. The case that I have discussed involves a philosopher with a comparatively positive inclination who is not without a certain critical flair and who possesses considerable logical capabilities. But the essence of the matter remains the same.

The better nature of our 'specialist' shows itself only in vague premonitions of the correct evaluation of her awful work that slip out here and there. In the introduction, she makes special mention of the 'significant number of debatable and doubtful elements that her judgements contain', and she attempts to console herself with the fact that this is caused by her striving 'to go my own way whenever there is a difficulty'. This is a poor consolation, since 'her own way', in this case, means having significance and meaning *only* for the author herself and for no one else – having only subjective value. 'Well', says the author, 'on the other hand, a short summary personally for myself might not be devoid of particular interest to a certain few people'. Alas, there is an unconscious falsity here: what is 'personally for myself' can be summarised in written form, but then why print it? Why publish it?

Further on, the author hints that of course she does not write only for herself but for a very few – for specialists, to be precise ('... this pamphlet is far from intended to be a popularisation' ...). But, after all, these specialists will also not essentially understand her, since each of them animates the world of philosophical abstractions in their own way and lives in it in their own way. 'Yes', says the author, 'but what is to be done? In general, philosophy is more of a system of disagreements than a system of agreements' ... But what is the task of philosophy in reality? Precisely in order to *harmonise* everything that people experience. How can a 'system of disagreements' possibly accomplish this?

But, nevertheless, the author is completely correct in regard to the *specialised* philosophy that is torn out of life and that she represents. Yes, that philosophy is a 'system of disagreements'. It is the realm of the *subjective*. It is a direct contradiction of its own task. It is a splendid example of the perversion of life – the deformed degeneracy – which the utmost development of specialisation brings.

One now observes in literature and in the public an unusually powerful passion for philosophy. There are different ways to think about this fact. One can rejoice at the 'deepening of spiritual culture' that must appear as a result of this passion, and one can grieve that a great many fresh, young forces are diverted down this path and away from immediate life with its burning needs and demands – needs and demands that are growing more and more and being satisfied less and less. Both points of view have much to be said for them, but both of them provide too little. Here it is all the more important 'not to cry, not to laugh, but to understand'.[1]

Philosophy expresses *life's need of monism* – the striving to connect, coordinate, and harmoniously unite the heterogeneous, varied, contradiction-ridden content of experience. In our time the disharmoniousness of life is terribly strong and is increasingly growing. The differentiation of social being and social consciousness is proceeding more quickly than ever before. Different interests and desires are interwoven and entangled so peculiarly and conflict with one another so harshly that it has become almost impossible for the human individual to sort them out and to reconcile to any extent the various points of view regarding them. This situation of things is more agonising for the intermediary groups of society in which the opposing tendencies of progressing life and obsolescing life intersect – for that 'intelligentsia', which until now has constituted the main part of the 'public' for literature. Here the 'need for monism' becomes acute to the highest degree but without any hope for it being really satisfied. The 'passion for philosophy' blazes up with particular force, but, having encountered overwhelming tasks, it soon degenerates and adopts abnormal forms. Not finding any unifying point of view on the basis of life itself, people begin to seek it *outside life*, some directly in the hereafter and others in the 'logical' world of empty formal abstractions. And, of course, everyone who goes off in that direction is lost to life.

There are other classes for whom contemporary development brings simpler, clearer, and more transparent contradictions and for whom life itself marks out the path toward resolving them. In those classes, the temporary intensification of the need for philosophy does not lead to its degeneration because it finds a way out along more healthy paths.

In our time, this 'passion' continues, and it will do so until such time as at least some tolerable order is established in our life – when life ceases to be a real 'organised disorder' as it is now. And until that time, everyone who must deal with this passion must be concerned with directing it toward normal development, toward positive creative work.

---

1   The reference is to Spinoza: 'I have striven hard not to laugh at human actions, not to weep at them, nor to hate them, but to understand them' [trans.].

Just as I have done several times in the past in regard to our metaphysicians, I now have intended to point out in regard to our 'positivists' – that is, what philosophy *must not be* and what it too easily becomes in the era of the differentiation of social being and the specialisation of human consciousness.

Philosophy changes its tasks and changes its own self as soon as it forgets that its material and its starting point is *in living experience* and that the *harmonisation of life* is its inalterable goal.

CHAPTER 9

Revolution and Philosophy

Revolution does its revolutionary work; philosophy does its philosophical work. What is the essence of the two? How are they related? And whence and wherefore is the possibility that they are related even brought up? It would appear that the relationship is clear: revolution is for stern fighters; philosophy is for meek thinkers. There is no point in looking for anything in common; there is no point in muddying up simple things with a forced comparison.

In reality, a serious and profound connection does exist between them. It not only involves a historical connection in which certain groups and classes carry on revolutionary struggle under the banner of a certain philosophy and in which philosophical ideas are reformulated under the influence of revolutionary struggle, and it does not only involve a connection between class struggle and class ideology. No, there is still another relationship here – the connection between the basic content and the basic meaning of philosophical work and revolutionary work.

I

From where does revolution originate, and what does it do?

Revolution is born in the contradictions of social life. The basis and the essence of these contradictions boils down to a discrepancy between the labour content of social life and the bounds within which labour is contained – between the development of society's 'productive forces' and its 'ideological forms'.

For the Great Russian Revolution,[1] this contradiction consists in the huge growth of the social division of labour and the development of machine production on the one hand and in the stubborn immobility of the semi-feudal governing and legal structure on the other.

The development of the social division of labour requires great flexibility and great mobility in labour relationships among people, and it requires this to an even greater degree in machine production with its ceaselessly changing technology. The fossilised forms of the bureaucratic structure, with its spon-

---

1 The Revolution of 1905 [trans.].

taneous crudeness and mindless routine, counteracts this development and continually fetters the life of the people with its restrictive regulation.

The growth of major industry means the necessity of a vast and continually expanding market, and, in a predominantly agricultural country like Russia, this means the necessity of a prosperous, enterprising class of peasants. The old feudal class of landowners and the bureaucracy that it has generated and that dominates the life of the state impoverish the peasantry and all the people, fundamentally undermining the internal market. A machine needs a conscious worker who is capable of conscientiously directing its complexly combined movements. Such a worker is a living contradiction in a political system that depends on its inhabitants being oblivious, but machine production, despite everything, *creates* this kind of worker, and the proletariat, unified by the factory and the city and revolutionised by bourgeois exploitation and government oppression, becomes a powerful organising force capable of bringing unity and consistency to society's struggle against the unendurable contradictions that it faces.

This is how the elements of revolution arise: its motive force takes the form of profound, continually sharpening contradictions of people's social being, and its organising force takes the form of social consciousness of classes directed toward these contradictions. When, after long painful development, both elements become mature, the revolutionary storm breaks. Its spontaneous blows destroy everything that stands in the way of advancing life, that fetters and chains it, and that engenders unbearable contradictions to it. The impetuous work of the revolution creates another, new container for the social process – new forms that organically correspond to its new vital conditions.

The social whole is raised to the next higher level of organisation. A new cycle of historical change begins. The accelerated progress of life, comparatively harmonious at first, later on begins once again to produce contradictions. Once again, the social body outgrows its clothing, once again the political and intellectual struggle of classes becomes acute, and once again social revolution is in the offing ... This continues until the arrival of the great, final revolution that *changes the very type of social development*, that replaces development through contradiction and class struggle with *harmonious development in a system of universal social collaboration*.

Revolution is social criticism and social creativity that at the same time attains the highest intensity in a burst of exhilaration that engulfs society. The critical work of revolution is to remove the general contradictions of social being and consciousness. The creative work of revolution is to create new forms of collective life. And they have the same meaning and the same goal: the *harmonisation of human existence*. But it will not be a minor, ordinary 'harmonisation' that eliminates small, partial contradictions of life and that creates small, partial adaptations at the margins of the old social forms. No, it will be the harmonisation of *the most general forms with general content.*

This is the work of revolution, and this is the fundamental difference between revolution and 'evolution' within the bounds of a society's day-to-day life.

II

Where does philosophy come from, and what does it do?

Philosophy is born from the cognitive contradictions of human experience. The essence of all these contradictions consists in the lack of correspondence between the content of people's experience and the historically elaborated cognitive forms of their experience, between the data that people find in their experiences and the general conceptions, ideas, dogmas that they have become accustomed to use to tie together and unify these experiences.

Thus, Karl Marx's social philosophy was engendered by a huge mass of contradictions in which people of his day were enmeshed in regard to knowledge of themselves and their social nature. The basic and universal contradiction, in which all other contradictions were summed up as its parts and ramifications, was this: people were accustomed to thinking that reason – if not the higher reason of God then at least the limited but progressive reason of people – *governs* their social life and fate. People's social worldview was thoroughly imbued with this conception, but, meanwhile, it was harshly and painfully refuted by the reality that they experienced. People became increasingly convinced that along with the progress of science and enlightenment it was possible for blatant irrationality to grow in the social structure itself, that in parallel with the spread of humanistic ideas it was possible for inhumanity to develop in the mutual relationships of people, that the most well-considered actions often lead to results that are the opposite of the stated goal, and that the most just wishes, wants, and endeavours of human individuals and of whole classes encounter a kind of fateful force that is elusive but at the same time insurmountable, that is impersonal and at the same time seemingly deliberately hostile. Countless cruel manifestations of imperfections and irrationalities in the social system excited a burning desire in all the victims of these cruelties – and in all who were capable of sympathising with these victims – for expedient social activity, for systematic work that would reform the structure of society in the interests of reason and justice. But the old social worldview was powerless to point out a path for such work. All attempts at social reform that were based on the old worldview inevitably collapsed, and the heroes of these attempts departed into the realm of history with the regretfully respectful sobriquet of *utopian*. The powerlessness of cognition deprived practice of a foundation; the contradiction between idea and experience was transformed into a severe real contradiction.

However, there was also material of another sort within human social experience. If the oppressed classes and all who were on their side achieved nothing in their attempts to rationally remake society, if from their point of view the entire course of social life turned out to be utterly unreasonable, then there were other classes who, just the opposite, *achieved everything* in their efforts to set themselves up in society as comfortably as possible and who even benefited from the liberating efforts of the oppressed and the utopians that did not deliver the desired results to those who fought for it. There were classes for whom there was not only a certain *logicality* but also a high wisdom in the *insanity* of social relationships and social development ... These were the classes who controlled the material forces of society. And at the same time there was a class among the oppressed classes that advanced, uniting ever more closely and standing up against the exploiting classes ever more resolutely. More than once this class compelled the exploiting classes to make certain concessions and achieved partial *rational* and *just* goals. This was the class that grew up and became organised due to the very process of the development of the material force of society in its struggle with nature. It was the class that was the real creator of that material force, the one who paid the price for it, and the one who supported its development. This class was the industrial proletariat. The insanity and injustice of the social system did not suppress it into hopelessness, although it experienced both insanity and injustice perhaps more than all the other classes. It sensed in itself the power to fight for its own *reason* and *justice*, and this power grew. And, as its numbers, its unity, its comradely solidarity, and its understanding of social relationships developed in the process of its labour and struggle, the ideals of class reason and justice became ever clearer in its consciousness.

Thus, at the same time that a basic contradiction existed between the people's social worldview and their social experience, elements of a new worldview took shape that removed this contradiction. The resolution of this task was provided by the social philosophy of Karl Marx. The contradiction disappeared as soon as it was established that the very 'consciousness of people is determined by their social being, not their being by their consciousness'. The spontaneity, *irrationality*, and *injustice* of the social process were now properly understood, and along with this it was possible for the first time to objectively and scientifically investigate the development of *social consciousness* – that is, ideology. The doctrine of the development of production and of the class struggle – the understanding of the real basis of social development and of its historically given general form – provided a solid support to the demand for systematic socially-creative activity. Marx's social philosophy provided all of this, and it thereby accomplished the *harmonisation* of social cognition that was vitally necessary for the new classes – those who carry social progress forward.

The constantly on-going development of science in every field of its endeavour is also a *harmonisation of human experience*. But only the act of cognitive work that creates or transforms *general forms of cognition* can be termed *philosophical*. This applies to Marx's theory in full measure. His theory did not transform only social science and forms of cognition of social life. *All* knowledge lies in the sphere of his reforming activity, and his theory provided new meaning and new significance to *all* cognitive forms (and especially to the most general cognitive forms) – not only those that must immediately change as a result of them but also those that continue to survive in a comparatively unmodified form.

If it is admitted that cognition is determined by people's social being, then everything absolute in cognition disappears. All its forms are transformed from the abstract models in which they had formerly appeared into real products of social creativity, into a living container of the developing social experiences that are organically engendered by that social creativity. Every cognitive combination is examined to determine how it originates in social being, how it is based on social labour. *All cognition is changed*, and at the same time all cognition is imbued with a new cohesive interconnectedness.

III

It is not at all accidental that I brought up Marx's theory in particular as an illustration of the vital significance of philosophy. Not one doctrine, not one system that existed before Marx was a *philosophy* in such a strict and complete meaning of the word as historical materialism. No one achieved such a unified point of view on cognition and life; no one opened up such a boundlessly expanding possibility of actively harmonising cognition and life. In Marx's doctrine, philosophy for the first time found a place for itself *in* nature and *in* society and not above them or outside them.

The old philosophy did not know its own origin. In striving to unite the content of experience into a coherent whole, it was unable, of course, to avoid dependence on the social environment in its work. Its unifying forms reflected – vaguely or clearly but inevitably – the structure and organisation of the *basic* realm of social experience, the basic vital relationships of labour in that society. Philosophy was unaware of this, however. Not understanding where the unifying forms came from and what their real significance was, philosophy was unable to really master them and began to be controlled by its own tools – concepts that had taken shape spontaneously. It became the plaything of social forces that it could not grasp and that had created its concepts. Because of this, philosophy always suffered from an essential incompleteness, always contained a contradiction in its very foundation, and was thoroughly imbued with a distinctive fetishism.

The fundamental incompleteness of its worldview consisted in the fact that, torn from the realm of the immediate struggle of humanity with nature – from the realm of social being that is the starting point of all social development – philosophy was unable to understand and *explain* the very fact of development, the most important fact in the life of humanity. It either ignored this fact, which was essentially a rejection of its main task, or it attempted to substantiate this fact with its customary logical processes, which was something it absolutely did not have the means of doing.

The basic contradiction consists in the fact that, taking its task to be the ideal unification of *all* that exists, philosophy was always built on a *rupture* between nature and cognition. This was expressed in either of two ways. One was dualism (obvious, as with Descartes, or disguised behind formal unity, as with Spinoza). In this case, it is impossible to speak of the real philosophical unification of all that exists, and, given the lack of a bridge between cognition and nature, the very possibility of cognition of nature was transformed into a sheer miracle. The other way was to mentally do away with one of the two sides. Either cognition appeared to be a combination of atomic movements and became utterly unlike itself, or nature was understood to be 'another form of being' of the cognising soul, but in this case it did not occur to nature to give up its own logic. Here the job of philosopher-systematisers boiled down to covering up the contradiction with ingenious verbal convolutions.

Finally, the same rupture of unifying philosophical forms from living life also led to those forms being transformed into fetishes of cognition: they acquired independent existence and absolute meaning. In the first religious philosophies, this rupture and this fetishism had a naïve, concrete character: the unifying forms – called gods – did not live on the earth but in the heavens and were clothed in flesh and blood no differently from people. In subsequent philosophy – abstract philosophy – these forms wasted away to the point of being abstract spectres, dressed only with the thin shell of words. But their pride did not diminish because of this. They did not permit the thought that they had any blood kinship with vulgar reality, and they opposed even more the idea that they were subordinate to it. They paid for this with complete life-lessness that, nevertheless, has often been progressive. When the old gods died, they often became vampires and continued for a long time to drink the blood of living people; when the metaphysical abstractions died, what remained of them, like insects, was only a comparatively harmless empty shell. In any event, both religious fetishism, reflecting the power of external nature over human-ity, and metaphysical fetishism, reflecting the rule of social relationships over humanity, became obstacles to development that was directed toward elimin-ating both forms of humanity's servitude.

Marx's philosophy, engendered by new social forces, pointed the way out of the blind alley in which the old philosophy – the ideology of the old classes – found itself. Cognition as an adaptation in the social labour struggle, cognition as a tool that processes lived experience and thereby causes success in further struggle with nature, philosophy as a special organising centre of cognition – all these found their place in living life. Cognition and philosophy, having merged with life and having become subordinated to life as an organ of a whole, was able for the first time to really embrace life in its entirety and to really master it.

Of course, Marx's idea did not provide this immediately and in a finished form, but it pointed out the problem and the path toward solving it. In regard to philosophy, the problem and the path can be formulated in the following demand: basing itself on the investigation of social development, to find the laws of development of cognitive forms and the conditions of their maximum perfection – their maximum correspondence to their vital goal.

The solution of the problem demands the intense labour of perhaps more than one generation of workers, and it demands unwavering consistency and resoluteness in this labour that is not restrained in its analysis by any habitual ways of thinking. It is necessary to investigate *all* forms of cognition and think-ing – from the most particular to the most general, from the most incidental to those that seem to be eternal and absolute – as *products and tools* of humanity's social labour struggle for existence.

In the realm of the simplest and lowest concepts that are characteristic of the most primitive human psyche, such a connection between labour and cog-nition is easy to see and is practically self-evident. But in the sphere of various 'pure categories' and universal forms, this connection is deeply hidden behind a long process of development of which frequently only the final result can be seen. In this case, therefore, the fetishism of cognitive forms reaches the highest degree, and it is all the more difficult to overcome it.

For example, without analysis, even the most determined and progressive philosophical thinking can seem inclined to turn away, as if insulted, from the

idea that all historically-prevailing forms of religious and philosophical dualism – the dualism of soul and body, god and the world, thing-in-itself and
phenomenon – are simple reflections of the customary social labour dualism of organisational and implementational work and its derivative form –
ruler and ruled. In truth, the cold-bloodedness of an anatomist is necessary
in order to find in the highest conception of God (Spinoza's substance, with its
all-embracing nature and elusive immediate content) the crystallised reflection of the necessary, unquestionable, and spontaneously sensed interconnectedness of all the elements of exchange society and of the content of social
labour, which nevertheless remains invisible and unintelligible to members of
this society because it is hidden by the struggle of individual interests and by
the fetishism that this struggle engenders. To understand this, it is necessary,
even in the sphere of pure science, to give up many attendant presuppositions.
The only consciousness that can be satisfied with a worldview with any sort
of atomistics or monadology[2] is a consciousness that is raised on the individualistic fragmentation of the life of the social whole that issues from the basic
anarchy and contradictions of exchange society ...

The point, of course, is not in these illustrations; they might be arguable, and
they might even be wrong. But the necessity of steadfast investigation in *such a
direction* remains unchanging. It is necessary to keep in mind that *all cognition
and all abstract thinking is reducible to the social labour existence of humanity.*
Before human society appeared, the ancestor of human beings was able to have
only the concrete consciousness and graphic thinking of an animal. What was
created on the basis of social being and dependent upon it must be so understood. Only when philosophy knows itself will it be able to go forward – not
gropingly but completely consciously and systematically.

∴

It is now a simple matter to formulate the basic and essential relationship correlation between the work of revolution and the work of philosophy.

In two different realms – in *practice* and in *cognition* – each of them fulfils the same task: harmonising the developing content of life with its general

---

2 'Monadology' was the idealist mirror image of atomism – the idea that reality ultimately
   consists in tiny, discrete, indivisible particles of inert matter moving in a void. It was a metaphysical outlook developed by the German philosopher Gottfried Leibniz (1646–1716), who
   held that matter is an illusion and reality ultimately consists of discrete, invisible psychical
   beings that move according to a pre-established harmony [trans.].

forms. The inseparable connection between both realms in the process of social labour creates a close mutual dependency in the realisation of both tasks.

Philosophy draws the elements for its unifying forms from life. The more intensely that harmonisation occurs in the sphere of practical life, the more profound and powerful is the demand for monism – i.e. for philosophy – and the higher is the energy and fruitfulness of labour toward it. The tenor of minds – monistic or eclectic, philosophical or philistine – is instilled by practical life. When all social life is imbued with a fundamental duality between its growing content and the stationary forms that clothe that content, then two contradictory tendencies are revealed in people's thinking. Those classes that benefit more from the existing situation and that defend a political, legal, and moral system that contradicts life have no problem at all with the real contradiction, and they deaden and lose their sensibility in 'ideal' contradictions. They are crude eclectics. For them religion is interwoven with science, absolute morality with the most vulgar opportunism and petty epicureanism. For them there is no *logic*, only *interests*. It is just the opposite with those classes in which revolution grows and matures, in which a new harmony of social life is engendered, and that strive to develop the progressive side of the basic social contradiction and to destroy the other. These classes are filled with monistic logic and a philosophical mood; they involuntarily and inevitably demand from cognition the same thing that they demand from life – harmony and unity. And the victory of revolution by harmonising life will create new stimuli and new material for harmonising knowledge.

Thus, revolution, from its invisible origin right down to its final triumph and completion, fulfils *not only the great work of life but also the great work of philosophy*.

The role of philosophy in regard to revolution is not so definite because it stands further from the primary creativity of life. The old philosophy was sometimes instinctively reactionary and sometimes instinctively revolutionary, depending on its connection with one or another social forces. Often, as the role of the social class that creates a given philosophy changes, the intrinsic conservatism of philosophy (which is more significant for philosophy than for many other narrower ideological forms) makes it reactionary.

But philosophy *that knows itself* – philosophy that understands its relationship to life, its origin in life, and its real significance in life – such a philosophy can *only be revolutionary*. It is conscious that vital contradictions are reflected in cognitive contradictions and that actual harmonious unification of all of people's social experience is only the *result* of the harmonious unification of people's entire life of social labour. *Such a philosophy, in doing its philosophical work, inevitably does revolutionary work at the same time.*

Neither revolution nor philosophy are eternal. Both of them are products of disharmonious social development. Both of them are characteristic of class society. In class society, forms of appropriation and forms of law and governance – because they are *class forms* and are linked with the conservative interest of the *rule* of specific classes – must inevitably be considerably more conservative than the labour content of social life. This is what revolution springs from. And cognition, which immediately organises social experience in the form of science, is unable – due to the severe atomism of social experience – to continuously create unifying conceptions in a scientific form that are capable of harmoniously embracing all of its contradictorily developing content. This is what philosophy springs from.

The revolution that will put an end to class society will, for the first time, create the possibility of harmonious social development. In the new society, as class rule disappears, so will the class conservatism of ideological forms, and the unity and coherence of social experience will be worked out by the comradely union of people in a system of organised labour. Then revolution will dissolve into the continuous and harmonious progress of organised social life, and philosophy will dissolve into the continuous and harmonious progress of scientific monism ...

PART 2

New World

•.•

From the Author

These three articles constitute one whole. I have striven to depict in them the development of a new, higher type of life, as I understand it. The first article is devoted to the transformation of the nature of human individuality – the elimination of that narrowness and incompleteness of human beings that has created inequality, heterogeneity, and the psychical disconnection of people. The second article speaks about the transformation of the nature of the social system – the removal of elements of compulsion from relationships between people. The third article outlines the transformation of the nature of human cognition – liberation from the fetishes that limit and distort cognitive creative work. In my explanation of these problems, I have attempted to follow the path that has been pointed out by Karl Marx – to seek the line of development of the 'higher' manifestations of human life, basing my analysis on how they depend on the development of the *basic* conditions of life. The point of my work, of course, is to deal only with the most general contours of the new living type.

CHAPTER 10

The Integration of Humankind

> So God created man in His own image ...
> Book of Genesis

••

> Social being determines people's consciousness ...
> K. MARX

•••

> Man is a bridge to superman.
> F. NIETZSCHE

•••

What is a human being? Some people's answers to this question are too simple and concrete, other people's answers are too complicated and abstract. Both types of answer agree with one another in many ways, not only in terms of real content but also in terms of the basic point of view from which they issue. They are *naïve* answers.

For the average person, a 'human being' is not a mystery at all. It is not an 'accursed question' but simply a living fact of their everyday experience: a 'human being' is oneself and other ordinary people and everyone who is sufficiently similar to them. This answer, obviously, is not only naïve but on the face of it is not completely determinate. To the average person, however, it is completely satisfying. Its simplicity corresponds perfectly to their uncomplicated needs; its narrowness corresponds to the cramped dimensions of the world in which they live.

For philosopher-metaphysicians, a 'human being' is a great mystery, but with the aid of 'introspection', 'speculation', and other methods, they answer it quite easily: a 'human' is a being with the gifts of 'reason', 'moral freedom', 'striving toward the absolute', and similar elevated qualities. These formulas are really not overly clear or overly precise but they are specific enough for metaphysicians; they satisfactorily sum up their personal experience, both theoretical and worldly. For metaphysicians, 'reason' means the capacity for the subtlety and abstruseness of scholastical exercises. 'Moral freedom' means the inclination to violate one's own practical principles and then to repent for not having behaved otherwise. 'Striving toward the absolute' means a general dissatisfaction with life, a vague consciousness of the emptiness and futility of one's existence, etc. In this case, the naiveté of thought consists in the fact that their small and wretched world – the real content of which they make no attempt to broaden and develop – is made, unnoticed by themselves, the measure for such a great thing as humankind.

The scientific perspective offers a contrast with these naïve points of view. Unfortunately, however, science so far does not have one, single answer to this question, but several. Thus, for the general science of life a 'human being' is characterised by specific anatomical and physiological characteristics, for the science of psychology a human being is a specific combination of facts of consciousness, for social science a human being is a set of specific relationships to other similar beings, etc. All these points of view, of course, are completely legitimate and satisfactory in their own field but in certain respects they are insufficient and are inferior to the naïve-everyday and the naïve-scholastical views: they are all partial.

A 'human being' is *a whole world of experience.* This world is not fully captured as an anatomical or physiological complex (a 'human body') or as a psychical complex ('consciousness'), or as a social complex ('social collaboration') ... And if we simply combine – mechanically connect – all these points of view, we still will not acquire a *holistic* conception. A collection of parts is still not a whole.

In this sense both the ordinary point of view and its variant – the scholastic point of view – have an undoubted superiority. Each of them *formally* takes a human being as whole and does not abstract one particular 'side'. But, unfortunately, this formal wholeness has very little use, since the *content* in both cases is meagre and indefinite. The very 'breadth' of these conceptions turns out to be narrow and one-sided: 'human' does not stand out in them as something that is infinitely developing but rather as something that is fundamentally stationary, a static datum. It is entirely limited in one case by the frame of naïve philistinism and in the other by the frame of philosophical philistinism. In the first case, humans are beings who are forever doomed to being 'full of fear and the hope that God will have pity on them', and, in the second case, humans are beings who are full of unnecessary reflections of pure reason regarding true cognition and hopeless dreams of practical reason regarding the overcoming of all instincts. The general presupposition is that 'all creatures have limits placed on them' that they cannot escape ...

The task is to provide a *scientific* but at the same time *integral* and not partial conception of 'human'. For this it is necessary to consider a human not only as a whole world of experience but also as a world that is unfolding, that is not limited by any *absolute* bounds.

A human being is a world but a partial world, a microcosm and not a cosmos, not everything but only a part and reflection of a great whole.

But why are human beings not a whole? What makes them a part is what connects them with the whole.

If individual human beings were all by themselves, each of them would not be a microcosm. Their experience and the world would coincide with one another. They might be able to distinguish their own body from other objects, but those objects would be exclusively objects of each individual's own experience. Any broadening of this experience would then be a broadening of the world as a whole.

Communication with other beings is what makes a person a microcosm.

Only this communication teaches people about things that do not belong to their experience but that nevertheless '*exist*' because they belong to the experience of other people. It teaches people that there are experiences that they do not undergo but that nevertheless are '*real*' because they occur in the consciousness of other people. People are convinced that there is not just one flow of experience but many of them, and they all merge together for all individuals in an endless ocean that they call nature.

Thus, a link is created between a 'person' (as an individual world of experience) and 'nature' (as a universal world) through the medium of communication, a social medium in the precise meaning of the word. And if we want to answer the question of what exactly a human is amidst the universal world process, then we need to ask yet another question: what is the relationship between the experience of individual people and the experience of other living beings?

These other beings are first and foremost, of course, people. To be precise, they are those people with whom they are in the closest vital communication, members of the society to which they belong.

II

At the dawn of the life of humankind, the difference between the experience of individual people and the collective experience of their 'society' was comparatively very small and very simple. It was a *quantitative* and not a qualitative difference.

Primeval clan society is a world in which people are exact copies of one another, repeated one after another with negligible differences. Forms of life are simple, elementary, and homogenous. Everything that is accessible to the experience of one member of the clan group is accessible to everyone else. What one does and is good at, everyone else does and is good at. What one knows, everyone else knows. The environment in which each of them lives and acts is identical: the same small group of people, the same small plot of nature. The resources which each have at their disposal are also identical: the same fund of spontaneously accumulated labour experience and the same primitive tools.

There is nothing here that would single out some people from the rest as having a fundamentally *broader* content of life, nothing that would distinguish some people from the rest as having fundamentally *different* material of experience. There are only insignificant quantitative differences of strength, dexterity, memory, quick-wittedness, etc. In essence, the experience of each is equal to the experience of all throughout the entire life cycle.

At the same time, people's thinking has a 'solid and continuous' nature. The group lives as a whole. There is *no human individuality* and no idea of an 'I' as a special centre of interests and desires. This is why there are no personal pronouns in primitive languages.

People have frequently attempted to idealise primeval life, presenting it as a *golden age* in our past. They interpret the absence of power and subordination as the reign of freedom and equality, and they interpret the absence of internal struggle and the close solidarity of the clan group on the basis of blood ties as the realisation of siblinghood. *This is all a huge mistake.* Our ideas of freedom and equality spring from the kind of experience in which there is oppression and inequality; they express active desires directed against these facts of *experience*. Our idea of camaraderie also springs from real contradictions of social life and expresses active desires directed against their factual rule. When experience does not provide a negative foundation for these ideas, they are empty and inapplicable, and this is how it is in regard to primeval society.

But life that is simple and elementary is still not a harmonious life. Harmony is the reconciliation of contradictions and not a simple absence of them; it is the unification of what is heterogeneous and not simple homogeneity. While harmony is not always incarnated in powerful motion, it nevertheless always *contains the possibility of powerful* motion. There was no such thing in the primeval life of humankind; it is stationary and spontaneously conservative.

The poverty of the content of life of primeval people – unimaginable poverty – was the basic cause of their conservatism. Progress and the creative work of life spring from a profusion of combinations of experience. When all the material of experience boils down to a small number of habitual associations of images, customary emotions, and actions, conditions do not exist for progress and creative work. When the entire construction of the psyche is based on habit, there is no demand for change. The basic tool of human development – cognition – does not exist in this world. Whatever lies within the limits of the habitual does not evoke the demand for 'explanation', and when something unexpectedly appears from the outside and destroys those limits, there is not enough data in the insignificant material of the psyche to provide an explanation. Life without cognition is spontaneous, and the power of nature over life is infinite.

III

Despite all its immobility, the primeval world possessed its own forces of development. They were, of course, elemental biological forces: reproduction, over-population, famine ... They forced development to occur, and development was accomplished – with unimaginable slowness – over the course of many millennia.

At first this development had a purely quantitative nature: the field of experience broadened, the sum of experiences grew, but 'society' remained a complex of *homogenous* units. A 'person' was an *integral* and *identical* being. This continued up to a certain limit after which change became *qualitative*.

The sum of collective experience grew to such dimensions that individual people mastered it only in the later stages of their life, and not everyone mastered it completely. At that point elders were singled out as the bearers of *all* the experience of the group, in contrast with the rest of its members who had only *incomplete* experience at their disposal.

The original homogeneity of relationships within the group gradually changed. One person, based on the built-up experience, began to direct, and the rest began to follow the elder's directives. This difference subsequently grew, since the heterogeneity of people's roles in life itself caused the heterogeneity of subsequent development.

In order to embrace the greatest sum of experience within the confines of their psyche, the one who directed the others narrowed their 'physical' activity to a great extent: they less frequently acted themselves and more frequently acted through others; the elder was transformed predominantly into a manager, into the *organiser* of group life. The rest of the group, on the contrary, retained increasingly less personal initiative and became accustomed to being subordinate; they became permanent *implementers* of the directives of other people. The comparative poverty of the content of their lives was favourable for such activity: greater automatism and less vacillation made it easier for the organiser to cope with their task.

This was how the first fragmentation of humankind – the division of the 'head' from the 'hands' – was accomplished. This was how the *authoritarian* form of life appeared. In the subsequent history of humanity, this form – developing and complexifying and disintegrating – appeared in countless variations. Up until now it has been the basic and principal division of society. In the form of a gentle matriarchy or stern patriarchy, in the form of priestly rule invested with religious mystery or of feudal rule invested with the force of arms, in the form of a system of slavery devoid of any formalism or a system of hired labour full of cold formalism, in the form of mindlessly unquestioning eastern despotism or the rule of elected representatives in Western culture, in the form of the of the arid paper-shuffling rule of the bureaucrat over the citizenry or rule based on the moral suasion of ideologists over their fellow citizens. In all these changing forms the authoritarian fragmentation of humankind retains the same foundation: the experience of one person is recognised – clearly or vaguely – as fundamentally unequal to the experience of another. The dependence of one person on another becomes one-sided; an active will is distinguished from a passive will.

IV

The fragmentation of humankind caused the fragmentation of the world.

It began when people's thinking ceased to be 'solid', when one person was singled out from other people in their consciousness as a special, distinctive world of experience. 'I' appeared as a centre of individual interests and desires, but it was still at the very start of its development. This 'I' was the human individuality of the organiser; it still did not have an antithesis in the form of other 'I's that could come into conflict with it as independent units. Organisers faced only subordinate units who were inseparably tied with them like lower organs of their organism. Organisers could not completely separate themselves from the implementers as independent 'I's. They were correlated with them. Organisers were inconceivable without implementers just as implementers were inconceivable without organisers. *Both an organiser without implementers and implementers without an organiser were logical impossibilities.*

This authoritarian fragmentation was extended to all of nature, maintaining the same correlation and interconnection.

The world presented itself to primeval thinking as a chaos of *actions*, because it is precisely in the form of actions that the struggle for life appears to human beings. Before this, 'action' had appeared in consciousness as a single and whole vital act among other such acts, but now, after the separation of organisers and implementers, 'action' was fragmented in experience and broke down into two separate phases – an active organisational will and the passive implementation of that will. And all nature, as a world of actions, took on that same duality: in every phenomenon the active will was taken to be what determined things and the passive force was taken to be what was determined. This was the 'soul' and the 'body'. People themselves – phenomena in a series of phenomena – were subject to the same bifurcation along with everything else. They acquired a 'soul', just as at the same time rocks, plants, animals, heavenly bodies did so. *Animism developed as a universal form of thinking.*

There is no need to specially prove that the relationship of 'soul' and 'body' is precisely the authoritarian relationship of domination and subordination, of superior and inferior. But, in fact, as far as we can tell from the history of primeval humankind, precisely *this dualism* sprang up in the consciousness of people wherever and whenever authoritarian fragmentation existed. And then – to the extent that authoritarian fragmentation developed, became complex, and changed its forms – the same thing happened with the authoritarian dualism of thinking. When consciousness grouped broad series of phenomena into complex unities, a higher power appeared behind each such series that organised it, and the divinities of polytheism took places of honour in human thinking. When cognition, as it developed, managed to unify all the series of experience into a *Universum* – into a world whole – the era of monotheism began. When the contradictions of social life, being reflected in the psyche of the human individual, engendered an *ethical* worldview, human beings divided their own consciousness into two, setting off higher strivings from lower ones, rational duty from blind instincts ... Dualism and religious consciousness are precious to precisely those classes of society that live in an atmosphere in which authoritarian relationships predominate and who have a propensity to power and subordination. Where authoritarian life flourishes, a dualistic religious worldview also flourishes, and when the former decays, the latter does as well.

Historically, authoritarian dualism is the first type of 'worldview'. Before this, the kind of interconnectedness of experience for which the term 'worldview' would be suitable did not exist. Along with authoritarian dualism there arose what we call 'cognition': distinguishing an active and a passive basis in phenomena. People now 'explained' the manifestation of the latter by means of the former. This, needless to say, was only the beginning of cognitive development. The chain of 'explanations' – the chain of causality – here is broken at the second link; if a phenomenon has a cause in its own 'soul', then one need go no further for an explanation other than this soul. But similar to the way in which authoritarian relationships, as they develop, unfold in a long series of successive links, so also the chain of causality unfolds and becomes more complex. In people's social life the authoritarian series of relationships always boils down to some sort of single, higher authority, and, in just the same way, people's cognition strives to reduce all causal series to one higher, original cause. Thus, cognition reflects the social life of people not only in its content but also in its forms.

V

In essence, authoritarian forms do not fragment the actual *content* of human experience as much as the *relationship* of people to the data of experience. Thus, those who command and those who submit inevitably perceive the same facts from *different* points of view.

The second phase of the fragmentation of humankind – specialisation – goes in another direction. Here the *content* of life narrows quantitatively for each person, and collective experience turns out to be divided among people in such a way that one realm predominantly falls to the lot of one person, another realm falls predominantly to the lot of another, etc. Cobblers know their lasts, merchants their counters, scholars their tomes, priests their prayers, philosophers their syllogisms. The microcosm is made small and narrow, and the world is screened off by lasts, counters, tomes. Thought revolves in a tight circle from which it cannot escape. This narrow existence is incapable of independence, and therefore it is even impossible to once and for all deliver someone from under the power of authoritarianism. Authoritarian power survives in the form of the patriarchal rule of the father in a family, the economic rule of the entrepreneur in an enterprise, the politically organising role of a bureaucrat, the intellectually organising role of ideologists, etc.

Specialised experience makes for a specialised worldview. In the consciousness of some specialists, life and the world appear as a workshop where everything is prepared for their particular tools. In the consciousness of others, it appears as a store where energy and dexterity buy happiness. In the consciousness of a third group, it is like a book written in different languages and different alphabets. In the consciousness of a fourth group, it is like a temple where everything is attained by invocations. In the consciousness of a fifth group, it is like a complex, ramifying scholastic task. And so on and so on. Utilitarians grow up in a world of trade and credit, and they arithmetically assess every manifest-ation of life according to its monetary value. Jurists grow up in the atmosphere of the specialised activity of the law, and they involuntarily view even the laws of nature as norms that are established for nature from without and that cannot be violated. Contemporary workers, amid the elementally powerful and har-moniously coherent work of machines, unconsciously acquire a mechanistic conception of nature ... Everyone *constructs the world* according to the form and likeness of their specialised *experience*.

At the same time, the possibility of people mutually understanding one another also narrows. Dealing with different content of experience and cre-ating dissimilar forms for this content, the members of a society in which specialisation is developing necessarily speak different languages. And if spe-cialisation could develop without end and if along with the fragmentation of collective experience a significant part of it did not remain common to all, then the story of the Towel of Babel would be repeated, and people would be forced to disperse because of the complete failure to understand one another.

VI

Specialisation did not destroy society, but all the same it fragmented it to the highest degree.

Although specialisation arose amidst authoritarian relationships, as it developed it ceased to be confined within the bounds of one or another author-itarian group. In each isolated sphere of experience, each specialist encoun-tered considerably less resistance than the previous integral people had en-countered in their diversified world, and therefore the broadening of exper-ience went incomparably faster under specialisation. The collective world, expanding simultaneously in different 'specialised' directions became huge in comparison with the former sum of collective experience.

Meanwhile, the powers of the old authority were limited, if only because its form was concrete and personal. Authority was embodied in a living person, and no human powers can grasp the whole sum of experience that the life of a specialised society presents. The collective whole now could not be controlled and regulated by a single will; it fragmented and broke up into independent groups – that is, individual enterprises.

A separate 'specialist' became the centre of each such group. Such specialists participated in social life as completely independent units who were not direc-ted by any outside will in regard to either the method or the means of their labour activity. Society as a whole became an unorganised, anarchical system, and it was therefore full of contradictions. Elements of society – living differ-ent lives and being independent in form but constantly clashing by virtue of necessary material relationships – turned out to be mutually unadapted and therefore mutually hostile. The collective world was then transformed into a world of competition, struggle of interests, war of all against all ...

It was then that the human 'I' developed and came to the fore.

VII

In a world of specialisation, it is only a difference in life experience together with its result – the incomplete mutual understanding among people – that profoundly distinguishes one person from another in their consciousness. This distinction gains strength because of the external independence of human individuals from other people in their labour activity, and it is brought to com-pletion on the basis of the mutual struggle among people that issues from the contradiction of their vital interests.

In being opposed to other 'I's in reality, the human 'I' becomes an independ-ent centre of interests and desires. The hammer of social antagonism forges individual consciousness.

This is not the relative 'I' of the authoritarian world that cannot imagine itself without an implementational 'you'; it is an absolute 'I', an 'I' *an und für sich* – in itself and for itself – that is unaware of its organic interconnectedness with other 'I's and with the whole world.

Old authority was unable to reconcile itself with this developing anarchical consciousness; it struggled against it and tried to suppress it. In the struggle with authority, individualism became a *liberating* movement, and in this role, it had huge historical significance. Its role, however, was historically fleeting. It appeared with full force in the old revolutions of the seventeenth and eight-eenth centuries, but in the revolutions of our times the struggle of individu-alism against the authoritarian past is increasingly giving way to its struggle against the socialist future.

VIII

The 'absolute' individual 'I' is an expression of socially fragmented experience and the opposition of one person to another in life. Understandably, the unity of the social whole is outside its field of vision. And this unity is not only invis-ible to the human individual, it is also imperfect, spontaneous, unorganised, and full of vital contradictions. The human individual is *beneath* these contradictions of the social whole, which is inaccessible to it and which it cannot understand. The human individual is powerless in the face of these contradictions; humanity is governed by the spontaneous forces of social life.

Experience and thinking are of the same sort. Thinking is individualistic. Its eternal centre is 'I', it is 'absolute', and it is torn from the social whole – and all the more from the world whole. This 'I' is a 'subject' that stands opposed to everything else as an 'object'. It cannot find a place for itself in the endless series of phenomena of reality. It agonisingly feels itself to be under the dominion of some kind of dark spontaneous forces, but these supra-individual forces go beyond the limits of an individual's experience. And people embody their vague conceptions of these forces in impersonal, metaphysical abstractions with indefinite, fluctuating content. All life and the entire world process are then conceived of by the consciousness as 'manifestations' of a mysterious, impersonally abstract reality deeply hidden beneath the surface of the 'visible' world as its unknowable 'essence'.

These metaphysical forms of thinking achieve the purest and most subtle refinement only in the heads of philosophers, but they are characteristic of *all* individualistic consciousness, no matter how vaguely and awkwardly they are expressed in the psyche of an uneducated, ordinary person.

IX

Individual consciousness, embodying fragmented, contradictory experience, necessarily becomes the victim of 'accursed questions'. These are the hopelessly fruitless questions for which 'fools have expected answers' for so many centuries. 'What am I?' a fool asks. 'What is the world?' 'Where did it all come from?' 'What for?' 'Why is there so much evil in the world?' and so on without end.

If you look closely at these questions, it becomes clear that they are the questions of an atomised person. These are exactly the questions that an organ that was separated from an organism would have to ask itself if it continued to live and could ask questions.

'What am I?' – is this not the most natural question for any finger of a hand that was separated from a body? 'What am I for; where did I come from?' How could this not be asked by a living part that has lost its connection with its vital whole? And other questions inevitably accompany these questions that are unavoidable but at the same time are inaccessible to its parts: 'what is the world?' 'what is the world for?' 'where did the world come from?' And wherever living tissue has been torn in the separation of an organ from a body, there is agonising and incomprehensible pain. This is where questions about evil in life come from. The hopelessness of these questions issues from the fact that it makes no difference what answers are given; no answers can satisfy an individualistic consciousness. After all, these questions express the torment of life that has been torn apart, and as long as it remains torn apart, no answer can end the pain because an answer to the pain is altogether impossible. In this case everything is useless. Even when progressive criticism proves that these questions are incorrectly posed, are meaningless, and are based on false premises – even then individualistic consciousness does not cease to ask them. This is because criticism is powerless to *really* transform this consciousness; it is powerless to convert it from a fraction of life to a whole.

X

Specialisation did not eliminate the authoritarian fragmentation of humankind, it only restricted its field and created new limits for it. A 'specialist' – an artisan, a peasant, a scholar – not only externally appears to be independent in their activity, but they are also the 'authority' within the confines of the small group with which they are connected by a direct vital link. They are the 'head' of their family, their household economy. The 'bourgeois world' is an authoritarian-individualistic world.

As I recall, Ludwig Börne,[1] a brilliant representative of this world, defined freedom as despotism in a certain, limited sphere. This sphere is first and foremost the family, and the great liberal therefore warmly defended the slavery of women and children.

The thinking of the bourgeois world naturally combines both authoritarian dualism and individualistic fracturedness. It is religious and metaphysical. Its *Universum* is bifurcated throughout and is full of mysterious contradictions.

XI

The fragmentation of humankind not only made life incomplete, bifurcated experience, and fractured the world, it also engendered real vital contradictions and, through them, progress.

---

1 Karl Ludwig Börne (1736–1837) was a German political writer and satirist [trans.].

The need to become whole sprang up with spontaneous force in the atomised person. It brought severe torment of discontent to individuals, but it also pushed them onto the road of struggle to redress that discontent. This is the path along which the *integration of humankind* is being accomplished.

This process is more vitally complex and therefore vitally more difficult than the process of fragmentation. Thus, while this latter develops progressively, the former unavoidably lags behind it more and more. As a result, although the integration of humankind is constantly evoked by fragmentation and follows after it, it has nevertheless been utterly *masked* during the course of long periods of the life of humankind. Only when the process of fragmentation slows and comes to a halt will the process of integration come to the fore and make its mark on the development of the life of humankind.

Modern times is the era of the integration of humankind.

XII

In a specialised society, the need to unify and gather atomised experience attains enough power to evoke *conscious* attempts in that direction. These attempts bear the name 'philosophy'. The task of philosophy – harmoniously unified thinking about the world – coincides with the task of the integration of humankind because the world is the entire sum of experience that is accessible to people.

As long as the fragmentation of humankind continued to develop, the work of philosophy was the work of Sisyphus. It was an agonising tragedy of heroic minds who repeated over and over again the hopeless effort of binding up the deeply torn tissue of the world, which was increasingly torn apart, with the delicate, bright threads of ideas.

At a certain stage of the development of this tragedy, a comic element appeared in it. Philosophers became *specialists*, and the further this developed the narrower they became. It turned out that their special realm of experience was the realm of *words* that expressed attempts at unifying experience. They ceased to be encyclopaedists as they had been before and now no longer strove to be. They became enclosed in specialties and became walking contradictions: a torn off bit seriously attempting to sew the whole together.

Proceeding along this path, philosophers became ever greater philistines. Their activity became a systematic mending of holes in the universe with the fabric of their nightcaps. This is the predominant type of contemporary epistemologists and metaphysicians. The uselessness of their efforts is only amusing; their fate is a farce and not a tragedy.

They all sincerely believe themselves to be successors to the philosophical geniuses of the past – heroes in the struggle for the unity of the world and humankind – and do not notice that in reality they are nothing more than bad tailors.

Philistine philosophy, it goes without saying, is useless and even harmful in regard to the integration of humankind, which is being realised outside of philistine philosophy and not by means of scholastic twaddle but by life itself. Life itself is becoming 'philosophy'.

XIII

We find the most vivid, typical, and brilliant example of the integration of humankind precisely where the fragmentation of humankind has gone to the ultimate extreme.

The pinnacle of the fragmentation of humankind is the detail worker in a manufactory.[2] Artisans were already 'narrow specialists', a fraction of humankind as far as the content and the extent of their experience is concerned. But the worker in a manufactory is turned into a minor part of an artisan. Some spend their whole life sharpening the points on needles; others spend their whole life making the eyes ... They have become human machines.

They also have become almost as stupid as machines. And the more that each of them becomes stupid – losing life and individuality – the better they are as machines and the more profitable they are for those who command them and make use of them. Profit also led to the complete elimination of individuality and life: a detail worker becomes a *machine*. And, to the extent that such a worker is atomised and simplified, this is both possible and comparatively easy.

But at the same time a new type of labour has appeared: the worker in machine production.

Workers in a manufactory were conceivable only as *implementers* of the orders of others; they were machines, and a machine must be operated. People who work with machines are also implementers, but that is *not all*. They *operate* the machine. They direct and supervise the activity of the mechanism. Their work has the same psychical content as the activity of an organiser who directs and supervises the labour of manufactory workers. 'Organisational' qualit-

---

2 'Manufactory' refers the first stage of capitalism, as discussed in Chapter xiv of *Capital*, 'Division of Labour and Manufacture' in which workers perform simple, repetitive, machine-like tasks, as opposed to 'machine production' in which workers are responsible for supervising the operation of largely self-regulating machines [trans.].

ies – intelligence, attention – are even more necessary to the machine worker than to the organiser. It is easy to understand a detail worker, and the detail worker almost always obeys, but it is often much more difficult to understand a machine, and the machine often ceases to obey ...

Thus, in the world of technology an important step has been taken on the path along which the fundamental – authoritarian – fragmentation of humankind is being overcome. A psychological type is appearing that combines the organisational and implementational points of view in one immediately whole activity.

And this is not all. While requiring intelligence and attention from a worker, a machine at the same time is not at all capable *by itself* of satisfying the needs that it evokes. Work on a machine is empty and not rich in content, it fully occupies the intellect and attention of the worker only occasionally. It is necessary to seek other nourishment for them in order to fill the emptiness. Intellectual interests and a striving to deepen and broaden experience develop – interests and desires that are directed toward the integration of humankind.

But how are they to be satisfied? Capital is seeing to this. Capital brings *people* together, and this leads to the integration of humankind.

Capital unites people in huge masses for common work. They need only *understand* one another in order to mutually broaden and deepen their experience. There are none of the previous obstacles to this mutual understanding, since we are now looking at people and not at specialised machines in manufactories. No matter at what different machines machine workers find themselves, the general nature and content of their labour is always very similar. And, to the extent that machines are perfected and approach their ideal – the automatic mechanism – this similarity continually grows. Therefore, there is sufficient commonality of experience for mutual understanding through communication. And communication develops.

Thus, the second form of the fragmentation of humankind – specialisation – is being gradually overcome.

XIV

Yet newer and more perfected forms of the integration of humankind appear on the basis of the commonality of experience – both that which is immediately given and that which develops by way of communication.

Group and class self-consciousness is the most typical of these forms. It extends individual experience to group experience and to broader class experience. It extends individual interests and desires to group interests and desires and then to class interests and desires. This is a necessary stage in the integration of humankind.

Various new forms and combinations of the integration of humankind – economic, political, and ideological unions, parties and doctrines – spring up on the ground of this commonality. Some of them turn out more viable, others less viable; some develop, others decay. But in the final analysis, directly or indirectly, they all serve the integration of humankind.

xv

The machine was born in the world of competition, of social antagonism. As is well known, the machine sharpened this competition and antagonism to the extreme. But in so doing, it sharpened and intensified *the need for development*.

Continuous, systematic improvement of technology becomes necessary for competition in every given realm, and this need is satisfied by the development of general technological methods.

General technological methods lead to a situation in which all machines gradually approach the highest type of machine, the automatic mechanism. This process not only directly and immediately diminishes the significance of specialisation by increasing the similarity of different forms of labour, it has still another importance – indirect but huge – for the integration of humankind.

At its foundation, science is the systematisation of technology. The material of science is 'labour that is experience and experience that is labour'. *Science expresses and reflects general technological methods in general methods of cognition.*

The universal law of the conservation and transformation of energy is precisely the universal technological principle of machine production. It expresses a fundamental fact of all human labour – that work is necessarily derived from some kind of existing supply of forces. And the universal limiting law of entropy, which supplements the law of energy, reflects the universal limitedness of human technology – the existing supply of energy can never be entirely and fully utilised by humankind.

Thus, all of collective experience is systematised in the unifying forms of cognition that are accessible to the psyche of an individual. Knowledge of general methods replaces familiarity with endless details. Consequently, non-specialists cease to feel alien in any special realm. Naturally, a lot of details and particulars are *unknown* to them, but everything in general is *understandable* to them, and it is easy for them to become as familiar as they please with each of these details and particulars. A specialist remains a specialist only in the sphere of details, but in the sphere of methods – i.e. in the entire *active* side of their special experience – a specialist is now a human being.

Specialists of the previous type become not only deformed but also useless figures; they are unable to create anything in their field since their techniques are all identical and their psyches are narrow and meagre. At best, they are still useful for gathering facts, but here also the usefulness is accompanied by harm. They are unable to sort out these facts, piling them up without meaning and even unconsciously distorting them according to their obsolete point of view. When they enter the realm of broad generalisations, they turn out to be openly reactionary. In biology they are vitalists, in economic science they are 'marginalists', in philosophy they are metaphysicians, and everywhere they are scholastics. Here they are still harmful, but they do not frighten cognition that is developing; their grand mien causes only the hearty laughter of youthful criticism.

A new type of scholar is taking the place of the old philistine specialist – a broadly educated, monistic thinker who is a social being. Such a thinker expresses the consciously systematic integration of humankind, and the further this process goes the more successful it is, since it finds support in the spontaneous social process. The best – almost ideal – embodiment of this type was the person who first provided a monistic understanding of social life and development – the great philosopher-fighter, Karl Marx.

XVI

The integration of humankind occurs along various paths. I have pointed out only the basic paths – in the sphere of technology and cognition. To trace all the derivative paths – in the realms of 'political', 'legal', and 'moral' relationships – would take too long. The important thing is that each new step on this path makes further steps easier, intensifying the interconnectedness and mutual understanding of those elements of humanity that are drawn into the process of 'integration'. Consequently, no matter how difficult, no matter how painful this process is from time to time, with each new phase its realisation becomes easier. Its speed is growing.

XVII

Where is this line of development leading? To the transformation of a human-fraction into a human-whole. But what does this mean?

Does this mean that there will be a return to the primeval type of element-ally whole life when the experience of each and the experience of all coincided, when each person was a stereotypically repeating element of an undifferenti-ated whole? Of course not!

As humanity conquers nature, the sum of collective experience has grown to such colossal dimensions that it is impossible to think that it could fully fit into each separate psyche. And the very process of the integration of human-ity, to the extent that we can know it, is definitely not headed toward such a monstrous swelling of the human soul.

The issue here has to do with a growing generality of the *basic content* of experience and not with innumerable particular experiences; it has to do with the possibility of the *full mutual understanding* of people and not their becom-ing psychically identical. The issue has to do with the *capability* of all individual people at any given moment of taking possession of whatever part of the exper-ience of other people that they want to and not about the actual possession of all this experience.

Primeval wholeness was based on the limitedness of life and was connec-ted with the extreme conservatism of life; the new wholeness to which the integration of humanity is leading must embrace the huge profusion of life and provide a space for life to develop without limit. The first wholeness was static; the second is dynamic. The first was *habitual*; the second is *plastic*. The essence of the first was simplicity; the essence of the second is harmony.

You look around and an endless world unfolds in your field of vision. Rays of light draw images of objects in your eyes. These are attenuated but 'true' images. Some objects are closer to us and are perceived in great detail; others are fur-ther away and only their general features are perceived. At any given moment, a third set of objects is inaccessible to our vision. For other people all these rela-tionships are different. They see objects that you do not see, and parts of the surroundings that appear to you only in the form of vague contours appear to them, just the opposite, in great detail. In a word, their field of vision is *different*. But you need only use binoculars or go up to the objects, and you will be able to clearly see any of the objects that are nearest to them every bit as clearly and in detail as they do. The visual world of both you and them is *identical*, and you both have at your disposal *common methods* of visually 'capturing' any part of this world.

However, if you live on a small island that you cannot leave, or if you do not know how to use optical instruments that other people use, then your visual world is not the same as for other people, and you will not *understand* their descriptions of other countries or the information they provide about forms and movements of the planets and other such utterances.

In both cases above, if you replace the visual world with collective experience, you will arrive at the antithesis between the harmonious life of the future – toward which the integration of humanity is leading – and contemporary, obsolete specialisation. If people master well-worked-out general methods of cognition and practice, they will be able to 'approach' any problem or vital task with these methods. They will resolve the problem or task even though it is outside their 'specialty'. Under the old specialisation a person is unable to 'approach' such things, since there are no general methods. To resolve a particular problem or task, it is necessary to master a whole new specialty, and it might take someone's whole life to achieve that.

When there is a true and harmonious – if attenuated – reflection of everyone's experience in every person's experience, when no one finds anything fundamentally inaccessible and incomprehensible in the experiences of other people, then 'specialised' labour will no more cut people off from collective life than a given field of vision cuts them off from the entire visual world. Then life can freely extend in any given direction, and it will not be deformed, distorted, or badly one-sided.

This is what the integration of humankind is leading to.

XVIII

A person is a reflection of society. What social relationships correspond to the new, developing type of human life?

The fundamental equality of experience united with the complete mutual understanding of people can only be the result of broad communication among people who are completely equal in their mutual position. These conditions correspond to only one type of human relationship – the relationship of *comrades*. These relationships are essentially hostile to any barriers between people, to any subordination and limitation, to any fragmentation of humankind.

The integration of humankind is also accomplished precisely where and precisely to the extent that authoritarian relationships and specialisation are replaced by comradely relationships.

This needs no proof, and there is no need to explain it in detail here.

XIX

There can be no doubt that universal comradely relationships and the complete mutual understanding of people mean that social contradictions and antagonisms will be destroyed.

Here the question of the *forces of development* arises.

Opponents of comradely relationships assert that these relationships are essentially stagnant precisely because they are harmonious. In their opinion, only struggle between people – in the form of war, competition, group antagonism, and, finally, athletic contests (although they are a weak psychical reflection of this struggle) – stimulates progress and guarantees that it will be continuous. Wherever there is harmony there will be nowhere to go and no need to go further.

Is this so?

Is it possible that the vital struggle will really cease when the struggle between people ceases? Is it possible that spontaneous nature will then make peace with human consciousness? Is it possible that suffering, death, what has not been discovered about our world, and what is not known about other distant worlds will cease to surround humanity? Is it possible that the great enemy will then take humanity into its embrace?

The struggle of one person against another is nothing more than the high price that is paid for *spontaneous* development. A huge amount of effort is fruitlessly expended on this struggle, and only a small part of it goes directly to make humanity stronger and more perfect. When such a waste of effort is brought to an end, an era of *conscious* development will begin.

Where the experience of each person continually obtains more content from the experience of all, where ever newer questions and tasks continually spring up from the mutual communication of people, where the harmonious unification of collective forces gives each person the ability to enter into the common struggle against elemental nature with confidence in victory, there can be no question that development will be stimulated.

Whoever considers the struggle among people to be a necessary condition of their development is simply generalising their own narrow experience, crudely carrying the past forward into the future. Frequently a person who has been taught with a birch rod considers it impossible to teach children anything without it. This is the same logic.

The integration of humankind will lead not to stagnation but to the replacement of one type of development by another – the disharmonious development of fragmented humanity by the harmonious development of united humanity.

Essentially, the fragmentation of humankind was never only fragmentation. It took place much more through one-sided development than through the curtailment of life, much more through hypertrophy of one of its sides than through atrophy of the other side. The *plenitude of life* did not thereby decrease; it grew.

Even the narrowest specialists of our times – any blacksmith who forges some nails or a dust-laden epistemologist who sees life only through the dingy window of their office – even they possess an incomparably greater profusion of experiences than the primeval whole person of long ago. And this is exactly how things must be in regard to the different scope of life for the one-sided, contradiction-filled people who are developing in our times and for the harmonious, many-sided beings that will replace them.

Because of huge quantitative differences of experience and the radical dissimilarity of types of life, someone from one phase of humanity's development of humanity cannot even understand someone from another phase. They cannot concretely imagine the other's psychical life, and when investigating that psychical life, one can only abstractly characterise its basic traits, as I do in regard to the type of life of the prehistorical past and to the type of life of the historically emerging future.

The question then arises: does it make sense to use the same word 'humanity' to indicate beings that are so heterogeneous?

Both yes and no. Yes, because the chain of development here is nevertheless continuous. No, because there is little use in a unifying 'concept' where real differences prevail over similarity, where the psychical interconnectedness and the unity that are necessary for the mutual *understanding* of living beings are lacking. It is obvious that '*no*' is truer here than '*yes*'.

So, what is humankind? The delineation of the entire picture of development serves to answer this question.

Do we accept that humankind is predetermined in the embryo, spontaneous, and alien to development? I do not think so.

Do we accept that a human is an incomplete being – a part torn from its whole – that develops disharmoniously? I do not think so.

But if we accept that humans are developing and not embryonically predetermined beings, whole and not fragmented, then our conclusion will be the following:

Humankind has not yet arrived, but it is near and its silhouette is clearly coming into view on the horizon.

CHAPTER 11

The Norms and Goals of Life

Only a few thousand years have passed since human life ceased to be a naked 'struggle for existence'. For thousands of years before that, the entire meaning – the content – of life boiled down to simple *survival*, to the assertion of life against the terrible and hostile forces of the external world. All people's efforts were aimed only at avoiding destruction and death, only at supporting life, supporting life *as such*. Given the weakness and instability of life, the smallest change threatened it with terrible danger, almost inevitable destruction, and people felt overwhelming terror in the face of anything new and unusual in their lives and in the natural world that surrounded them.

All this was completely natural and appropriate. When the light of life had just begun to gleam, any variation was dangerous and threatened to irreversibly extinguish it. From time to time, the elemental influences of the external world cannot but engender spontaneous changes in the nature of people and in their relationships with one another, but these changes are infinitely more often destructive than useful for life. They destroy the existing equilibrium of life, and if elements for producing a new, higher equilibrium are lacking, then the degradation of life is inevitable. Hence the *elemental conservatism* of primeval life; hence the huge internal resistance that it displayed to any development, to any transformation. Humanity was governed by this conservatism and resistance so completely for so long that all the movement of historical life has not been able to wipe them out, and they continue to leave their mark on the psychology of even the most progressive groups and classes of contemporary society.

In the era of primeval conservatism, the question of 'norms' of human life was extremely simplistic. To be more exact, it did not even exist. The given, existing form of life was *absolutely obligatory*; conservatism was its norm. Nothing could be allowed to change; everything had to be as it had been and as it was. This is the 'universal norm' of primeval psychology.

But, in essence, this is not even a norm. Any norm presupposes a more or less conscious formulation and presupposes the idea of the possibility of 'violations' of it. Primeval conservatism was free of any conscious formulation; there was no need of it, since there was no idea of the possibility that one could 'violate' this conservatism. It *existed*, and it was as little in need of being formulated into norms as was the instinct of self-preservation – of which conservatism is the purest form. For primeval people, anything that violated conservatism was an external and hostile force, and they spontaneously struggled against it. They obeyed the immediate impulse of their organisation and not the voice of conscience, legal consciousness, or even prudence that expressed their demands in the form of various 'norms'.

It is appropriate to characterise the situation as the rule of 'custom' over primeval life. But this 'custom' was not at all what is meant by that term in the contemporary world. It was not an old *norm* known to everyone. It was not a rule that people were guided by and that they tried not to violate. It was rather a thousand-year-old *habit* that constituted an inseparable part of human existence. There were cases in which this 'custom' was violated, but for primeval consciousness this was simply the violation of the natural order of facts just like the birth of a two-headed foetus or a solar eclipse. The baby with two heads was discarded. The violator of custom was killed or driven out. They shot arrows to try to drive away the dark force that obscured the sun. All these are psychologically similar actions, manifestations of the unconscious and unconditional conservatism of life, of the instinct for self-preservation in the initial phase of its development.

People who belonged to one primeval clan group were psychologically as identical to one another as they were identically organised physically. Because of this, their mutual relationships were infinitely simple and devoid of any contradictions. Norms are needed only where relationships are complex and contradictory. This is why primeval life did not know norms, and this is why it did not even know the basic concepts that constitute the necessary content of any norm making. In this world that was so very distant from ours, there was no place for the ideas of 'one must' and 'one must not', of 'compulsion' and 'freedom', of 'law' and 'transgression'. There was only immediate life that frantically struggled against everything that violated the uniform cycle of its spontaneous course as it repeated itself over and over.

II

The norms of human life express knowledge of 'good and evil', and they began to rule after the 'fall' of humankind.

The 'fall' was not accomplished in one day or in a thousand years. It was a long and extremely slow process. It consisted in life gradually ceasing to be true to what it had been – it ceased to be true to its primordial, fixed form ...

No matter how seldom and fortuitous *useful* changes of primevally conservative life were, they survived along with life because they helped life to survive, whereas all other changes harmed life and perished along with it. Through the endless accumulation of the infinitely small, new real magnitudes were created. The power of life grew and prevailed in the struggle with the forces of hostile nature.

A surplus of energy causes life to grow, and as it accumulates it engenders the need for new forms of equilibrium. The faster energy accumulates, the greater the need for new combinations and relationships and the less possible and expedient is the simple survival of given forms.

Thus, by necessity, life gradually began to change from a simple repetition of the unchanging cycles of life into development, from the naked struggle for the survival of what is into a struggle for more. What is *given* ceases to be the sole goal and norm.

The development that was being engendered could not be anything other than spontaneous development, an emerging struggle for more in life, and it could not be anything other than an unconscious struggle. Movement forward was involuntary and devoid of any planning. Therefore, at any moment, in any given manifestation, it turned out to be partial and one-sided and not whole and general. This movement forward *destroyed* the existing harmony of the vital system. Then the old instinct for the *survival what is given* appeared – the desire to defend and restore the previous harmony. But it was now utterly unable to do this because of the growing power of development. In its struggle with development, the old instinct of preservation retreated and was transformed into a new form – the desire to *place boundaries* on the destruction of existing harmony. This was the starting point for the formation of compulsory norms.

Thus, if in communistic clan communes, there were cases in which certain individual members were found to be using some extraordinary means of labour or consumption – tools, clothing, adornment – then there can be no doubt that these facts, which were historically completely progressive, deeply shook the entire structure of communal life and caused a severe reaction. But from the outset, the simple suppression of them did not, of course, attain its goal. The new means of labour or consumption were repeated more and more often, and the necessity of them entered the collective consciousness; collective consciousness was forced to adapt to them. Then the semiconscious creative work of collective consciousness led to a certain compromise: the 'new' was allowed, but up to a certain boundary, beyond which suppression began. A *customary norm* was the incarnation of that compromise: 'this is allowed, and this is forbidden'. 'Forbidden' signified the real sanction of a norm – social compulsion, violence against the violator of the norm. Such was the first fruit of collective creative work directed toward the struggle with the contradictions of social development.

III

What precisely was it that brought people to the kind of attitude toward transgression in which deviations from existing forms of life ceased to be an utterly extraordinary phenomenon and became part of a chain of natural events?

It began when the psychological identity of the people of one group disappeared and their thinking was no longer 'solid'. The *division of labour* gradually began to eliminate the former homogeneity, and at the same time it involved the *division of experience*. The content of people's labour activity continuously became more different. The material of the impressions upon which their thought had to operate was different for farmers than for woodland hunters, different for hunters than for fishers. In dealing with different material, the thinking of individual people increasingly led to dissimilar results. Society was transformed into a continuously more complex combination of increasingly heterogeneous elements. The manifestations of people's lives turned out to be ever less coordinated, and a profound and powerful need to coordinate them arose.

The division of labour often brought people into conflict even in the sphere of their immediate goals, when, for example, hunters pursuing game would trample a farmer's crops or cattle farmers leading their herds to watering places would interfere with the work of fishers. But the conflicts that were much more important and much more frequent and profound were those that appeared between the customs of different workers, between their points of view on life, and their means of responding to their surroundings. The roughness and callousness of soldiers was irreconcilable with the gentleness and prudence of their fellow members of the commune who were farmers. The heightened needs of skilled craftspeople caused bewilderment and aversion on the part of simple fishers, and so on and so on. The organic similarity of customs disappeared; they lost the characteristics of absolute stability and elemental immutability.

Under such conditions, the destruction of a former 'custom' was necessarily encountered more and more often, it ceased to seem to be something monstrously strange and incomprehensible, and the formerly unconsciously reflexive relationship toward it became impossible. The work of consciousness in this realm was inevitable and necessary; the *previous* form of the custom was unsuitable for the constant restoration of the vital equilibrium that had been upset.

A radical transformation of custom occurred here that was radical even though the very content of the custom continued to survive. From being a naked, immediate fact of life, it became a *norm* of life. An organic tendency attained a definite formulation.

'One must behave in such-and-such a way!' ... This 'must' contained not only the desire to *preserve* an historically given form of vital relationship but also the conception of the possibility of *violating* it. It reflected the struggle of two forces, an internal contradiction of life. Both sides of custom were objectively embodied when its norm was violated: 'compulsion' by which the violation was brought to a halt arrived on the scene. 'Custom' manifested itself as a compulsory norm with a specific sanction.

This inaugurated a whole new realm of human development

IV

At a certain stage, the development of the heterogeneity of elements of the social whole brought in its train the development of its *non-organisation*, and then the world of compulsory norms expanded to colossal dimensions.

To the extent that individual elements of society become increasingly less homogenous, they become more isolated in their vital activities, and it is all the more difficult to maintain constant interconnectedness among them. In a small clan or tribal commune interconnectedness is maintained by the activity of a general organiser – a patriarch or a leader. But the progress of production leads to a situation in which the dimensions of society grow exponentially and then the general organisation of labour becomes impossible. It is now utterly beyond the power of a human individual, and society as a whole, due to the heterogeneity of its elements, is incapable of carrying it out collectively. Society disintegrates into individual small groups – separate enterprises – in which each independently organises its labour activity and is not externally connected with others.

The material interconnectedness among enterprises remains. They form the links of one gigantic chain – a system of the social division of labour. Otherwise, they would be completely independent societies, and then each of them, because of their insignificant power, would be utterly helpless in the struggle for life against external nature. The unorganised nature of this labour interconnectedness finds expression in *exchange relations* among enterprises. The *distribution* of products of labour in society is also anarchic and unsystematic, i.e. not unified by any kind of conscious will.

Lack of organisation of life means the unproductive expenditure of life's powers, antagonism of its forms, and contradictoriness in its manifestations. This relates to all realms of life. In the sphere of production, social labour should satisfy social needs exactly and completely. But when social labour is not organised, when it is not distributed among the individuals in society with any plan or oversight, then it is impossible that its results can strictly correspond to social needs. It is inevitable that part of the accumulation is dissipated fruitlessly, creating excess in the realm of some social needs, while some other social needs, lacking a sufficient quantity of the necessary products of social labour, remain unsatisfied. 'Overproduction' exists side by side with 'underproduction'.

In the sphere of distribution, lack of organisation gives rise to new, profound disharmonies. Distribution itself takes on the form of struggle and competition – struggle between buyer and seller and competition among buyers and sellers themselves in which each strives to obtain more at the expense of the other. The result is unequal and disproportionate distribution. Even when there is a general surplus, the needs of many members of society remain unsatisfied, and many enterprises perish or experience a decline in their standard of living. The brute power of the market makes a mockery of people's efforts.

As it develops further, the same lack of organisation of the social system gives rise to a struggle of classes that becomes sharper to the extent that the powers of those classes grow. This struggle permeates *all* social life, from its most 'material' to its most 'ideal' manifestations ... The colossal progress of life and the power of humanity have always gone hand in hand with the colossal growth of social contrasts and contradictions.

It is not difficult to see what a huge significance for development would be possessed by anything that brings any order to this chaos, that brings any organisation to this lack of organisation, and that puts any limits on this disharmony in the way that compulsory norms would. This is why social creativity in this realm unfolds with huge force and gives rise to a huge profusion of forms. It is the result of severe vital necessity.

V

As we have seen, the basis of a world of norms was established when custom was transformed from an immediate manifestation of an organically whole life into an external, compulsory norm. Subsequently, this new, 'normative' custom became the progenitor of a whole series of other forms of the same type: customary rights and laws, decency and morality. Despite all specific differences of form, they are similar in that they are an external and compulsory force directed toward regulating the relationships of members of society. The significance of this regulation is that it strives to weaken and remove contradictions generated by development, to bring organisation to atomised and anarchical social being.

The primary and fundamental form of external compulsion that sanctions the prescription of norms is direct material violence upon those who violate the norm. This sanction survives entirely within the sphere of custom and law, while the compulsion that constitutes the vital basis for norms of decorum and morality has a different character. It boils down to social censure and contempt. This ameliorated form of social reaction to the 'abnormal' (from the point of view of existing relationships) behaviour of people applies only to those cases when divergent behaviour does not directly and harshly violate the fundamental vital interests of the collectivity as they appear in its consciousness – when these interests are touched on only weakly or indirectly. Appearing as a weak reflection of the crudely-material struggle of society against 'anomalous' activities of its members, this second type of compulsion does not, of course, exclude the first type and is usually combined with it in cases of 'crimes' and 'offenses' against the norms of age-old custom or law. Such crimes and offenses are not only stopped and punished by the physical force of society but are also stigmatised as something immoral and sometimes even indecent.

Violators of norms are themselves children of the society that punishes the violation of norms with censure and contempt. They are used to the norm, and they *accept* it even when, giving in to immediate impulses, they violate it. They therefore carry out upon themselves the 'compulsion', the punishment, or at least the nonmaterial form of censure and contempt that the given society has always applied to 'abnormal' actions. This is the objective basis of the painful feeling that is called a guilty conscience; it is the individual psychological reflection of how *society* reacts to actions that violate norms.

This is favourable soil for the individualistic fetishism that the Kantian philosophy of morality has formulated. It is only on this basis that moral norms, once they are laid down, acquire the inner sanction of a 'guilty conscience'. *Exclusively* internal obligation is ascribed to moral norms; they stand out as autonomous legislation belonging to the absolute human individuality that lies at the basis of human existence. In this way, the entire genesis of morality is ignored – how it descends in a direct line from custom, how it was later set apart from customary law (which was still far from being achieved in feudal-Catholic society, for example). The obviously *non-autonomous*, externally compulsive nature of moral norms that is clearly evident in the conflict of moral duty with instincts and desires of developing life are also ignored. Ignoring all this, the Kantian philosophy of morality was successful for a long time and for many people in obscuring the elementary and simple fact that 'internal' moral conflicts are conflicts of immediate impulses of life with the crystallised power of the social past that *is external to them*, even though they are encountered in one field of individual consciousness. In any event, the liberating struggle of contemporary *amoralism* (both individual and social) already appears as clear and living proof that the duty to obey of moral norms is only the historically transformed form of social compulsion.

In this sense, there is no essential difference between morality and all other normative forms – custom, law, etc.

VI

The organisational significance of normative forms for contradictions within people's developing social being is truly huge. In order to understand it fully, it is necessary only to imagine approximately what society would turn into if there were no norms. Society would go to pieces like a barrel without hoops; it would break down like a human organism that lacked the parts of the nervous system that unify and regulate life.

Exchange is a necessary condition of life in the cultured societies that are known in history, and competition and class antagonism are the motive forces of their development. But exchange takes the form of struggle among buyers and sellers in order to obtain the greatest possible value. If this struggle were not limited by compulsion laid down by custom, law, and morality, then society would naturally fall apart and exchange itself would become impossible. Analogously, competition would turn into the physical destruction of the competitors who one wanted to be rid of, and class struggle in any other form besides bitter and bloody internecine war would be inconceivable.

And all this is what will happen in reality if vital contradictions, temporarily intensifying to the extreme, burst though the shell of norms and unfold spontaneously and freely. Enormous destruction of the elements of life – not only of those that have grown decrepit but also those that have just come into being – will then reveal with striking clarity the real meaning of 'development through contradiction'.

Different norms are extremely unequal as far as the breadth of their vital significance is concerned. The legal norm of private appropriation embraces and determines all the life of contemporary society, while many norms – the rules of propriety, for example – relate only to a few particular cases of interaction between people. This does not create a fundamental difference between norms; as *organising adaptations for people's social life*, they remain fundamentally the same.

For us, to organise life means to regulate it in an orderly way, to harmoniously adapt some of its manifestations to others. But precisely from this point of view the organisational significance of compulsory norms can often seem very questionable. Moreover, in other cases, by bringing contradictions into the process of development, the role of compulsory norms becomes absolutely disorganising. Thus, in our time, a great many legal norms in the political life of society and many moral norms in the life of the family cause unbearable contradictions that profoundly disorganise developing life. Such cases are explained by an historical investigation of how norms originated, since their positive role belongs *to the past*. The norm continues to survive when the conditions that created it have already disappeared, its vital significance has disappeared along with them, and it remains as a useless anachronism in the way of development. Sometimes a norm grows decrepit very quickly, as happens with many legal determinations, and sometimes a norm does not lose its vitality for thousands of years, as happens with certain moral principles. This vitality, which differs in degree but is always historically limited, boils down to the same basic content – to its organising function in the social process.

Contemporary societies with their anarchical structure and system of collaboration are entirely supported by *compulsory norms*. Norms of *property and subordination to contract* constitute the soul of capitalism.

VII

In primordial society, custom/habit embraced the existence of all people in all spheres of their activity. Normative forms succeeded customs and gradually took over this vast realm. Normative forms regulated the technology of social labour, people's economic relationships, consumption, and thought. People began to encounter compulsory boundaries everywhere. They began to feel everywhere the power of external norms over them that they did not establish and that emerged independently of them in their social surroundings.

Since any deviation from the norm was 'criminal', 'crime' was definitely possible in all spheres of life. Any major improvement of technology was viewed as 'criminal innovation' and was bitterly persecuted until such time as the power of economic necessity forced normative compulsion to retreat – as vividly illustrated by the tragic fate of many inventions and inventors during the Middle Ages and at the beginning of modern times. The same relationship toward technological or economic innovations (only in an ameliorated form – social odium) is observed among contemporary peasants in backward districts who see 'devilish (i.e. sinful in the highest degree) tricks' in non-traditional improvements in farming. In the realm of consumption, there are various 'taboos' of habit, law, morality, etc., such as the religious customs in the Pentateuch that forbade Jews to consume pork, the blood of animals, and many other kinds of food, Medieval laws that punished luxury inappropriate to status (or, more accurately, estate), and in our own time the rules of propriety that do not permit the simplest and most comfortable clothing or certain methods of consuming food, the moral aversion by many cultured and uncultured people to alcoholic drinks. All these are typical examples of 'taboos', and a countless number of other examples could be added.

The all-embracing power of custom/habit originally determined not only people's *actions* but also their *internal experiences*. In this case, compulsory norms also descended from custom. In the eastern despotisms of antiquity, there were cases of capital punishment for 'criminal dreams' – when, for example, someone dreamed about killing the king. The Inquisition considered heretical thoughts to be criminal whether or not they were expressed. There was even a case in which an inquisitor informed on himself when he began to entertain blasphemous thoughts, and, because of this justice required that he be burned at the stake. And in our cultured world the conception of 'sinful' or even 'criminal' thoughts has far from disappeared. It is only the legal compulsion that punishes 'illegal' association of ideas that has disappeared; moral compulsion in the form of social censure and a guilty conscience remains in great force down to the present day. There is also the virtually indistinguishable compulsion associated with the violation of the norms of propriety.

Thus, the net of external norms – sometimes crude and rigid, sometimes mild and elastic – enmeshes all sorts of manifestations of human life.

VIII

External compulsory norms of all kinds serve to bring order into the disharmony of life that is generated by spontaneous development. But the order that it brings is still not harmony in the positive meaning of the word; it is only an external unification and regulation of heterogeneous vital processes. For example, a contradiction between directly egoistic and directly social desires – between the desire to turn one's back on the suffering of other people and the desire to make a certain sacrifice to help them – might arise in someone. The dictate of law or moral obligation subordinates some of these motives to others: people act according to those motives that correspond to the 'norm'. But within their psyche the struggle between motives does not cease, and it can even become sharper, if the power of norms gives the victory not to those motives that are growing stronger at the present time but to those that are growing weaker.[1] Thus, in smoothing over and suppressing the manifestation of internal contradictions, an external norm does not remove those contradictions. It might even add a new contradiction to them: a contradiction between the particular vital tendency that the norm suppresses and the norm itself.

Further, external norms are conservative. They emerge slowly, and, for the most part, they disappear slowly. They always live longer than the need that caused them, and they die only after a stubborn struggle. Our times are full of such struggle; almost all the political life of backward countries and even a significant part of the political life of advanced countries often boils down to this kind of struggle. The same is true in other realms of normative ideology. Legal organisations and systems of custom and morality that have outlived themselves do not regulate spontaneous development and do not smooth away its contradictions; they simply hold it back. Sometimes this resistance results in the colossal expenditure of the best forces of developing life, and the era that our country is experiencing provides many examples of this. Here is a new source of vital contradictions.

External compulsory norms are absolutely necessary for the survival of life amid the contradictions of spontaneous development, but they allow it to survive only at the cost of constraining, limiting, and holding back that very development. Consequently, these norms, by replacing external conflicts with the harsh struggle of internal contradictions that issue from compulsion, direct human consciousness with all the more force toward working out new forms of life and development, forms that are free from spontaneity, contradictions, and compulsion.

IX

It may be considered a general rule that the higher the level of life in which they are manifested, the sharper, deeper, and broader are the contradictions of spontaneous development. The beginning of sexual life produces considerably more new anxieties and dissonances in the spontaneous growth of the human organism than in the development of any other young animal. In exactly the same way, the progress of 'cultured' capitalist societies is purchased at the

---

1   The following was added when this article was republished in the 1925 edition of *O proletarskoi kul'ture*: 'for example, when people bitterly regret having given poor people some money that they themselves might have needed very much' [trans.].

cost of an incomparably greater sum of contradictions than the progress of 'pre-cultured' communes with a natural economy. For higher forms of spontaneously developing life, the accelerating growth of life is combined with accelerating expenditure.

It even often happens that expenditure outweighs the growth of life, development turns into degradation, and 'one step forward' is followed by 'two steps back'. The ills of growth sometimes lead to the profound and protracted exhaustion of a young, delicate organisation and then to its complete destruction.

What exactly sharpens the contradictions of the spontaneous development of the higher forms of life to such a degree? The very features that make these forms 'higher'.

First and foremost, they are less conservative and more supple and plastic. Stationary and conservative lower forms naturally possess considerably greater immediate stability. It is true that it is only immediate stability, like a rock that it is hard to break but once it does break it loses its previous form forever. However, such stability safeguards a vital complex from too rapid destruction under the effect of moderately strong harmful influences, i.e. precisely those that are the most usual and frequent. Thus, for city-dwellers or cultured people in general, with their more impressionable and less hardy organisation, the contradictions of the period of sexual coming of age are considerably more painful and acute than they are for pre-civilised people or peasants.

A second characteristic, operating in the same way, is the profusion of the vital content of higher forms of life – of the many elements and the diversity of the parts from which those forms take shape. In a given living system there are huge numbers of combinations that have already entered it, and any change that is spontaneously engendered in that system will naturally encounter a great many combinations that will turn out to vitally contradict it. Thus, a new idea, having sprung up in the head of a separate human individual, is likely to encounter considerably more opposition and contradiction in the sphere of the complex, broadly multipartite ideological life of society than in the narrow and less rich intellectual life of the circle of people who are closest to the author.

Finally, a third distinctive feature of higher forms that sharpens the contradictions of their spontaneous development is their internal unity, their organisation, and the close vital interconnectedness of their parts and elements. For example, the hypertrophy or atrophy of any of the organs or functions of the human organism, which has a high degree of interconnectedness and organisation, would have a more profound influence on all its other relationships and would be much more dangerous than it would be for, let us say, an annelid, with its comparatively minor vital interconnectedness and interdependence of separate parts.

It is obvious that these conditions, which sharpen the disharmony of spontaneous development, must become more and more intense in proportion to this very development. Contradictions must grow more and more.

If this is so, then is not the development of life on an inevitable path toward hopeless destruction? What is the way out from the fateful connection between the progress of life and the progress of its contradictions?[2]

The way out lies beyond the confines of spontaneous development; it will be provided by a change in the form of development itself.

X

The agonising oscillations of life that are engendered by spontaneous development and the great cost and increasing insecurity of that development give rise to a new need: to bring harmony and unity to the process of development itself, to make it harmonious and holistic, and to eliminate its randomness. Its oscillations must give way to continuity, its dissonances to full and clear concord. In a word, it is necessary that life should change from a spontaneous movement into a harmonious movement.

Only then will progress find unconquerable support in the entire sum of the accumulated forces of life, and only then will endless and continuous victories over nature open up before it: *the struggle for more will turn into the struggle for everything.*

In this consciously expedient progress of life, the question of the goals of life will have perfect meaning for the first time, and that question will find an answer that is free from contradictions – in an endlessly growing sum of felicity. We, who are people of one-sided and disharmonious development, people of an era of contradictions, cannot imagine this type of life with any kind of completeness or clarity, but we have a vague presentiment of it in moments of ecstatic contemplation or reflection when we are in living communion with natural beauty or a great genius, and it seems to us that our tiny being disappears and merges with the infinite.

---

2   This paragraph was omitted from the 1925 edition [trans.].

XI

It would be foolish, however, to talk about a higher type of life or about the har-monious progress of life if there were nothing in our experience other than a vague presentiment or indistinct desire for it – if it was impossible to mark out embryonic forms of it in the past and present and if there was no data that depicted its probable future development, if only in the most general and schematic terms. Fortunately, such embryonic forms and such data exist, and there are enough of them to provide the basis for absolutely definite conclu-sions.

First and foremost, where are the conditions that are creating the very *pos-sibility* of a transition from spontaneously contradictory development to sys-tematically harmonious development? *In the very same place* as the conditions for the progressive sharpening of the contradictions of spontaneously devel-oping life – in the growing plasticity, the multiplying profusion of content, and the increasing organisation of vital forms.

Only a high level of plasticity of life allows rapid and many-sided adapta-tion to the environment. Compare the flexible nature of an urban proletarian worker with the dull and awkward psyche of a peasant from a backward vil-lage. It is only in rich, complex, and heterogeneous vital content that one can always find the necessary elements for such adaptation. Compare, for example, the vital resourcefulness of someone who has seen and experienced a great deal under all sorts of circumstances with the typical obtuse perplexity of someone with little experience when they encounter any kind of new combination of conditions. Finally, only the growing organisation of forms makes individual, separate processes of development less and less isolated with the result that each process is no longer limited to the part of the vital whole in which it arises but is quickly reflected in all other parts and causes a series of correspond-ing changes in them. In this respect the contrast between the highly organised thinking of philosophers for whom a new phenomenon or a new idea can cause concordant changes or even transformations in all realms of their worldview and the comparatively weakly organised thinking of average people who put a new fact or new idea in one of the countless file boxes in their mind and then lock it up pending practical need, not worrying that there are other thoughts and facts in other file boxes that might profoundly contradict it or especially harmonise with it.

Thus, the transition from lower forms of life to higher forms, by intensify-ing the contradictions of spontaneous development, at the same time prepares for the radical removal of these contradictions along with the spontaneity that engendered them.

XII

For us, completely harmonious development that is free of internal contradictions is only an *ultimate goal* that expresses a certain tendency, familiar to us from experience, toward the liberation of processes of development from the contradictions that are associated with them. Therefore, it is possible to give a clear presentation of the harmonious type of development only by contrasting concrete cases that approach that type with those in which the lack of harmony is obvious.

In contemporary society a large-scale capitalist enterprise can serve as a model of a vital combination that is highly organised, rich in content, and plastic. In this limited sphere the processes of development are accomplished quite harmoniously. If a new technological device is introduced that exponentially reduces the expenditure of labour power in one of the operations of the given production, a series of further changes will immediately occur.

Change cannot be limited to the removal of old machines and installation of new ones; it is necessary to adapt the entire internal arrangement of the factory to these new machines. For example, the old building might not be suitable for them, and it would then be necessary to alter it with regard to the new needs. Correspondingly, partial alterations might be needed in other sections of the factory and in communication among them. The diminished need for labour power frees up some capital, and that labour power can be used for a more or less uniform expansion of the entire enterprise. The workers who are freed up by the new machine can be re-employed in significantly different applications than before, and in this change of roles, it is in the best interests of the enterprise to assign workers the function most suitable for them and perhaps to completely remove some workers from the production in question and put them to work on strategically chosen new tasks instead. All this redistribution of capital and labour is carried out quickly and easily due to the presence of engineers and directors who have a wealth of experience and knowledge regarding the organisation of business. Thus, development in one part of a system causes corresponding adaptations in all other parts, and progress of a part is transformed into progress of the whole. Progress is not accompanied by any significant interference or disruption in the technological life of the enterprise.

But things look entirely different when we take the given enterprise in relation to all the others. As a whole, the contemporary economic system is distinguished by *unorganisedness*,[3] and in this sense in comparison with the highly

---

3   In the 1925 edition, 'unorganisedness' was changed to 'anarchicalness' [trans.].

organised individual enterprises it represents a lower form of life, and its development is incomparably more spontaneous and contradictory. In this case, the technological progress of some enterprises causes the decline and even the death of others. It deprives a great many good workers of both their useful role in social labour and their ability to earn a living; it makes their labour unnecessary in the enterprises where the productivity of labour is increased and fails to give them a place in other backward and therefore declining enterprises. From time to time, this same technological progress leads to general crises of production – severe shocks to all social life. Finally, this spontaneous progress results in class contradictions, and although it is only the development of these contradictions that creates the possibility for society to escape from the power of spontaneous nature proper, they are, all the same, full of painful disharmony and contain a mass of elements that are destructive of life ...

Thus, the anarchy of the whole prevails over the organisation of the parts, at each step destroying or weakening the results of their systematically harmonious development by its spontaneous force. The general nature of the social process remains profoundly contradictory.

XIII

All the vital meaning, all the positive significance of compulsory norms is inseparably tied to the contradictions of spontaneous development. To the extent that these contradictions and this spontaneity retreats in one or another realm of life where there is organisation and planning, the social role of compulsory norms changes radically. Their meaning disappears, and their significance is taken away. Compulsion that represses contradictions is not needed if development itself does not generate contradictions. The conservatism of external norms clashes harshly with the continuous tendency of progress and then it becomes the source – in this case the fundamental and even the sole source – of profound vital contradictions. The need arises for other norms that correspond to the new type of movement of life. These new norms, obviously, must be free both from the compulsoriness and the conservatism of previous norms.

These are the *norms of expediency*.

Norms of external compulsion – legal, moral, etc. – can, of course, be 'expedient', i.e. useful for society, and they are actually 'expedient' to the extent that they occupy a stable place in life. This does not, however, make them norms of expediency. They compel, but they do not motivate or pay attention to conditions; they do not adapt their compulsion to changing conditions. 'You must do such-and-such, and you may not behave in such-and-such a way'. 'You must' and 'you may not' – completely independently of how expedient this is for you in each given case. 'You must' and 'you may not' and that is all – the imperative is absolute and categorical.

The norms of expediency have nothing in common with *this* imperativeness. Scientific technical rules are a highly typical example of such norms. These rules essentially do not compel anyone to do anything but only point out the best means to attain one or another *given* goal. The imperative is conditional and hypothetical; these rules say that if you want to attain such-and-such, you must act in such-and-such a way. Norms of external compulsion prescribe a person's very goals or at least the boundaries of these goals: 'thou shalt not covet your neighbour's wife' and the like. Norms of expediency present a person with a choice of goals: 'if you covet your neighbour's wife, then' ... etc.

There is a very clear connection between norms of expediency and a harmonious course of development. If development does not generate contradictions, then the goals that issue from it and reflect its tendency will not clash among themselves in interminable conflicts. Consequently, there is no need to limit those goals in the interests of life.

Nevertheless, to the extent that we are dealing with intermediate, interim goals, the norms of expediency can define the choice of those goals. If you want to attain such-and-such a final goal, then at the start you must set yourself such-and-such immediate goals and move from them to such-and-such subsequent goals, etc. It is obvious that in this case a directive has the same conditional character: it is an explanation of the necessary means that temporarily play the role of goals. Thus, one of the main goals for conscious political actors is the power of their party, but it is not at all a final goal. If necessary, they must forget about the former for the sake of the latter. If certain means cease to be necessary to attain the stated ideal and cease to be truly leading toward it, then expediency prescribes that those means be renounced.

Norms of expediency are entirely *subject to critique* by experience and knowledge; norms of compulsion *require supremacy over that critique*. These two tendencies of thought are expressed philosophically on the one had in the form of the 'primacy' of theoretical reason over practical reason and on the other hand in the idea of the 'primacy' of practical reason over theoretical reason.

XIV

If the norms of expediency do not in themselves prescribe certain goals to people, then does it not follow that they assume that the choice of these goals is totally capricious?

Both yes and no.

Formally, yes. Any goals – the most reasonable and the most monstrous – are logically thinkable, and so are the norms of expediency that fully correspond to those goals. If you want to sacrifice your life with the greatest benefit for the development of humanity, then this must be done with such-and-such a method; if you want to take the life of someone who is close to you, then such-and-such are the most convenient techniques, and so forth.

But, essentially, no. Of countless logical possibilities, only one equates to reality. Norms of expediency are not a mental game but specific *forms of life*. They appear in social relationships to replace norms of compulsion only under specific conditions of life and are historically and inseparably tied to those conditions. They correspond to the harmonious development of life, and they presuppose the harmonious development of life. They are entirely determined by the universal, ultimate goal to which the norms serve: the maximum of the life of society as a whole, which simultaneously coincides with the maximum of the life of society's separate parts and elements – human individuals. To the extent that there is no such concurrence, one cannot speak of harmonious development and consequently also of the social supremacy of norms of expedience. To the extent that such concurrence exists, the goals that these norms serve in all their concrete variety flow together into the higher unity of the *socially-agreed-upon struggle for happiness* – the struggle for everything life and nature can give to humanity.

XV

It is only at a specific stage of the development of humanity that norms of expediency must take supremacy over social life away from compulsory norms, but they appear considerably earlier than this stage. They follow a long path of development and spread out gradually into whole broad realms of life, while continuing to occupy a *subordinate* position in the overall system. This is completely understandable: wherever and to the extent that the goals and results of human actions cease to be mutually contradictory, wherever and to the extent that the disharmony of spontaneous development disappears, a place is freed up for norms of expediency ...

Norms of expediency conquered the realm of *labour technology* – the realm of humanity's immediate struggle with nature – most quickly. It is here that human efforts are primarily unified; it is here that the necessity of victory over the great universal enemy first overcomes both the direct conflicts of human goals and the vital contradictions that are indirectly generated by the spontaneous combinations of those conflicts.

The system of norms of expediency that systematically organises people's technological experience is called *science*. This includes not only the technological sciences, proper, which are set out in the form of a systematised series of practical directives by which one or another technological goal is more easily attained. The natural sciences – from mathematics and astronomy to sociology and the theory of cognition – have essentially *the same significance*. They represent a system of norms of expediency *of a higher order*, norms that normalise norms and are themselves in charge of how all practical rules are applied. When engineers work out a project of constructing a building or a bridge by means of mathematical analysis and the principles of mechanics, they create immediate technological norms of expediency by means of scientific norms. When politicians work out a programme of actions for a particular social group at a particular historical moment based on a specific socio-philosophical theory and on an analysis of corresponding social forces, they also create immediate practical norms of expediency based on scientific norms. In the final analysis, all scientific knowledge represents the creative work of norms of expediency for people's practical activity.

In our times, norms of expediency also predominate in the ideological life of society, but they do not entirely prevail there. In contemporary society people can *believe* what seems expedient for saving their souls, and they can *speculate* about what seems expedient for accurately understanding and evaluating the reality that surrounds them, but as soon as they begin to *express* the results of their ideological work, then, in addition to norms of expediency, they usually must still pay attention to certain compulsory norms – of law, decorum, and custom. In backward societies, these compulsory norms are greater and can even predominate decisively. In advanced societies there are fewer of them, and they are of secondary importance. Here development leads to the relative decline of compulsory norms and their replacement by norms of expediency; it leads to the *liberation* of human activity.

XVI

When the process of liberating people from compulsory norms has been accomplished in one or another sphere of life, and the very memory of them
disappears, then the idea of 'freedom' in that sphere is also removed from life
in practice. In advanced countries in our times, no one thinks about 'freedom'
of internal experiences (thoughts and dreams), about 'freedom' of technological inventions and improvements, and such. But the very process of liberation
inevitably proceeds in forms of compulsory relationships – moral and legal.

'Freedom' of conscience, speech, publication, and association exists in cultured countries. What is this freedom? It is a specific *law*. As a legal norm, it
must consequently include elements of external compulsion. What do these
elements consist of? Any attempt to violate this freedom is suppressed by social
force. For example, the juridical content of 'freedom of speech' is as follows:
no one can prevent anyone else from expressing their thoughts, and whoever
does so is subject to punishment. But the very thought of the possibility of preventing people from expressing their thoughts means that traces still survive
of the previous compulsory regulation of human expression – there is at least
a memory of previous forcible censorship of speech. When these traces and
memories finally disappear then society will no more think about freedom of
speech than it thinks at the present time about the freedom of breathing or
freedom of dreaming.

The general law of evolution manifests itself here: new content of life initially takes the elements for its organising form from old content and only
as these elements disappear are completely original forms developed in their
place. The new comes from the old and through the old. Legal compulsion
of censorship is overcome by legal compulsion that protects the freedom of
speech, and it is only together with this latter, negative compulsion that the
legal form altogether disappears in the given realm.

In the social sciences, metaphysical idealism turns the freedom of conscience, speech, etc. into a series of 'absolute' or 'natural' laws of humanity that
are immutable and eternally obligatory. It does not understand that real freedom that is fully realised is not a 'law' at all but a negation of law. It has attained
the level of development at which freedom that is limited by the police is
replaced by freedom preserved by the police, but in its flight of creative fantasy
metaphysical idealism is unable to ascend higher than the latter, and it naively
dreams of making it eternal. The peculiar narrowness of bourgeois psychology
reveals itself here; it does not allow the 'idealist' to escape the boundaries of the
ideological forms – legal, moral, etc. – that are typical of the bourgeois world.

XVII

Thus, in our times, the prevalence of norms of expediency is particularly notable in the sphere of technology and knowledge. Things are different in the realm of economics – the mutual relationships among people that arise in the labour process.

In contemporary society these relationships are characterised by lack of organisation, anarchy. Their development is associated with a great number of contradictions, and therefore there is objectively very little room for norms of expediency and a great need for norms of compulsion. And we already see how necessary these norms are for the exchange process that expresses the basic economic structure of present-day society – necessary because of the fundamental and unavoidable contradictions of its content.

The principle of property – the right of particular people to particular things – reigns here, and all other compulsory norms (legal, moral, etc.) are grouped around this principle as particular manifestations and variations of it or as necessary supplements to it.

Bourgeois economic structure is utterly inconceivable apart from the legal system. The legal system is its skeleton, the necessary link between its parts and the form that constantly embodies them.

XVIII

The transition from an economic system that is full of contradictions and that is therefore regulated by external norms to a harmonious system of collaboration for which such norms are not necessary can be realised only through a specific transitional phase in which new, incompletely established content still uses old forms. The transformation of the economic system must occur by means of new legal relationships, i.e. by means of politics. It therefore will be put forward as the goal of a particular *party*, and it is usually designated by the term *Zukunftstaat*, 'government of the future'.

In analysing this formula with the help of the same Marxist school that made it its slogan, it is easy to conclude that it is a contradiction. This school teaches that 'government is an organisation of class rule', while, at the same time, it promotes the elimination of classes as an ideal. How can this be reconciled with the idea of a *Zukunftstaat* that is, nonetheless, a '*Staat*', i.e. a 'government'.

The contradiction here is only apparent, of course. 'Government of the future' is really an organisation of class rule, but only of *the class that strives to eliminate classes*. Thus, it is a transitional stage; it assumes that there will be

vestiges of the old class ideology that stand in contradiction to the new organisation of life and that are subject to legal normalisation. When these vestiges
disappear, and the psychology of the entire society comes into correspondence with its new system of collaboration – general cooperation for general
development – the 'government of the future' will lose the elements of compulsion and will then cease to be a 'government'. It will be a society in which
the mutual relationships of people – like their relationships toward nature and
experience – will be determined by norms of expediency. Such is the ideal of a
socialist world, as far as contemporary people are able to understand it.

XIX

At this point, a contemporary person – the child of an era of contradictions and
compulsion – inevitably raises the question: is such a society conceivable? And
after this question yet another: is it likely to happen?

The first question expresses a demand to be shown now the elements of the
kind of social interrelationships that would be reduced to norms of expedience.

The second question is the demand to be shown now that it is objectively
possible that these interrelationships can expand to all reaches of society.

The first question can be answered by picturing the internal relationships of
a circle of comrades.

How is the distribution of labour accomplished in groups of this type? It is
completely independent of norms of compulsion and consistent with norms
of expedience. People get together and consider what precise part of the common task is most suitable for each of them to take on. The overall goal is the
starting point for all decision-making.

It is obvious on its face that there cannot be any talk here of legal compulsion.

The sort of compulsion that is known as the obligation of 'conditional agreement' is also excluded here. This obligation consists in people obeying the
decisions of their group as long as they participate in it: if they do not want
to obey, they must leave. There is none of this in the pure and advanced form
of comradely relations. If one or another member of the group declares that
the role that the others proposed for them was not suitable for them and that
they cannot carry it out, this does not entail their exclusion from the comradely
organisation.

There can be no thought of moral obligation; no absolute imperative directs
these people's actions. Some might take on a kind of work that is out of their
comfort zone or that is even outright unpleasant to them, but they do it either

because none of their other comrades are able to do the job – i.e. due to purely practical expediency – or because they want to spare the other comrades from work they find difficult – perhaps because they have a spontaneous liking for them – and this feeling, just like any other spontaneous feeling, of course does not include anything normative, anything formally obligatory.

Thus, the particular goals of individual people issue from their common work and upon the immediate relationships that have sprung up among them on the basis of that work. Their actions are determined by norms of expediency that correspond to those goals.

This is the highest type of organisation of labour in its *elementary form*.

XX

A second, more difficult problem now arises: is it possible for the comradely organisation of labour, free from compulsion, to expand to the dimensions of an entire society and beyond – to include all humanity?

At first glance, the only likely answer that presents itself is in the negative. There are so many arguments against the possibility that one does not know where to begin.

However, in investigating these arguments, it is easy to reduce them to two types. One type has its starting point in a specific understanding of comradely relationships themselves that attributes to them characteristics that exclude the possibility of expanding without limit. The second type of argument alleges that conditions in the nature of human beings and society impose narrow limits on such expansion.

Let us take a look at arguments of the first sort.

The most general and the most serious of these arguments is that comradely relationships are essentially the relationships of a *club*. They are based on the *personal feelings* of individual people for one another. Where there are no such feelings, comradely organisation is impossible or unviable. In addition, each individual's realm of personal feeling is limited, and the sphere of comradely connection is therefore also limited. It cannot embrace the millions and billions of human individuals who form society and humanity.

The entire force of this argument consists in confusing the particular, concrete form of comradely relationship (and its lowest form, at that) with comradely relationships in general – with the special type of development that they express.

The essence of comradely organisation consists in the unity around a goal that people freely take on without any compulsion and that goes beyond the bounds of the personal interests of any of them. In an atomised, anarchic society, the goals of human activity are extremely varied and are so disconnected that they encounter contradictions at every step, and in such a society it is natural that comradely unity around a goal appears at first only in small groups of people who are closely tied by kinship or friendship – by personal fondness and personal elements of life in general. This narrow immediate tie of sentiment strengthens the very unity around the goal: love of the general work flows together with love of the people who are carrying it out and finds additional support in it. Everything changes, however, as this work expands.

Now we see a personal closeness and a club-like relationship that not only ceases to serve as a reliable basis for common work but that often turns out directly harmful to it. Having become accustomed to connecting the striving toward a common goal with particular human individuals in one's consciousness and subjectively and one-sidedly valuing these individuals because of a lively friendship with them, people with a club-like psychology do not reconcile themselves to the unavoidable change of their role when the focus is on the common goal itself. The resentment that they bring in is a source of dissension and contradictions in the common life of the comradely organisation. Moreover, at this stage of development, the comradely tie is still not devoid of a certain authoritarian colouring. The position of some comrades as acknowledged leaders seems more 'influential' and 'respected' than the position of others, and frequently clubbish people are even ready to fight with comrades who are personally not close or friendly with them over 'positions' for 'their' people – for people who are closer to them and whom they like more.

This often happens in the life of professional and political organisations of the comradely type when they make the transition from a narrow group approach to something to a broader approach, especially when the party incorporates a number of separate 'clubs' that have worked independently of one another for a long time. This produces a strange picture: people who are apparently striving toward the same goal and do not even disagree on the fundamental means of achieving it but who struggle bitterly among themselves, senselessly wasting the forces of their collective whole. This struggle ends only when those groups prevail that are least steeped in the clubbish spirit and who are most imbued with the idea of the whole. Comradely organisation is then liberated from the rule of personal ties and friendships and emerges as a real collectivity made cohesive by real unity of work.

Incidentally, when the overall structure of society is anarchical and unorganised and individualistic psychology predominates in it, even a comradely organisation must, as it expands, take on impersonal forms that are of a conditional and normative nature – the forms of organisational 'statutes'. They seem to be similar to external compulsory norms such as legal, habitual, moral, etc. norms, but in essence they are really no such thing. From the outset, their *obligatoriness* is subordinated to their *expediency*; from the outset it is recognised that it would be possible – and even necessary – for these normative forms to be done away with as soon as they turn out to clearly contradict the common goal for which the organisation arose. These norms are not the dictates of personal or impersonal *power* which demands unquestioning obedience; they are *organisational norms of expediency* by which the most expedient means of *collaboration* are established. Under normal conditions, they do not contain the fetishism that constitutes the spirit of compulsory norms – that turns these norms into laws for how people should establish the goals of their activity rather than choosing only the best means for attaining their freely established goals.

Thus, the fundamental narrowness of club-like relationships does not at all mean that comradely ties are also narrow. It is just the opposite. It is only by removing specifically-club-like elements that comradely relationships are able to freely develop. But this does not mean one can completely remove elements of friendliness from comradely relationships or that the comradely relationship is essentially emotionally cold and narrowly business-like. No, it is only that in this case friendliness does not have the same kind of personally narrow and individualistic nature as, let us say, in relationships of personal friendship, natural kinship, or sexual love. Friendliness that is based on collaboration in a common struggle toward a common goal can be *no less* deep than friendliness based on habitual, pleasant impressions received from another person. At the same time, the comradely relationship is a more perfect type of friendship in the sense that it is considerably less sensitive to the contingencies of life and considerably more able to endure life's inevitable disasters. Mutual celebration – and *not commiseration* – predominate in it.

Comrades are valued by other comrades as active forces working harmoniously with them in a common struggle, as partial living incarnations of the common goal. Every success in their common struggle serves as a rich source of that common joy in which mutual expressions of joyful experiences deepen and strengthen their joyfulness. But failure or defeat does not cause grief or sadness to be manifested to nearly the same degree; the *active* nature of the comradely relationship does not permit this. If comrades are put out of action or die, the first thought that arises is how to *replace* them for the common task, how to fill the gap in the system of forces that is directed toward the common goal. There is no inclination to despondency or funereal emotions. All attention is directed toward action and not 'feeling' – hence the 'callousness' of active political warriors toward the sufferings of comrades that so shocks philanthropical philistines.

Thus, in essence, the comradely relationship is capable of the same limitless expansion as the conscious collaboration that constitutes its real basis. Narrowly personal friendly feelings are not only not a necessary condition for comradely relationships but, just the opposite, are somewhat antagonistic toward the tendency of such relationships to develop. Narrowly personal friendship inevitably plays a large role at the early levels of the development of a comradely organisation, but at subsequent stages it becomes an obstacle that must be overcome. In the place of such friendliness another friendliness appears that is alien to individualism and pettiness and that, as it develops, is capable of embracing an indefinitely expanding circle of human individuals.

XXI

Let us move on to the other series of typical arguments against the conception that I am defending.

Could there be fundamental conditions in the very nature of human beings and society that make vital contradictions among people inevitable, and, as a necessary result of these contradictions, there must be compulsory regulation of human relationships by external norms? Such arguments assert that these conditions cannot be eliminated as long as people are human beings and not angels. Egoistic instincts, they say, will always cause a conflict of personal interests and, in order that, as these conflicts progressively develop and sharpen, they do not turn people into regular wolves that are at each other's throats, it is necessary for there to be the external restraint of law, rights, morals, etc. Norms of expediency definitely cannot replace such restraint – they can specify the best means of helping one's neighbour in some conditions just as well as the best means of going for their jugular in other conditions. The conditional imperative of norms of expediency determines the means and not the goal; only the categorical imperative – unconditional compulsion – has the power to regulate the goal.

Those who advocate such views ask us to imagine a huge railroad network where thousands of trains are constantly moving and crossing paths, where the continuity of the whole is guaranteed only when all of the countless agents carry out their special role in the common work with the greatest precision and where the least negligence threatens thousands of human lives and a profound shock to the entire social system. What would happen if each of the agents was guided in their work only by norms of expediency – i.e. if they essentially pursued their own goals everywhere, trying only to attain them as quickly and completely as possible and with the least expenditure of energy? Suppose that experienced specialists put together the very best, most expedient timetable that indicated to all workers their individual function in the system in all of its detail. Who could guarantee that these directives would be strictly carried out by everyone? Everything would depend on the personal caprice of each of the many thousands of workers. Not feeling any kind of compulsory power over them, not fearing any kind of punishment, they would at each step give in to an individual, chance disposition or inaccurate computation, and the life of the whole would become impossible. Today a tired engineer finds it expedient to hold up a train for a few hours to have a rest, tomorrow a stoker prefers to contemplate the beautiful landscape, the day after tomorrow a switch operator considers it opportune to direct all trains onto spare tracks so they can wait there until the operator returns from an assignation, and so on and so on. Only severe compulsion can constantly keep everyone within the exact boundaries of their obligations.

The argument continues that the strong fits of passion – anger, revenge, sexual impulse, jealously – that in our times burst so easily through even the solid framework of law and morality, would encounter even less serious resistance from the flexible, elastic forms of pure expediency, which would allow complete freedom for crime. The kind of fear that saves one from committing crimes would not restrain people from extremity and impulse, and everything that is social would drown in the anarchical chaos of unbridled instincts. Madness and fear would set in in the place of reason and freedom.

All these considerations have their starting point in the idea that human nature is basically immutable and that in all social forms and in all historical conditions it will remain as egoistic and individualistic as what we see in contemporary society. Faithful to narrowly personal interest, human nature is alien to the idea of the whole, and social interest and social expediency begin to direct it only when – by means of punishment and compulsion, force and fear – they are transformed into personal expediency in the interests of the individual. Fortunately, the situation concerning human nature is not this bad, and the idea that it is immutable belongs to a level of cognition that is long past.

Contemporary historical theory teaches that human beings are derivative of their social surroundings. If humans appear to be essentially individualists in a given era, then this is precisely because they were made that way by their contemporary anarchic, atomistically splintered society that is built on competition and class hostility. Reflecting this social structure, humans cannot but be individualists. However, in another, differently structured, society such as the clan society of primitive communism, people were not like this. In that society, personal interest had not separated itself out from collective interest; individual humans organically blended with their whole – the group, the commune – just like cells blend together in living tissue. It required thousands of years of development in order for individual humans to begin to separate their personal goals from the common goals of their collectivity. This occurred when the primeval interconnectedness of society fell apart, when it changed from a small organised system into a huge unorganised aggregate.

There can be no doubt that in a new society from which the disuniting force of competition and class struggle has disappeared the psychology of division in which human individuals counterpose their own goals and interests to those of other individuals and of all society will also disappear. In becoming conscious of themselves as integral parts of a great whole and in living inseparably united with the life of the whole, individual humans will lose even the idea of egoistic, narrowly individualistic goals. At the same time, compulsory norms that regulate the struggle of these goals will also disappear.

Even in contemporary society the relationship of compulsion and violence predominates over the relationship of friendship and labour solidarity only by and large. In a great many cases the latter relationship entirely eliminates the former, and it is precisely then that collective actions attain the greatest power and systematic nature. Two armies clashed in the Great French Revolution. The soldiers of the backward countries of Europe were united and guided by the compulsory force of obligation, of duty and morality, while soldiers of the Revolution were united and guided by the vital, immediate consciousness of a common goal in the form of love for the motherland, and we know which of the two turned out in fact to be more organised and heroic. The consciousness of a collective goal is so much more vitally, clearly, and deeply manifested in a society not when this goal appears only in individual, exceptional cases but when it is immediately embodied in an organised system of collective labour and imbues all social life.

XXII

At this point, the argument against my conception of comradely relationships changes its form from an argument that is based on 'the nature of human beings' into one based on *the nature of society*. It argues that the very collective organisation of labour that alone is able to eliminate personal, group, and class antagonisms (and thereby would make possible the rule of norms of expediency) could not exist without precisely a huge development of compulsory norms and a huge expansion of their realm. In reality, this argument continues, social production must be organised in such a way that all social needs are fully satisfied. For this, human labour must be systematically distributed among all sectors of production, and how could such distribution be achieved apart from externally compulsory methods? If one proposes to allow all individuals to determine for themselves both the kind and the amount of their labour, the result would be that the most interesting and pleasant fields of labour would always be overcrowded with workers, while in other fields the lack of labour power would be an utterly unavoidable, chronic evil. It would therefore be undoubtedly necessary to establish a universal working day, perhaps not very long but obligatory for all, and, moreover, without the right for all individual people to choose their work according to whim. Such a compulsory working day, obviously, presupposes continuing complete subordination of human individualities to the power of the social whole that is external to them and that *excludes* the real governance of norms of expediency.

The hearts of present-day individualists are painfully alarmed by the terrible spectre of a government-military occupation implacably chaining human individuals to work that they hate, by the spectre of 'approaching slavery'. A great scientist spending eight hours every day doing stupefying work on a weaving machine, a talented artist exhausted from spending so much time digging coal in a dark mine, a brilliant novelist working in an accounting office and so on and so on – all these unbearable horrors reflect simultaneously both a spontaneous, instinctive aversion of today's individualists toward those higher forms that are being engendered in the depths of capitalistic society and a deepening *failure to understand* them.

Labour is an organic need of humankind, and society has no need to lash the individual human with the whip of governmental or even moral compulsion in order to force them to work. For a normal, self-improving, developing person, the working day is certainly not eight hours but significantly more. Look at workers who have become socially conscious, who in the past before the revolution would – often after ten or eleven hours of compulsory work at a factory – spend even more time at the most intense work of self-education. Look at active political workers who work so strenuously that they often can hardly find time to eat and sleep. The psychology of these representatives of future society living in today's society is enough to guarantee that the social structure that is in the offing will have a colossal sum of free labour at its disposal. Even with today's social relationships, members of the upper classes who are systematically brought up with a parasitic orientation are not at all, in the vast majority of cases, simple idlers. Even the purest rentiers usually work – even if they do work less than other people. It is only that they are free to choose the kind of labour, and, for the most part, because of class prejudice and other abnormal conditions of their life, they choose precisely the sorts of labour that are least meaningful and least useful for society. Thus, there is every reason to think that by and large future society will not experience any lack of labour and consequently will not have forms of compulsion.

It is true, however, that one might think that even this free labour, on the whole, will fall far short of filling all spheres of production equally – it will turn out to be too little in a great many sectors. And here the question of compulsory compensation for the deficiency does arise. The *advanced, collectivist society* that will still be organised in governmental, legal forms and that will still be an organisation of class rule – the organised power of the proletariat – will certainly find it necessary to establish a compulsory working day. But in such a society, compulsory labour will obviously involve only a certain part – and from the very beginning an insignificant part – of what is collectively necessary, so that it is doubtful that more than an eight-hour – or even a six-hour – 'working day' will be needed. In the distribution of this portion of labour, society nevertheless must necessarily – in the interests of the greatest productivity of labour – take into account as much as possible the individual inclinations and tastes of workers. Social obligatoriness and a compulsory norm will appear on the scene only if it turns out that the voluntary distribution of workers does not correspond to the real needs of production and only to the extent that it does so.

This, however, will only be a transitional state of society. Later on, a change must be made in two directions. On the one hand, the rapid development of productive forces in itself will diminish the need for compulsorily organised labour; machines will replace people, freeing them from work but not from sustenance as it does under capitalism. On the other hand, in the new social organisation human psychology itself will change as it becomes ever more social and ever less individualistic. In so doing, the free, voluntary distribution of labour will become ever easier; an insufficient quantity of labour in one or another realm of production will be quickly made up for by volunteer workers, who will not need to be brought in by the force of social compulsion but only by statistical tables that state the social need. And this will be attained all the easier as the endlessly progressive development of machines makes the transition from one kind of work to another ever less difficult and as the intensive growth of energy of the human organism will continually generate the desire in it for the continual exchange of some labour processes with others.

XXIII

Thus, there are no conditions either in the nature of humankind or in the nature of society that would exclude the possibility of development right down to the complete removal of external norms and compulsory relationships, right down to the complete rule of norms of expediency and comradely relationships among people. But one terribly important question still remains: how progressive will these higher forms of life be? They will provide limitless space for development, but will they provide sufficient stimulus for it? Will their harmony not lead to stagnation and their orderliness to immobility? If this is the case, then even the contemporary world with its unhealthy development and countless contradictions would be infinitely better than the harmonious and trouble-free 'higher' world in which meaningless cyclical repetitions proliferate.

Meanwhile, this is exactly what the defenders of individualism insistently assert. Is not social development born only from the contradictions of social life, and is not the movement of progress caused only by competition and the class struggle? Is it not the case that the clan societies known to history that did not have this struggle and these contradictions were really extremely stagnant? Is not technological progress – the basis of all other progress – really caused precisely by the competition that forces capitalists to seek every new means of keeping the market to themselves amid the desperate attacks of rivals? Is not the change of social forms itself really caused by the struggle of classes? And is it not obvious that the elimination of competition and class struggle and the elimination of the social contradictions of spontaneous development would mean to eliminate the progress of technology and social forms – to eliminate development altogether?

Not only competition and direct struggle but even simple competitiveness must disappear where individualistic feelings also disappear. Competitiveness has its source entirely in individualistic feelings, since there is no basis for it if some human individuals do not contrast themselves with others. Where will the stimuli for development come from?

The answer is very easy. Struggle, competition, and competitiveness of people are all only *secondary* stimuli of development and hidden behind them are others – *primary* stimuli – that lie deeper. These latter arise where people come face to face with nature – where people stand up as powerful and creative forces in the immediate struggle with nature. A tireless polar explorer carrying on a solidary, desperate struggle with nature, a fervent hunter hourly risking death in an exterminatory war with predatory beasts, a persistent inventor straining thought and imagination without rest in order to subordinate to humankind yet one more of the elemental forces of the universe, an idealistic scientist striving with inexorable energy to wrest a secret from nature – these people experience the most rapid and intense development, and is it really *only* competition or competitiveness with other people that motivate their wills? Of course not; these motives are of the least significance to them.

Progressive, creatively harmonising work of the psyche begins everywhere that new material of experience is provided and everywhere that disharmony in the old material of experience is revealed. Clan society lost its conservatism and began to transform technology when absolute overpopulation was manifested in general starvation – competition between individual people was not thereby required. The discovery of America, which brought a huge amount of new vital content to humanity and transformed the entire life of humanity was accomplished without any competitiveness. A human enemy does not propel a person down the path of development more powerfully or more certainly than another great enemy – and at the same time a friend full of mysterious fascination – nature.

When people in the social system of the future mutually understand one another completely, the breadth of comradely communication among them will guarantee that the human individual will receive a constant inflow of new experiences and new material of experience. At the same time, a subtle and complex harmony of life that will be historically worked out and will become a matter of habit will cause a higher sensitivity to any disharmony that arises. These conditions of highly intense development are the direct opposite of those that are created in our contemporary world. Here the 'atomisation' of people that is engendered by specialisation lowers the level of their mutual understanding and narrows the sphere of their communication. And, at the same time, *becoming habituated* to vital disharmony, which naturally springs up wherever people are constantly surrounded by contradictions, means the dulling of sensitivity to any new disharmony. We know well from the experience of our times – this era of acute social crises – how far the insensitivity of people to the most terrible, insanely monstrous manifestations of the contradictions of life can go.

The intra-social struggle that the individualist sees as the sole and absolutely necessary motor of progress is, in reality, not only a motor but also partly a brake on progress. It squanders people's *energies* and dissipates their creative *attention*. The former is clear in itself; the latter also becomes obvious to the highest degree if one clearly recognises that victory in the struggle between people – even in the economic struggle – is very often attained along routes that have nothing in common with social progress. So much intellect and ingenuity that is fit for better things is expended on speculation and stock market swindles!

And at the same time, the possibility of introducing machines into production is significantly narrowed because they are introduced not for their usefulness but for their profitability, not for using them to make workers' labour easier but to increase the rate of profit.

All these collateral harmful actions are utterly alien to the *universal* and *fundamental* motor of progress, which is the immediate struggle of humanity with nature.

The degree of progressiveness of comradely organisations is directly related to the breadth of communication among people that is achieved in those organisations. Narrow circles, having limited vital content, inevitably lapse into conservatism as they exhaust everything new that their members can provide one another. Large comradely organisations develop much further and more intensively – again in relation to their breadth. Communistic communities with several hundred members degenerate after several decades of flourishing. Political parties of a similar type with many thousands of members grow and strengthen and work out new forms ever more quickly and energetically without displaying any exhaustion.

All this leads to the absolutely unavoidable conclusion that the greatest speed and energy of progress, the greatest diversification and harmoniousness of progress, can be attained only in the kind of society that has comradely collaboration as its social form and the borders of humanity as its outer limits. There the forces of development will become limitless.

CHAPTER 12

The Accursed Questions of Philosophy

By the sea, by the desolate nocturnal sea,
    Stands a youthful man,
His breast full of sadness, his head full of doubt.
And with bitter lips he questions the waves:
'Oh solve me the riddle of life!
    The cruel, world-old riddle,
Concerning which, already many a head hath been racked.
    Heads in hieroglyphic-hats,
    Heads in turbans and in black caps,
    Periwigged heads, and a thousand other
        Poor, sweating human heads.
Tell me, what signifies man?
Whence does he come? whither does he go?
Who dwells yonder above the golden stars?'

The waves murmur their eternal murmur,
The winds blow, the clouds flow past.
    Cold and indifferent twinkle the stars,
        And a fool awaits an answer.[1]
HEINRICH HEINE

• •
•

The philosophical questions that Heine's hero asks of the ocean's waves –
after having addressed them to the contemporary German idealistic philosophy of Fichte, Schelling, and Hegel without success – are known as 'ultimate',
'supreme', or 'eternal' questions, but they have not always been characterised
as 'accursed'. In so-called 'organic' eras, when the social world stands firmly
on its pillars [whales],[2] these serious, phlegmatic animals are not disturbed

---

1   Bogdanov used the Russian translation by Mikhail Larionovich Mikhailov (1829–1865). I have
    used the English translation by Emma Lazarus (1849–1887) in Lazarus 1881, pp. 215–16 [trans.].
2   The Russian word for 'whale', *kita*, is an idiomatic expression referring to an important person,
    a 'pillar' of the community [trans.].

by the sharp harpoons of practical contradictions and intellectual critique and do not manifest a dangerous tendency to toss and turn and dive. Organic eras essentially do not know accursed questions. If our likeable young metaphysician addressed his questions, for example, to ordinary farmers in a natural economy unaffected by capitalism and culture, who in their time were real 'pillars' for a whole harmonious, hopeful worldview and who nowadays have turned almost into mythological beings, then the answers they obtained would be definite and perspicuous, devoid of any 'anxiety' or 'doubts'. True, these answers would probably not satisfy our hero and perhaps would seem to him even not to be answers at all, but this is precisely because he is the representative of a completely different 'critical' or 'transitional' era that has already carried out one half of the task. It has done away with the old answers but has not succeeded in carrying out the other half – to do away with the old questions.

There can be no doubt that the 'bitter youth' has had a philosophical and theological education. He is familiar with the huge variety of answers that have been given at one time or another by humankind's sages to the questions he is concerned with. Why can he not be satisfied with any of these answers? What brought him to such a hopeless lack of confidence in them that the waves of the ocean seem to him to be more competent in metaphysics than the wise authors of these answers and that he even considers it fair to classify the heads of the aforesaid wise people according to the hats with which they are adorned?

In all the answers of metaphysics and theology, he found one common and extremely deplorable feature: they unfold in an infinite series without getting anywhere.

'Tell me, what is the meaning of a human being?' he asks, for example, and let us assume that they answer, 'their immortal souls'. 'But what does the soul mean?' he then asks. We can suppose that the following answer is given: it signifies the eternal striving toward the absolute ideal of goodness, truth, and beauty. 'But what is this ideal?' he continues, and, when they give him the definition that the ideal is such-and-such and such-and-such, he cannot help but inquire further: 'What is this "such-and-such and such-and-such" that stands as the predicate of the subject "absolute ideal"?' – and so on without end. It looks to him like an endless series of reflections of images in two parallel mirrors. His mind is as little able to be satisfied with any of the answers he is given as his vision is able to come to a stop on any of the reflections. Just the opposite, the images become increasingly dimmer, the answers become increasingly less intelligible, and the feeling of dissatisfaction grows.

The same story is repeated with each of the 'accursed' questions, and our young philosopher, seeing that he cannot get any answers other than even more 'accursed' ones, falls into completely understandable despair. The wise ones try to explain to him that this is utterly unreasonable, that he himself is the one to blame in all of this. They say, 'Young man, by endlessly stretching out a chain of questions, you have made a very crude error. Of course, you can ask "what is this" or "what is that" in regard to any thing or any definition, but these questions do not always have a rational meaning. There are things that are immediately known, that are immediately obvious and understandable, and any attempt to define them is, first, pointless, since they do not need definition, and, second, unrealisable, since there is nothing more certain than them through which they could be defined. Once you arrive at them, you have achieved your goal and must stop; further questions are only an abuse of grammatical forms and our patience'.

'Wonderful!' our bitter youth remarks, 'then be so kind as to point out to me where is that immediately known thing that you are talking about. I asked you what is the meaning of a human being, and you told me that it is their immortal soul. So, should not this be immediately obvious and understandable to me?'

'Yes! Of course!' one of the wise ones agrees, 'Do you really not feel it in yourself? Are you really not yourself conscious of your spiritual "I" that so decisively and clearly stands out amidst the entire world? Is it possible that any kind of definition is still necessary?'

'Now then', the youth replies, 'imagine that for me this "I" is not at all clear and intelligible. Sometimes it seems to me that I really do feel it and distinguish it from everything else, but sometimes, just the opposite, it completely slips away somewhere and becomes imperceptible, and sometimes I notice that I do not have just one but somehow several of them. How can I not ask what my "I" is in its essence'?

'You are perfectly right about this', another wise one condescendingly replies, 'The empirical "I" that the old theologians confused with the soul does not have any kind of definition at all – it is no more than a chaos of experiences. It is necessary to single out the absolute, normative "I" that comprises the authentic essence of human individuality, its immortal soul. You are conscious of this "I" in yourself precisely when you subordinate your experiences to supreme ethical, aesthetic and logical norms – when you strive toward absolute goodness, beauty, and truth'.

'Alas, most venerable one', our hero answers sadly, 'I have a harder time with these absolutes of yours that with the soul in general. Yesterday it seemed to me that I strove toward absolute goodness, giving in to a burst of patriotic hatred for the enemies of the fatherland and suppressing all feelings to the contrary, but today I see that this was an orgy of vulgar chauvinism hostile to the true ideal. Yesterday I tried to restrain my sensual passions, striving, as it seemed to me, toward supreme spiritual beauty, but today I suspect that at the basis of this restraint lay simply in base cowardice in the face of the spontaneous forces of my own nature'.

It is obvious that the unhappiness of the young philosopher – and along with it the difference between him and the wise ones who offered him their answers to the eternal questions – boils down to his complete inability to find anything in his experience sufficiently definite and immediately intelligible to be able to serve as a reliable basis and criterion for all the rest. If someone in olden times used the expression 'my soul', they knew very well what they were talking about. It was today's consciousness that was imperceptibly different from tomorrow's and yesterday's, that was a solid and conservative complex of experiences that repeated itself, and it was therefore apprehended as something fully known and intelligible in itself. What was habitual did not arouse questions and puzzlement. People could not see any mystery in them, and by virtue of multiple repetitions even the vaguest concept ultimately took on the appearance of the greatest certainty and obviousness, as testified by the entire history of religious dogmas. The various minor divinities of the Catholic religion with whom Italian peasants entered into prayerful communion were no less real and undoubted for them than the neighbours with whom they conversed and quarrelled. The more conservative the consciousness, the more self-evident and self-explanatory is the material that it contains – material which does not give rise to doubts but, just the opposite, can serve as a support against any doubts, the basis for reliable and convincing answers to any question.

Our hero does not find anything sufficiently stable and conservative – nothing so 'immediately known' – in his psyche upon which he could come to a stop and say with a calm heart: 'this is intelligible to me and needs neither questions nor explanations, and everything that I am able to reduce to it will be equally intelligible'. All the abstractions that the wise ones entertain him with seem to him to be content that is *transient*, indefinite, and doubtful. All the definitions that they try to help him with seem to him to be a fruitless game with vague and hazy forms that lack the life or the force to be able to materialise. '*Mobilis in mobili*' – 'that which changes in a changing environment' – such is the tragic condition that, from his point of view, makes all the efforts of philosophical heads – no matter what caps they are wearing – completely hopeless as far as answering the 'eternal' questions – questions of what is unchanging and immovable in life – is concerned.

Now a new character appears on the scene – one for which the gloomy youth, to his surprise, had not found a place in his classification of philosophical heads. This is the critic-positivist, who, instead of concocting answers to the 'accursed' questions, calls into question the validity and logical justifiability of these questions themselves.

'You want to know what the "essence" of a human being, of life, of the world consists in', they say, 'but first try to explain to yourself what, as a matter of fact, you mean by the word "essence". It means the unchanging basis of phenomena – the absolute, constant substrate that is hidden beneath their changeable outer shell. The word "essence" had meaning for your predecessors who *did not know* that in reality there is nothing that is invariable, nothing that is absolutely constant. They singled out from reality the more stable elements and combinations and, because they had an insufficient store of observation and experience, they considered them to be absolutely stable and called them the "essence" of the given things and phenomena. You know very well that there are no constant combinations and that in every phenomenon each of its elements can disappear and be replaced by a new one, and if, in attempting to arrive at the essence, you remove from reality everything that is changeable in it and that therefore does not correspond to the very concept of essence, then *nothing* remains for you, except for the word "essence", which expresses your attempt to find something unchanging in that which changes. Your attempt is hopeless because of its inner, logical contradictoriness. And all of your questions that involve the word "essence" are just as logically contradictory as the concept that is expressed by it. There is no more rational meaning in them than, for example, in the questions of how large is the volume of a given surface or of what kind of wood iron is made.

'Your other questions in regard to the "origin" of human beings, life, and the world – origin not in the sense of scientific experience and the observable succession of phenomena but in the sense of an absolute, supra-experiential, creative original source – these questions express the desire to find the final cause of everything that exists. But the concept of cause arose from experience and relates to experience; it expresses the interrelationship between one object and others, between one phenomenon and others, and, outside of separate given objects and phenomena, it is devoid of all meaning. Meanwhile, the "everything" that you are inquiring about is not any given object or given phenomenon at all; it is the endlessly unfolding content to which all objects and phenomena belong. To apply the concept of cause to it means to accept it as something given and limited, and it is limitless and never given to us. And for all that, your ancestors knew what they were talking about when they posed the question of the cause of everything – of the creation of the world. Their "everything" seemed to them, in reality, to be something given and completely limited, even if only in their thought. The idea of the infinity of being was alien to them; for them nature was only a very large thing for which they tried to find a correspondingly large cause. But you, possessing the concept of both the extensive and intensive infinity of what exists, how can you ask a question about this infinity that can only be asked about the finite? Knowing that "everything" is not an object of possible experience but only a symbol of its limitless expanse, how can you want to handle this "everything" like one such object of experience? In truth, your question is like asking a child how many miles it is from the earth to the vault of heaven or many years old the Lord God is.

'The third series of your questions relates to the "meaning" – i.e. the "goal" – of the existence of human beings, life, and the world. Here the misunderstanding is even more obvious. The concept of "goal" is borrowed from psychological experience, from the realm of consciousness. It expresses the relationship between the *conceptions* of a conscious being and the results of its actions. Consequently, the question of the goal of the world and of life already assumes in advance the presence of some kind of conscious being that strives through its actions to attain specific results – i.e. obviously, that it possesses specific needs and that the world process and human life are the means, or one of the means, for achieving those results. But where did you find such a being, and what gives you the right to assume its presence a priori? This was completely natural and understandable for your ancestors. They lived in an atmosphere of slavery and subordination and were accustomed to play the role of a means to someone else's capricious goals in all sorts of life events. Across the board, they connected the observed actions of people and even the phenomena of dead nature with the idea of a despotic will that these actions or phenomena served. But you are someone who is familiar with the ideas of freedom and even with the struggle for freedom. In practice, you reject slavery and subordination, and in theory you recognise them as a past level of the development of society. Why do you pose questions in the sphere of highest generalisations as if you cannot conceive of yourself other than as a slave to the will of someone else? And, moreover, your question turns out to be as little justified and as poorly founded as if, for example, you were to ask a hungry person to say who it is who is pleading with him to go to dinner or to ask someone falling from a bell tower whose errand they were rushing to carry out.

'So, you must get rid of these nonsensical combinations of words, these so-called "eternal questions". They do not need answers, since they are questions only in their grammatical form and not in their logical content. And, any answer other than a denial that they should be posed at all would be just as absurd as the questions themselves'.

The inquiring young man, having passed through the school of Kant's *Critique of Pure Reason*, is unable to deny the validity of subjecting to critique the very questions that he has taken up. After several objections and attempts to defend these questions, he arrives at the conclusion that from a formal perspective defending them is a hopeless task. He then turns to his interlocutor with this declaration:

'I concede that logically you are perfectly correct and that the questions that trouble me are illogical and contradictory. But why do your arguments, which I am unable to object to, not convince me enough to give up even one of these questions? Why, when I force myself to take your point of view, do the rejected questions remind me of the anguish and pain of them in my soul, and after a minute they come to the surface once again, breaking through all logical questions? Why are they so *irremovable* from my consciousness and even seem more precious to me than all my other questions? I think that the problem is not with logic alone and that theoretical reason is not competent to reject or even subject to critique what is born in the profoundest depths of practical reason. Is it possible that the illogicality of the questions signifies only that they are higher than logic'?

'My friend', the critic-positivist replies, 'if you want to reject logic, then any argument with you or any attempt in general to convince you would be inappropriate. But look at how pathetic the semblance of an argument that you use to defend your questions is. Can the trouble and pain in your soul really prove anything but illness? Is the irremovability of something from your consciousness really not a characteristic of many illusions that have been refuted once and for all, like, for example, the illusion that the sun moves around the earth or the illusion that the moon and stars move along with you as you walk? And your belief that the illogical can be superior and not inferior to logic – tell me, what can be more pitiful as far as cogency is concerned, than such "could-be beliefs"? And it is in vain that you take refuge in the priority of practical reason over theoretical reason. This convenient dogma – and let it not incriminate the late Kant on Judgement Day! – can in no way abolish logic, since what is called reason must, according to the very concept of "reason", be subordinated to logic. So, give up your fruitless philosophising about questions that do not exist – your youthful energy could be used on something better'.

'Oh, leave me alone!' our questioner anxiously protests, 'Nothing in this world will mean anything to me until these questions are answered, and if they are absurd, it is what I want to do, and does it really matter how I spend my energy? There is no goal, no meaning to life, everything flows and changes, spectres are born from spectres, and there is nothing behind them other than endless, glaring emptiness. What is your logic, your science, your critique and your positive knowledge to me, then? I cannot believe you, even if you have evidence on your side. What is there for me in such cold, lifeless evidence?'

'And you know what', he suddenly adds, resting his fixed, fiery gaze on the sorrowfully amused face of his interlocutor, 'after all, you do not completely believe yourself. There, in the dark depths of your soul, what you are struggling against and what you so heatedly reject still remains. And I, by God's mercy, a psychologist and poet to whom it is given to penetrate the human heart further than other people, say to you: it is only your struggle against these accursed questions that saves you from their fatal influence. If this struggle came to an end, and you convinced everyone and your own self and there was no one else to whom you could prove what you have just tried to prove to me, your victory would turn into the greatest defeat. Hunger would possess your empty soul, an abyss would open before it, and from its dark depths all the same hateful, unavoidable, accursed questions would rise up.

'And *this* illness would not be cured by your pitiless surgery. You would have to dissect the whole patient, and all that would remain of them would be a system of properly applied bandages. It would be better for my incorrigible self to go and ask the waves. If they cannot answer me, then they will give me a moment of oblivion in the enraptured contemplation of all kinds of questions. And after that moment has passed, and my heart is again beset by the accursed visitors, I will turn to the waves for a different favour. In their cold embrace, I will be able to escape from anxieties and doubts forever. Clean and limpid, they will wash everything away' ...

The positivist withdraws, compassionately shrugging his shoulders, and the young philosopher remains alone with his thoughts.

Let us go, in our turn, to converse with him about these thoughts. It is true that in doing so we will fall into an obvious anachronism, but what do anachronisms matter where the 'eternal' questions are concerned? In addition, since we appeared in the world three generations later, we are three-quarters of a century older than him, and the greater experience behind us will perhaps provide some kind of directions or indications toward an exit from the agonising despair that so oppresses this sympathetic idealist of the past.

He asks about the essence of human consciousness, about its ultimate cause, about its final goal. What would he obtain in the case of a successful resolution of these questions? What is their vital meaning?

'Essence' – the unchanging substrate of change – would provide a firm, stable *point of support* in the chaos of constant movement, in the eternal change of forms in it, itself, and in the surrounding environment. He could appeal to an 'essence' and be at ease each time that his cognition and will was lost in this chaos, each time that a dangerous vertigo threatened his energy and joy in life.

And what about an 'ultimate cause' – this stop on the path of the infinitely unfolding knowledge of causes in the past? It obviously would also be a point of support, or to be precise – *a point of support in the past*.

The same is true of a 'final goal' – *a point of support in the future*.

Who, in anguish and apprehension, seeks points of support in life? People who do not have any. People who are being carried away and are being carried away against their will. Swimmers who voluntarily and joyously give themselves up to the waves are not then tormented by anguish and apprehension of the coastal rocks.

Carried away against his will, he knows not where! This is the tragedy of the situation of our idealist, and not of him alone ...

What is carrying him away? Cosmic forces – the movement of the earth around the sun, the movement of the sun around an unknown centre? ... Well, our philosopher is not especially concerned about this ... His consciousness has long since reconciled itself with this, and the laws of gravity seem to him a sufficient point of support in the infinite voyage through the astronomical abyss. He even sometimes allows himself to make flippant jokes regarding the cosmic 'perpetuum mobile':

> The glowing sun up yonder
> Is naught but a red drunken nose.
> The nose of the spirit of the universe,
> And around the red nose of the spirit of the universe
> Reels the whole tipsy world.[3]

What they gaily and light-heartedly laugh at is not, obviously, something they relate to with particular 'alarm and doubt', and the movement of the sun does not give birth to their fatal questions regarding points of support ...

And death? Is it possible that death – inevitable and merciless, filling the consciousness with instinctive fear, agonising and vague like a nightmare – brought these evil spectres into the world? But for humanity, death is not movement but an end of movement, a stop on the path, of course, and the task of finding a point of support in the movement of life does not arise from it. Death establishes indefinite but narrow boundaries to personal existence; it can stimulate and intensify the needs and riddles that spring up within these boundaries, but it cannot determine their content. The starting point of that content, in any event, is in the movement of life itself.

---

3 Heinrich Heine, 'Im Hafen' translated into Russian by M.L. Mikhailov as '*U pristani*' and into English by Emma Lazarus as 'In Port'. Lazarus 1881, p. 223 [trans.].

But perhaps our poet-philosopher is frightened and tormented by the unin-telligible, spontaneous forces of his own soul? No, he is not frightened by them but rather loves them. They give him the joy of creativity. They summon him to the joys of life, to struggle ... To struggle – but for the sake of what? To joy – but could it really be only for himself? Creativity – but where is it directed, what is there in it for one to base oneself on. This is where the accursed questions come in. Neither the eternal movement of the great cosmos nor the disturbances and outbursts of the idealist's own soul generate these questions in him – they only *lead* to them and no more. Their source lies *outside* the separate human indi-viduality and *outside* the indifferent spontaneity of external nature.

Where exactly it lies is clearly indicated in another poem of Heine, which is also dedicated to the 'accursed questions'. In it he formulates those question more closely to life:

> Away with your parables
> And empty hypotheses;
> Give us direct answers
> To the accursed questions:
> Why does the good man,
> All bloody, bear the burden of his cross
> Why is the dishonourable man
> Everywhere met by honour and praise?
> Who is to blame? Is everything on Earth
> In truth not accessible to God?
> Or is God playing with us?
> That is vile and despicable.
> So we fervently go on asking
> Until we become silent,
> Our mouths crammed full of earth ...
> But is this an answer, really? ...[4]

This is where what is irrational and illogical in life lies. It is in the social life of people, in their relationships with one another, and it is what fills the heart with anguish and doubt and arouses unanswerable questions in it. The unintel-ligible spontaneous forces that rule over social life lack both logic and justice; they carry people off to a fate that they neither want nor deserve, and, what

---

4   The lines are from Heinrich Heine, '*Laß die heil'gen Parabolen ...*', Bogdanov again used Mikhail Mikhailov's translation, and I translated Mikhailov's version [trans.].

is even worse, that they do not know ... A struggle is going on – but are the best victorious in it? Everyone works feverishly, but who gets the fruits of it? Time and again the answers of life turn out to be so absurd and so monstrous that the heart is gripped by pain and bewilderment. The contradictions of the social being of people – this is the root of the accursed questions that besiege the consciousness.

When nature ruled over humanity entirely, what was unreasonable and illogical hung over its life was entirely outside of each and every human being and was completely alien to them. It lay where they could not seek and demand either logic or rationality – where they could fear and pray but not ask questions. There were, therefore, no accursed questions at all in the religious worldview that expressed this phase of development. The questions that superficially corresponded to them had completely different and incomparably less complex content and permitted extremely simple, clear, and quite convincing answers. If, for example, it was recognised that human beings and all life existed in order to do the will of God, then this will was understood as pure self-will. It could be explained not by philosophical analysis but by immediate revelation. If it was established that the 'essence of human beings' consisted in their souls, then the further question of what the essence of such a soul was did not arise: it was not woven from mysterious contradictions, and its simplicity and vital stability did not engender doubts about its composition and the degree of its reality. Everything was in its place, and philosophical doubts could not make their way into heads that were entirely filled with anxiety concerning the immediate maintenance of life.

A series of decisive victories won by humanity over external nature proceeded inseparably from a radical transformation of the social nature of humankind. People became *logical and ethical* beings.

The first – the logical form of thinking – was the more immediate result of the growing power over nature. Fixed logical norms were expressions of the solid mastery of a vast number of interrelations and correlations among the complexes of nature. The principle of identity gave expression par excellence to the social and continuous nature of this mastery. 'What is A for me and at a given moment is exactly the same A in the *experience* of other people and also in my subsequent recollections of it'? This is the only possible meaning of the formula A = A, and outside of this meaning it turns into a useless and lifeless combination of signs. The principle of sufficient reason sums up the real vital meaning of the same mastery – the possibility of anticipating the future, the liberation from incomprehensible randomness and miracles.

Ethical consciousness was a more indirect effect of the development of labour of humanity. Society grew to huge dimensions and became deeply differentiated due to the division of labour among people. But this was precisely what made society a formally unorganised, anarchic system. The material vital interconnectedness of collaboration among members and groups of society remained, but it was completely concealed by their formal isolation and the struggle of their interests. Ethical consciousness expressed this dual nature of society appearing, as it did, in a form in which the material interconnectedness of labour solidarity limited and restrained the anarchic tendencies of groups and human individuals in the struggle of their interests. The fetishistic nature of this consciousness (the absolute imperative, whether religious or 'categorical') – its 'inscrutability' – issued precisely from the contradiction between the real interconnectedness of collaboration that comprised its basis and the formal independence of individuals in the labour process and the struggle among them that concealed this interconnectedness. As soon as the basis slipped from sight and appearance took on obvious vital reality and practical significance, then, quite understandably, that appearance represented a 'voice from another world' to the fetishist.

The unorganised, anarchic form of the social process put human beings, having escaped from subordination to the elements of external nature, under the dominion of the no less elemental forces of social life itself, and these forces propelled people 'they knew not where and against their will'. But logical and ethical beings could not relate to this situation with primeval fatalism and submissiveness. They began to clutch at what usually supported them in life – logical and ethical forms of consciousness. They began to put forth logical and ethical demands on the unintelligible and insuperable torrent of life that could not, of course, be satisfied, and because they could not be satisfied, they only became even more urgent and were felt even more painfully. The 'accursed questions' were the generalised form of these demands.

The huge differences in the life experience of people as members of a differentiated society led, to a greater or lesser degree, to an inevitable mutual lack of understanding in their collaboration and struggle. This, along with huge changes in the content of the experience of individual people in various phases of their existence, created an agonising need for something that was general and continuous, that would prevail over all these differences and changes, and that would *always and for everyone be the same* point of support in the chaos of life. This need, expressed in the 'eternal question' regarding the 'essence of things', is the transference onto 'everything' – onto the elemental stream of being – of the demand that logic formulates as the *principle of identity*.

The helplessness of the human individual in the face of the incomprehensible forces of social being – their inability to master them in cognition and in practice – intensifies the need to conceive of the movement of these forces in terms of causation, and it engenders another 'eternal question' regarding the universal 'cause of causes' that would serve as a respite and reassurance from the eternally flickering and elusive, wearingly intertwined, and hopelessly entangled particular causes. This is the transference to the infinite of the point of view in regard to ultimate phenomena that is expressed in logical terms in the *principle of sufficient reason.*

As far as the question of the supreme goals of being is concerned, its meaning is still more obvious: it is the impassioned cry of the impotence of *ethical consciousness* in the face of the hopeless prosaicness of the unfolding vital struggle. An ethical person cannot make ethical demands of social and human existence, and that existence silently jeers at them, punishing virtue and rewarding vice. The pain of this contradiction is embodied in the teleological question – 'accursed' and 'eternal' – because the very circumstances that engender it guarantee that it cannot be resolved.

Thus, the distinctive socio-psychological fact that is known as the 'accursed' or 'eternal' question of philosophy has a profoundly real basis in life. It is the rule of spontaneous social relationships over the individual and the individual's fate. As long as this basis exists, one cannot dream of the *complete* eradication of the aforesaid questions. The most subtle and powerful philosophical critique cannot destroy what was born altogether much deeper than the sphere in which criticism acts. In this sense, our hero was correct in his reproof of the positivist critics. These same positivists did not understand the true basis of the questions they were offering a critique of, and so in the depths of their souls they were not as free of an inclination toward them as they imagined and claimed. As children of bourgeois society, standing entirely on the ground of bourgeois relationships, positivists were as subject as everyone else to the insuperable spontaneity of those relationships. How could they not reproduce this subordination and this spontaneity in their psyches?

Their historical descendants – realists of the Marxist school – are in a different position. For them, it is not only the prevalent bourgeois-capitalist relationships that exist but also other relationships that spring out of them and that, at the same time, are the opposite of them. Side by side with classes that live entirely in the atmosphere of the competition and social labour anarchy that is caused when people are under the sway of their own relationships, another class steps forth – the proletariat. The proletariat represents growing comradely solidarity – the mass unification of forces – along with the tendency to subordinate the aforementioned social relationships to its organised will. The appearance of this class creates a new point of view that now makes it possible first to investigate the spontaneous forces of the social process and thereby to master them in cognitive terms and second to steadily carry on a conscious struggle against their actual rule. Thus, the very basis of the agonising 'eternal' questions is undermined, and for the first time the possibility appears of really and lastingly removing them.

Those who know the tendency of the changes that occur in life clearly understand where they lead. Such people have no objection to the basic direction of those changes, but, just the opposite, see in them progress, growth, and the expansion of life. They are not like swimmers who are carried off by the current against their will and into the unknown, and they do not desperately seek points of support, fictitious if not real. This is how it is with collectivists. They know the basic features of the line of development of social life, this knowledge is sufficient to permit them to successfully make certain important predictions, and the general meaning of these predictions turns out to be favourable for the growth of life and power of people in the given era. Where changes that take place are not horrible and not hostile, there is no striving to cling to the unchanging. What does an empty 'essence' of things matter to realists, when the full meaning and content of the laws of development of things are steadily being revealed to them? What does an unchanging 'final cause' matter, when, as they unwind the links of an endless chain of causes one after another, they experience with each new step a proud feeling of victory, a growth of power over hostile forces? What does a 'final goal' of life that is established from without and imposed by the will of another matter, when, freely choosing their own ideal of life, they are convinced that the objective course of the development of life is along a path heading toward this same ideal? The 'eternal' questions disappear and slip into the past. Space and energies are freed up for new, difficult, but resolvable questions, questions that are 'temporal' but that are alive and immediate – questions of life and not questions of what is outside life and above it.

All these conditions and reasons for a feeling of reassurance in the struggle and for the struggle exist in our time, but they did not, or practically did not, exist in the era of Heine's idealist. Therefore, if, in defiance of the laws of history, 'realists' of today could appear to him and try to expound their point of view, the young questioner simply would not accept it; he would not find in his psyche the experiences that make up the real meaning and content of the new understanding of life. He would shrug his shoulders and say 'You are speaking in my native language, and I understand each word, but what you say as a whole is completely impenetrable to me; it is really a meaningless collection of words'. Nothing could be done to help him, since new vital content cannot be created by words and arguments.

In 1848, amid the storms and gales of the 'crazy year', Heine's idealist died, while already in 1847, the Communist Manifesto had proclaimed to the world the appearance on earth of the contemporary 'realist'. New vital content quickly emerged, and the end to its growth and development is not in sight.

Everything has changed. Already there are no 'fools who expect an answer' any more from the waves of a cold, lifeless sea, but conscious swimmers who strive to master the waves of the foaming sea of life in order to make the ferocious power of those waves the means of moving toward their ideal. And on this path a new world is being born – a realm of harmonious and whole people who have been freed from contradictions and compulsion in their practice and from fetishism in their knowledge.

Even if this world is not as near as it is thought to be by people who visualise it too vaguely, its beauty and grandeur are not made any less because of it, and the struggle for this new world does not cease to be the most noble of all the goals that conscious beings can set for themselves.

PART 3

Contributions to *Studies in the Realist Worldview*

∵

Introduction to the First Edition

Realism is not a finished *system* of knowledge but a specific *path* toward the systematic knowledge of everything given by experience. And it is first and foremost the path of *labour*. For realism, knowledge is a living immediate struggle with nature to know its secrets in which the point is the real dominion of human beings over the world. Realism does not believe in the innate right of human reason to give nature its laws – it recognises only an *acquired* right, only a right won by struggle.

But real struggle – in knowledge as in life – is harsh; the enemy is terrible in its elemental grandeur and knows no mercy. The *weak* avoid a direct encounter with it and try to create for themselves another more comfortable arena for struggle, another more tractable and gentle enemy – an enemy in 'appearance' and not in 'essence'. Thus arose a world of cognitive dreams; thus arose a conception of nature in which thinking surrendered to fantasy. This was natural and inevitable in times when cognition was really weak. But in our times, realism cannot resign itself to this, and it condemns any return to the phantasmal world of metaphysics or to the realm of a natural world that metaphysics has falsified. Realism considers this to be a shameful flight from the field of battle and as a weakness that does not deserve pity.

From time to time such weakness develops to the extent that it is a kind of epidemic in literature. The social class to which the majority of the people of theory and the printed word belong – the professional intelligentsia – is a class that does not have an independent position in society and that has a highly strung and impressionable constitution. The tempests and storms of life produce a heavy, oppressive effect on the intelligentsia, and if, confronting this, it does not immediately find a firm point of support for itself in the surrounding environment, or if the previous point of support turns out to be unsuitable for its desires and interests, then flight from life – in practice and in cognition – becomes a common phenomenon for it. Then there arrives a time of enthusiasm for metaphysics with its castles in the air, with its fictitious points of support for real life, and with its idols that have taken the place of ideals. All this has been playing out before our eyes in recent years and still has not come to an end.

At such moments, a new important task arises for realism. It must not allow ideological weakening. It must not allow mental demoralisation to deeply penetrate the psyche of the thinking elements of society. It must not allow the impotence and uselessness of old fetishes that have once again been dragged into the light from the dungeons and graveyards of the past to stir up a harmful narcotic and to undermine the intellectual health of the working-class intelligentsia. This task is becoming especially important in such a culturally youthful society as ours, which does not have behind it a long tradition of serious mental work over many generations and which cannot resist diseases of thought with a powerful inherited immunity. Realism must show that a return to the type of ideas of one's ancestors is nothing other than degeneration and disease. Realism must explain the origin of this disease and elucidate of all of its manifestations. Realism must put forward the clarity and rigour of its own point of view against the confusion and capriciousness of thinking that suffers from the disease of metaphysics.

Realism teaches that cognition must first and foremost remain true to itself. It must be governed only by feelings that relate to the joy and pain of cognition and only by a will that is the will to knowledge. Realism unconditionally rejects the interference of any other feelings, any other will in the matter of cognition. Only truth and falsehood exist for it. Realism strives only toward pure truth no matter how harsh it might be, and it does not allow knowledge to be subordinated to any other need of the human soul whatsoever. In this sense it is alien to compromise and is the *pure idealism of cognition*.

History shows that in cognition and in practice where there are great antagonistic forces truth is never a 'golden mean' between them: not in the struggle of paganism and Christianity, not in the struggle of Catholicism and the Reformation, and not in any other struggle between immobility and progress. A force that is true does not change; it promotes its tendency to the end. Steadfast consistency in cognition and steadfast consistency in life are two manifestations of the same principle. Theoretical realism, as an expression of this principle in the sphere of cognition, and practical idealism, as its expression in the sphere of life, are siblings in spirit.

Contemporary realism finds that cognition is one of the manifestations of life and that the laws that it ascertains for the entire realm of life are also the laws that it ascertains for its own self. One of these laws says that the fullest and most powerful life is life that is whole and harmonious. This means that the most perfected and powerful cognition must be cognition that is unitary and orderly, and this means that truth is monistic. Contemporary realism is inimical to eclecticism; it considers eclecticism to be a mark of weakness, and expression of a pitiable, inharmonious life. It struggles for a *monistic ideal of cognition*.

Eclecticism is a sort of professional illness of the intelligentsia. The intelligentsia – a group that occupies an intermediate place between powerful social classes and constantly vacillates in its relationships with them – reflects these traits of its being in its thinking. It is true that purely philosophical eclecticism has few supporters here, but in the realm of sociology – a science that has attained the most important vital significance in our times – eclecticism is very stubbornly clung to. And, in defending its position, the 'Russian sociological school'[1] – regardless of serious defeats brought on it by obvious facts of life and by the polemics of its opponents – nevertheless enjoys significant influence. To do away with this eclecticism in its last refuges, having confronted it with real life and the precise methods of science, is one of the main tasks of contemporary realism in social science.

We mark out here only the most general contours of realism, as we understand it. This entire book is dedicated to the most immediate explanation of its basic ideas. Our task consists in providing the reader with an understanding of the conception of realism that we are profoundly convinced is uniquely true for the contemporary world. There will be a time when it will be replaced by a new, higher point of view, but it will arise precisely out of realism, as its natural born child, as a new, more complete and perfected realisation of the same vital tendencies. It is on the path of realism that knowledge conquers nature, and it will not turn away from this path. Truth is the sure path to victory over nature.

Realism – like truth – is unified, but at the same time – like truth – it is many-sided. In this book, readers will encounter various nuances and approaches of realist thinking, but these differences will not prevent them from clearly seeing the basic unity behind them – the unity of a vital tendency.

---

1   This is a reference to the thought of the great Narodnik publicist, N.K. Mikhailovsky (1842–1904), and the so-called 'legal populists' who are discussed in Mendel 1961 [trans.].

Introduction to the Second Edition

Our country is undergoing a profound crisis. An impetuously unfolding struggle, the ever-increasing conflicts of immediate vital interests of classes and groups, unavoidably demands the attention not only of every person disposed to action but also of anyone who is at all capable of seeing and hearing. On the surface everything entwines and clashes in a motley, contradictory chaos; in the depths muffled, threatening reverberations can be heard ...

Under such conditions the lively interest in theory and questions of worldview that our readers display – and a characteristic illustration of this is that we are undertaking a second edition of this collection one year after the first – might seem puzzling. It is well known that our readers belong mainly to the intellectual proletariat and the proletarian intelligentsia, groups that stand so close to the centre of the historical cyclone of our era that it would seem that from a simple sense of self-preservation they must necessarily focus all their attention on what is immediate and closest, on the events of the struggle. How can we explain such a peculiar bifurcation of interest between what is vitally concrete and what is theoretically abstract?

In reality there is no bifurcation. Whoever does not want to be powerless in the face of what is concrete must master it with the help of theory; whoever does not want to spin helplessly in the chaos of the vital crisis must get to know it in a realist manner. The most active interest in life requires the greatest consciousness. Realist theory makes it possible to sort out the tangle of contradictions, to reduce to a unity the fantastic combinations of different elements, to unite the best forces of life on the truest path of life. Realist theory is a powerful tool of struggle.

To give oneself up to life still does not mean to live; to react still does not mean to act. You will not see much if you do not anticipate; you will not move very far forward if you do not start walking. Where there is no knowledge, victory over spontaneity is fortuitous and fleeting. It is only where steadfast activity is based on rigorous knowledge that struggle is assured of victory and life flourishes to the highest degree ...

Exchange and Technology

The processes of exchange are one of the basic and most characteristic phenomena in the life of capitalist society. At the same time, these phenomena are extremely complex, and it is very difficult to subject them to analysis. The question of the laws of capitalist exchange has so far engendered many disagreements among investigators and has acquired the reputation of being the most tangled question of economic science. Our task consists in pointing out and justifying the means of deciding this question that seems to us to be the simplest and, moreover, the only reliable means.[1]

The idea of *social adaptation* lies at the basis of our work. Society is a complex system of mutually adapting elements and relationships, and it is therefore impossible to understand one or another aspect of social life outside of its inseparable connection with other aspects, outside of the adaptation of one aspect to another and vice versa. Thus, the laws of social life can be established by discovering the conditions under which the social whole is adapted, i.e. survives or develops. Laws of adaptation provide not only the possibility of understanding the processes of adaptation but also the necessary starting point for analysing the phenomena of unadaptedness. The entire realm of life – social life, just like all other kinds of life – lies within these bounds.

The same thing relates, in part, to the laws of exchange. Exchange is a specific, historically transitory, form of *distribution* in a society of products that are created by social labour. Distribution must not be understood in any other way than in an inseparable interrelationship with the process of social labour – with 'production'. Distribution must be adapted to production, otherwise, society could not survive and develop. Thus, the laws of exchange boil down to the expression of the conditions under which a system of production is adapted, i.e. that survives and develops. Along with this, it is easy to analyse contradictory cases – cases of the unadaptedness of systems of exchange and production with partial or general degradation that spring up because of that unadaptedness, through the destruction of elements of one system or another.

---

1 We do not consider it necessary to apologise to the reader for dedicating this article to the sort of question that 'everyone is fed up with', such as the question of price, value, etc. We are convinced that readers will be found who look at the matter not from the point of view of the hunger for new themes but from the point of view of the need for as complete and rigorous an explanation as possible of fundamental scientific questions.

The idea of adaptation, taken both in its positive and negative aspects, is sufficiently broad for all manifestations of life.

Our point of view does not represent anything *essentially new* in this realm of investigation. It has not been formulated with complete precision and has not been carried out completely, but it nevertheless factually predominates in the works of a whole vast economic school or, to be more precise, two schools that, each in its own time, have possessed the most vital and progressive tendencies. Most applications of the so called 'abstract method' of the classical and subsequently the Marxist school take the idea of adaptation as an implicit presupposition.[2] But we propose that only a completely conscious and consistent implementation of this idea can lead to a clear elucidation of the question, to a sound and completely reliable method of resolving it.

In order not to complicate this discussion and not to violate its unity, we will restrain ourselves from historical references to the development of various viewpoints on the question under examination. We will touch on these viewpoints only to the extent that they have a direct bearing on our task, and each time we will take them in their most developed and finished from.

---

2 Precisely for this reason, both schools always studied exchange as inseparably interrelated with production. Such an approach to the question has been particularly disliked by modern Russian 'critics'. In his article '*K kritike nekotorykh osnovnykh problem i polozhenii politicheskoi ekonomii* [Towards the critique of certain basic problems and the condition of political economy]', *Zhizn'* [*Life*], 1910, Mr Struve wrote: '… to the extent that scientific analysis is limited – consciously or unconsciously – to economic intercourse, a fetishistic point of view is methodologically and uniquely correct. Investigating the abstract form of economic limitations with the aid of inter-economic categories, political economy can and must take the position of fetishism' (p. 264). To translate this into generally understandable language: exchange must be studied outside its connection with production and, moreover, from a fetishistic point of view. And why do so? Because, in exchange, fetishism 'is a psychological necessity' (p. 264, above). If, in exchange, a seller and a buyer inevitably turn out to be fetishists, then, in Mr Struve's opinion, the economist, when studying their relationships, must also not rise above fetishism. Following this logic, the life of children must necessarily be studied from a child's point of view, the life of ants from an ant's point of view, etc. Not an easy task!

Developing his idea, Mr Struve remarks, '… Marx was not aware of the profound fundamental difference between various "economic categories" – between enterprise, inter-enterprise, and social categories. This explains the scientific unsoundness of his construction, in which a social category – capital, as a social relationship – is inferred from an economic category – value' (p. 266). So, Marx did not grasp this. He did not grasp what Heine describes as a bookish state of mind in which all 'categories' are distributed around the head in separate file boxes, and the key to each box is completely unique. God forbid that a link should be found between 'capital', which for Mr Struve lies in one box, and 'value', which lies in another. Mr Struve calls these categories 'sharp tools of analysis' (p. 272). We doubt that anything can be cut with them.

I

The social process is first and foremost the process of labour; its basic content consists of the consciously expedient activity of people in their struggle for existence with nature and with other people. The broadest and most important realm of this process is designated by the word 'production'.

The activity of labour of human individuals is directed in a great many cases not only toward the survival and development of the individuals themselves but also the survival and development of other people. Sometimes people are fully and clearly aware of this direction of labour, and they set themselves goals that go beyond the bounds of their own personal benefit. Sometimes the social nature of labour escapes their consciousness, their immediate goals are egoistic, and the useful results that other people gain occur in spite of these goals. For example, in clan society, all members feel themselves to be a part of an indivisible whole for which they carry out their productive activity. In exchange society, all people have in mind their own interests, but in producing for sale – for the market – they actually are also working for other people who will use the products of their labour. We will use the term 'productive labour' – or, more concisely, 'production' – to refer to any labour that has results that are *socially-directed*.

Thus, labour that is useful *only* for workers, themselves – labour for personal consumption, for example – is not within the sphere of production, and labour that is socially harmful – destruction or theft, for example – is even further outside production. As far as socially useful labour is concerned, it is all within the realm of production whether it is 'physical' or 'mental', whether its products are material or not material.[3]

In order for labour to be really socially useful, its products must in one way or another be *distributed* in society for consumption. The system of production

---

3 We note this, in view of the fact that in economic science up until now a much narrower understanding of production has been retained to a significant degree. Many people use the word 'productive' to refer only to labour that has *material* results, and any other labour – purely intellectual labour, for example – is designated as 'unproductive'. Traces of this point of view are even encountered in Marx, although with him there are also direct indications in support of the opposite point of view, which we think is correct. The 'materiality' and 'non-materiality' of products has nothing to do with their *social* features and therefore cannot serve as the basis for a discrimination of types of labour in *social* science. In the social struggle for life and the development of labour, 'physical' and 'mental' have *essentially the same* significance and are really inseparable. V. Bazarov deals with this in greater detail in *Trud proizvoditel'nyi i trud, obrazuiushchii tsennost'* [*Productive Labour and Labour that Generates Value*] (St. Petersburg 1899). [Bazarov 2019.]

is inseparably tied to the system of distribution and is necessarily complemented by it. The social nature of the labour of human individuals or even of a whole group is fully revealed only when the products of this labour are situated in a system of social distribution. At the same time, the individual or group can carry out their socially productive labour only if they obtain a certain share of social product from the realm of distribution sufficient for maintaining their capability of labour. Productive labour requires, first, sufficient 'means of production' with which labour is carried out – its material and tools – and, second, sufficient 'means of personal consumption' that maintains people's labour power. All this is obtained by human individuals and groups through the distribution of social product.[4]

From all this, it is already clear that there is a fundamental connection of adaptation that exists between the sphere of production and the sphere of distribution. This connection can be expressed in the following form: *what is distributed in society is what is provided by productive activity, and it is distributed in such a way that productive activity can continue.* We will develop this formulation to make it completely clear.

The first part of the formula is, of course, very understandable, but it can be shown to be not completely precise. It might be asked whether there are also things that are distributed but that are not created by social labour, and whether individual members of society also appropriate untilled land, virgin forests, the power of flowing water, and other 'gifts of nature'? But there is a misunderstanding that springs up here because it is inappropriate to apply the word 'create' to production. Labour altogether cannot 'create' anything; labour, as was explained long ago, only relocates and combines the objects of labour. But everything that enters into the sphere of distribution necessarily underwent the process of social labour and, consequently, was *provided* by it in one way or another. Untilled soil, which becomes the object of appropriation, and so of distribution, necessarily must at least have been previously discovered and attained by people. From our point of view, the labour of a traveller – the labour of a discoverer of new lands – is not essentially distinguishable from other forms of social labour.[5] And here, as in all other cases, the sphere of distribution is completely determined by the sphere of production.

---

4   And let us note once again that all this relates identically to physical and mental labour, to material and non-material products. Both types of labour require means of production and means of consumption, and both kinds of product can serve as the conditions of maintenance or growth of people's capacity for work, as an object of consumption.

5   Of course, in our time, it is possible to appropriate, buy, and sell the North Pole even before it is in fact reached. But in reality, the North Pole does not thereby enter into in the realm of

The second proposition of our formula – that products are distributed in such a way that production can continue – expresses the idea of adaptation: obviously, society survives or develops to the extent that the course of events corresponds to this formula in its most direct meaning. If things occur differently, if the law is not observed, then the system of production will break down and change until some kind of correspondence between the two spheres of life is attained or until society fails. Consequently, the law, as a norm of phenomena, would then arise from a negative perspective, but its meaning would nevertheless remain the same.

In general, all laws of adaptation are *abstract* laws, i.e. they express tendencies of phenomena and are not simple empirical correlations. The broad general meaning of abstract norms depends precisely on their depicting phenomena in an idealised, simplified form, conceiving of them as if their tendencies were fully realised.

Such abstract laws do not exist only in the social sciences; they play no less a role in the natural sciences. Analysis in the natural sciences strives to find the basic tendency in each series of phenomena and to express it as a norm of that series. In subsequently introducing other, complicating tendencies into the analysis, one gradually crosses over from norms to the concreteness of phenomena. Thus, for example, the abstract law of fall speaks of the evenly accelerating movement of falling bodies, but this is only a norm of phenomena; not a single one of our experiences and observations will strictly correspond to this formula. Nevertheless, the fewer the complicating tendencies (resistance of air, collateral stimuli, attraction of nearby objects ...) and the weaker they are, the closer a phenomenon will conform to this formula. Keeping all these secondary aspects in mind, we can analyse and describe the real processes of falling with endlessly increasing approximation, but in no case may we demand that an abstract law precisely express the entire concreteness of the series of phenomena. Such a demand would be simply contradictory, since an abstract norm is precisely an abstraction from the concreteness of a real process, from a concreteness that is infinitely complex for cognition.[6]

---

distribution. Besides that, even such a fictitious 'distribution' of the North Pole presupposes, at least, the labour of theoretical investigation relative to this doubtful object of consumption. And, in any case, it is impossible not to accept that in our time the North Pole already 'costs' not a little labour.

These remarks are directed, by the way, against one of the banal objections to the labour theory of value – against the assertion that there are commodities that have exchange value but 'absolutely do not cost labour'. The unconditionally universal characteristic of commodities – as objects of distribution – is altogether to be a product of labour.

6 One of the common objections against the labour theory of value is this: the price of goods in

Having explained the meaning that we must attach to the law we have formulated and how it must be used in analysis, we return to a precise formulation
of it. For the goals of our investigation, it must be made somewhat more definite and concrete – in the following form, to be precise.

*In a society that is surviving or developing, each human individual or produ-
cing group obtains from all social labour the means of production and the means
of consumption in a sufficient quantity in order to fulfil their social role.*

To the extent that producers do not obtain a sufficient amount of the means
of production and consumption and to the extent that they are not able to participate in production as previously, society does not survive or develop but
deteriorates. At first glance, this proposition is almost a tautology, but in reality
it is far from tautological. Because it contains the idea of adaptation, further
conclusions that are far from self-evident can be drawn from it and applied to
certain other conditions. This is no greater a tautology than, for example, the
principle of natural selection, which says that what is adapted survives while
adaptation is precisely the capability of life to survive. This principle, however,
contains idea of *regularity* in the survival and failure of life, and it can therefore
lead to new and important conclusions.

II

The organisation of the ancient patriarchal clan commune can serve as a direct
illustration of the general law of distribution.

A patriarch – the head of a clan – appears here as the organiser of production
and distribution. He assigns the role in communal labour to each member of
the group and gives them the means for carrying out this role. If some of them

---

fact diverges from the value of labour, and so the law of exchange according to the labour rate
is not true. It is clear that this objection boils down to ignorance of what a scientific law in
general is and ignorance of the extent to which an abstract norm can correspond to a concrete
phenomenon.

A somewhat less common form of this objection is this: average prices of goods do not
completely correspond to their labour value, and so the labour theory of value is not true.
What is going on here is the confusion of two characteristics of cognition – rates and averages.
A rate, as we have pointed out, expresses the *fundamental* tendency of a series of phenomena, and an *average* is the resultant of all the various tendencies that appear in this series.
It is clear that in the majority of cases the two will not coincide. Thus, if we observe the fall
of a body near the surface of the earth and empirically find an average value of acceleration,
then this average will not at all correspond with the rate of acceleration ($g = 9.81 \, \mathrm{m/s/s}$) but
will turn out to be less than it. The rate corresponds completely to unimpeded fall, without
any complicating influences, while the average is derived from all complicating influences –

must undertake field work, he provides them with communal ploughs, seeds for sewing, etc. If others are preparing to go fishing, he gives them communal nets, boats, and so forth. Besides this, he permits each worker to take from the communal reserves sufficient bread, meat, clothing, and other products that are necessary for maintaining the appropriate labour capacity of all producers.

In so doing, the organiser must bear in mind the unequal nature of the labour of individual workers. Some peoples' labour is easier; others' is more strenuous. Some peoples' labour is simple; others' is more complex. Labour that is more strenuous or more complex can be successfully carried out only with more significant consumption. Each type of labour corresponds to specific needs – exactly which, the patriarch knows on the basis of his past experience. Women who must carry out work that is usually simple and less intensive receive predominantly vegetable food and in a lesser quantity. Men who undertake more significant movement and experience the burdensome influences of external nature to a greater degree need to eat meat and a greater amount of food, besides. Fishermen who often must carry out extremely tiring work in cold water additionally need certain supplementary stimulation – intoxicating drink, for example. The organiser, himself, in order to be fit for his complex and highly demanding activity that demands special mental effort and that would be deadly for a less developed psyche, must inevitably have broader, more varied, and more refined needs, and he must, of course, not refuse to satisfy them.

Here we run into one of the most difficult questions of economic science. The head of a commune must accomplish this task: to commensurate the participation of individual producers in communal labour and to distribute the common product among them in correspondence with their participation.[7] The patriarch can, of course, accomplish this task *in practice*, based on clan traditions and on his personal experience. But from the point of view of *theoretical* investigation, the matter is not so simple.

Is it possible to establish any commensurateness between types of labour that are as different as, let us say, the mechanical labour of women who spin

---

and the most important of these influences (resistance of air) acts to slow the speed of falling bodies. In exactly the same way, the *normal* length of life, corresponding to its full physiological cycle, is not at all equal to the *average* length of life, etc. But we will subsequently have even more to say about this and in considerably greater detail.

7   The communal product is not consumed only by the actual producers alone but by 'unproductive' members of the group – children, those who are ill, and old people. But there is no need to dwell on all the complicated aspects of production. Future and potential producers are also necessary elements of the business of labour, and all people (perhaps with insignificant exceptions) are, over the course of their existence, producers.

wool and the mental labour of the organiser of the group? Should it not be acknowledged that different forms of labour are quantitatively incomparable because they are qualitatively heterogeneous? Adherents of the labour theory of value hold that, in the analysis of a social system, complex labour must be viewed in general as a multiple of simple labour. Is this idea permissible? How can such commensurability be found? We will attempt to provide a precise and reasoned answer to these questions.

Labour is a specific form of expenditure of human energy. The continuous *expenditure* of energy is realised only under conditions of the *assimilation* of energy by the organism, and, in addition, where there is a greater expenditure there must be a correspondingly greater assimilation. And, just the opposite, where the need for greater assimilation is observed, it means that there is also greater expenditure. In general, as long as the equilibrium of these two sides of life is not destroyed, we can draw conclusions about the magnitude of one of them according to the magnitude of the other.

But in economic analysis we obviously are not able to speak of expenditure and assimilation of energy from a general point of view of physics; in economics our investigation is carried out from a specifically social point of view, and we can speak only of the expenditure and assimilation of social labour energy. The expenditure of social labour energy, as we know, is labour – to the extent that it is social labour. But what is the assimilation of social labour energy?

Assimilation of social labour energy is the consumption of a social product. Social labour is embodied – 'crystallised' – in a product, and the human individual, in consuming the product, consequently acquires the labour energy put into it by other people. Capacity for labour is created by this assimilation of social labour energy, and thus the 'labour power' of producers is subsequently spent in those other people's labour.

If the assimilation and expenditure of energy correspond, then it is obvious that, as well as making a direct quantitative comparison between of the labour performed by the organiser and the labour performed by an implementer, it is also possible, for example, to compare the quantity of labour that they assimilate, which is embodied in the products they consume and which creates the labour power of both. The first relationship can safely be replaced by the second without risking error, and, besides, the second relationship is fundamentally easier to discover, since the issue here is the sum of consumed products.

There is, however, a big difficulty here. Organisers not only consume more than implementers, but in part they consume different products. The former need silk cloth, fine wine, and white bread in order to maintain their labour power; the latter need only linen, vodka, and black bread. Both sorts of products are, yet again, produced by different forms of labour. Is not a comparison made even more confusing by replacing the one with the other?

But nothing prevents us from descending even further and, instead of comparing the labour of the producers who make silk and linen, wine to the labour of those who produce vodka, black bread and white bread, to compare the means of consumption of those producers. Here the comparison can turn out to be easier, since the needs of the producers of silk and linen are not nearly as different as the products of their labour. If things are not simple enough here, one should go even further down the path of indirect comparison and continue to the point where quantities that are suitable for comparison are obtained.[8] Thus, ultimately, we can be convinced that complex and simple labour are really commensurable – that the qualitative differences of forms of labour from a social point of view are fully capable of being reduced to complex, quantitative differences. This gives us the right to view labour of any degree of complexity as a multiple of simple labour.[9]

---

8   If such a path of comparison seems never-ending to anyone, one must keep one more thing in mind. Each stage of this path, as we have seen, provides us an equation in which the relationship of some forms of labour is equalised in relation to others. One can obtain as many equations as you want, but the number of forms of labour is limited. It is obvious that a certain number of equations will always allow the possibility of resolving the question of the quantitative comparison of individual forms of labour.

At this point, we can foresee the possibility of yet another objection. We substituted the relationship of the labour of the organiser and implementer for the relationship of social labour that is embodied in the products they consume, but their own labour – the very labour that we want to quantitatively compare with the help of the substitution we have made – can be partly embodied in these products. Is this not a vicious circle? Of course not. An equation does not cease to be a legitimate equation because its unknowns enter into its second part and not only in the first. It would be meaningless only in the event that unknowns entered into both parts to an equal degree, with equal coefficients – then they would simply be cancelled out and the equation would be indeterminable. But this obviously is not what is going on here.

The question of the complexity and difficulty of equations are of no interest at all to us here. It is obvious that there is no need to subsequently resolve them. We need only to contradict the error of those who consider the equation of the commensurability of labour to be formally impossible and on this basis to deny the very concept of the commensurable social labour value of all commodities.

9   From this point of view, one should consider the relationship of labour of greater intensity with labour of lesser intensity. Usually, when it is said that one worker accomplishes twice as much in a day than another, it means that that worker works twice as intensely. This view is wrong. In order to carry out twice as much external work in the same amount of time, three or four times the labour energy usually needs to be expended, not two times. Experience shows that beyond a certain limit any supplementary external work costs the organism considerably more dearly. Therefore, in comparing work of different intensities, an indirect comparison is

We do not at all propose that Messrs Economists apply the above method to every concrete case. Life itself can accomplish the difficult task, and in our times the market – valuing the labour power of an organiser at 3,000 roubles and of an implementer at 300 roubles – establishes the quantitative relationship between the two kinds of labour with sufficient precision.[10] For us it was important only to explain the extent to which the idea of commensurability of all forms of labour is valid in abstract investigation, and we saw that its validity was unquestionable.

Let us return to our example of distribution – to the patriarchal clan commune. It was pointed out that producers must receive no less an amount of means of production and means of consumption than is necessary for their labour activity. But could they not receive more than this? If a surplus remains after all the essential needs that are sufficient for maintaining the production of the commune are satisfied, how will distribution be accomplished then?

Here we encounter a concept hat will play a very important role in the theory of distribution – the concept of surplus labour.[11] Surplus labour means the possibility of social *development*. Instead of a simple equilibrium in a social system, the energy of the system is elevated so that the assimilation of energy

---

necessary: one must investigate how much the consumption of a worker must grow in order to create two or three times more products in the same amount of time. This is how we can obtain the most reliable measure of the increase in the intensity of labour.

10   In order to remove a possible objection, let us note in advance that the sum of products that are actually obtained by one or another producer (and, in contemporary society, the sum of monetary compensation) might not correspond to the magnitude of the normal needs that it is objectively necessary to satisfy in order to fully maintain a worker's energy at its given height. For example, organisers of production often obtain considerably more than is required from this point of view, and workers often receive considerably less. But for our conclusions what is sufficient is that this norm *exists* and that any given worker's energy *factually corresponds* to a certain level of consumption, that a deviation below this level means that the worker's energy will be exhausted, and that a deviation above it means either the possibility of qualitative and quantitative *development* (and not simple preservation) of a worker's energy or socially useless luxury. *This level is the rate of social adaptation.*

11   Surplus labour is the excess of all social labour above the labour that produces the means of consumption of producers. This is the first and direct meaning of the term, and it relates only to the system of production as a whole and not to the labour of individual people. But if one acknowledges the commensurability of all forms of labour – the existence of a common measure of it – then one can also speak of the surplus labour of individual producers. One need only express individuals' own labour and the labour that is embodied in their means of consumption in the same labour units, and then the excess of the first quantity over the second represents the surplus labour of given producers. This second, derivative and more abstract, meaning of the term 'surplus labour' has a particularly important meaning for us.

more than covers its expenditures. At the same time, the question of distribution obviously becomes more complex.

But in regard to clan society, of which we have just been speaking, surplus
labour did not represent a particularly important phenomenon. The technology of clan society was not developed and was extremely conservative. The
quantity of surplus labour was insignificant and the result of surplus labour
boiled down to the strengthening of the commune by means of reproduction.
In this case, Malthus's law, which corresponds precisely to stagnant technology – is fully applicable. When productive forces attain a level at which surplus
labour becomes a significant and not a chance quantity in production, the old
organisation can no longer survive and breaks down and transforms into a new,
historically higher form. The higher form is exchange society, and, before we
continue further, we need to dwell a little on how it is organised.

III

In exchange society the means of distribution is very different from the one
that rules in clan communes. The conscious will of an organiser who adapts
distribution immediately to the needs of production is replaced by the socially
spontaneous force of the market. Individual producers organise their small
enterprises independently of others and then, entering the sphere of social dis-
tribution/exchange with their products, strive only for the benefit of their own
enterprise and not for the survival and development of the social whole. So, is
distribution for society as a whole not organised?[12] In the act of exchange there
are only mutually conflicting interests; there is no conscious regulation of their
interaction.

How can the general law of distribution – that producers must obtain sufficient means of production and consumption from the social product to be able
to continue their social labour activities – be realised under such a system? If
there is no conscious actor, who directly applies this norm (in the manner of

---

12   With exchange, one producer gives their product to another, as occurs with any process of distribution. Products are distributed in society by means of exchange, and what
is unique here is only the form of the process, which is unorganised and therefore full
of struggle and contradictions. But it pleases Mr Struve to call unorganised distribution
'pseudo-distribution'. Unorganised production he also calls 'pseudo-enterprise'. Mr Struve
seriously considers such 'pseudo-terms' that he delights himself with to be a 'critique'.
Pseudo-critique!

the organiser of a clan commune), then it is obvious that the law of distribution can only govern over phenomena in a spontaneous and indirect manner. And this is actually what happens.

Enterprises that are incapable of drawing sufficient means from the sale of their products to be able to continue their vital activities either perish and disappear from the social system or degrade to the extent that their diminished needs are just covered by the results of the sale of their goods. Adapted enterprises that receive sufficient means of production and consumption survive, and by means of this 'selection', distribution in exchange society corresponds with the norm. This correspondence is, of course, only approximate for each separate case, and the norm is realised only in general and on average and only at the cost of constant fluctuation in one direction or the other. But this does not prevent it from remaining a law of these phenomena, i.e. from expressing their basic and constant tendency.

Because of the distinctive organisation of exchange society, the question of distribution must be posed in a new way that has a different form from the previous one. Commodities are exchanged for commodities, and for each individual case of exchange one must ask not about the general correlation between the sum of products of an enterprise and the sum of its needs but only about the particular exchange relationship of the two commodities. This is the question of 'exchange value'.

It stands to reason that the essence of the question cannot be changed by its new formulation. As before, the point is to explain the necessary relationship between production and distribution, and it is only how this interrelationship is expressed that is considered in new terms.

From the point of view of production, a commodity is the result of social labour; from the point of view of exchange it is a value. It embodies a certain number of units of social labour energy, and it is equal in value to a certain number of units of other commodities. In other words, a commodity has such-and-such a labour cost and such-and-such an exchange value.[13] How are these facts interrelated?

Let us consider a member of exchange society – a cobbler, let us say. In one year, he makes 100 pairs of boots. In so doing, he uses up leather and thread and works with a knife, an awl, and other instruments. Suppose that the quantity of all these 'means of production' that is used in a year embodies 6,000 hours of simple labour. And suppose that the sum of living labour that is applied to

---

13   We will use the term 'labour cost' to designate in general only the sum of social labour that is embodied in a commodity and so is purely a relationship of *production*. We will use the term 'exchange value' to signify the ratio of exchange – a relationship of *distribution*.

the material and tools by the cobbler and by other members of his household equals 4,000 hours of simple labour. Thus, objectively, the sum of labour that the given merchandise costs comes to 10,000 hours of simple labour, and for each pair of boots 10,000 ÷ 100, i.e. 100 hours. If this is the labour cost of the merchandise, what is the magnitude of the exchange value?

In order for production to be maintained, the cobbler must sell his commodities in the market for enough to cover his means of production and consumption. The leather, thread, and instruments represent a labour cost of 6,000 hours, and he must consequently receive from the sphere of exchange the same quantity of means of production costs an equal amount of labour. Besides that, he must purchase a sufficient quantity of bread, meat, clothing, and other objects of consumption to maintain the labour power of the members of his household. What can the labour cost of these objects of consumption be? *As long as there is no surplus labour*, the means of consumption must be equal to the same sum of labour as is used in production by the workers themselves. If their labour cost is less than the sum of living labour, then surplus labour *now exists*. If it is greater than the sum of living labour then it means that the given enterprise is unviable, because it cannot develop as much labour as is needed for its own maintenance.[14] In brief, if there is no surplus labour, then the labour cost of the means of life necessary for the maintenance of all the labour power of the enterprise is just equal to the sum of labour that is developed by this labour power. In our example, this would consist of 4,000 hours of simple labour.

Thus, the entire labour value of the commodities that the cobbler must obtain from other people in making their 100 pairs of boots comprises 6,000 + 4,000 – i.e. 10,000 – hours of simple labour or 100 hours per pair, while the labour value of these same boots, as we saw earlier, is 10,000 hours or 100 hours for each pair. The two quantities are equal. Hence the conclusion: *the exchange price corresponds to the value of labour*. The relationship of exchange in a simple mercantile society is qualitatively determined by the relationship of labour crystallised in individual commodities.

In reality, as we know, commodities are at first exchanged for money, and subsequently money serves as the means of buying other commodities. But does this change anything in our calculations? Money is a commodity that costs labour just like other commodities and is exchanged according to the

---

14   Of course, such an enterprise could exist by exploiting other enterprises – by, for example, selling its products at an excessive price, but then the surplus labour that would allow the exploitation to be accomplished would have to exist in these other enterprises, and we have taken an example where there is no surplus labour in the given society.

very same law. True, it is a special commodity and precisely the kind that serves as a tool of exchange. But precisely because it is a *tool* of exchange, it cannot essentially change anything in the in the quantitative *results* of exchange: it is through the means of money that commodities are exchanged for commodities. It is obvious that the quantitative relationship between the commodity that is being sold and the commodity that is then purchased cannot essentially change merely because of the circumstance that money appears in the capacity of an intermediary link between them. The conditions of adaptation do not change at all.[15] Therefore, at the present level of analysis we can place the question of the influence of money to the side (we will return to it again in the future).

We have established the law of commodity exchange in the case where there is no surplus of labour in the system of production, but how do things stand if surplus labour exists? The fundamental principle would then appear to be inadequate. Suppose, for example, that the labour value of a product that is produced in an artisan's enterprise is 10,000 hours, and the labour value of the necessary means of production and consumption is only 9,000 hours. Then we can confidently say only one thing: that the product, which is worth 10,000 hours, must not be sold for less than the 9,000 hours of the means of production and consumption that are embodied in the commodities of other people. If the artisan sells it more cheaply, then the enterprise will not be maintained. But must the product not be exchanged just for that sum of commodities that corresponds to its real labour value? This we cannot say for sure.

Further analysis here is quite difficult, but it also is not of very great interest. A simple commodity society is a scientific abstraction of quite a high level of abstraction, and all real social organisations that are close to its model to any extent – city communes of the middle ages, for example – are themselves variable. A petty enterprise of an isolated commodity producer is weak and unstable precisely because it is small and its productive power is insignificant. In the presence of any unfavourable combination of the spontaneous forces of

---

15   The monetary form of exchange has the property of being able to extremely confuse eclectic economists, who tend to dwell on the surface of phenomena. Thus, Mr Frank (*Teoriia tsennosti Marksa i ee znachenie* [*Marx's Theory of Value and Its Significance*]) suggests that the investigation of the question of exchange value must begin with an historical study of the psychology of monetary fetishism, and this will be only the first step toward answering the question – a step, which, in Mr Frank's opinion has not yet been made. Mr Struve was previously able to tell Mr Frank that money was not of the essence, that commodities are exchanged for commodities. Now Mr Struve, as we know, says something different. Now he advises Mr Frank to be inspired with monetary fetishism – and not to try to extricate himself from it. And things are indeed calmer now.

nature (fire, flood, crop failure, illness, and the like) or of society (the collapse of market demand for the commodities it produces), it undergoes a profound shock from which it can recover only with great labour and far from always successfully. And since such unfavourable combinations must inevitably occur from time to time, the majority of petty enterprises reach a condition of chronic unfitness. This destroys the normal conditions of exchange and the majority of socially weak commodity producers sell their commodities at less than their value. Because of this a few more fortunate and stronger enterprises turn out to be in an exceptionally favourable position; through exchange they appropriate to themselves all the product of the surplus labour of the first (if it is present) and usually part of the product of necessary labour. On this basis, new social forms – *commercial and usurious capitalism* – expand their domination. Weak enterprises are economically subordinated to stronger ones.

The further weakening of less fit enterprises and the strengthening of the more fit ones leads to the complete absorption of the former by the latter. This is accomplished in the form of the development of *industrial capital*. The former independent or semi-independent petty producer becomes a simple element of a major enterprise – a hired worker, the object of exploitation. The more that surplus labour develops in production the more quickly and decisively such absorption occurs, since surplus labour creates the basis for exploitation and so motivates major enterprises to absorb minor ones. Thus, the forces of development lead to the transformation of a commercial society into a capitalist society.

For this latter, surplus labour cannot be considered to be an accidental phenomenon; it is an essential necessity and a permanent characteristic, and without it one cannot even speak of capitalism. Therefore, it is all the more reasonable to investigate the significance of surplus labour in exchange precisely in capitalist society, which, in addition, is historically closer to us than any other.

IV

The basic feature of capitalist organisation is the distinctive role of labour power as a commodity. There is no need to dwell on the history of this commodity, which at the same time is a history of capitalism. For the time being one thing is important for us: labour power is exchanged for wages, which serve workers as the only means of buying the things that make it possible for them to maintain and reproduce their labour power. The 'labour value' of labour power is the sum of social labour necessary for labour power to be fully maintained –

i.e. the sum of social labour necessary for the production of the normal means of consumption of a worker. Since labour power in general must be replaced precisely for these means of consumption – otherwise it could not be maintained – we can therefore draw the following direct conclusion: *labour power in capitalist society is a commodity that is exchanged according to its labour value.*[16]

But are other commodities exchanged in this way? In order to figure this out, we must use the same method that we applied previously – to be precise, we must analyse under what conditions of exchange a capitalist enterprise can survive and develop.

Let us suppose that over the course of a year a capitalist purchases a quantity of means of production in which 900,000 hours of social labour is crystallised and let us signify it with the formula $c = 900,000$. Meanwhile, in order to maintain the labour capacity of all the producers in the enterprise, a quantity of various objects of consumption embodying 100,000 hours of social labour are required: $v = 100,000$ (we note that in this general sum we must also consider the satisfaction of the needs of the capitalist, personally, to the extent that he actually works as an organiser of labour and his needs are really caused by their organising role). It is obvious that if the capitalist does not obtain back though sales-purchases the same quantity of means of production and consumption as he spends, then the enterprise cannot survive. Consequently, he must without fail make a net gain from the market of at least the sum of commodities from other people that equals 1,000,000 hours of social labour. And how large is the labour value of his own output? If there is no surplus labour, then the amount of living labour that is carried out in the enterprise would equal 100,000 hours (the value of the objects of consumption) and the general labour value of the commodities that are produced would be 900,000 (the means of production) plus 100,000 (living labour), i.e. 1,000,000 hours. Thus, for the survival of the enterprise, a commodity in this case must be sold for its whole labour value. However, since surplus labour exists, it must be introduced into our analysis.

The relationship of the magnitude of surplus labour to the labour value of labour power is s/v and is called the 'rate of surplus labour'. In our example, let the rate of surplus labour be 100 per cent. The labour value of the entire output is represented in the following form:

---

16   The possibility of individual deviations from the norm is implied, but these deviations cannot be steady and prolonged, since a capitalist is not inclined to pay more than is necessary to preserve a worker's health and full capacity to work, and to give less would mean to destroy the labour power that is needed for production.

Labour value of the means of production c = 900,000 hours	Labour value of the means of consumption v = 100,000 hours	Surplus labour s = 100,000 hours	General sum = 1,100,000 hours

We know that *no less* than 1,000,000 hours of labour value must be obtained in the form of other commodities in exchange for this output, otherwise the enterprise could not survive. But it is easy to show that the exchange value of the output must be *greater* than this magnitude.

In a capitalist system, the development of production becomes a requirement of production. Each enterprise must grow, or it will die. The strong destroy the weak in pitiless competition, and only a force that continues to grow can maintain itself. Hence the irrepressible, colossal growth of capitalist production. Enterprises must expand in order not to fall behind others and not to weaken in the struggle.

Production expands in relation to society's surplus output. Of course, not all surplus output is used precisely in this way; some of it is spent unproductively. On the one hand, parasitic consumption – i.e. consumption that is not governed by the needs of production and not connected with a corresponding participation of the consumer in social labour – exists in the capitalist system. On the other hand, due to a distinctive feature of capitalist organisation, there is sometimes a useless waste of products that cannot be sold in time because of market conditions and that spoil and become useless. In the developed societies that we are familiar with, these unproductively consumed portions of surplus output are relatively small in comparison with those that are productively consumed. In any event, at the moment we will leave unproductive consumption to the side and concentrate our attention on productive consumption.

The expansion of capitalist production conforms to a specific regularity. Pursuant to the idea of adaptation, it is easy to show what this regularity consists in.

There is a very close connection between the various sectors of capitalist production: they deliver tools, materials, and objects of consumption to one another. The production of coal and iron provides materials for the production of instruments and machines, and the latter, in turn, provides tools for many other sectors, and for the first two sectors as well. The production of bread and meat delivers a necessary means of consumption for workers in all sectors of production, in general, and itself obtains tools and materials from machine, chemical, and many other sectors and means of consumption form the textile and housing sectors, from the salt industry, etc. The same can also be said of all other sectors in the social labour system: *each of them serves as a market for the others and finds a market for its own products in them.*

The expansion of production of each sector needs a corresponding expansion of its own market and presupposes an equal expansion of those sectors for which it serves as a market. For example, let us consider a 5 per cent increase in the production of cotton yarn. First, the production of cotton fabric that is made from the yarn must increase by precisely 5 per cent. It cannot increase by more since there is not enough cotton yarn to permit it, and if it expanded by less than 5 per cent, then part of the yarn that was produced could not be marketed and would be lost without being used. Second, the production of the raw cotton that cotton yarn is made from must have expanded by 5 per cent even earlier, so that there would be a sufficient amount of material for the production of yarn. If the production of cotton had increased by less than this, there would not have been enough material for the production of yarn, and if it exceeded this, the excess supply of cotton above 5 per cent could not be sold, since the market for it had only increased by 5 per cent. With appropriate changes, the same relates to all other realms of social labour. The fact that each sector serves as the usual market not for one but for several other sectors and also finds a market for its goods not in one sector but in several makes no difference: it is only that instead of a relationship between one separate sector and another, there is a relationship between one separate sector and whole complexes of other sectors.

In this way, each realm of production in a capitalist society can successfully expand only in a *certain proportionality* with the other realms that are interrelated with it – those that serve as a market for it and also those for which it serves as a market. And since *all* sectors of capitalist production are united – directly or through the means of other sectors – by the stated kind of interrelationship, we are fully justified in drawing the following conclusion:

For a given capitalist society, there exists a specific rate of expansion, a rate of capitalist accumulation which is the same for all the various spheres of production.

This rate, like all rates, is not unconditional. Not only individual enterprises but whole sectors of production can diverge from it in one direction or the other. However, the rate governs these fluctuations. The sectors of production that expand further than the rate inevitably undergo a certain crisis because they cannot find sufficient sales. The sectors that begin to fall behind the general rate that has been established necessarily hold back the development of others by not supplying them with the quantity of means of production or consumption that they need. The conditions of the market then turn out to be particularly favourable for the sections that are lagging. Demand for their products is more than the supply, prices rise, and the possibility arises of speeding up accumulation as long as the amount of it does not reach the general rate or even go beyond it. If, by virtue of any special circumstances, accumulation does not grow to a sufficient degree, then a phenomenon of another kind occurs: the very rate of accumulation for other production declines – partly as the result of an insufficient market and partly as a result of insufficient means of production. The rate obviously continues to decrease until an equilibrium is established.

It might seem that the law of the equality of rates of accumulation relates only to an ideal, closed capitalist society that lives exclusively by means of an internal market. It might seem that exporting commodities to other countries, capitalist or non-capitalist, must check the tendency of this law, permitting an indefinite expansion of production. The law would be irrelevant to all contemporary cultured societies. But such a thought is utterly wrong, and, in order to refute it, it is sufficient to ask the question: what exactly is the export of commodities?

Commodities are exchanged for commodities. An 'external market' is not a monster that simply devours the commodities it receives. It gives back their soul – their value – only in a new material shell in the form of commodities or money. Export means import, since capitalism never gives anything away for free. The market is in general simply an apparatus for the transmigration of the souls of commodities, and it therefore cannot eliminate the action of the technological-industrial law of rates of accumulation. Production for an external market is the indirect production of imported goods. They enter into the general system of production and consumption in exactly the same way as products that are produced internally. If production for an external market grows above the rate of accumulation, then the importation of foreign products also increases above this rate, and those products do not find a sufficient market in the capitalist system of the given country, which has in general expanded no more than in correspondence to the rate and cannot devour more new means of production and consumption than the rate allows. Thus, although the equilibrium is temporarily broken, it is inevitably restored again. The external market only expands the action of the law; it does not limit it in principle.[17] This is why no external markets can save contemporary capitalist societies from crises

---

17 Sometimes export exceeds import for a long period of time, or the other way around, but this signifies only the relocation of capital, the transformation of non-capitalist countries into capitalist countries, and the development of mass production in new place. And this, obviously, only leads to a new and more complete triumph of the laws of capitalism.

In exactly the same way, the transfer of capital from some sectors of production to others does not contradict the tendency toward equality of the rates of accumulation but, just the opposite, helps it to be realised. The transfer of capital appears precisely where accumulation in one sector falls behind the real demand for it (falls behind an expanding

of overproduction in which the limits of accumulation are only most crudely and spontaneously established.[18]

It is not difficult to see that the rate of accumulation immediately depends mostly on the sectors of production that under the given technology are the least elastic, the least capable of expanding. But this dependence, of course, is far from absolute. Technology can change, and, once the need for more rapid expansion of enterprises arises, science, in the service of capital, tries to eliminate technological difficulties.

Of considerably more importance is the connection which exists between the rate of accumulation and the general sum of surplus labour in a given system of production. If the entire surplus output is devoted to the expansion of production, then this connection would be expressed very simply: the rate of accumulation would be exactly the same as the ratio of the sum of surplus labour to the entire sum of labour that is embodied in social 'capital' – the means of production and consumption that is expended in a given period of time (a year, for example). But the surplus output is not always applied productively. Part of it is lost without any benefit, and part of it is consumed parasitically. Because of this, the question becomes significantly more complex.

---

market), whereas, in another sector accumulation is ready to exceed this demand. Thus, the rate of accumulation is preserved in both sectors with considerably fewer fluctuations.

18   I must make a small explanation in order to avoid possible confusion. My idea about the meaning of the proportionality in *accumulation* is not at all connected with the theory of crises that Mr Tugan-Baranovsky proposes, which, as is well known, states that the root cause of crises consists in the uneven *distribution of capital*. My understanding of crises is as follows. The production of the means of consumption cannot expand beyond the extent of its market – i.e. the extent of *personal consumption in society*. The production of the means of production also cannot favourably expand further than its market, and *in the final analysis* the production of the means of consumption is the same. But by virtue of the spontaneous tendency of capitalism to expand, production nevertheless proceeds in both cases farther than these limits, and, of course, the divergence from the norm is stronger in the realm that is further from the ultimate regulator of the system – personal consumption – which is precisely the realm of production of the means of production. And this is the realm that most directly expresses the *productive forces of society*. In the end, consequently, the question of crises boils down to a lack of correspondence between the growth of the productive forces of society and the growth of personal consumption, the boundaries of which are determined, in turn, by the capitalist *form of appropriation*.

Thus, it is completely possible that production could expand completely proportionally and yet a crisis would still break out. For this to occur, it would be sufficient for personal consumption not to expand in the same proportion (as occurs, for example, due to the replacement of workers by machines). This remains unclear to Mr Tugan-Baranovsky, and therefore his theory of crises takes a step back from Marx's theory.

Both 'unproductive' parts of surplus output express a partial *unadaptedness* of capitalist society – expenditures of its energies that do not contribute to the struggle with nature through labour. But the capitalist world grows, develops, and conquers nature. In short, it turns out as a whole to be highly adapted for the struggle with nature. From this we can a priori draw the conclusion that the 'unproductive' portion of surplus labour must be relatively small. Observations confirm this. We know that the fruitless loss of social output is significant only in eras of crises, and we can easily see how small parasitic consumption is in comparison with productive consumption if we contrast the colossal amount of surplus output in the form of all the tools, machines, materials of production and ordinary objects of consumption of productive workers with the yearly production of objects of pure luxury.[19] Our analysis will not depart too far from concrete reality, if we ignore elements of unadaptedness for the time being and consider the matter as if surplus labour is entirely expended for productive goals and postpone reservations about unadaptedness until we clarify the issue of rent.

Let us return to our example in which we are investigating the conditions of the capitalist sale of commodities. Suppose that in the society given in the example the annual rate of accumulation is 5 per cent. The labour value of commodities in that example was 900,000 (c) + 100,000 (v) + 100,000 (s), or 1,100,000 labour units, of which 1,000,000 corresponds to expended capital and 100,000 to surplus labour.

Since the rate of accumulation is 5 per cent, in the following year the enterprise must carry on within the rate of 5 per cent, i.e. the amount it must expend on the means of production and consumption cannot be the former quantity (1,000,000 labour units) but 5 per cent more (1,050,000 labour units). These means of production and consumption must be gained through the sale of manufactured goods. That is, since we have so far proposed that there is no unproductive consumption, these commodities must ultimately be exchanged precisely for these means of production and consumption. Consequently, commodities that have a value of 1,100,000 hours of simple labour must be exchanged for other commodities of the general value of 1,050,000 hours. Ex-

---

19   In speaking of pure luxury, we have in mind the kind of consumption that absolutely does not issue from the needs of production. Many of the products that are usually ascribed to the sphere of luxury are in part socially necessary as the customary objects of consumption by the group of the actual organisers of production. We know that organising activity is associated with broad needs, and, to the extent this is so, consumption by the necessary organisers of production cannot be considered unproductive. An exact investigation into the boundaries of luxury is, of course, impossible for the time being. For us, however, an approximate calculation is sufficient.

change is not completely according to the labour rate, but diverges from it – in the given case by 5 per cent (to be exact, by 4.54 per cent): the exchange value of the given commodities is lower than the rate, and the value of the commodities for which it is exchanged is higher than the rate by the same amount.

It is not difficult to explain how the size of this divergence is determined. Under the given rate of accumulation, it depends on the so-called 'organic composition' of capital, i.e. the ratio of labour value c to labour value v. For capital of a specific organic composition, which is easily calculated, this magnitude is equal to zero – i.e. exchange occurs strictly according to labour value: c = 950,000 hours, v = 50,000 hours, s = 50,000 hours, and the labour value of commodities is 1,050,000 hours. With expansion at 5 per cent, c and v will now no longer add up to 1,000,000 but to 1,050,000 hours. This is the labour value of the commodities that come from the outside in the form of means of production and consumption for which the commodities of the given enterprise must be exchanged, and the labour value and the exchange value fully coincide.

It is also not difficult to establish the limits of the divergence of exchange value from labour value if the rate of accumulation and the rate of surplus labour are known. These limits correspond to two extreme cases of the organic composition of capital: capital which consists entirely of c – i.e. represents only means of production – and capital which consists entirely of v – i.e. is spent entirely on means of consumption of producers (wages). Both cases are inconceivable in a pure form, but we can view them as limits.

(A) Entirely variable capital: c = 0, v = 100,000, s = 100,000. The labour value of the output, consequently, is 200,000 hours. With a rate of accumulation of 5 per cent, output is exchanged for a quantity of commodities from the outside (means of consumption) that has a labour value of 105,000 hours. The deviation from the labour rate is 200,000 minus 95,000 or negative 47.5 per cent (lower than the labour rate).

(B) Entirely constant capital: c = 100,000, v = 0, s = 0. The labour value of the output is 100,000 hours. With a rate of accumulation of 5 per cent, the output is exchanged for a quantity of commodities from the outside (means of production) that has a labour value of 105,000 hours. The deviation from the rate is 100,000 plus 5,000 or positive 5 per cent (higher than the labour rate).

In our calculations we have taken the period of capital turnover to be one year. Needless to say, in individual cases it could be more or less than this, and corresponding changes would consequently have to be made in our calculations. This is very easy to do. One need only replace the yearly rate of accumulation with a rate of accumulation of a different period of time – the period of capital turnover. Let us take, for example, all the numbers from our previous example but assume a capital turnover equal to half a year: c = 900,000, v =

190,000, s = 100,000. The labour value of commodities is 1,100,000. The rate of accumulation for half a year is 2 ½ per cent (for an annual accumulation of 5 per cent). Commodities are exchanged, ultimately, for the means of production and consumption in an amount that corresponds to 1,025,000 hours (900,000 s plus 100,000 v plus 2.5 per cent of this sum). The divergence from the rate is around 7 per cent (to be precise, the exchange value is 6.82 per cent lower than the labour value).

Let us take a similar example with a turnover time of five years: c = 900,000, v = 100,000, s = 100,000. The labour value of commodities would be 1,100,000. The rate of accumulation over five years would be 25 per cent.[20] In exchange for these commodities, in the form of commodities from outside, a labour value of 1,250,000 hours would be obtained; this amount would be larger than the labour rate by almost 14 per cent (13.64 to be precise).

It is also not difficult to determine the extreme, maximum amount of deviation from the labour rate. Assuming the same rate of surplus value and the same rate of accumulation, we can, with simple but boring calculations find the following values:

For a turnover time of half a year, the greatest deviation upwards is 2.5 per cent, and the greatest deviation downwards is negative 48.75 per cent. For a turnover time of five years, the greatest deviation upwards is 25 per cent, and the greatest deviation downwards is negative 37.5 per cent.[21]

These examples are sufficient in order to see how easy it is to establish the relationship of exchange value and labour value under a variety of conditions both technical (the organic composition of capital, the turnover time) and economic-social (the rate of accumulation, the rate of surplus value).[22]

---

20   To be more precise, it would be about 27.6 per cent, since the process of accumulation increases geometrically (according to the law of compound interest).

21   For our analysis neither the variable capital turnover time nor the *annual* rate of surplus value separately are significant. For us, v signifies the general labour value of what is consumed by producers in the course of one cycle of the means of subsistence, and the magnitude of this value does not change depending on how much the capitalist receives from selling his commodities and how often the money that they pay their workers returns to them. In relation to this general value v, the only important thing is the general rate of surplus value (the rate for one cycle of production).

22   Let us note that by 'exchange value' we do not have in mind here the incidental, particular price of a commodity that appears in one sale or another and not the abstract rate that corresponds to labour value, but the magnitude of the exchange relationship *under which production and exchange are adapted to one another* – the rate toward which, consequently, the process of social adaptation gravitates. This meaning of 'exchange value' does not entirely coincide with the Marxian meaning.

What is the scientific significance of these conclusions? They establish the fundamental law of capitalist exchange. What is the content of this law? It can be designated as the principle of labour value or, more precisely, the *principle of the technology of production.*

At first glance, such a conclusion does not seem to be completely accurate. Exchange values, as we have seen, do not coincide with the labour rate. In the majority of cases, they deviate from it, and, what is more, they do not deviate from it by accident but by necessity. But if we turn our attention to the *conditions* that determine them and the nature and the magnitude of these deviations, then it turns out that they lie in the labour process in such a way that the exchange relationship is governed by the labour principle, except it is governed indirectly and not directly.

In reality, as has been explained, still other aspects besides labour value turn out to have an influence on the exchange value of a commodity: the organic composition of capital, the rate of surplus labour, the rate of accumulation of capital, and the length of time of capital turnover. The first two, obviously, represent the relationships of labour value c, v, and s. The rate of accumulation, in turn – following our assumption that surplus product is not expended uselessly or consumed parasitically – boils down to the relationship between the labour value of all social surplus product and all the capital that is invested in production. Finally, the capital turnover time – yet again assuming the absence of wasteful expenditure – depends entirely on the technology of production and is one of the conditions of technological labour. In general, if one ignores elements of *unadaptedness* of society in its struggle with nature, then it turns out that all the conditions that determine exchange value lie in the sphere of the labour process, and the most basic of these conditions is the immediate labour value of the product.

v

The preceding conclusions provide the possibility of analysing, step by step, the concrete conditions of exchange in any particular historically given society.

So, for example, if we examine the most cultured countries, taken as a whole, as one system of production, then, on the basis of existing statistical material, it is possible to establish the following approximate rates in regard to it (very approximate, since this material is never gathered and processed with the same goals as we have here):

The rate of surplus value is between 100 and 130 per cent, and the rate of accumulation is between 2 and 3 per cent. The organic composition of capital is generally already very high. Constant capital seems to predominate over variable capital everywhere, and there are whole sectors where the latter has almost disappeared in comparison with the first (commercial and credit concerns and production using automatic machines). The capital turnover time is extremely variable; only in a few cases – mostly in certain sectors of commercial and credit concerns – can it be considered to be less than a year, in a majority of cases significantly longer; usually, however, it is not more than 5 to 40 years.

Regardless of the crudeness of these data, the conclusion can be drawn from them that in the huge majority of cases deviations from simple labour rates cannot be large – no more than 20 to 30 per cent. The fact is that a high organic composition of capital in conjunction with a low rate of accumulation leads to the least deviation from this rate, and also the influence of the remaining two conditions – the rate of surplus labour and the capital turnover time – is comparatively small.[23]

It is necessary to add to this that, in accordance with the theory of probability, given a great number of cases, smaller deviations from the rate must significantly predominate over major deviations that are close to the limit. Thus, the labour rate even in its direct, immediate meaning really expresses *the basic tendency of adaptation in capitalist exchange*.

And this is not all. It is not difficult to show that capitalist development of technology strives to realise the basic tendency of exchange with ever greater completeness and rigour. This occurs principally by two means: change in the organic composition of capital and change in the rate of accumulation. Let us explain the direction of both processes.

First and foremost, the technological process strives toward decreasing capital's need for labour power, which it realises through the introduction of

---

23 We can verify this in comparatively extreme cases which must already be quite rare in the contemporary capitalist system.

1. Constant capital 990,000, variable capital 10,000, rate of surplus labour 100 per cent, rate of accumulation 3 per cent, duration of capital overturn 10 years. Labour value of output 1,010,000 units; accumulation over 10 years 30 per cent. Exchange value of the output 1,300,000 units (capital increase of 30 per cent). Deviation from the norm is positive 28.7 per cent.

2. Constant capital 750,000, variable capital 250,000, rate of surplus labour 130 per cent, rate of accumulation 2 per cent, turnover time 1 year. Labour value of output 1,325,000 units (750,000 + 250,000 + [(250,000 × 130) ÷ 100]). Exchange value 1,020,000 units (capital + 2 per cent of its value). Deviation from the norm is negative 29.9 per cent

Taking other values within the same parameters that are indicated in the text for contemporary society, we will in all cases obtain significantly smaller deviations.

machines and other improvements. At the same time, the constant part of capital grows in comparison with variable capital, and the means of production begins to increasingly predominate in comparison with the means of consumption of producers. The organic composition of all capital increases.[24] And, under normal conditions, capital with the highest organic composition – as will be easy to see in subsequent examples – provides smaller deviations of value from the immediate labour rate.

But although the dominating tendency in capitalist society is to increase the organic composition of capital, things stand somewhat differently for individual enterprises. It is possible to show that especially highly organised businesses strive to lower their organic composition while the least organised businesses strive with particular force to increase it, so that both kinds reveal the tendency toward an average composition. Let us take a look as some very simple examples.

Imagine a capitalist business with an organic composition that is particularly low for a given society, let us say 750,000 c and 250,000 v. This means that for the given enterprise a particularly large amount of living labour – labour power – is needed. Under such conditions even the *simple replacement* of part of v with an equal amount of c (replacing workers with machines), would, even though it did not constitute a direct economy, nevertheless bring considerable benefits. The more the machines and the fewer the people, the easier it would be to run the enterprise; people always cause more trouble than machines. The issue is not only the number of workers but also their quality. The more that production is carried on with machines, the less often a worker with the knowledge and skill of a craftsman is required. Both of these factors lead to a situation in which it is easier for a capitalist to replace some workers with others (in the event of conflict with them) or to hire new ones (in the event of an expansion of production). In both such cases, the capitalist with an enterprise at a low level of organisation experiences significant inconvenience. Because their enterprise uses more labour power in general, it is comparatively more difficult to obtain new workers, and, because the capitalist needs manual

---

24   Capital thus approaches the limit at which it would be reduced to only constant capital. Certain forms of capital exist – commercial capital and especially credit – which play a particularly important role in developed capitalist society and which almost coincide with this limit. Complete coincidence with the limit, however, is impossible: without living human labour, even though taken in a very small amount, capital altogether cannot function in a social system, and even credit capital is still driven by living labour (the labour of account management and relations, the transfer of money, the supervision of operations, etc.). Besides this, as we will subsequently see, the tendency toward the increase of the organic composition of capital has limits of its own.

labourers with a specific skilled trade specialisation, the fact that there are not very many of them means that the reserve from which he must draw workers is considerably less. Just the opposite, with a higher organic composition, fewer workers are needed. Moreover, they do not need to be as specialised as in the first case but simply sufficiently intelligent in order to operate a machine. There are always considerably more such workers in the reserve army of capital. Further, capitalist credit is more available to enterprises with a higher organic composition; machines can be used as collateral for borrowing money, whereas labour power cannot. And in capitalist competition creditworthiness is hugely important and often is the decisive factor in whether the enterprise lives or dies.

Things are different with capital of an especially high organic composition. Imagine an enterprise in which c comprises 999,000 labour units and v only 1,000 – i.e. an enterprise in which there are very many machines and very few workers. In this case, the capitalist has no interest in reducing his variable capital by eliminating labour with machines; variable capital is so insignificant that there would be nothing to gain by doing so. It would be much more important to be concerned with the reduction in cost of tools and materials of production – i.e. reduction of the constant part of capital. Because of its large scale even a comparatively small reduction of the elements of constant capital would present very large benefits. For example, the capitalist must especially strive to replace expensive machines with less expensive ones (in order to economise on construction), to decrease expenditures on coal, and so on. If he succeeds in this, then notwithstanding the increase in the productivity of labour, the constant part of capital will not predominate over variable capital by as much as it did formerly: the organic composition of capital shrinks and approaches the average magnitude for that society.

Thus, while capitalists with capital of a lower organic composition have an especially powerful interest in eliminating workers by using machines and so decreasing the variable part of capital, enterprises with a higher organic composition face a technological task that is just the opposite. They are exclusively motivated to reduce tools and materials as much as possible and so to relatively decrease constant capital. Science, in the service of capitalist technology, is usually very successful at satisfying these needs. As a result, both extreme types of capital strive to acquire a makeup that is closer to the mean. And as we know, it is precisely at the mean makeup of capital that exchange value most closely corresponds to the simple labour rate.

But in the same sense, the general and basic conditions of technological progress act on the capitalist system incomparably more powerfully. As we have said, for society as a whole the increase in the productivity of labour is linked

precisely with an increase in the organic composition of capital. In this way
the living labour of producers represents an ever-smaller magnitude in comparison with the dead labour that is embodied in the means of production
and consumption – in the elements of capital. Thus, the rate of profit, which
expresses the relationship of these two magnitudes, must diminish, and so the
rate of accumulation, which for us for the time being merges with the rate of
profit, must also diminish. Only raising the rate of surplus labour (the rate of
exploitation) can counteract this tendency, but, as experience shows, it cannot, generally speaking, keep up with the growth of the organic composition of
social capital. As a result, in reality the rate of profit usually declines with the
course of technological progress.[25] But, as our examples show, the lower this
rate is the smaller the maximum magnitudes of deviation of price from labour
value, and the closer the labour rate is to reality.

---

25   Mr Struve saw an 'antinomy' or, to put it differently, 'clear nonsense' and also an 'absurdity'
      in the idea that a decrease in the rate of profit accompanies an increase in the productivity
      of labour (see *Zhizn'* 1900, February). What this 'antinomy' – i.e. a *direct formal contradic-
      tion* – consists in, Mr Struve unfortunately did not say. Meanwhile, it is obvious that the
      productivity of labour and the rate of profit are not the same thing, and that is why the
      increase of the one along with the decrease of the other – even from the point of view of
      the capitalist – might perhaps be a regrettable fact, but it is not at all a contradiction of
      formal logic.
          It is not difficult to reduce the productivity of labour and the rate of profit to a relation-
      ship in which it becomes clear that it is completely factually possible for the two values to
      simultaneously change in opposite directions. The productivity of labour can be expressed
      by a fraction in which the numerator is the amount of all the newly produced output and
      the denominator is the amount of the living labour expended in production, or – replacing
      these amounts with others that are completely proportional to them – a fraction in which
      the numerator is the quantity of surplus product and the denominator is *the quantity of
      surplus labour*. The rate of profit can be expressed as a fraction in which the numerator
      is the *quantity of surplus labour* and the denominator is the general sum of labour that is
      crystallised in capital (the labour value of capital). Thus, there are two fractions in which
      the numerator of one corresponds with the denominator of the other, and it is clear that
      these fractions not only can but under certain conditions *must* change in opposite direc-
      tions. Mr Struve's 'antinomy' lies not in the 'labour theory of value' as he proposes but in
      the basic laws of algebra.
          And, by the way, this 'antinomy' can be found even deeper, in reality itself. After all,
      the fact of the simultaneous increase of the productivity of labour and the decrease of
      the rate of profit is obvious. And Mr Struve does not even contradict this fact but seeks
      another explanation for it. But if it is a fact, then what criterion gives him the right to
      declare, without any evidence, that the explanation that he does not like is 'nonsense'?
          But perhaps we misunderstand Mr Struve; perhaps he is not speaking about a proper
      'antinomy' – i.e. not a logical contradiction – but about a psychological contradiction. Per-
      haps he is saying that capitalists would have no reason to raise the productivity of labour
      if that increase would lead to a decline in the rate of profit? We cannot vouch for it – Mr

Under certain circumstances, of course, the opposite phenomenon can sometimes also be observed. An increase in the rate of profit (and accumulation) occurs because the rate of surplus value goes up faster than the organic composition of capital. On the one hand, capitalists can sometimes quickly increase exploitation by lengthening the working day or increasing the intensity of labour, but, if they follow this path, they encounter resistance that sooner or later scotches their efforts. On the other hand, the labour value of labour power – i.e. the means of consumption of producers – can fall. If the productivity of labour increases in sectors of production that acquire these means of consumption, then labour power becomes socially cheaper and the 'necessary working time' in which the producer earns their value decreases, and the surplus time increases. This second means of increase in the rate of surplus value has no definite limit, but so far it has not in fact won a very large (although not small) role in economic life. This is because technological progress in the most important sectors of production of objects of consumption by workers has proceeded quite slowly (especially in agriculture).[26]

In investigating this question, it is necessary in any case to keep in mind that neither an intensification of exploitation nor an increase in the pro-

---

Struve's means of expression is not distinguished by clarity. But then it would be necessary to assume that Mr Struve absolutely did not understand the elementary explanation of this question in the simple expressions provided by Marx. Marx pointed out that an individual capitalist has every reason to elevate the technology of their enterprise, since their own profit will increase because of it: for the entire period of time before the given improvement becomes generally adopted, the capitalist will sell their merchandise for more than its *individual* value, for its social value. And the question of whether the rate of profit will subsequently decline for the *class* of capitalists does not interest the individual entrepreneur at all. For them it is important to increase their profit and their capital, and the class of capitalists loses little from the decline in the rate of profit, since, due to the huge growth of capital with the development of production, the general *mass* of profit turns out nevertheless to be greater than before, even though it constitutes somewhat less a per centage of capital.

26 In 1899, Mr Tugan-Baranovsky made the 'discovery' that the rate of profit cannot fall in relation to the increase of the organic composition of capital, that the rate of profit "automatically" increases from an increase in the organic composition of capital exactly enough in order to support the rate of profit at the former level'. (*Nauchnoe obozrenie* 1899, No. 3). He formulated this 'discovery' in a whole series of computations that I subsequently analysed in detail (*Nauchnoe obozrenie* 1899, 9 and 1900, 8). I pointed out that two absolutely new hypotheses for Marx's theory lie at the basis of Mr Tugan-Baranovsky's computations. One is that as soon as new tools that can be used to perform labour are produced – tools, for example, that are twice as productive – the labour value of all existing capital (tools, materials, and means of consumption) immediately falls by half 'automatically', since, *going forward, they can be reproduced* with half the expenditure of labour than before. I showed that this hypothesis is altogether false, since it would mean that what is real and

ductivity of labour can occur by such leaps as might appear at a superficial glance. If an entrepreneur increases the working day by two hours, then the rate of surplus value hardly grows in even an approximate proportion to this amount: labour turns out to be less intensive and less productive than before. If a new machine is introduced in which one worker does as much as three workers did previously, this does not mean that the productivity of their labour increases by three times: the machine itself costs labour that must be considered and that significantly changes the evaluation of the phenomenon.[27]

---

actual (the exchange value of all capital) is determined by *what is possible and in the future* (expenditures of labour under the new, only just created conditions of production which have just been applied). I also pointed out that this hypothesis (the theory of 'expenditures of reproduction') pertains not to Marx but to Carey [Henry Charles Carey, 1793–1879, an American economist (trans.).] Mr Tugan-Baranovsky's response to this was that the point of view of expenditures of production was precisely the point of view of Marx, and he cited Volume Three of *Capital* (*Nauchnoe obozrenie* 1900, no. 3). Unfortunately, he cited Marx inaccurately both in form (distorting Marx's words by the inaccurate use of italics) and in essence (not understanding the citation that I provided in my answer in *Nauchnoe obozrenie* 1900, no. 8 and that he did not try to refute). Mr Tugan-Baranovsky's second hypothesis is that the replacement of workers with machines can occur without any change in the equilibrium of the market. In response to this, I explained that workers are responsible for a significant part of consumer demand, and that their replacement by machines and unemployment means that consumer demand is curtailed and there are losses for the capitalists who produce workers' means of consumption and for many other entrepreneurs indirectly. A machine as a 'consumer' of coal, oil, etc. can never replace the living consumer-worker that it displaces. After all, when a worker is replaced with a machine, another machine is also replaced – the machine that was used to produce the means of consumption of the now unemployed worker. As a result, all of the 'consumption' of this machine (analogous to the 'consumption' of the first machine) is also eliminated. In both cases, Mr Tugan-Baranovsky has lost sight of the organic interconnectedness and unity of a social system of production as it develops. This is why he arrived at an unbelievably fast and easy increase of the productivity of labour occurring through some sort of sudden leaps. The psychological basis of all this confusion (like Mr Struve's 'antinomy') is the old bourgeois-apologist idea of the *productivity of fixed capital*.

In essence, Mr Tugan-Barankovsky raises no objection against the critique of both hypotheses. He only announces (in *Pomoshch'*, 1901) that he finds the entire critique to be unconvincing, and he repeats anew all the confusion of the first article. Such an answer would not be found convincing even if it had been given by such a great scientist as Darwin or Marx, and, by the way, neither Darwin nor Marx ever, of course, permitted themselves to refute the objections of other people only by reference to their own authority.

27   In Mr Tugan-Baranovsky's article of 1899 cited above, he committed quite a gross error in regard to this question. He says, 'The very fact that a machine replaces living labour makes this labour more productive *even if the costs of production of a unit of output remains as before*' (the italics are Mr Tugan-Baranovsky's, p. 982). Of course, if half of the workers who are making silk cloth are replaced by machines, then twice as much cloth passes

The predominant tendency in the historical development of capitalism is unquestionably not an increase but a decrease in the rate of profit, just as the organic composition of capital does not decrease but increases. Both are proven by a multitude of facts. But it is precisely the low rate of accumulation when there is a high composition of capital that results in the least deviation from exchange according to labour value. Consequently, here also the progress of capitalist life does cause exchange relationships to diverge from the rate that the labour theory of value indicates but causes them to converge.

VI

Let us now dwell on the very moments when technology changes and examine how the labour rate plays its role as a regulator of exchange relationships.

Suppose that the annual production of an enterprise is expressed in the following figures: 900,000 c + 100,000 v + 100,000 s = 1,100,000 labour units. This is the labour value of the output. If the rate of accumulation is 5 per cent, this output is exchanged for 1,050,000 labour units that are embodied in other commodities (means of production and consumption).

Technological improvement is introduced, and it decreases the variable part of capital and increases the constant part. This benefits capitalists only in the event that the decrease of the variable part more than compensates for the increase of the second. For example, suppose that c increases by 20,000 labour units, and v decreases by a whole 50,000. Then the labour value of annual output would appear in the following form: 920,000 c + 50,000 v + 50,000 s = 1,020,000 labour units.

However, the market price that is established in society cannot change of its own accord, and at first it remains as it was previously: the output is exchanged for 1,050,000 labour units. Thus, the profit of the capitalist turns out to be 80,000 for 970,000 units of capital – i.e. 8.25 per cent – considerably more than the usual rate of accumulation. The possibility of expanding the enterprise is

---

through the hands of each of the remaining workers, but this does not at all mean that the productivity of labour in the production of silk cloth has doubled. If the machine cost the same amount of labour as it replaces, then, obviously, no growth in the productivity of labour has occurred. It is only that the labour of weavers is replaced by the labour of workers who operate the machines, and the general sum of labour that a given quantity of cloth costs remains as before. Mr Tugan-Baranovsky continues to forget about the interrelationship of the various enterprises and of the sectors of production.

greater than could be previously managed, and the capitalist takes advantage of the possibility of rapid expansion because the increase in profit excites a thirst for accumulation and gives him the hope of eliminating his competitors.

These competitors are not pleased with the prospect, and they, in turn, hurry to transform the technology of their enterprises and also speed up their expansion. But the entire sector of production cannot, as we have seen, expand above a general rate of accumulation. The market cannot of its own accord increase to the same degree as the mass of produced merchandise has grown. Therefore, either part of the merchandise will remain completely unsold or its exchange price will decline. And this will continue until such time as the given sector of production arrives at a rate of accumulation equal to all the others. Merchandise with a value of 1,020,000 labour units will then be sold not for 1,050,000 units but for 970,000 (the amount of capital) plus 5 per cent of 970,000 (the amount of accumulation), i.e. for 1,018,500 units.

In reality, the process of decline must proceed still further. It turns out that in the entire sector of production the organic composition of capital has increased. Consequently, the structure of all social capital is no longer the same as before, and on average it is somewhat higher. If the change in the productivity of labour is not altogether large enough to counterbalance this increase in the organic composition, then the rate of accumulation must decline somewhat, for example, from 5 to 4.9 per cent. How does such a change occur?

It can be accomplished in two ways. On the one hand – although this would seem to be the less important aspect of the matter – the elimination of some workers by machines at the beginning of the process we have described entails a contraction of the consumer market. Since they are not receiving pay, the workers who have lost their jobs cannot buy consumer goods. Capitalists who produce these goods suffer constraint and hurry to transfer their capital to other spheres of production where there is no constraint. This therefore increases the competition of capital in other sectors and so causes a decline in profit in them as well. This is especially so since the capitalists, themselves – due to the constraint they are suffering – are also poorer consumers than before, and they therefore worsen the condition of the market for everyone. On the other hand, the intensified accumulation in the sector of production in which the new improvement is introduced creates excessive capital that seeks to be applied and thus increases the general competition of capital, and it would seem that this second path of decline in the rate of profit would generally be of much greater significance than the first. One way or another, the rate of accumulation declines.

We thus see that when technology changes, the exchange price of individual commodities does not immediately adapt to the changing labour value and the rate of profit in individual sectors of production does not immediately adapt to the changing composition of capital. But gradually this adaptation must necessarily occur.

VII

Until now, we have intentionally described the situation as if commodities were exchanged directly for commodities; we have ignored the role of money as a tool of exchange. How do our conclusions change if we take money into account?

We know that money is not only a tool of exchange but also a commodity in a series of other commodities. The production of money (monetary metal) is organised in a capitalist society in the same way as any other sector of production. Therefore, everything that we have established regarding the labour rate of exchange – and deviations from it – also applies to money. If the output of an enterprise is not directly exchanged for commodities that are necessary for the continuation of production, but are sold for money, which now serves as a means of purchasing these commodities, then the divergences from the labour rate cause complications for one another, so to speak. Adding the deviations from the rate of exchange that are inherent in money as a commodity to the deviations that are inherent in a given commodity, we could easily determine the exchange relationship of the given commodity to money. In so doing, the relationships of exchange turn out in some cases to diverge somewhat higher than the ideal direct rate of exchange, and in other cases they are somewhat lower.

But each additional deviation that is dependent on the intermediary role of money balances in the opposite deviation. A purchase follows a sale, the role of money changes in the opposite direction, and thus the exchange of money changes nothing in regard to final results. Consequently, it was not only fully valid to ignore the influence of money in the foregoing, but there will be no subsequent need to dwell on it.

VIII

We now need to take a new step forward in our analysis. We must introduce two facts that are usually considered a serious difficulty for the labour theory of exchange relationships – taxes and rent.

In regard to taxes, things are quite simple – at least from the most general theoretical point of view. Taxes represent the portion of the social output that is expended not on the individual needs of one or another particular enterprise but on the general needs of the entire system of production that is contained in a given political whole. And, to the extent that the satisfaction of these common needs is necessary for each individual enterprise, the corresponding part of the labour that is embodied in taxes also obviously goes into the labour value of the output of each enterprise. For example, if roads and law and order are necessary for the output to be socially-useful – so it can fulfil its social purpose – then the production of roads and law and order directly enters the process of production of this output (not as a whole, of course, but as a corresponding part). There is no justification for measuring the labour value of a given particular product only according to the quantity of labour that is immediately expended on it in a given individual enterprise: labour value is the whole amount of social labour necessary for production of products. Thus, the principle of labour value is still not limited here, but, just the opposite, reveals its significance completely.

But then the question arises: are taxes really distributed *in correspondence* to the participation of each enterprise in the general system of production? Of course unevenness is possible here, and in contemporary governments it is more often the rule than the exception, and because of this certain groups of enterprises – precisely those on which the greatest portion of taxes falls – are forced to sell their output at a relatively higher price in order to be able to develop normally. This is how additional divergences of value from the labour rate occur, and they are subject not to abstract analysis but to concrete investigation that deals with historically given economic and political organisation. Here one can take note of only two fundamental facts: first, that such deviations are usually insignificant,[28] at least in the best organised social systems, and, second, that development strives to diminish and eliminate these deviations by working to equalise the distribution of taxes.

It remains to make note of still one more important circumstance: often a part of taxes is not 'socially-necessary' and does not serve the real needs of production but serves the goals of parasitism that is used to support the life of certain groups that have lost their real vital significance in the system of social labour. In decaying societies, this part of taxes can turn out to be huge (for example, the Roman Empire in the era of its collapse and disintegration),

---

28   In individual cases they are very significant (excise taxes on vodka, tobacco, etc. in Russia, for example).

but it can also be quite large in progressive societies in which development has not yet done away with many vestiges of the past (for example, in England at the beginning of the nineteenth century, the 'corn laws' that were indirectly imposed on the entire population to benefit landlords, and countless sinecure positions that were also reserved for landlords). The amount – and also the distribution – of this unproductive portion of taxes cannot, of course, be established by abstract analysis. In each particular case, the amount and distribution must be determined empirically. Once this is done, it is not difficult to figure out the influence of these taxes on the system of production and distribution. But for such an investigation it is more appropriate to consider each given fact in its relationship to other similar economic facts – with the phenomena of 'rent'.

IX

The term 'rent' is used by economists in various meanings. For Rodbertus,[29] for example, it means capitalist income in general. Usually, however, in the expressions 'land rent' and 'rent from capital', this term signifies the kind of income that is not connected with any productive activity by the one who receives it but is based entirely on the fact of ownership of property. The term 'rentier' is given both to a landowner who is paid for allowing the application of productive labour on a parcel of land that he owns and to a capitalist who receives interest on capital that he has deposited in a bank, i.e. who personally is paid for allowing the productive use of his capital in other people's enterprises. 'Rentier' should also be applied to anyone who holds a sinecure position in private or government service, anyone who is paid a pension that is not conditional upon socially useful activity, etc.

Since our investigation is conducted from the point of view of social production, we must also define the concept of 'rent' to correspond to this point of view. To be precise, for us 'rent' will not designate one or another means of *appropriation* but, in general, *the portion of surplus product that is unproductively consumed.* Landowners can appropriate to themselves a certain part of the social product exclusively by right of their ownership of a certain piece of land, but we do not count this as rent as long as the appropriated part is applied productively – to the expansion of any sort of enterprise. Most of the income of a

---

29   Johann Karl Rodbertus (1805–1875) was a German economist and scientific socialist [trans.].

capitalist who runs an industrial enterprise does not come from their personal labour, but – from the point of view of production – we must count as rent only the part of income that is spent completely unproductively on the consumption of objects of pure luxury.[30] Thus, for us, the sum of the surplus product in society is divided into two parts: one goes toward 'capitalist accumulation' – to the expansion of production (and so also to the expansion of the consumption of productive workers) – and the other goes to unproductive goals. This latter we call rent – a usage of the term that is not quite usual but at the given stage of analysis is the most useful.

Suppose that all the 'capital' of a society at a given moment is 100 billion hours of simple labour. Of this, 95 billion are embodied in the means of production – tools and materials – and 5 billion in the means of consumption of producers. Over the course of a year, producers maintain their labour power with this means of consumption and apply their living labour to the means of production in the amount, let us say, of 10 billion hours. This means that the sum of surplus labour is 5 billion hours and the rate of surplus labour is 100 per cent.

The question now has to do with what part of the general sum of surplus labour goes to productive goals – to the development of production – and what part makes up 'rent'? This question cannot be answered by theoretical reasoning – it is decided by a struggle of interests. These conflicting interests are embodied partly in different classes of society, partly in different groups or members of one class, and partly in different aspects of a single psyche. When a capitalist struggles with a landowner over the size of profit and so called 'ground rent', the former is predominantly a representative of accumulation and the latter is mainly a representative of unproductive consumption, i.e. 'rent' in our meaning of the word. In many cases, this relationship exists between different groups of shareholders in a joint stock enterprise in which some strive more for the development of the enterprise and others for an increase in the immediate dividend. And individual capitalists contain the same contradiction in their own souls when they face the question of what part of their profit they should invest in their business and what part they should use for the pure enjoyment of life.[31]

---

30   We remind the reader that from our point of view a capitalist's income can also include the element of wages to the extent that they actually participate in production as an organiser and to the extent that it satisfies needs that are necessarily connected with this role, i.e. they would not be able to carry out this role unless they satisfy those needs. Except that this part of income is usually comparatively insignificant.

31   The tragedy that is thereby performed in the soul of the capitalist serves as the basis for the well-known crude theory of the origin of profit – or the theory of 'abstemiousness'.

The outcome of this struggle of interests is decided by the entire totality of historical conditions – the advancing force of competition, the conservative force of tradition, etc. It is only possible to point out the tendency of development of this struggle: the further capitalist relationships develop and the more intense the mutual competition of enterprises becomes, the more accumulation must gain over 'rent' in the general sum of profit. In the pitiless capitalist struggle, the stronger defeat the weaker, and each strives to become stronger in order not to perish. And in order to become stronger they must accumulate and accumulate and spend as little as possible unproductively. This tendency embraces even those groups that are predominantly representatives of rent (the remnants of feudal groups, for example). As for the capitalist society in which we live, it can be confidently stated that productive consumption greatly predominates over unproductive consumption.

Thus, suppose that in our example the goals are that 80 per cent of the surplus product (with a labour value of 4 billion hours) goes to accumulation and 20 per cent (with a labour value of 1 billion hours) goes to rent. In this case, the system of production must expand at 4 per cent of its magnitude in a year (since the general sum of capital is 100 billion units), or, what is the same thing, the rate of accumulation equals 4 per cent. As regards rent, we so far know only its general magnitude,[32] but we do not know if it makes any sense to talk, for example, about the 'rate of rent'. We still need to find out the laws according to which this remaining one billion labour units is distributed in the price of commodities. In other words, how is 'rent' reflected in the exchange of commodities?

At this point, we must above all keep the following considerations in mind. So far, we have established the laws of exchange starting with the idea of *adaptation* – i.e. proposing that the social whole and its elements constantly and effectively adapts to the conditions of the struggle for life. Now the situation is somewhat different. No matter what form it takes, unproductive consumption is obviously a fact of social *unadaptedness*; it is the useless expenditure of social labour energy. It is impossible, at first glance, to establish laws of unadaptedness, since its forms can be endlessly varied – something that is already obvious a priori. But we cannot stop here.

The life of society consists of such a huge number of elements of development that it is impossible to talk in general about *absolute* unadaptedness in

---

32   Statistics could establish the relative magnitude of all 'rent' in our meaning of the word by comparing the value of objects of pure luxury produced in a year with the general annual sum of capitalist income.

it. The matter always has to do either with incomplete processes of adaptation or of colliding tendencies within it – relative unadaptedness that is subject to analysis from the point of view of the idea of adaptation. 'Rent' expresses the unadaptedness of society as a whole and is the result of the adaptation (of a special type) of its elements – private enterprises. Therefore, we can investigate it to a significant extent, but in order to do so we must dwell on a few phenomena of private economic life – the phenomena that were analysed by Ricardo and Marx under the term 'land rent'.

X

Capitalist production is carried on under the most varied natural conditions. That is why, as is well known, the productivity of labour in various enterprises of each sector of production does not turn out to be the same. One industrial enterprise next to a river has the ability to productively use the force of flowing water; another enterprise lacks this possibility. One is located near a market and requires only a minimal expenditure of labour for transporting its output; another is located far from a market and the additional expenditure of labour for transportation is very great. In one mining enterprise the ore is richer in metal and is easier to process; in another the ore is poorer and processing it is more difficult. One agricultural enterprise is carried out on more fertile soil; another on less fertile soil. Therefore, the unit of output – a pud[33] of iron, for example – produced in one enterprise represents one sum of implemented labour while a unit produced in another represents a different sum of labour – for example, 8 or 10 hours of simple labour.[34]

However, the market does not recognise these differences, and two units of output that are produced under very different natural conditions are exchanged in the same social conditions and have the same exchange value. To which of the two labour values must the exchange value correspond?

If the rate of accumulation is 4 per cent, then only those enterprises which grow at a yearly rate of at least 4 per cent can enjoy a solid position and main-

---

33   A Russian measurement of weight, 16.8 kilogrammes [trans.].

34   Social-technological conditions – the application of better or worse machines, better or worse organisation – also engender differences in the productivity of labour of individual enterprises; but these differences, as we have seen, are only temporary and are eliminated by development. Just the opposite, those differences that issue from the heterogeneity of natural conditions can to a certain degree be viewed as unavoidable and permanent.

tain themselves in the struggle to survive in the general system of production. Enterprises that lag in development must be considered to be unstable and unadapted. Amid the constant fluctuations of the market, in especially sharp moments of competition, it is the weakest enterprises, those that have accumulated the least amount of power, that will inevitably fail. Hence, we can justly draw the conclusion that enterprises that carry on production under the *most profitable* conditions, must have the ability to accumulation capital at 4 per cent a year, i.e. must obtain no less than 4 per cent profit.

It is obvious that enterprises that carry on production under *more favourable* natural conditions for the productivity of labour will thereby obtain more than 4 per cent return (for example, 5, 8, or 10 per cent). The excess they obtain constitutes *rent* for these enterprises – rent not in the socially productive sense, in which we used this term above, but in a different, narrowly economic sense adopted by the majority of economists.

But what kind of connection is there between the two kinds of rent, between social and narrowly economic rent? We can express this connection in the following proposition:

The sum of the narrowly economic rent of all individual enterprises must tend to correspond to the sum of social rent – unproductive consumption.

The following considerations can prove that this tendency really exists and that the two kinds of rent must generally correspond. If, apart from profit, any significant part of the rent of individual enterprises is used for the goal of accumulation, then the usual relationships in the sphere of accumulation will be destroyed. The unevenness of accumulation will cause partial crises (as we saw above) and either those enterprises that exceeded the rate will return to the old rate or a new rate will be established. If, just the opposite, the amount of unproductive consumption surpasses the amount of rent of individual enterprises, then this means that in certain realms of production accumulation does not reach the usual rate (since in each enterprise its rent is just the excess above the usual rate of accumulation), and the unevenness of accumulation in this case must cause some kind of reaction – either the enterprises that fell below the rate of accumulation will return to the previous rate, or a new rate will be established. It must therefore be conjectured that the amount of narrowly economic rent really corresponds to the amount of unproductive consumption. Meanwhile, there is no question that part of the rent of individual enterprises – and, generally speaking, not a small part – is expended toward the goal of accumulation, and, at the same time, part of the profit, proper, is spent on unproductive goals; it is obvious that the two magnitudes must approximately balance one another. To the extent that they do not balance, the equilibrium in the sphere of accumulation is upset, and, at the same time, spontaneous market forces

CHAPTER 13

appear on the scene, attempting to restore the equilibrium by decreasing accumulation where it is excessive and increasing it where it is insufficient.

Our theory is proved by this, and the usage of the same term 'rent' in two such different meanings as socially productive (as we have used it) and narrowly economic (the customary usage) is justified.

XI

It is appropriate to distinguish between 'absolute' and 'differential' rent of individual enterprises, and this distinction has the following justification. In a completely differentiated capitalist society, it is usually landowners who receive rent, proper, on individual enterprises. They appropriate rent to themselves as payment for the application of social labour to the land that belongs to them, and they do not give away gratis even the parcels of land that are least favourable for production. The payment they demand for these parcels constitutes 'absolute' rent. Therefore, in those enterprises that work under the worst natural conditions, the amount of all capitalist income must be higher than the rate of accumulation since it includes absolute rent. In enterprises with more favourable natural conditions, rent, of course, is more significant than in the first case, and this difference constitutes 'differential rent'.

We can take it as undoubtedly true that in contemporary society the size of absolute rent is very insignificant for a majority of enterprises, and for any industrial enterprise that occupies several hundred square metres and is hugely productive, it is an almost infinitely small amount. In overall accounting, rent becomes at all noticeable only in enterprises that are spread out over a large expanse, such as agricultural enterprises, for example.

It would be accurate, in essence, to accept that absolute rent is utterly absent in the capitalist societies that we know of. What the term properly means is only *a particular form of differential rent*. Actual 'absolute rent' is possible only in a completely closed capitalist society, limited to a specific territory, which is entirely in the hands of private property owners, and, again, this is not what contemporary societies are like.

In reality, what determines the amount of rent for the worst parcels of land in a given country? Within what bounds do capitalists agree to pay 'absolute' rent? If rent becomes too large, they can transfer their capital to another country where rent is lower. In an extreme case, they might even find completely vacant land – provided the expense of transporting people and the means of production to there and transporting manufactured goods from there are less than the rent that they are required to pay in their home country. And this really is one of the causes of the transfer of capital from a country with high rent to a country with low rent. Thus, this 'absolute' rent is determined by a *differential relationship* – the difference between the conditions of production in a given country and in other countries where there is still free land (of course, the difference is not only in relation to the cost of shipping operations, as in our example, but also in regard to natural wealth – fertility and the like.)[35]

Having explained the basic content and types of the phenomena of rent, we can now move on to the question of how these phenomena are reflected in the process of exchange, in the market value of commodities.

XII

The social labour value of commodities that are produced under worse or better natural conditions must be considered identical: the rate represents the quantity of labour necessary under average natural conditions. Thus, identical quantities of labour that is actually performed have a different social significance depending on whether they must overcome the relatively greatest, average, or least resistance on the part of external nature.

Suppose there are three enterprises in one sector of production. All of them have an *average* organic composition of capital, but one of them operates in *average* natural conditions, another in less favourable conditions, and the third in more favourable conditions.

A) Production under conditions of average resistance on the part of external nature. The labour value of the means of production, c, is 950,000 hours. The labour value of the means of consumption of the producers, v, is 50,000 hours. The rate of surplus labour, s, is 100 per cent. The value of the output

---

35   P. Maslov [Petr Maslov (1867–1946) was a Menshevik economist (trans.).] proves that absolute rent is impossible in contemporary societies from another point of view. Since the 'natural forces' of land have so far nowhere been entirely used up, capitalist tenants anywhere can apply an ever greater amount of capital to the parcels of land that they lease, and as long as they obtain at least the usual profit on newly applied capital, it would be exactly the same as if they had applied this capital to a free but even worse parcel of land for which they would not have to pay rent. Thus, for the worst parcels of land rent turns out to be in fact differential, and it is based on the difference in the profitability of the application of the first quantity of capital invested in it and the last.

As we see, in the end, absolute rent dissolves into differential rent and remains absolute only for those particular cases and temporary conditions when there is nowhere that tenants can obtain capital for increasing the intensiveness of their operations. But for these kinds of cases there is no need to create a special economic category – they relate to the realm of fluctuations in the sphere of supply and demand of capital.

is 950,000 + 50,000 + 50,000 = 1,050,000 labour units. Imagine that this output consists of 105,000 puds of cast iron. The question is: what is the exchange value of the given merchandise?

In order to restore the capital that was consumed during production plus the usual accumulation (4 per cent), the amount of merchandise that is required from outside embodies 1,040,000 hours of labour. But, besides this, the given enterprise must pay rent precisely consistent with average natural conditions – average rent.[36] The average rent in the given society, according to our assumption, is 1 per cent of capital (1 billion units in 100 billion). This means that in the given enterprise, rent has a labour value of 10,000 units. In total, the labour value of 1,050,000 hours is exchanged for the labour value of 1,050,000 hours. And each pud of cast iron, according to the labour rate, is exchanged for 10 hours of labour that is embodied in commodities from the outside.

Expressing the amount of rent in terms of output, we can say that in the given enterprise rent in its natural form consists of 1,000 puds of cast iron.

B) Production under conditions of the most significant resistance on the part of external nature. Let us say that the labour value of capital is the same as in the preceding example: 950,000 c + 50,000 v. Thus, the sum of labour that is actually carried out in the production of goods equals, as in the preceding case, 1,050,000 hours. But the *social labour* value of the output is not the same but a little less, and it is not difficult to determine precisely how much. The given enterprise, if it is operated under the most unfavourable natural conditions is obliged to pay absolutely no (or *almost* no) rent. Consequently, those 1,000 puds of cast iron that represent the natural form of rent in the preceding case, do not need to be obtained here with the given expenditure of capital and labour. The sum of output that is produced thus consists not of 105,000 but only of 104,000 puds of cast iron. And since under average social conditions the production of a pud of cast iron embodies 10 hours of labour, then the social labour value of the output in the given enterprise equals 1,040,000 puds of cast iron. How much will the output be exchanged for? The renewal of capital plus the usual accumulation requires a sum of commodities – means of production and consumption – which includes 1,040,000 hours of labour (capital = 1,000,000 and accumulation = 4 per cent of this amount). Since there is no rent, then the entire exchange of this sum boils down to the value of the merchandise that

---

36   If there is no absolute rent, the average amount of rent will be altogether equal to average differential rent; if there is absolute rent, then in order to determine the average rent it is necessary to add the amount of absolute rent (all absolute rent is a part of the average amount, since it is present in all cases) to the amount of average differential rent.

is manufactured: the value of 1,040,000 labour units will be given up for a value of 1,040,000 of the same units, i.e. it corresponds to the labour rate.

Of course, the *individual* labour value of merchandise is not the same; this, as we have seen, equals 1,050,000 units. But we already know that this does not represent the rate for a social relationship such as exchange, and therefore the issue of exchange need not occupy us.

C) Production under conditions of the least significant resistance on the part of external nature. As before, capital consists of 950,000 *c* + 50,000 *v*, and the amount of labour that is actually used is 1,050,000 hours. The amount of output is, of course, more than in the first case. How large it is obviously depends precisely on how favourable the natural conditions are. Let us say that it consists of 108,000 puds of cast iron. The social labour value of this output consists, in accordance with the preceding, of 1,080,000 labour units. The enterprise's rent consists of a full 4,000 puds of cast iron or 40,000 labour units, it has capital of 1 million units and accumulates 40,000 units, and, as a result, it has an exchange value equal to 1,080,000 units, i.e. this again corresponds to the labour rate. Once again, this does not correspond to the individual labour value for the same reason as in the preceding case.

Thus, the phenomenon of rent obviously could not cause special deviations of exchange value from the labour rate. But one circumstance which we have ignored in the preceding considerations still remains. We assumed that the average rent of enterprises of a given sector corresponds to the average rent of a given society as a whole and equals 1 per cent. But one cannot say that this is *altogether* the way things are. It is rather the opposite: rent is distributed unevenly among different realms of production.

The fact of the matter is that the appropriation of rent is mainly connected with the right of ownership of the land that enterprises occupy. And the distribution of land under enterprises cannot be equal because of technology. Agriculture requires a far greater expanse of land compared with manufacturing industry, cattle raising requires more land than mining operations, etc. Therefore, a more significant part of social rent falls on some sectors of production, a less significant part on others. For example, with an average social rent of 1 per cent, the rent for agriculture in general could turn out to be 2 to 3 per cent and even more, while for the textile industry, for example, it could be 0.5 per cent, 0.25 per cent, or even less.

This undoubtedly brings new complications into our calculations, new deviations of exchange from the labour rate. In consequence of the different effects of rent, exchange value of some commodities goes slightly up and others go slightly down. The degree of such deviations is determined by the degree of inequality of rent. To figure out the amount for different cases is a matter for concrete economic investigations. The abstract method cannot, needless to say, carry this out – it can only point out the basic form of the link between the magnitudes of rent and of exchange value. It is easy to see that an increase of exchange value occurs precisely for those commodities for which the technology of production requires a comparatively large expanse of land, and a decrease occurs for those for which production requires comparatively less space.

Suppose that a specific sector of production in which only 25 per cent of social capital and living labour is invested is responsible for 75 per cent of all social rent.[37] In such a case the average amount of rent of individual enterprises in this sector is not 1 per cent but 3 per cent on invested capital. An enterprise with an average organic composition of capital that is operated under average natural conditions would then appear in the following form: $c = 950,000$ labour units, $v = 50,000$, $s = 50,000$, for a total of 1,050,000. When exchanged, the same quantity of social labour (crystallised in goods from the outside) must be obtained: for the renewal of capital – 1,000,000 units, for normal accumulation (at 4 per cent) – 40,000 units, and in the form of rent (a 3 per cent average for the given sector) – 30,000 units. This adds up to 1,070,000 labour units. Thus, in this case, narrowly economic rent raised the exchange value by almost 2 per cent. This is the result of the particular technological conditions of the given sector of production, i.e. using a relatively much greater expanse of land. Thus, the determining factor of the deviation of exchange value from the norm here is still the *technology of production*.

In the general system of exchange, the smaller the general sum of unproductive consumption – rent in the social meaning of the term – the smaller the deviations from the norm.

A completely analogous series of considerations relates to the question of the influence of taxes on exchange relations. Unequal distribution of taxes has approximately the same significance as unequal distribution of rent. It is only the origin of the inequality that is different. As far as taxes that are socially useless are concerned, they represent nothing other than one of the particular forms of social 'rent'.

---

37   Purely economic rent is nevertheless not distributed in accordance with the technological distribution of the land under enterprises. For example, if in a given society the various sectors of agriculture occupy 90 per cent of the general area of the country, this still does not mean that 90 per cent of the rent will fall to agriculture. The greatest differentiation of rent applies to land that is occupied by the major centres of social life – centres of industry, trade, etc. Thus, less 'rent-bearing' land remains under agriculture, and the amount of rent in agriculture will be, for the case we have proposed, not 90 per cent of the general amount but, for example, 75 or 50 per cent.

By means of the abstract method, based on the idea of adaptation, we investigated the question of exchange relationships and arrived at the following conclusion:

*The exchange value of a commodity is determined by the conditions of the
technology of production: labour value is the most basic of these conditions, and,
moreover, its significance grows as capitalism develops.*

It is not difficult to see that these propositions could not correspond more
completely with the theory of historical monism, logically merging with it as
one of its particular conclusions. If the technological process is the basis of all
other social phenomena, then it also determines the processes of distribution,
among them the conditions of exchange.

The significance of abstract conclusions is that they provide, first, a starting
point for concrete investigation, and, second, a reliable guiding thread amidst
its entangled specific details. All of this is attained only when the premises from
which the abstract investigation itself begins are an essentially valid – if generalised and abstract – expression of concrete reality. We propose that the theory
we have presented satisfies this demand, and we therefore continually pointed out possible applications of it in the sphere of concrete investigation. The
degree of success of these applications serves as the ultimate criterion of the
validity of the theory itself.

XIII

As we have shown, the views on the nature and the laws of exchange that we
have presented are, in all essentials, a further development of the cycle of ideas
that is known by the term the 'labour theory of value'. For as long as it has
existed, this theory has been the subject of fierce critique from one side and
energetic defence from the other. In passing, we have already more than once
dealt with this criticism on one or another particular point, using correspondingly particular arguments in defence. It is now appropriate to take a more
general look at the system of critique and the system of defence as a whole.

The critique of the labour theory of value has been expounded most completely and systematically, and also with the most scientific appearance, by
Eugen von Böhm-Bawerk, to whom we will now turn our attention.[38] In fol-

---

38 See his *Kapital und Kapitalzins*, I, 18, the chapters on Rodbertus and Marx, and 'Zum
Abschluss der Marx'schen Theorie', an article in the collection *Festgaben für Karl Knies*.
His Russian populariser is S. Frank, *Teoriia tsennosti Marksa i ee znachenie*.

lowing his exposition, we will trace the basic elements of his critique without dwelling on details, since the size of this article will not allow it.

As is well known, Marx provided a simple and original justification for the labour theory of value, a justification which in a few words boils down to the following. Exchange presupposes the *equivalence* of two commodities that are exchanged, i.e. the presence of something *in common*, that is *measurable* in magnitude, and that is found in both commodities *in an equal amount*. But what can be common to all commodities of the most varied kind? Marx found two features: use value and labour value. Since the first, in his opinion, 'obviously' cannot be the basis of exchange equivalence – people *pay no attention* to this during exchange and it is not identical in goods that are exchanged – the second value remains, and it determines the relationship of exchange. Labour value turns out to be the basis of exchange value. Our point of view permits us to manage without this argument, but all the same we suggest that it is essentially valid, if somewhat abstract. How does the Austrian professor refute it?

He begins with a play of words on the theme that exchange does not at all presuppose equivalence but precisely inequality, otherwise why should there be an exchange? To obtain equal for equal is not worth the labour – someone wants to make an exchange when they calculate that they can obtain more than they give. There is no need to look into this argument in detail, and Böhm-Bawerk, himself, does not attach any particular significance to it. The fact of the matter is that, as Marx showed, exchange actually does presuppose a difference in commodities, but a difference in precisely use value: there is no point in exchanging iron for iron, but it might be exchanged for an equivalent amount of bread. To find it necessary to receive more than you give in each act of exchange is possible only for someone who has been thoroughly saturated with the atmosphere of exploitation, a person for whom exploitation has becomes a necessary form of thinking, an a priori category that contains their entire social experience.

Another of Böhm-Bawerk's objections directed against Marx's idea is considerably more serious – that in the process of exchange people 'abstract' themselves from use value. The critic finds a logical error in Marx – the confusion of two cases of 'abstraction'.

> What Marx would say to the following argument? At the opera, three prominent singers, a tenor, a bass, and a baritone, receive identical remuneration – 20,000 florins each. They ask me, what is the common condition by virtue of which their remuneration turns out to be equal, and I answer: as far as remuneration in concerned, one good voice has the same significance as any other good voice. A good tenor is the same as a

good bass or baritone, as long as in general its quality is in a corresponding proportion. And so, in the given case, people 'obviously' in general abstract out a good voice and consequently a good voice cannot be the general cause of a high remuneration. The falsity of such argumentation is utterly clear. But it is no less clear that the Marxian course of reasoning, which the argument exactly imitates, is not any more valid. In both cases the mistake is the same: to confuse abstraction from a certain condition in general with abstraction from a special form (*Modalität*) in which this condition appears. (*Kapital und Kapitalzins*, vol. I, p. 435. The translation is, as much as possible, verbatim.)

If we were playing a purely scholastical game of definition and inference, the critic would of course be right. But Marx never played such a game. Böhm-Bawerk did not understand the broad empirical backing of Marx's argument. When Marx says that in the act of exchange people 'obviously' abstract themselves from use value, he did not have in mind simply the qualitative difference of the use value of commodities. Rather, he found that it is simply impossible to discover any objective correspondence between quantitative relationships of exchange, on the one hand, and use values, on the other hand. If we are talking about the *magnitude* of use value – i.e. the usefulness of commodities – then exchange relationships systematically diverge from it and diverge sharply. A glittering little crystal of polymeric carbon costs more than 100,000 puds of bread in a locality that is hungry, objects of luxury are almost always more expensive than objects of necessity in an equal quantity. It is true that if one takes an individual psychological point of view and sets in motion the protean 'marginal utility', then all this can be reconciled and discrepancy can become correspondence. But Marx always proposed that the regularity of social exchange relationships can have only a *social* and *objective* – and not an individual and subjective – basis.[39] And 'marginal utility' had not yet appeared in the science of the time when he substantiated the theory of labour value.[40]

Further on the critic finds a new objection. If one recognises that use value cannot lie at the basis of exchange value, he asks, does there then really still remain only one trait they have in common – the trait of being the products of labour? Are there no other common traits, such as, for example, of being

---

39 Mr S. Frank, with a semi-conciliatory inclination, seeks, with the aid of Stoltzman, a social but *subjective* basis.

40 It will be necessary for us to talk about marginal utility later on.

objects of supply and demand or being rare in relation to the need for them, of being objects of acquisition, or that they are derived from nature, etc.? Is it not possible that any of these common traits also could serve as a basis of exchange value just as well as the trait of being products of labour? (*Kapital und Kapitalzins*, vol. I, p. 426)

But let us examine these 'common traits' that the critic offers to us in such abundance. Two of them – the trait of being 'derived from nature' and the trait of being 'private property' – cannot be 'just as good' as labour value for determining exchange value because they cannot in general be the basis for *quantitative* determination in the way that the exchange value of a commodity can. The trait of commodities of 'being rare in relation to the need for them' in exchange obviously coincides with the trait of 'being an object of supply and demand'. But what kind of trait is this? 'To be an object of supply and demand' means to be bought and sold, which means to be commodities. Thus, it is necessary to seek the basis for exchange ratios in the fact that commodities are commodities. It is doubtful that we can get very far ahead by going down this road.

Yes, says the bourgeois critic, but can the *quantitative* relationship of supply and demand determine the exchange value in each given case? Unfortunately, it would be impossible on this basis to talk about establishing the regularity of exchange. The theory of competition, the leading principle of the classical economists and pre-eminently developed by Marx, shows that supply and demand continually strive to *be adapted* to one another, and they therefore fluctuate around a certain common level that does not depend on their fluctuations but that exactly expresses the regularity of exchange. If, as a result of the predominance of demand over supply, the price rises higher than the norm, and then, because supply increases in reaction, the price falls lower than the norm, the *norm* can under no circumstances be explained by these fluctuations.

Those who believe in marginal utility, however, do not take this view. They consider the notion that competition involves the concept of supply and demand in an objective sense – the correlation in the market between the quantity of actually offered and actually demanded commodities – to be false. Those who believe in marginal utility see in supply and demand a complex correlation of the most complicated psychological facts that play out in the souls of sellers and buyers: a desire to acquire somebody else's 'good', a willingness to 'sacrifice' their own good for this, a struggle of various motives, vacillations relative to what it is worth and what it is not worth to give up for a given purchase, etc. This school insists on a 'subjective' understanding of supply and demand and seeks in it a basis for objective exchange relationships. It is exactly the same as if a biologist undertook to explain the objective facts of the survival of this species of animal or the extinction of that species of animal not by the objective conditions of the environment but by the subjective experiences of individual animals – that one is ill and feels hungry, that another feels itself to be in good health, etc. Science never gains by reducing what is objective to what is subjective, because its task is essentially opposed to such a reduction. In appealing from social and definite fact – exchange value – to the indefinite and elusive personal moods of individual people, we can obtain only an imaginary explanation of the facts and not a real one, only a theory of 'infinite uselessness' and not a theory of exchange value. Economic science is a science of objective relationships in the social struggle for existence, and it can take relationships of supply and demand only as objective relationships. For economic science, competition is an objective process of adaptation and not the subjective play of personal moods.

Thus, all of Böhm-Bawerk's proposed 'common traits' of commodities, which he supposes are capable of competing with labour value as the basis of exchange value, must be excluded from economic analysis, and all that remains is, once again, that same labour value. But the indefatigable critic continues to pursue it. 'Is it really true that the common trait inherent in all trade goods is to be the product of labour? Are, for example, virgin soil, gold deposits, coal deposits really products of labour? And yet they often have, as everyone knows, a very high exchange value' (op. cit., p. 437).

We already pointed out at the beginning of this article that this is in fact utterly false. Nothing enters the sphere of exchange that does not pass through the sphere of production. Virgin soil, gold deposits, deposits of coal only become objects of exchange when, at minimum, their discovery and investigation is carried out by physical and intellectual labour, no matter how insignificant that labour is. It is therefore possible to speak here only of the lack of correspondence between the magnitude of labour value and the magnitude of exchange value.[41] We must deal with this in particular in regard to Böhm-Bawerk's objections that are relevant here, but, for the time being, we will again point out a purely logical defect in his argument. He asserts that the single fact that 'non-labour' goods that possess exchange value exist is enough to fundamentally do away with the labour theory of value. But this would be untrue

---

41   For greater persuasiveness, Mr Frank uses the expression 'a good not created by labour' instead of 'a good that does not include the expenditure of labour power'. Unfortunately, labour does not in general 'create' anything but only changes the relations of objects and their elements.

even if such non-labour 'goods' existed. In reality, this would mean only a certain *limit* to the applicability of the theory, and that is all. It would mean that the theory does not have an *absolute* character. But the evolutionary world-view, with which the labour theory of value is associated, altogether does not acknowledge absolute formulas; it even proposes that concrete reality and cognitive abstractions cannot coincide unconditionally.

Finally, the fundamental meaning of such proposed limits to the labour theory of value would diminish even more if it turns out that 'non-labour goods' have trade value only because they are definitely related to labour goods – for example, if they are a necessary condition for labour goods to appear ('virgin soil', a 'mine', a 'coal pit'), if they are necessary objects for the support and restoration of labour (fertility of the soil, a virgin forest that is cut down), or if they are objects that only in certain cases are attained 'without labour' and in other cases are produced by the labour process (a fortuitously found diamond in the rough or gold in general). And so, even if one ignores the small labour value of such commodities and considers it to be zero, this still does not undermine the fundamental meaning of the labour theory of value, and stronger arguments are necessary.

And the bourgeois critic finds a whole mass of them. For convenience, we will begin to review them by first excluding one of them that has only a purely verbal character and that mainly testifies to the degree of antipathy of the critic to the labour theory of value. Here is the argument:

> ... Secondly, all those goods that are produced not by ordinary but by skilled labour form an exception to the principle of labour value. Although the output of the daily work of a sculptor, engraver, violin maker, mechanical engineer, and so forth embodies no more work than does the daily product of an ordinary artisan or factory worker, nevertheless the exchange value of the product is higher – often many times higher – in the first case than in the second (p. 438).

But it is well known that from the point of view of the labour theory of value, skilled labour is considered as a multiple of simple labour. In regard to this, Böhm-Bawerk adds:

> There is, of course, no doubt that the working day of a sculptor in certain regards – in the sense of valuation, for example – can *be taken as equal* to five working days of a ditch digger. But certainly no one can assert that twelve hours of work of a sculptor *constitutes in reality* sixty ordinary working hours (op. cit., p. 439).

With this objection, Böhm-Bawerk wants to prove that Marx himself did not sustain the labour principle of his theory and introduced foreign elements into it. But if the objection were valid, it could have meaning only for the question of what the theory is called – is the term 'labour' completely appropriate for it or not. But the objection is based on an error. From his individual point of view, the critic continually looks only at individual workers and forgets that with Marx the issue has to do with socially necessary time – with the social expenditure of labour energy – and this necessarily presupposes the reduction of individual labour to some kind of social labour unit, and it is self-evident that such a unit cannot be simply a unit of time independent of the intensity and complexity of labour. In the second section of this article, we pointed out how the very concept of social labour energy requires the reduction of complex labour to a multiple of simple labour, and we cannot spend any more time on this topic.

The remaining objections, which follow in a straight line from the objection that has just been analysed, boil down to pointing out various 'exceptions' – or, more accurately, deviations – from the labour norm that supposedly undermine its significance. But here, in order to clearly understand the significance of these objections, we must first become familiar with how Böhm-Bawerk understands the laws of social phenomena in general – in particular with what he demands from the scientific expression of exchange.

The critic admits that 'there exist certain real deviations from the theoretical formula, which the theorist really has the right to abstract: these are the fortuitous and transient fluctuations of market prices around their true, long-term, lasting level' (*Zum Abschluss der Marx'schen Theorie*, p. 171.)

But, in the opinion of the critic, the process of abstraction can in no case go further than this. Böhm-Bawerk considers invalid Marx's point of view that 'due to fluctuations of supply and demand, the exchange value of commodities sometimes rises above the level that corresponds to the quantity of labour that is crystallised in them and sometimes drops below that level' and that 'the latter signifies only the point toward which exchange value gravitates, and not its constant magnitude' (*Kapital und Kapitalzins*, vol. I, p. 440). Böhm-Bawerk proposes that this alone would make it necessary for an economist to investigate 'whether or not a more general principle of exchange value exists to which not only the "true" formation of prices but what seems from the point of view of the labour theory of value to be the "false" formation of prices could both equally be reduced' (op. cit., p. 441). We thus see that the critic insists upon a *monistic* explanation of the processes of exchange ... What does this mean? Could it be that a cloistered academic and a man of genius have changed places: the former standing out as a monist, the latter as an eclectic?

Several years ago, I wrote the following in regard to this:

Cognition is not required to deal with completely isolated phenomena. All processes of nature are really interconnected with one another and mutually influence one another. It is therefore utterly senseless to explain any one group of phenomena in its entirety (without leaving any of them out) from one principle that is specifically established for that group of phenomena, since it will turn out that various influences on the part of other surrounding phenomena cannot be fit into the confines of this special principle. Thus, for example, the explanation of the concretely observed facts of falling bodies must not be limited to the basic abstract formula of falling bodies (that expresses the action of gravitation in a pure form) but must pay attention to the entire sum of real conditions. A full explanation must take into account the form and density of the falling body, the density of the air, the presence of random gusts of wind, the closeness of mountain masses that deflect (although insignificantly) the line of fall from a strict vertical, and so on and so on. In this way, the basic principle of the explanation of singularities is not only altogether insufficient but sometimes is completely obscured by collateral influences.

The sole principle of explanation that absolutely does not need limitations for an individual group of empirical facts, would, at the same time, turn out to be a universal principle for explaining all the phenomena that are associated with this group in one way or another and so for all nature in general. Such, for example, is the principle of causality. But each group of similar phenomena needs, in addition to this too-general principle, one that is specific and more particular, and this latter principle necessarily conflicts with other specific and particular principles and is limited by them.[42]

Thus, if Böhm-Bawerk applied his criteria of 'scientific law' to the most developed of the natural sciences – mechanics – then the existing theory of falling bodies, for example, would be utterly unsatisfactory. He would say:

The formula of uniform acceleration toward the centre of the earth is obviously invalid. There are so many exceptions to it that the rule loses

---

42   Bogdanov's citations come from his review of Semen Frank's *Teoriia tsennosti Karla Marksa i ee znachenie*, Bogdanov 1901a [trans.].

all meaning. Exceptions from it include: (1) all bodies that fall within the confines of the atmosphere (that is, almost all cases that are actually encountered in our experience), (2) all bodies that fall in water, (3) all bodies that have some sort of movement of their own before the moment they being to fall, etc. Moreover, these are not tiny, fortuitous deviations, but in a huge number of cases almost nothing remains of the pure formula for falling. Examples include: raindrops or ice crystals that form different kinds of clouds, specks of dust, falling dry leaves, parachutes, balloons, etc. No, it is obvious that this false 'law' does not deserve to be called a law at all.

To this, a reader familiar with the methods of the natural sciences would answer the critic approximately as follows: 'of course the given formula does not apply absolutely to reality, but it accurately marks out the basic, most general tendency of the given series of phenomena. Having made it the starting point of analysis, and by introducing complicating influences into the analysis one after another, we can always arrive at an adequate understanding of the concrete facts of falling'. And the critic, in turn, would answer: 'no, it is necessary to find a more general principle which would embrace all the facts of falling bodies – those that correspond to the given formula and also those diverging from it – with insignificant "fortuitous" exceptions'. The natural scientist would then explain the following: 'such a role could be played only by the most general laws of mechanics, but precisely by virtue of their great generality they in themselves are insufficient for analysis of the given special group of phenomena and must certainly be supplemented by more particular formulas of which the basic one that specially characterises the given series of facts is the formula of gravity'. The critic continues to demand: 'No, you give me one particular law that entirely embraces the facts of falling'. Only one thing remains for the exhausted natural scientist to declare: 'If you want the moon, you have to get it yourself'.

If the indefatigable critic is not at a loss here and quickly supplies the principle that was demanded, then we can conclude a priori that he has fallen into a misunderstanding, and what he proposes instead of the given scientific formula must turn out to be either a false principle that contradicts the facts or a formula that is imaginary and completely empty and that is therefore useless for investigation ...

But perhaps this is the situation only in regard to the natural sciences. Perhaps things are completely different for the social sciences, and the rigorous demands of the critic are completely pertinent here? But one can only answer this with a question: is it possible that one or another group of social facts –

exchange relationships, for example – are so isolated that they are different from physical, biological, etc. phenomena? It is just the opposite: here also all sorts of influences that deviate from the norm both in a considerably greater amount and of a considerably more varied nature, so that everything that was said about the limits to the meaning of particular principles in the natural sciences applies to an even greater degree to social-scientific principles. Therefore, the all-embracing, universal exchange principle of 'marginal utility' that is proposed by the marginalists already a priori by virtue of general methodological considerations must be considered unsuitable. But we will have to pay particular attention to this later.

For now, it is clear to us what the further objections the learned critic has against the labour theory of value must be like. He fishes out all sorts of exceptions and deviations from the labour rate, drags them into one pile, and, pointing at them in triumph, declares: what kind of law can it be when there are so many exceptions to it? But for us the question appears in a completely different form. We want to know whether it is possible to make the labour principle the starting point of the systematic analysis of exchange relationships, whether the given idea really expresses the basic, most general tendency of the processes of exchange, and whether it is altogether expedient to apply it to a given series of phenomena. The entire preceding exposition brought us to a convincing answer to this question, and therefore there is simply no need for us to analyse in detail the particular groups of deviations that Böhm-Bawerk brings up. Besides, we have already analysed the most important of them – the deviations that depend on the inequality of the organic composition of capital, on the differences of their periods of circulation, and on the influence of rent. But, all the same, we think it useful to dwell a little on the two most significant of the remaining groups.

'Above all, "rare goods" (Seltenheitsgüter) are excluded from the sphere of action of the labour principle – goods that, as a result of insurmountable obstacles of a factual or legal nature cannot be reproduced at all or at least cannot be reproduced in an unlimited quantity' (*Kapital und Kapitalzins*, vol. I, p. 538, 1).

To the extent we are dealing with property in land, we know that its exchange value depends on rent, and, to be precise, on differential rent, since absolute rent, if it even existed, would, in the capitalist societies that we know of, be relatively very small – so small that it could be disregarded with almost no loss of accuracy of the analysis. And differential rent, as we explained, arises entirely on the ground of the labour principle of value and not at all in spite of it; it arises precisely from the difference between the social labour value of output and the individual labour value of output in the conditions of one or another individual enterprise. Here, therefore, the matter has to do not with an exception to the labour theory of value but with a special application of it.

To the extent that Böhm-Bawerk has in mind such 'rare goods' as remarkable works of art, unusually rare luxury items, aged wine, etc., these are all 'exceptions' of which it would be highly accurate to say that they 'prove the rule'. In reality, if the law of value in its pure form revealed itself to be fully applicable for the most exceptional and most complicated cases, if the law of value, having been established for the world of competition, turned out to be completely applicable in the sphere of almost pure monopoly, it would be a very doubtful law. Such an absolute and at the same time particular principle *could not* exist for one separate but not absolutely isolated group of phenomena such as the phenomena of exchange. It is possible, of course, to create an imaginary principle that because it has no content will apply identically both to typical and exceptional cases, but this is because it explains neither of them.

Another 'exception', which the critic endows with particular significance, is formulated as follows: ... 'The necessary means of existence of workers can also be sold according to those costs of production that are less than necessary working time. In this case, according to Marx's theory, the variable part of capital (i.e. paid wages) can be less than its value' (*Zum Abschluss des Marxschen Systems*, p. 141).

In reality this is, if one can use the expression, the very tiniest exception. Workers receive enough pay, generally speaking, to satisfy their existing needs, i.e. for the purchase of the usual objects of consumption, and this is precisely what they spend their wages on. Thus, the monetary phase of exchange is completely unimportant here, and things work out as if workers had exchanged their labour power directly for their means of consumption. In this case, the principle of labour value, as Marx formulated it, turns out to be in full force, since the value of the vital means necessary for a worker is at the same time the value of their labour power. If in the exchange of labour power for money there is a deviation downward from the labour rate, then it is inevitably subsequently compensated for by a deviation in the other direction with the exchange of this money for objects of consumption. But the critic goes no further than the monetary facade of exchange – the fetishism of this façade prevents him from seeing more deeply into it.

Meanwhile, the critic places this error at the basis of a complex argument that must prove that the rate of profit – and after it the cost of production as well – is not related to the labour principle. From Marx's point of view, the rate of profit is determined by the relationship of surplus value to the labour value of all social capital, since the general sum of profit (if it is not singled out from other forms of capitalist income) is equal to the general sum of surplus value.

The critic finds that if overall wages do not correspond to the normal labour value of labour power, then the sum of capitalist incomes *does not equal* the sum of surplus value. But this latter proposition, as we just saw, is completely wrong and is based on a superficial understanding of the facts.

There is no need to follow the Austrian critic any further in all his more minor raids – from the rear and from the flanks – on the labour theory of value. To all his pronouncements regarding one or another particular deviation of the market price from the labour rate, we can once and for all provide this answer: Worthy professor, our science does not set as its goal an explanation of the principle according to which patron A pays artist B so many dollars for a painting, or landlord C pays so many pounds for a bottle of wine from the last century, or even every case when a merchant clears a thousand thalers less than he expected for his goods, or when some manufacturer, having eliminated his competitors, receives 100,000 roubles more than their commodities cost. All this might be very important from an 'individual psychological' or a commercial point of view, but *in itself* it interests us very little – and not even because, as representatives of a specific class, there is not the tiniest risk of us obtaining all these thousands. We are properly occupied with the questions of the structure of society, of the social forces that struggle in it, of the broad class interests that engender this struggle, of society's possible and probable development, and of its various conceivable outcomes. We demand from our theory the answer to the question of what objective and general causes, conditioning people's decisive motives, direct their actions in society, and what objective and general results spring from such actions. We want to know what stimulates social development, and what is the direction and course of social development. And the labour theory of value, in our opinion, helps us to look into these questions more deeply and better than any other theory of exchange. This theory, in showing us how a single value, having sprung up in production, is subsequently distributed among various classes without changing in its general magnitude, reveals to us with complete clarity the origin of class antagonisms and the fundamental irreconcilability of those antagonisms in light of the existence of the classes, themselves, each of which can increase its share only at the expense of the other. In depicting the alignment of whole classes and individual social groups on the basis the one general fact of exploitation, this theory provides us with the possibility of conceiving with great precision the structure of capitalist society and the general stimuli of the struggle between the progressive and regressive tendencies that are created in it. The labour theory of value really *explains* the regularity of the phenomena of exchange because it not only permits a step by step approach to understanding the individual processes of exchange but to conceiving of these processes in connection with basic manifestations of social life as links continuously entering into one great chain of the social labour struggle for existence. And this is why we take a stand on this theory, until another one is proposed to us that can provide this and even much, much more than this ...

The worthy critics would raise a great many objections to us about all this. First, they would repeat all their previous arguments, and, pointing out that there are a huge number of them, would attempt to convince us that even if each of the arguments cannot be considered particularly significant when taken separately, still, taken as a whole, they would be sufficient to overwhelm the labour theory of value. But we would not agree with this, finding that a bad argument is not a positive magnitude but a negative one, and therefore a multitude of bad arguments is not a positive but only a larger negative magnitude. Second, they would declare to us that what we see as the benefit of the labour theory of value – its conclusions in regard to social antagonisms – constitutes its greatest deficiency, that this is a harmful, demagogic theory that inflames the contradictions of social life and prevents them from being ameliorated and reconciled, and that a *scientific* theory must not be like this. But this would not convince us, and it only would explain to us what, as a matter of fact, these worthy critics are striving for. We, in turn, would not see them as people of science but as conscious or unconscious apologists for existing relationships and the ruling classes. Third, the worthy critics would propose their own 'subjectively psychological' theories of exchange and value to us as being infallible and immediately explicative of everything. In order to resolve the issue of these theories, we would have to examine their actual bases, and this is what we will now do, although because of insufficient space, only in the most general features.

XIV

The theories of the psychological school seek the basis of exchange value in the individual psyche. A commodity has a specific 'subjective value' for each individual person as a means of satisfying specific needs. In regard to each commodity, the individual person considers what it would be worth to sacrifice from their property in order to acquire that commodity, or, the other way around, what other usefulness it would be worth to give up in exchange for it. Thus, there is one valuation for one buyer, another valuation for another buyer, etc., and it is exactly the same with the various sellers. To explain how the subjective valuations of various commodities compare in one psyche and how the subjective valuation of one commodity compares in various psyches, the concept of 'marginal utility', which plays the main role in the theories of this school (the marginalists), is introduced. With the aid of this concept, various cases of valuation are analysed, and a path is indicated for working out of the market price from individual valuations.

The magnitude of the 'usefulness' – and so also of the 'subjective value' – of a good is determined for each person by the intensity of the need that this can satisfy. But the same good usually serves to satisfy not one but several needs, and for each of these needs its strength changes, diminishing to the extent it is satisfied and increasing to the extent that the needs remain unsatisfied. Thus, for example, a piece of bread could serve, first, for satisfying actual hunger, second, for entertaining guests (the need to be hospitable), third, to deal with a beggar (the need to be philanthropic), and so on. Moreover, if the issue is to alleviate one's own hunger, then the first half-pound of bread satisfies the most acute need, the second half-pound satisfies a weaker – and already partly satisfied – need, etc. In such a case, what determines the 'subjective value' of the commodity – bread – for the given person?

It is determined by the *least intense* of the needs that could be satisfied with a given availability of goods – in other words, by the good with the least utility, or in the appropriate terminology, the *marginal utility* of that good. Thus, in our example, if there is sufficient bread for the complete satisfaction of all three needs that we enumerated, then the subjective economic value of bread would depend on the 'utility' of the last piece which satisfied the last minimal degree of the last and least intense need. If it turns out that there is less bread, of course, the given individual sacrifices less intense needs at their lowest levels for the sake of more intense needs at their higher levels. Consequently, the marginal utility and subjective value goes up, and, correspondingly, the marginal, lowest need that still factually can be satisfied also goes up – for example, the philanthropic need is replaced by the hospitable need or a lower level of need is replaced by the need to satisfy one's own hunger, and so on.

When the marginal utility of any good is lower for someone than the marginal utility of another good, then that person gladly exchanges the first for the second; but in so doing exchange takes place only if the situation is reversed for the seller of the second good. This is what market relations are based upon.

Suppose, for example, that a given person, having a lot of fish, is in need of bread and goes to the market with the goal of acquiring, let us say, two pounds of bread to satisfy their own appetite, one pound for guests, and a half a pound for the poor. For this the person proposes to give up no more than seven fish, since the marginal utility of the next, eighth, fish, as an object of possible consumption, is not lower or is even a little higher than the utility of the last half pound of bread that they need. The seller of bread has no objection to exchanging it for fish, but, complying with their marginal utilities, they want to obtain not two fishes for each pound of bread, as the first person proposes, but four. Then our first marginalist sees that they will not succeed in satisfying their need to the degree that they had proposed, and now they want to give up their philanthropy – i.e. to buy only three pounds of bread. But it turns out that the marginal utility of bread has thereby now increased, since it is determined by another more intense need that he has in mind to satisfy – the need to be hospitable; and, keeping in mind the marginal utility of fish for him, he goes up to a price of two and a half fish for a pound of bread. But the buyer of fish, also, seeing that the first marginalist cannot entirely obtain what he wants, decides to give up their lowest level of need for it, so that now its marginal utility goes up for them, and they are now prepared to concede a pound of bread for three and a half fish. This is the process of the change of the marginal utility of commodities, and the subjective value of those commodities can continue on even further until both marginalists either come together on price or go their separate ways once and for all.

The process occurs – only with corresponding complications – in a similar manner in the real market where there are a great number of sellers on the one hand and a great number of buyers on the other. Subsequently, by means of various theoretical conversions, those cases where commodities are exchanged that are not subject to direct personal consumption – for example, money, the means of production, etc. – are brought under the formula of marginal utility, and it turns out, as a result, that everywhere the subjective economic value of a commodity to an individual person is directly determined by the marginal utility of that commodity, and objective exchange value arises from the interaction of subjective valuations.

But there is no need for us to go any further in elaborating this theory. What is important for us is the basic method that lies at its base, its fundamental concepts. Altogether how valid is it to reduce socio-economic facts to individual psychological phases? Is it possible to look in the individual consciousness of individual people for the determining conditions of such socially spontaneous processes as the life of the market?

It is necessary to keep in mind that the human individual is born, lives, and develops in society and not outside of it, and that is why they are necessarily determined psychologically by society. From the very beginning of their lives they are enveloped on all sides by objective relationships that are independent of their will, and they must constantly adapt to them. The exchange value of commodities for each given human individual is one of these relationships. It is something given from without, something that the individual finds ready-made in their social surroundings. This external fact cannot but influence the 'subjective' evaluation of commodities; the individual cannot escape from it into their 'subjective' definition of value. Prices that objectively exist in the market, independently of the will of the individual seller or buyer, determine the individual's 'subjective' evaluation of commodities to an infinitely great degree than prices are determined by the individual. And, since this is so, 'subjective value' inevitably boils down entirely to exchange value, which is what 'subjective value' is supposed to explain. A vicious circle results, which the method of marginal utility cannot get out of in any case. It is utterly useless to argue that, although purely individual influences in each separate case are very small, yet by accumulating and piling up over hundreds and thousands of years their interaction can determine social exchange evaluation. These individual influences are either incidental and indefinite – in which case they cannot determine anything, since as a whole they must balance one another out according to the law of large numbers – or these influences are subordinate to a definite and objective regularity. But then it is necessary to find this defining regularity, and without this they, once again, explain nothing.

All of this becomes especially obvious if one keeps in mind that in a great many cases the human individual is altogether unable to make an evaluation of the usefulness of one or another commodity. How large is the 'subjective value' of a yard of cheap cotton print to the millionaire capitalist who sells it or the 'subjective value' of luxurious fabric to the poor milliner who sews it, or the 'subjective value' of a ready-made coffin to the coffin-maker who sells it? It would take an enormous number of scholastical tricks to pack all such cases into the confines of 'marginal utility'.[43]

---

43   E. Böhm-Bawerk's brilliantly worked out theory of profit on capital (*Kapital und Kapitalzins*, 2 vols.) can serve as a model of such scholasticism. The fundamental idea of this theory is as follows. When one or another good is at hand, it has significantly more subjective value than the same good that is in the prospect of being obtained in the future. One hundred roubles in the present are not the same as 100 roubles in the future but represent a larger amount. Therefore, any entrepreneur giving a loan of 100 roubles or spending that amount on production must be paid back or must gain from the sale of output not 100 roubles but more. The entrepreneur is exchanging present goods for future ones, and, in order for the exchange to proceed in accordance with subjective value, it is necessary that future goods be obtained in a greater amount. In the final analysis, therefore, the size of the per centage of profit is determined precisely by the difference between subjective values and future goods.

     The nature of this particular theory could not correspond better to the general theory of 'marginal utility'. The same vicious circle is present. Why does a given person who loans one hundred roubles value them at 105 roubles that must be obtained after a year? Precisely because in the given society the usual per centage on capital has already been formed. In another economic system, where the per centage of interest on credit has been established differently, the individual would evaluate present goods differently – after a

But if the explanation of social facts by the individual psychological peculiarities of individual people is impermissible for science in principle, then an
explanation of what is specific and comparatively stable by what is indefinite
and variable is even less permissible. The theory of marginal utility leads us
from the sphere of facts that are accessible to direct objective observation to
the realm of facts that are inaccessible – from the visible to the invisible. You
see a chain of plainly formed and quantitatively definite exchange processes;
you want to understand the causes and the laws that govern these phenomena.
They invite you into the secret compartment of the internal, spiritual life of
individual people, and they propose to seek in its indefiniteness the determining moments of what is definite, to seek in the qualitative variety of its elements
the causes of given quantitative relationships, and to seek in its variations and
transformations the relative permanency of these relationships. In this secret
compartment you find 'subjective value' – a reflection of *that same objective
exchange value* slightly distorted by the individuality of a given person, and they
say to you 'Here is your explanation! Now do you understand'?

What we obviously have before us is a false theory that can neither be proven
nor disproven, since the very criteria of truth and delusion do not apply to it. It
can never be verified – either directly or indirectly – by any objective experiences and observations, and this is its *advantage*. It is as invulnerable as a
shadow or a ghost. A natural scientist would be ashamed to propose such a
theory.[44]

---

year an entrepreneur would not want to receive 105 roubles for the loan of 100 roubles
but rather, for example, 103 roubles. In societies that have become partially commodity
societies but that are still not capitalistic, charging interest on capital seems to people to
be an extremely unnatural thing that contradicts nature and reason. Does this mean that
these people are mistaken in their subjective evaluation of present and future goods? But
then any 'subjective value', in general, can seem mistaken, and where is the criterion of
truth here?

In societies where there is no exploitation, it would not enter anyone's head that 100
puds of bread in the present are worth more than 100 puds in the future. Both signify the
nourishment of such-and-such number of people over the course of the same interval of
time, which is the same in both cases. If things stand differently in bourgeois psychology, it
is precisely because there is the possibility of using these 100 puds of bread to extract surplus value from the labour of other people. Profit in the form of a mass of surplus product
is something that is utterly objective and 'subjective' bases are a bad foundation for it.

The self-serving character of the theory is obvious. Profit does not enter the theory as
the result of exploitation but as a result of the simple passage of time, on the one hand,
and of 'subjectively-psychological' nuances, on the other. And since time is the legitimate
property of any person, the right to 'subjective' evaluation of goods is an 'inalienable natural right', as Mr Berdiaev would say, and then profit also turns out to be the 'natural right'
of capital.

44   The situation does not improve even when they 'supplement' the theory of marginal util-

The staggering lack of familiarity of the huge majority of economists with precise scientific methods that have been worked out in the more developed realms of science has unarguably provided extremely favourable conditions for the survival of economic theories like the theory of marginal utility, but the basic cause of the factual predominance of such theories in the academic world is the power of class interests that dominate people's psyches.

Thus, we must acknowledge that a subjective psychological theory not only cannot replace an objectively productive theory in economic analysis but cannot even supplement it. It must simply be rejected.

As concerns the theory we have adopted, because it is a profoundly vital theory, it takes us considerably further than its immediate tasks. It not only points out a reliable path for us toward the knowledge of economic reality, but it also fulfils a great organisational role in the intellectual life of whole classes of society. And there is every reason to think that its significance will continue to grow even more in the future.

In reality, once the path for crossing over from labour value to exchange value has been established, it is, after all, possible to travel in the opposite direction. In our time, the production of each commodity boils down to countless atoms of labour applied by millions of people, and to take these atoms into immediate account is an utterly inconceivable job. How, for example, does one take into account the portion of labour lodged in the value of a given product by a worker who is building the road along which that product will be transported (since there is no question that this portion enters into the general labour value of the product)? The technologically productive theory of exchange creates the possibility of indirectly summing up such atoms. From the global prices of a given commodity we can – introducing corrections according to the principles of the theory itself – go back to the labour value of the given commodity and explain with growing precision its real magnitude. Only along this path can a precise picture be drawn of the system of distribution of the labour value of a given commodity in the developing capitalist production of various products,

---

ity with the theory of the costs of production. This latter 'explains' the price of each good by the price of the means of producing it plus 'customary profit'. The price of these means of production are subject to exactly the same 'explanation'. In this way, the theory points out – and quite vaguely, at that – only the interrelationship between the prices of various commodities, while this provides exactly nothing for understanding *prices in general* or for explaining *the bases of exchange*. In this sense, the naïve formula – 'prices come from other prices' – is obviously just as useless and empty as the formula of marginal utility, and no matter how harmoniously the emptiness of what is 'subjectively psychological' is combined with the emptiness of what is 'objectively economic', it is obviously impossible to obtain a real theory of value from it but, once again, only a theory that is *false*.

and only along this path can conditions be found for the rational distribution of the labour power of society in the further planned organisation of that labour power. Without the scientific resolution of these tasks, the process of the conscious transformation of social forms that gradually must replace the spontaneity of contemporary capitalist development will be impossible.

Legal Society and Labour Society

In our times, few thoughtful people would deny that in the struggle for social development, theory serves as a necessary organising and regulating aspect of practice. Because of this correlation, the selection and the critique of theories of the nature and development of society attain the kind of vital significance that there is no need to prove and explain. Our task is to critically compare two theories that vehemently compete with one another in this realm, each of them energetically claiming to be the most progressive. We designate them as the legal and labour conceptions of society. In order to compare them, we will look at a very famous work by Professor Rudolf Stammler, *Wirtschaft und Recht* ... In it, Stammler thoroughly expounds the bases of the legal conception, of which he is a major representative, and criticises the labour conception. In a word, he makes the same comparison that we have just now taken on as our task, only from his own point of view.

∴

The basic course of Stammler's thoughts is as follows.

The first task of socio-philosophical investigation consists in rigorously and precisely establishing the *subject* of social science as a particular, independent realm of knowledge. For this it is necessary to single out what is *distinctive* in it, what distinguishes social phenomena from 'natural' phenomena, what makes the point of view and methods of the natural sciences unsuitable for the study of social life. To figure out what is 'distinctive' means to simultaneously define both the formal starting point of social knowledge – its logical 'a priori' – and its boundaries. Once the 'boundaries' and 'a priori' are found, the 'epistemological bases' for social knowledge are given, and social science for the first time thereby becomes 'possible as a science in the true, Kantian meaning of the word'.

So, what defines a social phenomenon as the subject of a special social science? It is obvious on the face of it that there can be no social phenomenon if there is no *relationship between people*. It is also obvious that if this relationship is one of struggle between people, then it still does not in itself provide a social phenomenon: sociality presupposes a certain positive interrelationship that unites people in their vital activity. In reality, no matter what social phenomenon we begin to examine, from the most elementary forms of production to the most complex movements in socio-ideological life, we find everywhere that people unite – directly or indirectly, consciously or unconsciously – for the attainment of various goals. Thus, the *universal content* of social phenomena is the joint activity of people; it is the 'material' of social phenomena, in Stammler's expression.

But 'material' that has no 'form' is only formless matter, i.e. chaos, devoid of any regularity and useless for scientific investigation. There still is no 'social phenomenon' – an subject for a special social science – as long as only collaboration, i.e. formless material of sociality, is present. This does not mean that there is altogether nothing to investigate here, but only that there is no ground here for a special *social science* investigation.

We will explain this with concrete examples. Suppose that you see someone who is carrying a weight that is beyond their strength. In accord with an immediate altruistic impulse, you help the exhausted person, even though nothing obligates you to do this, and the rules of propriety, which you have completely forgotten about at this moment, even forbid a person of your social position to play the role of a porter. The fact of joint activity is present, but, according to Stammler, a 'social phenomenon' is not. You act in conformity with your personal inclination, and the person who accepts your help acts in conformity with their immediate benefit. The investigator sees only human individuals with their motives, desires, and wishes – material for *psychological* investigation. But there is nothing besides these individuals and there is nothing outside of them that would create the necessity for a new point of view or new methods: there is no necessity for a special social-scientific investigation. People can act in one way or another way, and so their actions are not *socially determined* and therefore are not *subject to social regularity*.

Let us take another example. Several people who are going for a walk in a forest are attacked by a pack of wolves and have to desperately defend themselves. Even though these people had formerly not known one another in the least and were not in practice bound together by anything, still here, in the face of a common enemy, they are compelled to act jointly and without any mutual agreement and to attempt as expeditiously as possible to mutually coordinate their actions. What we see here is not only collaboration but a certain specific form of collaboration, which depends on the purely technological conditions of struggle with hostile wild animals. However, in Stammler's opinion, 'social knowledge' has nothing to do with this: there are people with their purely personal – even though mutually intertwined – motives and wishes, and there are wolves and other external natural conditions. These are objects for the investigation of psychological, biological, etc. knowledge, but not for special social-scientific knowledge.[1]

---

1 Both illustrations are mine. Stammler presents these propositions abstractly.

Where does this 'special' knowledge begin? In order to provide a graphic answer, we will again return to our examples but will take them in a somewhat altered form.

Let us suppose that at the very same moment you, obeying an immediate impulse, are about to go and help someone who is carrying a weight too heavy for him, you remember how 'inappropriate' this is for you, and you summon your servant to go instead of yourself. The fact of joint activity is present as before, and the participation in it of a third person – a servant – essentially changes nothing. But a new element is involved of an utterly special kind. This element is a *social norm that entails external obligatoriness (äusserlich verbindende)*. Your behaviour is determined not by your immediate wishes but by the rules of propriety that impose on you a certain obligation *from without*, which you are *compelled* to follow, even though you might completely disagree with it. The behaviour of your servant is also determined not by his own wishes but by the rules of propriety that *compel* him to obey you within the bounds of contract, even though he is not at all inclined to do so. In so doing, it is completely unimportant by what compulsion the given norm is sanctioned – the pressure of social opinion as a rule of behaviour or the force of judicial institutions as a legal form. Only one thing is essential: that this norm is *external*, that it demands purely *external obedience* – external legality – independently of the personal motives of the human individual.

The situation is similar if you participate in an organised hunt for wolves in which you have a leader to whom you are obliged, on the basis of common agreement, to unquestioningly obey. A norm created by this agreement stands above your individual will; once it arises it becomes an external compulsory force for you, no matter how small the objective means on which this compulsion depends. You can, of course, violate it; one can resist any external compulsion. But this does not at all change the character of the norm itself or of the form of its demands. It is not interested in your psychology, in your motives and desires; it demands that you follow it externally and nothing more. You can subordinate yourself to it with complete conviction in its rationality or only reluctantly with annoyance and dissatisfaction; it is all the same. What is essential is that there is something in the phenomenon that goes beyond the bounds of human individuals with their immediate preferences and desires, something, consequently, that is not contained within the bounds of individual psychological investigation and that requires a special point of view, a special method. It is here that the necessity arises for a special science – a social science – and for a special form of knowledge – social-scientific knowledge.

Thus, Stammler finds the special subject of social science: external norms that regulate collaboration. External compulsory norms – this is the basic concept that 'makes possible' special social knowledge and that defines its boundaries at the same time. This is the social-scientific 'a priori'. Externally obligatory norms (and only they) impart to formless social material (the joint activity of people) the specific definiteness that is characteristic of a 'social phenomenon'. They are the universal form of sociality, and any investigation of social regularity must begin with them.

Citing marriage, crime, trade, and industrial activity as typical examples of 'social phenomena', Stammler remarks: ponder these concepts, and you will immediately note that they have no meaning independent of external norms.[2]

Before we can follow the development of Stammler's views any further, we must dwell a little on his *basic* conception, which we have just presented.

What, properly, should be understood as an externally obligatory norm? Stammler considers it unnecessary to subject this concept to a general logical analysis and genetical investigation, and in this he, as always, is true to the spirit of Kantianism, which teaches that once you reach the 'a priori' there is of course no further you can go and no reason to try. Of course, Kantians would not deny that in the given case it is possible to go further, but from their point of view this 'further' is completely useless and unnecessary for 'social knowledge' and can have meaning only for some sort of other realm of knowledge. But we will nevertheless try to go farther – to the extent necessary.

From the aspect of logic, any externally obligatory norm presupposes the cognitive possibility of people not following it. Therefore, we should not ascribe such norms everywhere that we observe objective uniformity and regularity in people's actions. For example, all or almost all people walk on two legs, but, regardless of the universality of this fact, it is not related to 'external norms'; everyone acts this way by virtue of how they are objectively organised, and that is all. However, an 'external norm' could be possible in this case. Suppose that you find silly people who stubbornly prefer to walk on all fours or even on their hands, thereby causing significant difficulties and concern for everyone else. Then the other members of society would begin to struggle against the unpleasant eccentrics and create an 'external norm' in the form of a juridical rule or rule of propriety with approximately the following content: anyone who walks must, to the extent possible, use their lower extremities to do so. This norm has become logically possible because there is something it can be opposed to.

---

2 If one keeps in mind that, according to Stammler, not only do altruistic instincts not constitute a 'social' relationship, but that, with their exclusively 'inner' compulsoriness, those instincts also do not provide grounds and moral norms for a social relationship, then one must admit that the concept of the worthy thinker regarding marriage ('it makes no sense without external norms') is not devoid of a noticeable philistine tone.

Why do we find these elementary considerations to be necessary? Stammler treats the externally obligatory norms of social life, among other things, as *forms of speech*. He bases his argument that there is no sociality without external norms on the fact that no systematic collaboration is possible without the aid of language, and, in his opinion, forms of language are such norms in themselves.

> Language, in this case, represents nothing other than *primary agreement*. A simple sound of the human voice does not thereby have any meaning – at any rate, no more meaning than any other sound a person makes. But a sound acquires social meaning as soon as everyone *must* denote it as something, since in this lies the idea (explicit or tacit) of conventional norm making (*W. und R.*, p. 103).
>
> ... grammatical laws are external conventional rules for mutual communication between people – *jus et norma loquendi*[3] – and have the same meaning for the expression thoughts as rules of politeness, propriety, and etiquette have for human behaviour (p. 104).

The reader can imagine this touching scenario. Some cavepeople gather together and enter into a 'primary agreement'. They establish 'conventional norms' – to call a person a 'person' and to decline the noun 'person' a certain way and to call a dog a 'dog' and decline 'dog' a certain way. This agreement might proceed 'openly' or 'silently'. The first is hard to imagine, since what language will they use to 'come to an agreement'? The second is also hard to imagine, since how can the agreement then make it into people's consciousness?

But, the Kantian reader contemptuously remarks, you simply don't understand Stammler; he is not talking about the *historical* fact of agreement at all, but about the *logical* meaning of forms of speech as conventional norms of communication between people. This objection is extremely 'critical' but, unfortunately, it simply clashes with logic. Logic above all requires that words be used in their *precise meaning*. It does not allow one to speak about conventional agreement where there is no kind of 'agreement', and about 'obligatory' norms where there are no necessary logical elements of this concept. And one cannot talk about such norms if there is no conception in the consciousness of people of the possibility of acting 'otherwise'. The development of language is a spontaneously organic phenomenon, like the development of any organ or

---

3 Law and rule of speaking [trans.].

reflex. A baby who says 'mama', hardly thinks that it could call the being closest to it by another name, but this would then violate the 'external legality' that requires 'conventional agreement'. When we, ourselves, speak or think in our native language, we also do not think about 'external legality'.

It goes without saying that it is another matter when the child learns a foreign language or the 'native' language as it is taught in educational institutions. Here, in reality, an 'external norm' with its fatal 'obligatoriness' and even 'compulsoriness' arrives on the scene. This compulsoriness sufficiently corresponds to its 'logical meaning' so that a peculiar type of teacher-sadist is often formed on its basis who enjoys the tears and sobbing of the children 'entrusted' to them. But if on this basis one considers the language one is born with – the language of our thoughts – an 'external norm' then walking on two feet must be considered the result of the same kind of norm, since it can be 'regulated from outside' as happens with training in marching.

Thus, Stammler's resolute assertion that systematic collaboration is impossible without external forms because it is impossible without forms of speech turns out not to be 'critical' because the assertion is based on a confusion and distortion of concepts. This is the result of the 'logical' analysis of the concept of 'external norms'. Meanwhile a 'genetic' investigation leads to still other, and more decisive, conclusions.

'What is the law? It was added because of transgressions'. This is what the Bible says.[4] This thought expresses more truly than anything else the historical meaning of everything 'external' – and not only external norms. The 'social norm' arrived on the scene only where the immediate harmony of social being was destroyed. Stammler includes *custom* as an external, normative form. This is far from the truth. In its pure, primary form, 'custom' is not at all a social form that is external to people. In the primeval group, custom has the character of social *habit*, even instinct; it was the same kind of organic adaptation, taking shape spontaneously, as, for example, language. People in primeval groups followed custom not at all because they were subordinated to its external compulsion but simply because they had become accustomed to behaving in precisely this way and could not conceive of the possibility of acting differently. One cannot speak of external compulsoriness here – or even of internal compulsoriness, either – the matter had to do simply with the factual organisation of people in which a given custom appeared as an integral element. The 'general social validity' of custom for human behaviour at this stage of development was every bit as immediate and full as it is for us – the 'general social valid-

---

4   Galatians 3:19 [trans.].

ity' of forms of thinking or speech that take shape and that we unconsciously acquire. For the stereotypical person of a clan group, a custom is just as much an external obligation as the laws of logic are 'customs' of thinking for us.

But sooner or later the Fall occurs: the 'monolithic member' of the clan commune ceases to be monolithic. Individual nuances – new needs and desires – appear and under their influence individual people sometimes diverge from a social habit – a 'custom' – that had taken shape. At first, this was simply incomprehensible to the other members of the group; it seemed to be a strange abnormality to them, something like a baby that has two heads or is all covered with hair. The person who violated a custom was not 'punished' but simply driven away or killed, just as there was no attempt to fix a baby with two heads, but it was simply thrown away. But to the extent that the violation of customs becomes more frequent, the necessity of a new form of adaptation arises. It is then that an 'external norm' is created that requires an 'external legality'. It is a testament to the fact that the system of collaboration has ceased to be harmoniously whole and that contradictions have arisen in social life. It is a patch on the torn fabric of people's social being.

At this stage of development, 'custom' loses its spontaneously organic character. It attains the colouration of *customary law*, and only due to such a change does it become an 'external norm' that did not exist earlier.

Thus, we see that collaboration that is organically whole and without external norms precedes – both logically and genetically – collaboration with external norms. Neither language nor primevally pure forms of custom imply 'external regulation'. From this perspective, since it does not embrace the entire sum of facts that require explanation, Stammler's concept of sociality must be recognised as unsatisfactory and insufficient.

But, on the other hand, might this concept not fully apply to all forms of sociality that are at all developed and so be completely sufficient for the study of *cultured societies*, precisely those that present the greatest vital interest for science? Then we would be able to set primeval organic collaboration to the side, designate it as a 'pre-social' phenomenon, and calmly follow Stammler in all questions regarding sociology of the cultured world. Let us see if this is so.

Stammler emphatically rejects the possibility of a society of people that is based exclusively on a *moral* interrelationship among them. This idea is completely natural for him, since he, as a Kantian, considers moral norms to be the 'internal legislation of an individual' and considers sociality as an interrelationship of the external regulation of life. But Stammler's very argumentation is full of strained interpretations – to be more precise, it consists only of strained interpretations. We have already become familiar with one of them, the assertion that language – a necessary means of communication for any form of collaboration – is an external norm requiring external legality. Another argument boils down to the following: the collaboration of human individuals with moral freedom is realised in one way or another through *agreement* among them, and this agreement is already 'external norm making'. The unfoundedness of this argument is obvious and needs no special analysis: if a *moral* ideal is placed at the basis of each agreement, and the obligatoriness of it for each of 'those who agree' is accepted as exclusively *moral* obligatoriness and as a question of 'moral duty', then how can we talk about a social regulation that is non-moral and has only an 'external' nature?

But we willingly yield 'ethical society' to Stammler. We are not interested in it for two reasons. First, from *our* point of view, it is historically impossible since it presupposes such a high level of cultural development that of course would turn out to be sufficient to overcome the fetishism of the 'absolute', and since this fetishism constitutes the necessary basis of any ethical norm making, then precisely 'ethical' norms would turn out to be utterly unsuitable for a society which in the level of its development *could* become ethical. Second, from *our* point of view, ethical norms are also external norms. We do not see in them the 'inner' legislation by an absolute 'I', but only one of the products of social development. We consider the compulsoriness of ethical norms – to the extent they stand in opposition to 'subjective inclinations and desires' – to be external compulsoriness in the same sense in which it is possible to talk about norms of propriety. The 'empirical' person is not an Absolute, and a command of the Absolute for that person is always an 'external' norm, just like the command, for example, of a personal god, a government, or social opinion.

So, we will not dwell on the contradictions into which Stammler falls regarding the question of 'ethical society'. Here he is only a victim of that cant which rules among the Kantians under the brand name of Kant.[5] We will examine the question of the limits of external norm making from another point of view.

External norms, as we have seen, appear on the scene when the harmony of collaboration breaks down, when contradictions are revealed in the social system. An external norm is an *organising adaptation* for society; it restores harmony. How? Not directly but indirectly. When acting in conformity to a norm, people come to an agreement among themselves. If discipline requires that a soldier instantly carry out a command, then following discipline and command a soldier will act identically with other soldiers and in complete harmony with them. In this way the harmony that is obtained is not full harmony, but,

---

5   *The Critique of Practical Reason, The Metaphysics of Morals,* and, in general, the entire conservative side of Kant's philosophical activity.

generally speaking, only external harmony: it coordinates the actions of people but not their feelings and wishes. As far as the norm is concerned, it makes no difference what motives there are for following it or whether it is willingly or unwillingly done. The mood of each soldier could be completely different from the mood of any of their comrades whatsoever; they nevertheless do the same thing. Internal disunity is concealed behind external unity.

Thus, social organisation is attained through external regulation only *by an indirect route* and *in an external manner*. This is utterly necessary, and it does not prevent external norms from having huge vital significance as far as the organisation of humanity in the struggle with hostile nature is concerned. But, all the same, must we accept that this makes no difference in practice?

In organising the activities of people only indirectly, a norm can never attain the kind of complete adaptation to reality that is obtained by a *direct* adaptation. The more complex reality becomes and the more varied and unexpected the obstacles that reality puts in the way of humanity, the more significant the fundamental drawbacks of all norms become. The programme of any given high-school class might be brilliantly put together, but nevertheless insofar as it is put into effect, it might exhaust the energy of those students whose psyches are comparatively dull and weak, it might not satisfy the intellectual needs of those who possess a particularly lively and supple frame of mind, and, for those students in whom different sides of the psyche are unequally developed, it might to a certain degree correspond to both deficiencies. Needless to say, things might be helped by various supplemental norms that would allow one or another deviation from the unity of the programme, but this would allow the goal to be reached only partially, and the individual traits of the students would always remain to a greater or lesser degree outside the regulatory norms and beyond the bounds of feasible action. The greatest conceivable adaptedness would be attained only if teachers possess a sufficiently rich and supple psyche to be able to completely understand each of their students in the entire uniqueness of their mental constitution, if they are not limited by external norms, and if they freely and directly adapt their activity to that uniqueness and thus impart to their students the lived experience of humanity. This would be a *directly creative* type of social activity, the direct opposite of the externally normed, inevitably conservative type that keeps within the bounds of norms.

Further, as we have said, the harmony that is achieved through external regulation has an inevitably external character. The uniting of human actions through 'external legality' can conceal very large differences in attitudes and motives – even attitudes and motives that are in direct contradiction. These differences and contradictions become more significant as social differentiation

proceeds, and meanwhile it is precisely the development of social differentiation that causes the *need* for external norms. Thus, the development of socially
normed life does not inevitably lead to where external harmony increasingly
corresponds to internal harmony. For contemporary cultured society, one could
sooner assert the opposite – that the hidden disharmony of social being is growing. And this has huge vital significance.

There is no need to especially prove that the more that the external unity
any collectivity *issues* from internal unity (and does not exist *despite* a lack of
internal unity) the more power it displays. When Roman legions transformed
into motley conglomerations of people of various races and nations and of various interests and desires, iron discipline turned out to be insufficient to save
them from defeat in the struggle with elementally whole barbarian hordes that
were tied together with the 'solid' psychology of clan life. The entire psychology of class domination and class antagonisms is based on the external nature
of 'normative' social unity: some groups of society create and support external
norms that suit themselves, other groups, who are subordinated to the power
of the former, observe 'external legality' in spite of their own basic inclinations
and desires, but to the extent it is possible they carry on a struggle against the
former and their norms. As a result, society lacks internal unity. It is a class
society, and a great deal of social energy is expended not on the struggle with
external nature but with manifest social conflicts and latent social contradictions. In short, the external nature of social norms signifies, in any event, that
the unity of elements of society is far from complete or harmonious. And in this
regard also external normative unity is the direct opposite of the unity that is
achieved through immediate, conscious, and free mutual adaptation of people
in their striving toward common goals.

External norms are always conservative, and they thereby strengthen the
conservatism of the human psyche. This conservatism creates unnecessary res-
istances to any change of norms that are caused by the needs of life. They consequently also create unnecessary expenditures of energy. History shows that
both in the sphere of law and in the sphere of propriety, custom, etc. norms that
are essentially needed by no one often survive for a long time and needlessly
inhibit many people. Certain ludicrous remnants of feudal law in eighteenth-
century France could hardly have been more upsetting to the peasantry than
suzerain rights that were upsetting precisely because of their pointlessness and
especially since they really meant nothing to the feudal lords. And unnecessary
formalities – to whom are they useful or desirable in our times? And yet this
does not prevent them from surviving.

Just the opposite, direct and free conscious adaptation of people to one
another is fundamentally alien to such conservatism. Manifestations of such

adaptation easily change in accordance with changing conditions. Human creative work unfolds freely in it, and this is precisely why we call this type the 'creative' type of adaptation.

This this is all very well, says the astute reader, but what does it prove? After all, Stammler admits that in many cases it is better to do without unnecessary norm making, allowing people to settle their own affairs in accordance with their individual motives and inclinations, but this does not depart from his basic position that 'sociality' is inconceivable without external regulation. From the preceding discussion, of course, certain fundamental deficiencies can be seen in this regulation, but what is not seen is how any developed system of collaboration could altogether manage without it. For example, the illustration from the sphere of school life provided above points out only that more freedom should be introduced into these relationships, but the basic relationship – of student and teacher – is already assumed, and it is already an external norm. We can admit that everything cannot be confined to external norms, but must we not admit, along with Stammler, that something that is precisely 'specifically social' in phenomena is hidden here?

We have tried to show that in the process of joint labour, there are *two different types* of mutual adaptation of people: immediate, freely conscious coordination and indirect, externally normative coordination. We can leave unanswered the question of whether or not it is possible for a society to be organised exclusively according to the first type without any externally normative elements. To us – people of an era of external norms – it is in any event difficult to conceive of such organisation. But for us only one thing is important: both types of coordination of people can in fact *replace* one another in one or another concrete manifestation of collaboration. Whatever has been realised through immediate coordination could subsequently be carried out through normative organisation and vice versa. Such a change is not always practically possible. It depends on the nature of the people who are united together, on the concrete goal for which they have united together, and in part even simply on how many people there are. This is not changed by what is most important: that the social relationship among people when they act together does not boil down only to a form of 'external regulation' with the help of 'externally obligatory norms'; this relationship is also manifested in another form – immediate coordination.

But perhaps this second form should not be considered 'social' or, at least, 'socially deterministic'. Of course, all terms are subject to convention and if someone does not want to apply the term 'social' to immediate collaboration, they cannot be forced to do so. But in that case the real, historical meaning of the concept would be completely eliminated. We see that wherever it is possible, the fullest coordination and most harmonious unification of human *activity* is attained precisely in immediate collaboration, whereas under normative collaboration unity is less perfect and the interconnectedness of people is less complete. And if the expression 'sociality' is applicable to the second type of collaboration, it is much more applicable to the first. This aspect of the matter is sufficiently clear in itself and cannot be doubted. More doubtful, at first glance, is the question of whether or not 'social regularity' is inherent in immediate collaboration, which is the only thing that should interest social science.

From Stammler's point of view, the actions of people only conform to social regularity if they are regulated by an external norm. If there is no norm, the actions of people – no matter how 'social' their goal – are 'socially fortuitous'. Their actions depend on individual motives and inclinations, on individual peculiarities – on conditions devoid of social regularity. Such regularity is brought into human acts only by an external norm that does not take into consideration individual conditions, that does not depend on them, that is as if 'abstracted' from them, and that prescribes to people one or another form of action. The acts of people who are subordinated to norms cease to be conditioned by causes of a fortuitous, individual nature – and this makes them 'not fortuitous' and subject to social regularity.

At the basis of this reasoning lies the mistake that was recognised earlier – the idea that everything other than 'external norms' is nothing but 'individual' and 'fortuitous'. Meanwhile, this is not so. Something else exists that is able to bring regularity into the social life of people to a much greater degree than external norms, and this something is *collective experience*. Collaboration is inseparable from the commonality of experiences. Social labour means social experience. The human psyche is a product of the life of social labour, and no matter how 'individual' it is, a multitude of threads continuously tie it together with the psyches of other people. The basic similarity of biological organisation, the same spontaneous forces of external nature that people struggle against and overcome, the constant exchange of thoughts and impressions – all of these things form a massive amount of common experiences in the life of any given society (and, in particular, of a given class, of a given social group). And compared with these common experiences, what is 'individual' and 'fortuitous' in the experience of individual people is comparatively insignificant. Common experience engenders common goals and common methods of action that all the more clearly and obviously testify to the 'class psychology' of people. This is what constitutes the real basis of 'social regularity'. In regard to external norms, they are, from the point of view of each separate human individual, only a part of this common experience, and that experience is a necessary 'premise' of external norms. Without it, they are simply inconceivable, since they are inconceivable without the mutual understanding of people and the commonality of their basic, vital goals.

We must decisively reject the exclusively normative concept of 'sociality' that constitutes the basis of all of Stammler's conclusions. External norms, in general, and legal norms (which are basic among them), in particular, make up only one of the types of human social adaptation. Such norms must necessarily have arrived on the scene with the appearance of social differentiation, and they must have developed together with it over a long period of time. In this period of culture, external norms appeared in the necessary form of the *broad* unification of people in the struggle with the spontaneity of external nature and of social nature. But along with those norms the other type of social coordination – the immediate conscious adaptation of people in the process of joint activity – never completely disappeared. The more the experience of individual people became fundamentally heterogeneous, the less they mutually understood one another, and the more different their interests and desires, the more the second type of social coordination retreated in the face of the first. We can suppose – and life provides many indications of this – that the further development of humanity will bring with it a new harmonisation of the experience of different people. The narrowness of specialisation is disappearing little by little, and human individuality is becoming integrated. Through broad communication and the unifying methods of cognition, the experience of individual people will broaden to the extent that each will become a real 'microcosm' of social experience. With all the variety in the concrete content of people's experience, each person will be able to understand everyone else. The breadth of the common goals of humanity will be distinctly reflected in each human psyche, contradictions of personal desires will be removed, and the space for a diversity of desires will be left behind. Then the normative type of life must once again give way to the immediate, freely creative coordination of human labour. The old conservative norms will become superfluous and unnecessary, just as heavy, stationary rails are of no use for those who are able to once and for all overcome the force of gravity and are freely and lightly carried into the air.

The long and the short of it is that the collaboration of people is not just 'material' for external norms and, by the same token, that external norms are not the universal form of sociality. The process of social struggle with nature engenders various social adaptations, and external norms are one of them. It is true that such norms have huge vital significance within the scope of the history of humanity that we know, but, all the same, they are not *exclusively* important. Often the same combination of labour actions of different people can, in some cases, be the result of direct, immediate coordination, while, in other cases, they can be the result of external regulation. Moreover, they can sometimes appear in one of these forms and sometimes in the other – for example, in the form of a legal norm or in the form of a conventional agreement. All this permits economists who are investigating collaboration, when necessary, to *pay no attention at all* to the external norms that regulate people's labour. They then see 'productive relationships' in their pure form and as they are objectively manifested to an outside observer who knows nothing about the 'external obligatoriness' or 'external legality' in these relationships.

Stammler's system of socio-philosophical views, as a whole, is constructed in an extremely logical manner, and, precisely for that reason, since its basic position is wrong, it must inevitably collapse. We have no need, therefore, to specially retrace and analyse Stammler's further conclusions in their entire succession. We will limit myself to those conclusions that he directs against the theory of historical materialism.

From Stammler's perspective, the view of legal life as one of the superstructures of social economy naturally appears as the fruit of 'theoretical lack of clarity' and 'lack of careful consideration'. Legal 'form' in his opinion, can no more be a superstructure upon socio-economic 'matter', than, let us say, the external shape of the body is the superstructure over its substance. We have already sufficiently explained the misunderstanding that this consists in: law with its norms is not at all a 'constitutive feature' that is a part of the very concept of social economy but is one of the real adaptations that are generated by social labour life – an adaptation that appears at a specific stage of development and that under specific conditions progresses or degrades. Stammler's mistake is explained to a significant degree by two circumstances: first, that we live in an era of colossal development of legal life, and, second, that the law itself is in its very content an *organising adaptation* of social life. For any commodity-producing society – and especially for capitalism – law is the really unavoidable 'constitutive' sign, the social form without which it cannot exist, which holds its contradictory elements in check. Without the compulsory force of law, capitalism, because of its basic lack of organisation, would instantly fall apart like a barrel without hoops. Stammler has taken the specific conditions of commodity-producing society as the universal conditions of any social life whatsoever – a typical mistake in the ideologies of ruling classes.

But even in contemporary life, law is not the only externally organised adaptation. Norms of custom and also norms of morality, which Stammler fundamentally contrasts with legal norms, have essentially the same significance. And all these forms have their 'premise' in *internally organised* adaptations – in language and in cognition. Language creates the conditions for people to communicate with and mutually understand one another, and without this rational collaboration would be inconceivable. Cognition directly unifies and harmonises collective experience, which defines the methods of all subsequent collective labour. In this sense, *an entire ideology* must be viewed as a system of socially organised adaptations. And at the same time an ideology is a system of *superstructures* over the process of social labour, since it arises from the attainments and needs of that process, serves it, and is vitally conditioned by it.

The very form of the relationship of the 'basis' and 'superstructure' has perplexed many critics of historical monism. If this is a causal relationship, they reason, then why do ideological superstructures not change *immediately after* the economic basis changes and *in proportion* to its change, and how can it 'survive' its basis and start to contradict it. Their perplexity will be easily removed if they recall that what we observe is a form of causality that is characteristic of any *development of life*. Any form of life is conservative and 'outlives' the real conditions upon which it took shape. Biology knows a great many cases where organs outlive their function or where the function of an organ, even though it survives, becomes of no use for life and even harmful for the organism. Ideological forms are also forms of life – forms of the adaptation of life – and also are really conservative and capable of outliving the vital conditions that originally generated them. In this regard, norms of law would seem to yield only to forms of custom and moral consciousness.

From Stammler's point of view, naturally, a contradiction between the economy and the law is impossible: both are inseparable for him, as the material and the form of social life. The question of a contradiction between the economy and the law simply does not exist for Stammler. But after everything that has been explained, we cannot see any considerations that have fundamentally resolved this question. From our point of view, a contradiction between the economy and the law is not only conceivable, but under some conditions it is vitally necessary. It is the lack of correspondence between basic primary developing functions of the social organism and one of its secondary, derivative functions. But with certain moderate followers of Stammler, one can encounter his basic idea of the link between economy and law in a weakened, eclectically ameliorated form, in which the method of argument against the ideas of historical monism is correspondingly changed. In this regard, the views of Mr Struve can be of special interest to a Russian reader.

Since the article by Mr Struve that offers a critique of the foundations of historical materialism is not particularly distinguished as far as clarity is concerned, We will state his basic propositions, staying as true to the text as possible.[6]

---

6 'Die Marx'sche Theorie der socialen Entwicklung', P. von Struve, *Braun's Archiv f. soc. Gesetzgebung*, 1899.

The central point in Marx's theory of social development is the correlation – properly, the contradiction – between the economy and the law. Marx recognised the economy as the cause and law as the effect. But Stammler brilliantly showed that from a logical point of view (*logischerweise*) it is utterly impossible to conceive of the relationship between a given economy and a given law (*die Wirthschaft und das Recht*) as the relationship of what does the conditioning to what is conditioned. The proper expression for the relationship between the two should rather be the relationship of content to form (of 'regulated material' to its 'conditioning form' ...) (p. 667).

It would seem that Mr Struve has adopted the point of view of Stammler. However, it then turns out that he has not completely adopted it. 'The social phenomena that can be considered to be economic phenomena *do not always* represent socially regulated relationships' ... (p. 669).

The category of 'content-form' is far from sufficient to reduce this multifarious relationship (of economy and law) to one formula. This formula leads to the rejection of a genetic, causal relationship between individual economic and individual legal phenomena; it does not allow the possibility of socio-economic acts, independent of legal regulation ... (p. 668).

But if this is so, then how can Stammler be used to disprove Marx? Even if Stammler 'brilliantly showed that a given economy was regulated by a given law' – probably no one ever knew of such a thing before him – why does it follow *from this* that Marx was wrong to recognise the social economy as a cause and law as a result? The preceding economic life of a society *causally conditioned* the appearance of such-and-such norms of law, and they, while they exist, *regulate* subsequent social life. What kind of contradiction is there in this? And why '*logischerweise*' is the latter made into an objection against the former? (*Es ist aber von St. treffend ausgeführt u.s.w.*)? If my life experience brought me to where I produced certain practical and cognitive norms for myself, and my subsequent experience is regulated by them, must I not think that this is the result of previous experience? It is clear that the objection that exists here is only grammatical and not '*logischerweise*'.

Nevertheless, quite a lot from Stammler remains with Mr Struve:

That the economy, as a whole, cannot exert an influence on law, as a whole, follows from the fact that both generalised concepts (*Gesammtbegriffe*) express the same real substrate: 'law is already contained in the economy, and vice versa' (p. 669).

CHAPTER 14

As opposed to Marx and his formula of contradiction, we can advance the consideration that, according to the basic outlook of 'historical materialism', the antagonism of individual concrete economic phenomena with individual legal provisions inevitably leads to the overcoming of this very antagonism. The conception that the system of law as a whole might not correspond to the social economy as a whole is not realistic: legal organisation and social economy are abstract concepts; they are not reality and not a relationship (p. 671).

In all the quoted propositions of Marx (regarding the relationship of productive forces to industrial relations and to ideology, A.B.) there is the following obscurity: material productive forces, on the one hand, and relations of production, on the other, present themselves as nothing more than abstract expressions for the totality of concrete economic and legal relationships that are elevated to the rank of independent, particular realities or 'things'. Only because of this does it become possible to conceive of them as a whole as either corresponding to or contradicting one another ... (p. 666).

Thus, on the one hand, in the opinion of Mr Struve, Stammler's opinion that the economy and law are inseparable is wrong (and that there can be economic relationships without legal relationships), and, on the other hand, that the economy and law as a whole are inseparable, since they have the same substrate: law is already contained in the economy and economy in the law. And later he says that individual economic and individual legal phenomena really exist and can be antagonistic but that the economy and the law as a whole do not really exist and cannot be antagonistic, since they are abstract designations for the *totality* of concrete economic and legal phenomena. Such is Mr Struve's logic.

    Let us take a look at the individual propositions of this astonishingly coherent conception. 'The economy already contains law, and vice versa', and 'their substrate is the same'. That the social economy, taken in the total meaning of the word, comprises a system of legal relationships, is quite true for commodity societies that we know of in history. For example, the capitalist economic system is utterly inseparable from specific property relationships and necessarily assumes them. But, truthfully speaking, it is difficult to understand how a legal organisation can 'contain' all economic phenomena in all their concreteness. How can the system of legal norms of contemporary society wholly contain the fact that such-and-such a capitalist expands production, and the workers in that factory thereupon talk about a raise in pay? Law regulates these facts, places them within certain boundaries, guarantees that they will be realised without restraint, etc. But in order for law to 'contain' (*enthalten*) the fact of development of productive forces and relations of production – this is utterly beyond belief.

This is obviously a play on the word '*enthalten*'. The law 'contains' the social economy in the sense that it forms its factual limits but not at all in the sense that the economic content of life of society is identical with the legal content. The development of the productive forces of society is not at all the same thing as a particular activity that is intended to regulate those forces. The possibility that the forces of development can contradict a fundamentally conservative system of norms that contains and regulate those forces of development is so obvious that for Mr Struve, of course, there is nothing he can do other than to declare this possibility 'unrealistic'.

A strange thing! Less than half a century ago serfdom still existed in Russia, and our times are still full of reminders and even partial remnants of it. A legal system, as a whole, was constructed on it at that time, and serfdom was its basic, defining principle. But productive forces grew, they were cramped by the bounds of serfdom, and they needed new forms of life and a new legal organisation. It would seem that this is a classic example of a contradiction between economic and legal life, and an example that is so close and familiar to us. And what of it? Mr Struve declares that it is 'unrealistic'. With the aid of a few banal terms, like 'substrate', 'realistic', 'critical', etc., the greatest historical facts are calmly eliminated and 'disproven'.

However, is not Mr Struve correct when he proposes that 'the adaptation of law to the social economy does not cease even for a minute, and the development of economic phenomena not only occurs within the bounds of the old social order but also transforms and extends those bounds'? Well why not! This is approximately true, and, for example, in feudal Russia small 'adaptations' of the law to developing productive life were made here and there. But if this is so, then what kind of contradiction is there between 'law' and 'economy' as a whole? This, apparently, is out of the question? *This could not be*, if all life consisted of the kind of individual small pieces into which it is splintered in the mosaic thinking of Messrs Struve, Bernstein, and their ilk. But life is an organic whole and the system of feudal law could not be eliminated through the tiny little adaptations on which the Struves and Bernsteins of that time placed their hopes. Any adaptation is accomplished *within the bounds* of a given legal structure and is limited *in its bases*, and such an adaptation therefore cannot even weaken the contradictions between these bases and developing life. How should the peasant reform occur according to Mr Struve? Give peasants a little bit of freedom and little pieces of land today, do the same tomorrow, and so, gradually, after 500 years, there will be no more serf system, and no one will have seen where it disappeared. This could hardly be less 'realistic'.

Nevertheless, for Mr Struve the word 'realistic' has a completely special and very original meaning. He proposes, for example, that in the 1840s altogether no kind of social optimism was realistic, only social pessimism was realistic, and at worst – '*der Zerstörungssozialismus*'[7] (p. 662). Consequently, in those times, a 'realist' could not believe in the possibility of social development, could not find any elements of development in life, and did not have the right to point out those elements. If Marx did all this, then it was only by virtue of his utopianism. But, as we know, Marx *factually* and accurately pointed out the elements of development and the classes that were the bearers of them. As we know, development was *factually* accomplished, and Mr Struve's 'realist' was *factually* disproved by real life. After this, what does it mean to 'be a realist'? Evidently, from Mr Struve's point of view it means to see no farther than your nose. If it is in this sense that Mr Struve rejects the realism of the theory of the intensification of fundamental contradictions, then perhaps he is right, and his own theory of the 'blunting' of contradictions is then actually 'realistic' ...

But here is life ... It stubbornly does not want to be 'realistic'. Perhaps it is a secret 'Marxist'? Who knows? In any event, in the years that followed, life harshly mocked the 'blunting' of the Bernsteinians. Mr Struve proved very well, with the aid of a great many arguments, the very best terminology, and even special diagrams, that there were no obstacles to the 'blunting' of the great antagonisms. But life paid no attention to this and behaved *just the opposite*. And life treated Bernstein in just the same way when he found that for a 'rigorous realist' there were insufficient grounds to expect new general crises of production. Life answered this with precisely such a crisis and a huge crisis at that!

In Mr Struve's arguments regarding the blunting of contradictions, there is one small drawback. To be precise, he comes at it not from an historical but from an 'epistemological' point of view. He does not deal with real contradictions but with concepts and formulas, with various 'contradictions in general'. This is now called 'criticism', but in the future it will be called 'scholasticism'. This sort of thing can be used to mesmerise oneself and many others, but it cannot explain things. From an historical point of view, its essence is quite simple and boils down to the following. If two great classes develop in mutually contradictory directions – one, to be precise, in the direction of production, and the other, let us say, in the direction of 'consumption' – then each new step on the path of development rends an ever greater chasm between

---

7   The destruction of socialism [trans.].

their vital interests and strivings. An about face in the other direction becomes increasingly less possible for each of them, and the 'blunting of contradictions' becomes an increasingly more pitiable 'sober utopia'. It is possible, of course, that the weapon of either of the two classes might become blunt, but in no way will the opposition of their basic interests do so. That opposition can only grow. Life is not a kindly eclectic; it is severe and consistent in its logic. It files all daydreams away in the 'archive'.

But enough about Struve's article in *Braun's Archiv*. Let us turn to the original source – to Stammler's ideas. The second part of his work, *Wirtschaft und Recht*, is devoted to the question of the *fundamental regularity of society*. It is an attempt to apply the fundamental ideas of Kant's *Critique of Practical Reason* to the theory of social life. To examine the very foundations of this aspect of Stammler's views would mean first and foremost to subject the entire theory of 'practical reason' to critique. There is no room to do this here, and we will limit ourselves to what is most closely related to the critique of historical materialism.

Stammler proposes that two different kinds of regularity exist in human experience. One relates to the realm of cognition, the other relates to the realm of will – the regularities of theoretical reason and of practical reason. The essence of them both consists in the reduction of all the material of human experience to a systematic unity, the ascertainment of 'objective interconnectedness' in each of them. When people 'cognise' phenomena, they strive to unite them in their consciousness in such a way as to correspond not to random, 'subjective' experiences, in which there is so much that is illusory, but to their 'objective' conformity to regularity. Based on this regularity, a person connects the uncoordinated scraps of their experience into one harmonious whole, into one continuous chain of links spliced together by the highest necessity that flows from the very foundations of the cognitive organisation of a human being. This chain is a chain of causes and effects, and the objective regularity in the sphere of cognition is the universal principle of causality. To the extent that one succeeds in correctly unifying this regularity, one arrives at the *truth*. This is what relationships in the realm of cognition are like and what Stammler finds completely analogous relationships in the realm of will.

In Stammler's opinion, each individual goal that people set themselves, as their consciousness develops, necessarily becomes the *means* for another, broader and more general goal, and this goal, in its turn, becomes the means for yet another, and so on. Thus, an unwinding chain of goals and means is obtained in the realm of the will, just as there is a chain of causes and effects in the realm of theoretical cognition. The first is ruled by the regularity of the telos of expedience, just as the second is ruled by the regularity of the causal relationship. And just as both 'subjective' and false conceptions and 'objective' and correct conceptions are possible in cognition, so desires that are both purely subjective and false and desires that are objectively valid are possible. In the world of cognition, what is objectively correct is *true*, and, in the world of will, what is objectively correct is what is *obligatory*. The task for cognisers consists in singling out of the motley fabric of experiences that follow one after another what is true from what is apparent, what is objective from what is subjective. When people feel desires, their task consists in singling out and delimiting objective, 'obligatory' goals – the truth of the will – from the material of random and subjective desires. And if they can prove the objective truth of their conceptions to other people, then they can also prove the objective correctness of their desires. In the first case, the inviolable and universally valid laws of logic are the judge; in the second case the similarly inviolable and universally valid demands of moral duty are. In both cases, people can err in their opinion and evidence, but this does not change the objective meaning of the very principles of what is true and what is obligatory.

In a similar manner practical reason emerges in parallel with theoretical reason: causal regularity along with the regularity of goals, the kingdom of truth along with the kingdom of duty. In both realms what is objectively correct is established by means of systematic *investigation* and *scientific explanation*. Yes, *scientific* explanation even in the realm of will! Stammler more than once uses the term '*wissenschaftlich*'[8] and speaks of '*Erkenntnisswerth*'[9] of the point of view of the regularity of will.

The fact of the matter is that with Stammler practical reason often is so carried away with its own 'rationality' that it forgets its 'practical' character and begins to seriously compete with theoretical reason. Practical reason not only adopts the 'scientific' exterior of the latter but also tries to limit its freedom, keeping in mind, of course, its own primacy by the grace of Kant. That is to say, in those cases when something is treated as the object of a desire ('*als zu bewirkende*') it is, in Stammler's opinion, thereby already taken out from under the rule of theoretical reason and its law of causality. This is said not in the sense of the undeniable truth that in the case of will, as such, there is no room for cognition but in the sense that, from the point of view of telos, this particular cognition *precludes* usual cognition as far as causality is concerned. Stammler proposes that it is impossible to simultaneously recognise any phenomenon as causally *necessary* in the future and at the same time make it one's *goal* that

---

8   Scientific [trans.]
9   Cognitive value [trans.]

one actively strives toward. If we want something and strive after it, we thereby recognise that this 'something' either could or could not be – that it lies outside a causal chain, that it *is theoretically not inevitable*. Thus, a Kantian finds a certain *theoretical* element in a volitional experience (*'Wollen, Streben'*) even if it is of a negative character – the recognition that what is desired stands outside causal regularity. In the opinion of a Kantian, it is impossible to wish for what is 'causally necessary'. The regularity of telos is jealous and exclusive; it cannot bear to be *alongside* causal regularity, and it turns away in indignation as soon as it encounters the latter.

Here is the central point of Stammler's views regarding the question of the relation of cognition to practical activity; this is also the starting point of his objection against the form of active idealism that characterises the advocates of historical monism. As is well known, historical monists propose that the social structure that they make their practical ideal must replace capitalism by virtue of *the necessity of social development*. They find evidence of this by analysing those tendencies of social development that can be factually established in regard to the contemporary social structure as a whole and in regard to its separate classes. Stammler thinks that this uniting of a social ideal with the idea of historical necessity is a fundamental contradiction within Marxism.

Stammler justly proposes that all practical ideals – and social ideals among them – lie in the realm of active desires – in the realm of *goals*. But from this he draws the conclusion, based on the ideas of the two regularities of experience that have been presented above, that the social ideal consequently lies *outside the realm of historical necessity* and outside the sphere of *causality* altogether. In his opinion, to recognise the historical necessity of the appearance of a new structure in place of what exists and at the same time to actively strive toward that structure is essentially no different from some political party taking as the basis of their programme a lunar eclipse that had previously been predicted by astronomers. A practical ideal, once it belongs to the sphere of the will, can be recognised exclusively from the point of view of *its* particular regularity, and this regularity is a *moral requirement* and not causality. A practical ideal must therefore not be recognised as something that is historically necessary at a certain stage of development of society, but only as something *obligatory* that we are called upon to realise but that in itself might or might not be. If there is historical necessity, our interference in the course of events makes no difference; if our interference is required, this means that there is no historical necessity. Stammler considers this dilemma to be utterly inescapable and does not admit the possibility of any third thing outside it.

We can see that all this is a completely logical conclusion from the idea that practical reason conflicts with theoretical reason, and, as we have pointed out, this idea consists in the fact that to want something means not only to 'want' but also to recognise something – to be precise, to recognise that what is desired is located outside of objective historical necessity. But how accurate is this idea? To answer this question, let us turn to the immediate experience to which Stammler refers.

Our experience teaches that a feeling is the decisive authority in the question of 'desires'. We desire what is pleasant and gives us pleasure, and we do not desire what is unpleasant and causes pain. When different motives struggle in consciousness, the power and the possibility of victory of each of them is determined by the force of the feeling that lies at its basis. The process of 'choice', or, what is the same thing, the state of indecision, boils down to the fact that neither of the differently-directed motives possesses a *sufficient preponderance* of force – of the force of the feeling connected with it, to be precise – in order to overcome the inertia of the psychical whole. As soon as such a preponderance of feeling appears, the decision is determined and the choice is made. As long as the struggle of motives continues, their force still does not become clear, and a person would declare that either one of the two resolutions was 'possible'.

But 'choice' is not always involved. Sometimes, a spontaneously powerful burst of feeling takes immediate possession of the psyche and immediately determines the goal of action; a person 'gives in' to an unrestrainable impulse of love, hatred, attraction, or repulsion. Ask such a person about their mental state then, and they will tell you that it was *impossible* for them to strive toward anything other than the goal toward which the given feeling directed them. In this way, this person simultaneously had an intense desire and the consciousness that this desire was organically necessary – that the goal of the desire was *causally* conditioned – and that if there were no other external *causes* that interfered with them, the attainment of the goal would also, yet again, be necessary in the sense of *causal* regularity. In so doing, it would never occur to such a person that their mental state was absurd – that it is impossible to actively strive toward something that had become a goal by virtue of organic necessity.

But let us leave these people who are 'blinded by passion', who, of course, only by virtue of the insufficiency of 'critique' makes their goal something that they cannot not desire. Let us pass on to more conscious people who 'chose' and already arrived at a decision. The entire psychological process of choice and the act of decision already relates to the past as far as they are concerned, and, consequently, as Stammler recognises, the choice and decision have 'entered' the general causal series. Subsequent actions of the people who have made the decision are *causally* determined by this very decision, and the attainment of the goal is causally determined by these actions. In this way, if they begin to reflect on their position, then in all conscience they must admit that they are striving toward a 'lunar eclipse' – to what will be realised by virtue of causal regularity previously known to them. Of course, it may be that their actions did not attain the goal, or, perhaps, they themselves changed their decision, but both the one and the other cannot occur without a cause and necessarily because of some kind of external causes that interfere in the course of things and that they have not yet foreseen. After all, due to some kind of unforeseen events in the solar system, a lunar eclipse might not take place. In regard to the question of a lunar eclipse, they and any decision that they make is a quantité négligeable, but in the question of them setting a goal, they are a significant quantity, and, since this quantity already belongs to a causal chain, this does not change anything in the fundamental meaning of causal regularity.

All right, suppose this is so. But is it not true that until the time that a decision is made a person recognises that in making the decision two courses of events are after all possible, and consequently they do accept it as something that is necessarily caused? And people surely do not say to themselves: both my decision and all decisions that follow occur in conformity to the law of causality. This general formula is of no use at all to them as long as they do not know *precisely how* the causal regularity was determined. But rejecting the causal conditioning of their subsequent decision is also of no interest to them; it is every bit as pointless a pursuit. They simply experience a 'non-theoretical', emotionally volitional mental state. The principle of causality does not direct them but neither is it subject to limitation; it is simply outside their field of consciousness. But, from a from the point of view of one who cognises it – for example another person who is keeping an eye on this struggle of motives by observing the person's utterances – the matter occurs in strict correspondence with causal regularity, and, based on this, this other person can even guess what the decision will be while the person who is making up their mind is still vacillating.

Stammler's mistake is that, in his desire to discover a temporal rejection of causal necessity, he tries to draw a logical and, consequently, theoretical conclusion from a *volitional* state. This is an error that goes against logic and against experience.

But let us return to Stammler's opponents. They strive toward a particular structure of social life. Why? Probably because it is pleasing to them. No, says, Stammler, they do not think this. According to their own pronouncements, they strive toward this structure because it is an approaching historical necessity. Stammler errs, as even very conscientious thinkers often err, when they expound the ideas of their opponents.

Here is what these opponents say. 'Our ideal is such-and-such. We do not doubt that it will be realised because historical development is leading toward it'. If something is called one's ideal, then this shows with sufficient clarity that this such-and-such is a goal that is striven toward *because it is pleasing*. If they subsequently make reference to the objective course of historical development, then what they mean is that they have a powerful ally on their side in the form of the spontaneous forces of history, an ally whose voice will be decisive. This is the practical point of view regarding an ideal. When one takes a *cognitive* point of view, one finds that both the formulation of the ideal and the striving toward it are expressions of the progressive tendencies of historical development. 'Our idealism, our tasks', say these fanatics of objectivism, 'are causally conditioned by the course of historical development as the ideological reflection of its progressive tendencies'. What? You look at what is most sacred to you – your ideals and your idealism – from the point of view of causality? 'Yes, when we relate to them *in cognitive* terms, and in so doing we are only carrying out the precept: know thyself. And when we relate to our ideals in practical terms, we act by trying to realise them. It pleases us to be agents and exponents of the progressive forces of development'. But what does your labour matter if your ideal must be realised without it? 'My personal actions, of course, will not resolve the matter, but they will enter as a positive addend to the general sum of causes that will lead to my ideal. I would rather be an active person than an idler, and it would please me more to be a positive quantity in the chain of development than a negative quantity or a zero. Imagine that you see a person who is carrying a great weight for a long distance. You know that there is no absolute duty and no moral world order. You know that vital necessity forces them to bear their burden, and you know that they have the strength to carry it to the end, even at the cost of great exhaustion. Would it be so strange if you wanted to share their labour? Would you be obligated to stand with your arms folded only because the matter would surely be carried out to the end without you? This is our practical relationship to social development: to lighten the labour, to lessen the sacrifice and weariness, to strive so that more forces and elements of development would bring society to a new phase of its life, so that society can take advantage of life as fully as possible. We are not at all saying that you *are obligated* to do the same. Questions of "duty" are not very comprehensible to us and are not particularly interesting. But we reserve the right to categorise you as a plus, a minus, or a zero as far as social development is concerned'.

This is what the aforesaid fanatics say, and they are immediately rebuked by Stammler and other 'social idealists' of the school of natural law. 'What kind of fetish is this "social development"? Why do we make it our goal? Prove – based on the regularity of the will – that it is objectively correct, that it is a "proper" goal and not random, subjective, and false. Then you will have convinced us'. To this are added the following kind of considerations. In favour of social development, it is of course possible to say that it leads to the growth of the vital capacity of society. But what comes from this? 'Greater vital capacity and adaptedness are not at all the same as better and ethically valuable. One need only recall the example from natural science cited from Huxley – under certain conditions of development lichens could turn out to be the most adapted to life everywhere. All this has been repeated many times and hardly needs a detailed explanation'.[10]

Alas, it is actually needed very much – as usually happens when Messrs epistemologists and jurists make reference to biology, which they endure rather than respect and which they study hardly at all. Mr Novgorodtsev, like many of his predecessors using the 'ethical-biological argument', confuses two very different things: 'adaptability in general' and 'increase in vital capacity'. *Adaptability* expresses the relationship of an organism to a given, specific environment; an organism, species, etc. is adapted to a given environment if it survives and reproduces and does not die out and, consequently, adequately corresponds to this precise environment. *Vital capacity* is a relationship not only to a given environment, but also to all possible changes of the environment; an organism, species, etc. has vital capacity if it easily adapts to any variations in conditions and successfully reacts not only to the usual but also to any new influences of the environment. A parasite is adapted to a given environment – to the specific tissues of the organism that it is parasitic upon, but its vital capacity is almost infinitely small, since it is tied to an infinitely narrow environment and sometimes requires millions of generations for it to be adapted to even minimal variations of the conditions that are unusual for it. Therefore, with many adapted species of lower organisms – i.e. they have not at all died out – of billions of embryos only those individuals factually develop that have found a *completely* suitable combination of conditions. Just the opposite, in the whole biological world human beings have the most vital capacity because they are able to create expedient reactions for the most varied and variable conditions, because the realm of their victory of life is the widest. From the point of view of vital capacity, there is no reason for humanity to fear 'lichens'.

Vital capacity depends on the quantity of *elements of development* that a given form of life contains, the degree of richness and plasticity of the material for adaptation that it has at its disposal. And this material consists of already existing adaptations. Thus, the maximum vital capacity boils down to the max-

---

10   *Problemy idealizma*, article by P. Novgorodtsev, p. 264. [Poole 2003, p. 293 (trans.).]

imal variety of adaptations, the maximal energy of their actions, and their maximal versatility; in other words, it is identical with the *maximum of life*.

Frequently, so-called 'regressive development' is encountered in nature, when an organism loses part of the adaptations that had been previously developed – part of its elements of development – because during a *particular* long period when the environment was stable they were not necessary. The atrophy of organs of sight of fish and amphibians that live in underground lakes can serve as an example. In such a case, an increase in adaptedness is attained alongside a decrease in vital capacity. The sphere of life is narrowed, and it takes only a small change of circumstances, only a small broadening of the system of external influences, for the unfortunate atrophication to turn out to be decisively unadaptive. Temporary stability, purchased at the cost of the reduction of life, is transformed into ever greater instability; regressive development turns out to be internally contradictory and is a step toward degradation. *Progressive* development, in which the sum of life and the variety of its elements continuously grow, constantly broadens its basis and strengthens its material and the plasticity of its material; it is has no internal contradictions.

And now humanity has progressively developed over so many centuries, its life has become fuller and more diversified, and elements of possible progress are accumulating ... Is it possible that this does not speak in support of those who propose that further progressive development will continue and who suggest that attention be paid to the possible paths of this development? But for people whose entire interest consists not in life that is eternally progressing but in something else, all these indications cannot, of course, have fundamental significance. Such people can say, 'all this makes no difference to me', and it is useless to try to convince them, since their point of view is based on feeling, and feeling is not knowledge and is not susceptible of proof. This, however, does not give them the right to distort the views of their opponents and replace the ideal of the endless growth of life with the ideal of the stationary adaptedness of life to a given limited environment.

Stammler proposes that an ideal can be 'proven', that human will can be directed toward 'scientifically valid' goals, and that proof and substantiation boil down to an explanation of how this ideal and these goals are 'objectively the best'. But the question of better and worse is decided in the sphere of feelings, so that the matter has to do with objective proofs of feelings in life. Stammler's opponents, of course, tend to think that it is possible to show that the vital meaning of an ideal is progressive or reactionary, but it is impossible to prove the feeling that this ideal must be considered to be 'best'.

Stammler, relying on *The Critique of Practical Reason*, accepts the 'objectivity' of moral duty. His opponents, based on experience, consider the consciousness of 'duty' to be based on a feeling and consider any feeling to be 'subjective'. It is clear that there is no common ground not only for agreement but even for a polemic. The question is: do you or do you not believe in the objectivity and universal validity of the dictates of the feeling of 'duty'. Believers can call people who do not believe this moral idiots or animals – as our idealists forbearingly prefer to express themselves – as much as they like, but they cannot refute them. Stammler himself admits this with undoubted annoyance. Be that as it may, even from the time of Schopenhauer – who proposed that 'practical reason', 'objectively correct goals', and other formulae of Kantian ethics must be reckoned as a variety of wooden iron – the number of people who are 'like animals' has undoubtedly grown and, moreover, grown among the most active and progressive elements of society.

Thus, regarding the question of the social ideal, two sharply opposing points of view are depicted before us. One recognises that the 'substantiation' of this ideal consists in the proof that a given ideal is 'objectively obligatory' in the sense of moral valuation and that the direction of historical development is irrelevant. The other proposes that the 'substantiation' of the ideal can consist only in the ascertainment of its vital progressiveness and the historical necessity of its development. For the human individual, the question of the subjective valuation of this feeling is to either accept or not accept this ideal, to struggle for it or not. It would seem that these two points of view are so mutually irreconcilable that it is impossible to conceive of any compromise between them. However, it turns out that this is not so. The author of the article in *Braun's Archiv* contrives to find and take an eclectic position on this point.

In his opinion, science is obligated, of course, to figure out the necessity of historical development and to ascertain the social ideal of that path. But science is not capable of predicting the future entirely and therefore, 'the future is not entirely painted with the colour of necessity'; a certain space for 'free creative work' still remains in it. On this basis, 'a utopia also is legitimate. It represents the *autonomous* space of the social ideal ... Utopia must not contradict science, but it cannot help but be and is obligated to be autonomous in its space' (p. 703).

Thus, the weakness of our cognition, which is not able to fully foretell the historical necessity of the future, guarantees us a little piece of 'freedom' in defining our ideal, which we are able to use for constructions of a 'utopian' nature. The author of the article in *Braun's Archive* then admits that the basic features of the social ideal are correctly discovered by historical monists from the point of view of the historical necessity of development. Consequently, the realm of 'utopia' (1) must be limited to particulars that cannot be clarified, and (2) will become narrower as that same direction is investigated with more precision. In other words, the head of an ideal, unfortunately, is predetermined by ascertained tendencies of historical development, while we can 'freely' decorate its tail, for a while, with the fantastic plumes of 'utopia'. We doubt that such a moderate utopianism could entice anyone other than the 'little ones'.[11]

In any event, such utopianism, for all its modesty, could not be more 'utopian' since, being based exclusively on incomplete knowledge, it obviously can create nothing but illusions. Or perhaps Mr Struve proposes that this realm of what is not ascertained is really *not subject* to historical necessity? It obviously can be understood in this way. In this case, Mr Struve's philosophy of history presents itself in the following form: the future is defined partly by the necessary relationship of cause and effect and partly by 'free' manifestations of our will. Or, as one of the astronomers of the seventeenth century said, 'the centre of a comet is unarguably a natural phenomenon, and there is no justification to consider it an omen of God's wrath, but its tail, perhaps, might be recognised as such'.

Let us now return to the starting point of the positive and critical constructions of Stammler and his followers. It is a distinctive conception of society that has prevailed for several past centuries – for the whole era of bourgeois culture. To be precise, it is the *legal* conception of society, and its essence boils down to the following.

External norm-making, and specifically law – its especially typical form – is the basis of any social relationship. It is accepted that law, and nothing else, is the ultimate regulator of social life, that it alone creates objective unity and the regularity of people's social being.

In so doing, first, the possibility of seeking social bases of legal life anywhere deeper than the law is eliminated; the realm of law is considered to be socially independent and even socially deterministic of other realms of people's life. Second, the activity of the lawmaker acquires the character of pure social creative work with the special colouration of 'freedom'. The conditioning of society by causes that lie *outside* legal life is either rejected or becomes imperceptible.

From this issues the necessity to seek *a different* regularity for the development of law than the basic principles of cognition, than the necessary connection of cause and effect. 'The regularity of will', 'the principle of practical

---

11   Mr Struve does not notice the total modesty of his 'utopianism', otherwise he would not be able to so contemptuously reply to Bernstein, 'As a whole, this mixing of poorly understood theoretical idealism with timid practical realism produces – and forgive me for this expression – the impression of a certain philistinism' (p. 702). But life subsequently transformed these words into quite a vicious irony! After all, this is a most caustic definition of our ex-Marxist 'idealists'.

reason', 'the ethical ideal of law', etc. appear on the scene. *The contemporary school of natural law* – of which Stammler is one of the representatives – grew up on this basis.

In the words of Mr P. Novgorodtsev, one of the most prominent Russian adherents of this school, the school of natural law is characterised by 'the a priori method, ideal strivings, and the recognition of an independent meaning behind moral principles and normative consideration' (*Problemy Idealizma*, p. 250). Except for the fact that 'ideal strivings' is difficult to consider as a *distinctive* feature of this school in comparison with its contemporary opponents, the characterisation is quite precise and clearly indicates the logical connection of ideas of this school with the normative or, what is the same thing, legal conception of society.

In the words of the same Mr Novgorodtsev,

> The question of natural law does not at all consist in providing a theory of legislation *that explains* the natural development of legal institutions but in establishing moral requirements that *prescribe* ideal paths of development ... Here it is necessary to turn to a priori directives of moral consciousness that are essentially independent of all experience and contain information for the evaluation of any material of experience (p. 255, *passim.*).

Unfortunately, the worthy theoreticians of this school do not limit themselves to innocent 'prescriptions of the path' on the basis of 'a priori directives'. They continually transform the aforesaid 'directives' into the principle of 'explanation' (p. 270), 'investigation', 'study', etc. of legal life (p. 273). In a word, they transform 'directives' into a principle *that has to do with cognition and that seeks to replace the principle of causality*. Here its activity becomes scientifically reactionary. This is expressed all the more clearly in their struggle against evolutionism, to which they stubbornly try to prescribe 'boundaries'.

It is impossible to discuss all the constructions of this school here. It is clear that they survive or fail along with their general foundation – the legal conception of society. For my goal, it is sufficient to counter it with the *labour conception of society*.

The labour conception of society considers social life to be the collective labour process of the struggle of people for life and development, and it recognises that the *content* of social life determines its *forms*. It sees in legal and any other norms only *organising adaptations* that are worked out in the labour process and that have only conditional and temporary meaning. For the labour conception of society, the absolute ideal of law is a logical contradiction, since it does not find anything absolute in the law, itself. It is not attracted to the idea of the 'eternal' development of legal relationships, since it cannot fundamentally reject the likelihood that society will develop beyond the bounds of the form of law, itself. As far as the labour conception of society is concerned, the practical side of the question of legal development is not to 'prescribe the paths' of legal development a priori, but, in analysing reality, to discover and then to actively realise those legal forms that are most capable of facilitating the progressive development of the process of social labour. From this point of view, the search for new legal forms must proceed in the light of a broader social idea than one that is purely legal.

Bibliography

Bazarov, V.A. 2019, *Productive Labor and Labor that Generates Value*, Alden, MI: Independently published.

Berdiaev, Nikolai A. 1901, 'Bor'ba za idealizma', *Mir bozhii*, 6, pt. 1: 1–26.

Biggart, John, George Gloveli, and Avraham Yassour 1998, *Bogdanov and His Work: A Guide to the Published and Unpublished Works of Alexander A. Bogdanov (Malinovsky) 1873–1928*, Aldershot: Ashgate.

Bogdanov, A.A. 1899a, *Osnovnye elementy istoricheskogo vzgliada na prirodu*, St. Petersburg: 'Izdatel'.

Bogdanov, A.A. 1899b, 'Osnovnaia oshibka Tugan-Baranovskogo', *Nauchnoe obozrenie*, 9: 1758–66.

Bogdanov, A.A. 1900, 'Novye tochki zreniia v ekonomicheskoi nauki', *Nauchnoe obozrenie*, 8: 1435–48.

Bogdanov, A.A. 1901a, 'Iz mira kriticheskikh uvlechenii', *Zhizn'*, 3: 187–200.

Bogdanov, A.A. 1901b, 'Chto takoe idealizma?', *Obrazovanie*, 12: 24–43.

Bogdanov, A.A. 1902a, *Poznanie s istoricheskoi tochki zreniia*, St. Petersburg: Tip. A. Leiferta.

Bogdanov, A.A. 1902c, 'Razvitie zhizni v prirode i v obshchestve', *Obrazovanie*, 4: 33–46; 5–6: 91–110; 7–8: 66–83.

Bogdanov, A.A. 1903a, 'Novoe srednevekov'e: po povodu "Problemakh idealizma"', *Obrazovanie*, 3: 9–28.

Bogdanov, A.A. 1903b, 'Aftoritarnoe myshlenie', *Obrazovanie*, 4: 40–56; 5: 88–105; 6: 15–34.

Bogdanov, A.A. 1903c, 'V pole zreniia', *Obrazovanie*, 11: 1–7.

Bogdanov, A.A. 1904a, 'O pol'ze znaniia', *Pravda*, 1: 112–14.

Bogdanov, A.A. 1904b, 'Otzvuki minuvshego', *Obrazovanie*, 1: 56–71.

Bogdanov, A.A. 1904c, 'Sobiranie cheloveka', *Pravda*, 4: 158–75.

Bogdanov, A.A. 1904d, 'Filosofskii koshmar', *Pravda*, 4: 255–9.

Bogdanov, A.A. 1904e, 'Prokliatye voprosy filosofii', *Pravda*, 12: 240–52.

Bogdanov, A.A. 1904f, 'Obmen i tekhnika', in *Ocherki realisticheskogo mirovozreniia: Sbornik statei po filosofii, obshchestvennoi nauke, i zhizni*, St. Petersburg, Izdanie S. Dorovatovskogo i A. Charushnikova.

Bogdanov, A.A. 1904g, 'Obshchestvo pravovoe i obshchestvo trudovoe', in *Ocherki realisticheskogo mirovozreniia: Sbornik statei po filosofii, obshchestvennoi nauke, i zhizni*, St. Petersburg, Izdanie S. Dorovatovskogo i A. Charushnikova.

Bogdanov, A.A. 1905a, *Ocherki realisticheskogo mirovozreniia: Sbornik statei po filosofii, obshchestvennoi nauke, i zhizni*, St. Petersburg, Izdanie S. Dorovatovskogo i A. Charushnikova.

Bogdanov, A.A. 1905b, 'Normy i tsely zhizni', *Obrazovanie*, 7: 265–98.

Bogdanov, A.A. 1905c, *Novyi Mir*, Moscow: S. Dorovatovskogo i A. Charushnikova.

Bogdanov, A.A. 1906a, *Iz psikhologii obshchestva*, 2nd ed., supplemented, St. Petersburg: 'Delo'.

Bogdanov, A.A. 1906c, 'Revoliutsiia i filosofiia', *Obrazovanie*, 2: 54–63.

Bogdanov, A.A. 1925, *O proletarskoi kul'tury (Stat'i 1904–1924)*, Moscow: 'Kniga'.

Bogdanov, A.A. 2016, *Philosophy of Living Experience*, Leiden: Brill.

Bogdanov, A.A. 2019, *Empiriomonism: Essays in Philosophy, Books 1–3*, Leiden: Brill.

Böhm-Bawerk, Eugen 1949, *Karl Marx and the Close of His System*, New York: Augustus M. Kelley.

Heidelberger, Michael 2006, 'Kant and Realism: Alois Riehl (and Moritz Schlick)', in *The Kantian Legacy in Nineteenth-Century Science*, edited by Michael Friedman and Alfred Nordmann, Cambridge, MA: MIT Press.

Heidelberger, Michael 2007, 'From Neo-Kantianism to Critical Realism: Space and the Mind-Body Problem in Riehl and Schlick', *Perspectives on Science*, 15, no. 1: 26–48.

Howard, D. 2004, 'Fisica e filosofia della scienza all'alba del xx secolo', *Storia della scienza*. Vol. 8, *La Seconda revoluzione scientifica*, Rome: Instituto della Enciclopedia Italiana. Available in English as 'Physics and the Philosophy of Science at the Turn of the Twentieth Century' at: http://www3.nd.edu/~dhoward1/Phil-Phys-1900.pdf [accessed 9 April 2018].

Kindersley, Richard 1962, *The First Russian Revisionists: A Study of 'Legal Marxism' in Russia*, Oxford: Clarendon Press.

Lazarus, Emma 1881, *Poems and Ballads of Heinrich Heine*, New York: J.J. Little & Co.

Mach, Ernst 1897, *Contribution to the Analysis of the Sensations*, Chicago: Open Court.

Mendel, Arthur P. 1961, *Dilemmas of Progress in Tsarist Russia: Legal Marxism and Legal Populism*, Cambridge, MA: Harvard University Press.

Pipes, Richard 1970, *Struve: Liberal on the Left*, Cambridge, MA: Harvard University Press.

Poole, Randall A. 1999, 'The Neo-Idealist Reception of Kant in the Moscow Psychological Society', *Journal of the History of Ideas*, 60, no. 2: 319–43.

Poole, Randall A. (ed. and trans.) 2003 [1902], *Problems of Idealism: Essays in Russian Social Philosophy*, New Haven, CT: Yale University Press.

Read, Christopher 1979, *Religion, Revolution, and the Russian Intelligentsia, 1900–1912*, London: Macmillan.

Richardson, Alan 1997, 'Toward a History of Scientific Philosophy', *Perspectives on Science*, 5, no. 3: 418–51.

Richardson, Alan 2008, 'Scientific Philosophy as a Topic for History of Science', *Isis*, 99: 88–96.

Riehl, A. 1894, *The Principles of the Critical Philosophy: Introduction to the Theory of Science and Metaphysics*, London: Kegan Paul, Trench, Trübner, and Co.

Rosenthal, Bernice Glatzer 1975, *Dmitri Sergeevich Merezhkovsky and the Silver Age: The Development of a Revolutionary Mentality*, The Hague: Martinus Nijhoff.

Solovev, Vladimir 1896, 'Lichnost, *Entsiklopedicheskii slovar'*, Vol. xviia, St. Peterburg: Brokgauz i Efron, pp. 868–9.

Solovyov [Solovev], Vladimir 1996, *The Crisis of Western Philosophy: Against the Positivists*, Hudson, NY: Lindisfarne Press.

Stammler, Rudolf 1896, *Wirtschaft und Recht Nach der Materialistischen Geschichtsauffassung*, Leipzig: Verlag von Veit & Comp.

Struve, P.B. 1894, *Kriticheskie zametki k voprosu ob ekonomicheskom razvitii Rossii*, St. Petersburg: Tip. I.N. Skorokhodova.

Struve, P.B. 1897, 'Svoboda i istoricheskaia neobkhodimost', *Voprosy filosofii i psikhologii*, 1 (January–February): 120–39.

Vucinich, Alexander 1970, *Science in Russian Culture, 1861–1917*, Stanford, CA: Stanford University Press.

White, James D. 2019a, *Marx and Russia: The Fate of a Doctrine*, London: Bloomsbury.

White, James D. 2019b, *Red Hamlet: The Life and Ideas of Alexander Bogdanov*, Leiden: Brill.

Williams, Robert C. 1986, *The Other Bolsheviks: Lenin and His Critics, 1904–1914*, Bloomington: Indiana University Press.

Index

Lightning Source UK Ltd.
Milton Keynes UK
UKHW021259141222
413922UK00028B/275